Adsensory Urban Ecology (Volume One)

Adsensory Urban Ecology (Volume One)

By

Pamela Odih

Cambridge
Scholars
Publishing

Adsensory Urban Ecology (Volume One)

By Pamela Odih

This book first published 2019

Cambridge Scholars Publishing

Lady Stephenson Library, Newcastle upon Tyne, NE6 2PA, UK

British Library Cataloguing in Publication Data
A catalogue record for this book is available from the British Library

Copyright © 2019 by Pamela Odih

All rights for this book reserved. No part of this book may be reproduced, stored in a retrieval system, or transmitted, in any form or by any means, electronic, mechanical, photocopying, recording or otherwise, without the prior permission of the copyright owner.

ISBN (10): 1-5275-2317-9
ISBN (13): 978-1-5275-2317-3

This book is dedicated to Professor David Knights, with appreciation for his academic supervision and inspiration.

A share of royalties will be donated to the charity United Nations Children's Fund (UNICEF). Established in 1946, UNICEF is dedicated to furthering the rights, wellbeing, prosperity and creative potential of children.

"If the new language of images were used differently, it would, through its use, confer a new kind of power. Within it we could begin to define our experiences more precisely in areas where words are inadequate" (John Berger, Ways of Seeing, 1972).

Contents

List of Illustrations ix

Preface xx
Dialogic Configuration, Aestheticisation of Urban Ecology

Prologue xxxvii
By Composition of Forces

Acknowledgements li

Introduction 1
Post-Industrial Urban Ecology

Part One: Adsensory Dimensions of Urban Ecology

Chapter One 8
Post-industrial Society and the Aestheticisation of Urban Ecology

Part Two: Adsensory Façades in Post-industrial Urban Space

Chapter Two 20
Façade as the Gentrification of Post-industrial Urban Space

Chapter Three 51
Cladding Façade, Red Herring? Market-based Managerialism
and the Gentrification of Post-industrial Space

Chapter Four 115
Urban Ecological Façade as an Adsensory Gentrification
of Post-industrial Space

Part Three: Adsensory Financialisation of Absolute Boarder Controls

Chapter Five 172
Garden Bridge, Rentier Capital as the Adsensory Financialisation
of Urban Decay

Chapter Six 222
Garden Bridge, Subverting the Adsensory Privatisation of Our Riverway

Chapter Seven 251
Garden Bridge, Culture Industry Mediations: Framing Televisual
Ecofeminist Care Ethics

Chapter Eight 294
Garden Bridge, Forecasting Troubled Waters: English Ethnic Nationalism
in European Union Brexit Times

Conclusion 301
Adsensory Façade Gentrification: "History always constitutes the relation
between a present and its past" (Berger)

Epilogue 306

References 391

Index 431

LIST OF ILLUSTRATIONS

All photographic images and video imagery by Pamela Odih ©

Book Front Cover: Adsensory Time Reve'ls, Pamela Odih © 2017.

Preface

Figure P.i.: "Publicity has another important social function. The fact that this function has not been planned as a purpose by those who make and use publicity in no way lessens its significance. Publicity turns consumption into a substitute for democracy" (John Berger, *Ways of Seeing*, 1972). Photographic Image, Vicinity of Grenfell Tower; Lancaster West Estate, North Kensington, London, June 2017.

Figure P.ii.: "It supplies us with our archetypes of 'artistic genius'. And the history of the tradition, as it is usually taught, teaches us that art prospers if enough individuals in society have a love of art. What is a love of art?" (John Berger, *Ways of Seeing*, 1972). Photographic Image, Vicinity of Grenfell Tower; Lancaster West Estate, North Kensington, London, June 2017.

Figure P.iii.: "Etiquettes of modesty are not merely puritan or sentimental: it is reasonable to recognize a loss of mystery. And the explanation of this loss of mystery may be largely visual" (John Berger, *Ways of Seeing*, 1972). Photographic Image, Vicinity of Grenfell Tower; Lancaster West Estate, North Kensington, London, June 2017.

Figure P.iv.: "It is seeing which establishes our place in the surrounding world; we explain that world with words, but words can never undo the fact that we are surrounded by it" (John Berger, *Ways of Seeing*, 1972). Photographic Image, Vicinity of Grenfell Tower; Lancaster West Estate, North Kensington, London, June 2017.

Figure P.v.: "But a work of art also suggests a cultural authority, a form of dignity, even of wisdom, which is superior to any vulgar material interest; an oil painting belongs to the cultural heritage; it is a reminder of what it means to be a cultivated European" (John Berger, *Ways of Seeing*, 1972). Photographic Image, Vicinity of Grenfell Tower; Lancaster West Estate, North Kensington, London, June 2017.

Figure P.vi.: "Our vision is continually active, continually moving, continually holding things in a circle around itself, constituting what is present to us as we are"

x List of Illustrations

(John Berger, *Ways of Seeing*, 1972). Photographic Image, Vicinity of Grenfell Tower; Lancaster West Estate, North Kensington, London, June 2017.

Figure P.vii.: "But there is also another sense in which seeing comes before words. It is seeing which establishes our place in the surrounding world; we explain that world with words but words can never undo the fact that we are surrounded by it" (John Berger, *Ways of Seeing*, 1972). Photographic Image, Vicinity of Grenfell Tower; Lancaster West Estate, North Kensington, London, June 2017.

Figure P.viii.: "Yet this seeing which comas before words, and can never be quite covered by them, is not a question of mechanically reacting to stimuli … We only see what we look at. To look is an act of choice. As a result of this act, what we see is brought within our reach - though not necessarily within arm's reach" (John Berger, *Ways of Seeing*, 1972). Photographic Image, Vicinity of Grenfell Tower; Lancaster West Estate, North Kensington, London, June 2017.

Figure P.ix.: "Perspective makes the single eye the centre of the visible world. Everything converges on to the eye as to the vanishing point of infinity. The visible world is arranged for the spectator as the universe was once thought to be arranged for God" (John Berger, *Ways of Seeing*, 1972). Photographic Image, Vicinity of Grenfell Tower; Lancaster West Estate, North Kensington, London, June 2017.

Figure P.x.: "The camera isolated momentary appearances and in so doing destroyed the idea that images were timeless. Or, to put it another way, the camera showed that the notion of time passing was inseparable from the experience of the visual (except in paintings) … What you saw was relative to your position in time and space. It was no longer possible to imagine everything converging on the human eye as on the vanishing point of infinity" (John Berger, *Ways of Seeing*, 1972). Photographic Image, Environmental Activist, Central London, August 2016.

Figure P.xi.: "According to the convention of perspective there is no visual reciprocity. There is no need for God to situate himself in relation to others: he is himself the situation" (John Berger, *Ways of Seeing*, 1972). Photographic Image, South Bank, Central London, August 2016.

Figure P.xii.: "The inherent contradiction in perspective was that it structured all images of reality to address a single spectator who, unlike God, could only be in one place at a time" (John Berger, *Ways of Seeing*, 1972). Photographic Image, South Bank, Central London, August 2016.

Figure P.xiii.: "Adults and children sometimes have boards in their bedrooms or living-rooms on which they pin pieces of paper: letters, snapshots, reproductions of paintings, newspaper cuttings, original drawings, postcards. On each board all the images belong to the same language and all are more or less equal within it, because they have been chosen in a highly personal way to match and express the experience of the room's inhabitant. Logically, these boards should replace museums" (John Berger, *Ways of Seeing*, 1972). Photographic Image, South Bank, Central London, August 2016.

Prologue

Figure Pro.i.: "One may remember or forget these messages but briefly one takes them in, and for a moment they stimulate the imagination by way of either memory or expectation" (John Berger, *Ways of Seeing*, 1972). Photographic Image, South Bank, Central London, August 2016.

Introduction

Figure I.1.: "A people or a class which is cut off from its own past is far less free to choose and to act as a people or class than one that has been able to situate itself in history" (John Berger, *Ways of Seeing*, 1972). Photographic Image, Vicinity of Grenfell Tower; Lancaster West Estate, North Kensington, London, June 2017.

Part One

Figure P.I.: "Yet this seeing which comes before words, and can never be quite covered by them, is not a question of mechanically reacting to stimuli" (John Berger, *Ways of Seeing*, 1972). Photographic Image, North Kensington, London, June 2017.

Chapter One

Figure 1.1.: "Publicity is addressed to those who constitute the market, to the spectator-buyer who is also the consumer-producer from whom profits are made twice over — as worker and then as buyer. The only places relatively free of publicity are the quarters of the very rich; their money is theirs to keep" (John Berger, *Ways of Seeing*, 1972). Photographic Image, North Kensington, London, June 2017.

Figure 1.2.: "Publicity speaks in the future tense and yet the achievement of this future is endlessly deferred. How then does publicity remain credible - or credible enough to exert the influence it does? It remains credible because the truthfulness of publicity is judged, not by the real fulfilment of its promises, but by the relevance of its fantasies to those of the spectator- buyer. Its essential application is not to reality but to day-dreams" (John Berger, *Ways of Seeing*, 1972). Photographic Image, North Kensington, London, June 2017.

Figure 1.3.: "The entire world becomes a setting for the fulfilment of publicity's promise of the good life. The world smiles at us. It offers itself to us. And because *everywhere* is imagined as offering itself to us, *everywhere* is more or less the same" (John Berger, *Ways of Seeing*, 1972). Photographic Image, Vicinity of Grenfell Tower; Lancaster West Estate, North Kensington, London, June 2017.

Figure 1.4.: "Capitalism survives by forcing the majority, whom it exploits, to define their own interests as narrowly as possible. This was once achieved by extensive deprivation. Today in the developed countries it is being achieved by imposing a false standard of what is and what is not desirable" (John Berger, *Ways of Seeing*, 1972). Photographic Image, Vicinity of Grenfell Tower; Lancaster West Estate, North Kensington, London, June 2017.

Figure 1.5.: "We never look at just one thing; we are always looking at the relation between things and ourselves. Our vision is continually active, continually moving, continually holding things in a circle around itself, constituting what is present to us as we are" (John Berger, *Ways of Seeing*, 1972). Photographic Image, Vicinity of Grenfell Tower; Lancaster West Estate, North Kensington, London, June 2017.

Figure 1.6.: "A people or a class which is cut off from its own past is far less free to choose and to act as a people or class than one that has been able to situate itself in history" (John Berger, *Ways of Seeing*, 1972). Photographic Image, Vicinity of Grenfell Tower; Lancaster West Estate, North Kensington, London, June 2017.

Part Two

Figure P.II.: "We only see what we look at. To look is an act of choice. As a result of this act, what we see is brought within our reach – though not necessarily within arm's reach. To touch something is to situate oneself in relation to it" (John Berger, *Ways of Seeing*, 1972). Photographic Image, Vicinity of Grenfell Tower; Lancaster West Estate, North Kensington, London, June 2017.

Chapter Two

Figure 2.1.: "The inherent contradiction in perspective was that it structured all images of reality to address a single spectator who, unlike God, could only be in one place at a time" (John Berger, *Ways of Seeing*, 1972). Photographic Image, North Kensington, London, June 2017.

Figure 2.2.: "Alternatively the anxiety on which publicity plays is the fear that having nothing you will be nothing" (John Berger, *Ways of Seeing*, 1972). Photographic Image, North Kensington, London, June 2017.

Figure 2.3.: "Publicity helps to mask and compensate for all that is undemocratic within society. And it also masks what is happening in the rest of the world" (John Berger, *Ways of Seeing*, 1972). Photographic Image, Vicinity of Grenfell Tower; Lancaster West Estate, North Kensington, London, June 2017.

Figure 2.4.: *Love Assisst(f)*: "One may remember or forget these messages but briefly one takes them in, and for a moment they stimulate the imagination by way of either memory or expectation" (John Berger, *Ways of Seeing*, 1972). Photographic Image, Vicinity of Grenfell Tower; Lancaster West Estate, North Kensington, London, June 2017.

Figure 2.5.: "This has the effect of closing the distance in time between the painting of the picture and one's own act of looking at it. In this special sense all paintings are contemporary. Hence the immediacy of their testimony. Their historical moment is literally there before our eyes" (John Berger, *Ways of Seeing*, 1972). Photographic Image, Vicinity of Grenfell Tower; Lancaster West Estate, North Kensington, London, June 2017.

Figure 2.6.: "To great Omnipotence a debt can owe? Or owing, can repay it? Would'st thou dare Barter upon equality!" (Ann Yearsley, *On Jephthah's Vow, Taken in a Literal Sense*, 1787). Photographic Image, Vicinity of Grenfell Tower; Lancaster West Estate, North Kensington, London, June 2017.

Figure 2.7.: "But there is the evidence of the paintings themselves: the evidence of a group of men and a group of women as seen by another man, the painter. Study this evidence and judge for yourself" (John Berger, *Ways of Seeing*, 1972). Photographic Image, Vicinity of Grenfell Tower; Lancaster West Estate, North Kensington, London, June 2017.

Figure 2.8.: "These relations between conqueror and colonized tended to be self-perpetuating" (John Berger, *Ways of Seeing*, 1972). Photographic Image, Vicinity of Grenfell Tower; Lancaster West Estate, North Kensington, London, June 2017.

Figure 2.9.: "The artificiality is deep within its own terms of seeing, because the subject has to be seen simultaneously from close-to and from afar" (John Berger, *Ways of Seeing*, 1972). Photographic Image, Vicinity of Grenfell Tower; Lancaster West Estate, North Kensington, London, June 2017.

Figure 2.10.: *Love Assisst(f)*: "One may remember or forget these messages but briefly one takes them in, and for a moment they stimulate the imagination by way of either memory or expectation" (John Berger, *Ways of Seeing*, 1972). Photographic Image, Vicinity of Grenfell Tower; Lancaster West Estate, North Kensington, London, June 2017.

Chapter Three

Figure 3.1.: "No other kind of relic or text from the past can offer such a direct testimony about the world" (John Berger, *Ways of Seeing*, 1972). Photographic Image, Vicinity of Grenfell Tower; Lancaster West Estate, North Kensington, London, June 2017.

Figure 3.2.: "The compositional unity of a painting contributes fundamentally to the power of its image. It is reasonable to consider a painting's composition. But here the composition is written about as though it were in itself the emotional charge of the painting" (John Berger, *Ways of Seeing*, 1972). Photographic Image, Vicinity of Grenfell Tower; Lancaster West Estate, North Kensington, London, June 2017.

Figure 3.3.: "On each board all the images belong to the same language and all are more or less equal within it, because they have been chosen in a highly personal way to match and express the experience of the room's inhabitant" (John Berger, *Ways of Seeing*, 1972). Photographic Image, Vicinity of Grenfell Tower; Lancaster West Estate, North Kensington, London, June 2017.

Figure 3.4.: "A people or a class which is cut off from its own past is far less free to choose and to act as a people or class than one that has been able to situate itself in history" (John Berger, *Ways of Seeing*, 1972). Photographic Image, Vicinity of Grenfell Tower; Lancaster West Estate, North Kensington, London, June 2017.

Figure 3.5.: "A people or a class which is cut off from its own past is far less free to choose and to act as a people or class than one that has been able to situate itself in history. This is why – and this is the only reason why – the entire art of the past has now become a political issue" (John Berger, *Ways of Seeing*, 1972). Photographic Image, Vicinity of Grenfell Tower; Lancaster West Estate, North Kensington, London, June 2017.

Figure 3.6.: "This value is affirmed and gauged by the price it fetches on the market" (John Berger, *Ways of Seeing*, 1972). Photographic Image, Vicinity of Grenfell Tower; Lancaster West Estate, North Kensington, London, June 2017.

Figure 3.7.: "Yet the spiritual value of an object, as distinct from a message or an example, can only be explained in terms of magic or religion" (John Berger, *Ways of Seeing*, 1972). Photographic Image, Vicinity of Grenfell Tower; Lancaster West Estate, North Kensington, London, June 2017.

Figure 3.8.: "It is the final empty claim for the continuing values of an oligarchic, undemocratic culture" (John Berger, *Ways of Seeing*, 1972). Photographic Image, North Kensington, London, June 2017.

Figure 3.9.: *Love Assisst(f)*: Volunteering my time at the Grenfell Tower tragedy site. Heartbreaking and, according to my interviews, there were much higher losses. PamxXx (15 Jun 2017). "Today the attitudes and values which informed that tradition are expressed through other more widely diffused media – advertising, journalism, television" (John Berger, *Ways of Seeing*, 1972).
https://twitter.com/geraldi23591291/status/875385080717463552

Figure 3.10.: *Love Assisst(f)*: Words cannot express the devastating imagery of Grenfell Tower. JC is right … we need to know why so many lives lost xXx (15 June 2017); @Robert_W_Nelson: "So true". "Every image embodies a way of seeing" (John Berger, *Ways of Seeing*, 1972).
https://twitter.com/geraldi23591291/status/875410180296585218

Figure 3.11.: *Love Assisst(f)*: (16 June 2017): "One may remember or forget these messages but briefly takes them in & for a moment they stimulate the imagination" (John Berger, *Ways of Seeing*, 1972).
https://twitter.com/geraldi23591291/status/875782215577239552

Figure 3.12.: *Love Assisst(f)*: (16 Jun 2017): "One may remember or forget these messages but briefly takes them in & for a moment they stimulate the imagination" (John Berger, *Ways of Seeing*, 1972).
https://twitter.com/geraldi23591291/status/875787769729220609

Figure 3.13.: *Love Assisst(f)*: (16 Jun 2017): "One may remember or forget these messages but briefly takes them in & for a moment they stimulate the imagination"; "What is a love of art?" (John Berger, *Ways of Seeing*, 1972).
https://twitter.com/geraldi23591291/status/875789312465526785

Figure 3.14.: *Love Assisst(f)*: (20 Jun 2017): "One may remember or forget these messages but briefly one takes them in, & for a moment they stimulate the imagination"; "What is a love of art? … What does it show?" (John Berger, *Ways of Seeing*, 1972). https://twitter.com/geraldi23591291/status/877184335681662980

Figure 3.15.: *Love Assisst(f)*: (20 Jun 2017): "One may remember or forget these messages but briefly one takes them in, & for a moment they stimulate the imagination"; "Not only personal experience, but also the essential historical experience of our relation to the past: that is to say the experience of seeking to give meaning to our lives, of trying to understand the history of which we can become the active agents" (John Berger, *Ways of Seeing*, 1972).
https://twitter.com/geraldi23591291/status/877185458333245440

Figure 3.16.: *Love Assisst(f)*: (21 Jun 2017): "One may remember or forget these messages but briefly takes them in & for a moment they stimulate the imagination"; "The compositional unity of a painting contributes fundamentally to the power of its image. It is reasonable to consider a painting's composition" (John Berger, *Ways of Seeing*, 1972).

https://twitter.com/geraldi23591291/status/877592798291251210

Figure 3.17.: *Love Assisst*(f): (21 Jun 2017): "One may remember or forget these messages but briefly takes them in & for a moment they stimulate the imagination"; "A people or a class which is cut off from its own past is far less free to choose and to act as a people or class than one that has been able to situate itself in history" (John Berger, *Ways of Seeing*, 1972).
https://twitter.com/geraldi23591291/status/877594903974465536

Figure 3.18.: *Love Assisst*(f): (23 Jun 2017): "One may remember or forget these messages but briefly takes them in & for a moment they stimulate the imagination"; "This has the effect of closing the distance in time between the painting of the picture and one's own act of looking at it. In this special sense all paintings are contemporary. Hence the immediacy of their testimony. Their historical moment is literally there before our eyes" (John Berger, *Ways of Seeing*, 1972). https://twitter.com/geraldi23591291/status/878257462322880512

Chapter Four

Figure 4.1.: "Both media use similar, highly tactile means to play upon the spectator's sense of acquiring the real thing which the image shows. In both cases his feeling that he can almost touch what is in the image reminds him how he might or does possess the real thing" (John Berger, *Ways of Seeing*, 1972). Photographic Image, Vicinity of Grenfell Tower; Lancaster West Estate, North Kensington, London, June 2017.

Figure 4.2.: "Capitalism survives by forcing the majority, whom it exploits, to define their own interests as narrowly as possible. This was once achieved by extensive deprivation. Today in the developed countries it is being achieved by imposing a false standard of what is and what is not desirable" (John Berger, *Ways of Seeing*, 1972). Photographic Image, Vicinity of Grenfell Tower; Lancaster West Estate, North Kensington, London, June 2017.

Figure 4.3.: "We only see what we look at. To look is an act of choice. As a result of this act, what we see is brought within our reach - though not necessarily within arm's reach. To touch something is to situate oneself in relation to it" (John Berger, *Ways of Seeing*, 1972). Photographic Image, Vicinity of Grenfell Tower; Lancaster West Estate, North Kensington, London, June 2017.

Figure 4.4.: "Not only personal experience, but also the essential historical experience of our relation to the past: that is to say the experience of seeking to give meaning to our lives, of trying to understand the history of which we can become the active agents" (John Berger, *Ways of Seeing*, 1972). Photographic Image, Vicinity of Grenfell Tower; Lancaster West Estate, North Kensington, London, June 2017.

Figure 4.5.: "A people or a class which is cut off from its own past is far less free to choose and to act as a people or class than one that has been able to situate itself in history" (John Berger, *Ways of Seeing*, 1972). Photographic Image, Vicinity of Grenfell Tower; Lancaster West Estate, North Kensington, London, June 2017.

Figure 4.6.: "One may remember or forget these messages but briefly one takes them in, and for a moment they stimulate the imagination by way of either memory or expectation" (John Berger, *Ways of Seeing*, 1972). Photographic Image, Vicinity of Grenfell Tower; Lancaster West Estate, North Kensington, London, June 2017.

Figure 4.7.: "One may remember or forget these messages but briefly one takes them in, and for a moment they stimulate the imagination by way of either memory or expectation" (John Berger, *Ways of Seeing*, 1972). Photographic Image, Vicinity of Grenfell Tower; Lancaster West Estate, North Kensington, London, June 2017.

Figure 4.8.: "One may remember or forget these messages but briefly one takes them in, and for a moment they stimulate the imagination by way of either memory or expectation" (John Berger, *Ways of Seeing*, 1972). Photographic Image, Vicinity of Grenfell Tower; Lancaster West Estate, North Kensington, London, June 2017.

Figure 4.9.: "One may remember or forget these messages but briefly one takes them in, and for a moment they stimulate the imagination by way of either memory or expectation" (John Berger, *Ways of Seeing*, 1972). Photographic Image, Vicinity of Grenfell Tower; Lancaster West Estate, North Kensington, London, June 2017.

Figure 4.10.: "One may remember or forget these messages but briefly one takes them in, and for a moment they stimulate the imagination by way of either memory or expectation" (John Berger, *Ways of Seeing*, 1972). Photographic Image, Vicinity of Grenfell Tower; Lancaster West Estate, North Kensington, London, June 2017.

Part Three

Figure P.III.: "Yet this seeing which comes before words, and can never be quite covered by them, is not a question of mechanically reacting to stimuli" (John Berger, *Ways of Seeing*, 1972). Photographic Image, Environmental Activist, Central London, August 2016.

Chapter Five

Figure 5.1.: "Serving as a bridge between two intense imaginative states" (John Berger, *Ways of Seeing*, 1972). Photographic Image, Environmental Activist, Central London, August 2016.

Figure 5.2.: "The world smiles at us. It offers itself to us. And because *everywhere* is imagined as offering itself to us, *everywhere* is more or less the same" (John

Berger, *Ways of Seeing*, 1972). Photographic Image, South Bank, Central London, August 2016.

Figure 5.3.: "Colour photography is to the spectator-buyer what oil paint was to the spectator-owner. Both media use similar, highly tactile means to play upon the spectator's sense of acquiring the *real* thing which the image shows. In both cases his feeling that he can almost touch what is in the image reminds him how he might or does possess the real thing" (John Berger, *Ways of Seeing*, 1972). Photographic Image, South Bank, Central London, August 2016.

Chapter Six

Figure 6.1.: "If one moment of that process is isolated, its image will seem banal and its banality, instead of serving as a bridge between two intense imaginative states, will be chilling" (John Berger, *Ways of Seeing*, 1972). Photographic Image, Southbank, London 2016.

Figure 6.2.: "This was the time when the ocean trade routes were being opened up for the slave trade and for the traffic which was to siphon the riches from other continents into Europe, and later supply the capital for the take-off of the Industrial Revolution" (John Berger, *Ways of Seeing*, 1972). Photographic Image, Southbank, London 2016.

Figure 6.3.: "Publicity is, in essence, nostalgic. It has to sell the past to the future. It cannot itself supply the standards of its own claims. And so all its references to quality are bound to be retrospective and traditional. It would lack both confidence and credibility if it used a strictly contemporary language" (John Berger, *Ways of Seeing*, 1972). Photographic Image, Southbank, London 2016.

Figure 6.4.: "Publicity is addressed to those who constitute the market, to the spectator-buyer who is also the consumer-producer from whom profits are made twice over — as worker and then as buyer. The only places relatively free of publicity are the quarters of the very rich; their money is theirs to keep" (John Berger, *Ways of Seeing*, 1972). Photographic Image, Southbank, London 2016.

Chapter Seven

Figure 7.1.: "Publicity images also belong to the moment in the sense that they must be continually renewed and made up-to-date. Yet they never speak of the present. Often they refer to the past and always they speak of the future" (John Berger, *Ways of Seeing*, 1972). Photographic Image, Environmental Activist, Central London, August 2016.

Figure 7.2.: "The world smiles at us. It offers itself to us. And because *everywhere* is imagined as offering itself to us, *everywhere* is more or less the same" (John

Berger, *Ways of Seeing*, 1972). Photographic Image, Environmental Activist, Central London, August 2016.

Figure 7.3.: "Let us first be sure about what we are not saying. We are not saying that there is nothing left to experience before original works of art except a sense of awe because they have survived" (John Berger, *Ways of Seeing*, 1972). Photographic Image, Southbank, London, 2016.

Figure 7.4.: "Capitalism survives by forcing the majority, whom it exploits, to define their own interests as narrowly as possible. This was once achieved by extensive deprivation. Today in the developed countries it is being achieved by imposing a false standard of what is and what is not desirable" (John Berger, *Ways of Seeing*, 1972). Photographic Image, Southbank, London, 2016.

Figure 7.5.: "A people or a class which is cut off from its own past is far less free to choose and to act as a people or class than one that has been able to situate itself in history" (John Berger, *Ways of Seeing*, 1972). Photographic Image, Southbank, London, 2016.

Chapter Eight

Figure 8.1.: "Publicity images also belong to the moment in the sense that they must be continually renewed and made up-to-date. Yet they never speak of the present. Often they refer to the past and always they speak of the future" (John Berger, *Ways of Seeing*, 1972). Photographic Image, Environmental Activist, Central London, August 2016.

Figure 8.2.: "Capitalism survives by forcing the majority, whom it exploits, to define their own interests as narrowly as possible. This was once achieved by extensive deprivation. Today in the developed countries it is being achieved by imposing a false standard of what is and what is not desirable" (John Berger, *Ways of Seeing*, 1972). Photographic Image, Southbank, London, 2016.

Conclusion

Figure C.1.: *Love Assisst(f)*: "One may remember or forget these messages but briefly one takes them in, and for a moment they stimulate the imagination by way of either memory or expectation" (John Berger, *Ways of Seeing*, 1972). Photographic Image, Grenfell Tower National Memorial Service, St Paul's Cathedral, December 2017.

PREFACE

DIALOGIC CONFIGURATION, AESTHETICISATION OF URBAN ECOLOGY

Figure P.i.: "Publicity has another important social function. The fact that this function has not been planned as a purpose by those who make and use publicity in no way lessens its significance. Publicity turns consumption into a substitute for democracy" (John Berger, *Ways of Seeing*, 1972). Photographic Image, Vicinity of Grenfell Tower; Lancaster West Estate, North Kensington, London, June 2017.

Figure P.ii.: "It supplies us with our archetypes of 'artistic genius'. And the history of the tradition, as it is usually taught, teaches us that art prospers if enough individuals in society have a love of art. What is a love of art?" (John Berger, *Ways of Seeing*, 1972). Photographic Image, Vicinity of Grenfell Tower; Lancaster West Estate, North Kensington, London, June 2017.

Grenfell Tower Refurbishment Case Study

Figure P.iii.: "Etiquettes of modesty are not merely puritan or sentimental: it is reasonable to recognize a loss of mystery. And the explanation of this loss of mystery may be largely visual" (John Berger, *Ways of Seeing*, 1972). Photographic Image, Vicinity of Grenfell Tower; Lancaster West Estate, North Kensington, London, June 2017.

Interviewer: I just wondered; it is just so sad.
Interviewee: It is yeah.

Interviewer: It is quite beautiful what people have done [referring to the Grenfell Tower floral tributes and annotated portraiture tributes].
Interviewee: You should have seen it on Wednesday, Thursday.

Interviewer: People need to express themselves.
Interviewee: Yes, exactly, in the space of; people started to leave them things and things like that you know.

Interviewer: Hmm [agreement] ... I don't know why it happened.
Interviewee: No, no I don't. There is speculation going on about fridges exploding and things like that; but there's no proof to that yet ... Nobody really to say: Yes, that really happened.

Interviewer: Some people talk about the cladding don't they?
Interviewee: Oh the cladding; oh yeah well, there was a lot of talk about that. Mind you looking out to it, if you saw the fire; the fire would not breach like that. You know what I mean? ... People were saying that they put the fire out inside; but when they came out the fire was still burning outside.

Interviewer: Have they been looking after the buildings?
Interviewee: Yeah.

Interviewer: Why this building?
Interviewee: I don't know; some sort of regeneration programme. I think they just wanted to bring the building in line with the surrounding area.

Interviewer: Have they done something to the surrounding area?
Interviewee: They don't want to see, bare, bare walls anymore.

Interviewer: Did it have bare walls?
Interviewee: It wasn't like; [bare wall is] something that is ugly to look at you know.
[pause: we stand quietly].

Interviewer: That man seems to be sad. Has he lost his family?
Interviewee: It is very difficult to talk about these things.
[pause: we stand quietly].

Interviewer: The Council helping? The company seem to be organising things?
Interviewee: I have seen Council workers round the back; they were taking pictures and things like that. I don't know what they are going to do.
[pause: we stand quietly].

Interviewer: There's a lady sitting there and she's crying.
Interviewee: One of her friends, or something like that is missing or something? They say that a lot of that is going to happen anyway. Cos they say about 70 is missing or something like that? There's going to be a lot; there's going to be a lot more than that.

Interviewer: Really? How many do you reckon?
Interviewee: Probably about a 150? Estimate. But a lot of them won't be recognised or nothing like that.

Interviewer: How do you think the community is going to come to terms with it?
Interviewee: It's going to take a long time. There's a lot of scars to be healed. I don't know. I don't really know how they are going to understand ever again.

Interviewer: What do you think they should do with the building?
Interviewee: I think they should really knock it down. And build a shrine around it. And in that area [epicentre of the building's location], leave it like that, like 9/11. Shouldn't build anything again; just knock it down. Because I don't think people are going to want to live there again; not that high up anyway.

(Unstructured Qualitative Interview: Vicinity of Grenfell Tower; Lancaster West Estate, North Kensington, London, June 2017)

Figure P.iv.: "It is seeing which establishes our place in the surrounding world; we explain that world with words, but words can never undo the fact that we are surrounded by it" (John Berger, *Ways of Seeing*, 1972). Photographic Image, Vicinity of Grenfell Tower; Lancaster West Estate, North Kensington, London, June 2017.

Figure P.v.: "But a work of art also suggests a cultural authority, a form of dignity, even of wisdom, which is superior to any vulgar material interest; an oil painting belongs to the cultural heritage; it is a reminder of what it means to be a cultivated European" (John Berger, *Ways of Seeing*, 1972). Photographic Image, Vicinity of Grenfell Tower; Lancaster West Estate, North Kensington, London, June 2017.

Figure P.vi.: "Our vision is continually active, continually moving, continually holding things in a circle around itself, constituting what is present to us as we are" (John Berger, *Ways of Seeing*, 1972). Photographic Image, Vicinity of Grenfell Tower; Lancaster West Estate, North Kensington, London, June 2017.

Figure P.vii.: "But there is also another sense in which seeing comes before words. It is seeing which establishes our place in the surrounding world; we explain that world with words but words can never undo the fact that we are surrounded by it" (John Berger, *Ways of Seeing*, 1972). Photographic Image, Vicinity of Grenfell Tower; Lancaster West Estate, North Kensington, London, June 2017.

Figure P.viii.: "Yet this seeing which comas before words, and can never be quite covered by them, is not a question of mechanically reacting to stimuli … We only see what we look at. To look is an act of choice. As a result of this act, what we see is brought within our reach - though not necessarily within arm's reach" (John Berger, *Ways of Seeing*, 1972). Photographic Image, Vicinity of Grenfell Tower; Lancaster West Estate, North Kensington, London, June 2017.

Preface

Garden Bridge Reclamation Case Study

Figure P.ix.: "Perspective makes the single eye the centre of the visible world. Everything converges on to the eye as to the vanishing point of infinity. The visible world is arranged for the spectator as the universe was once thought to be arranged for God" (John Berger, *Ways of Seeing*, 1972). Photographic Image, Environmental Activist, Central London, August 2016.

Interviewer: *... So firstly if you can just tell me about Folly for London?*
Interviewee: *It actually has two names; it started off as Folly for London and that's my twitter handle [@follyforlondon]; and now I have this website called: A Bridge too Far [abridgetoofar.co.uk]. So the reason for that transition was, about May 2015, so two and a bit years ago. I had an exhibition on the South Bank with some friends; I am an artist. Sorry the North Bank, the Thames, near Somerset house. And it was a sight specific artwork, so it was about this particular architectural place. And a friend came along and she said: "oh this is brilliant, I have never seen an artwork which is about a place or politics like this. You should do something to help us stop the Garden Bridge". And she lived on the South Bank and she lived in that Coin Street Community Builders area. And she didn't really know what that meant, because she is not an artist; and I didn't really know what that meant, I hadn't really heard of Garden Bridge; which I am now ashamed of. Because at that point it had already*

Figure P.xi.: "According to the convention of perspective there is no visual reciprocity. There is no need for God to situate himself in relation to others: he is himself the situation" (John Berger, *Ways of Seeing*, 1972). Photographic Image, South Bank, Central London, August 2016.

Figure P.x.: "The camera isolated momentary appearances and in so doing destroyed the idea that images were timeless. Or, to put it another way, the camera showed that the notion of time passing was inseparable from the experience of the visual (except in paintings) ... What you saw was relative to your position in time and space. It was no longer possible to imagine everything converging on the human eye as on the vanishing point of infinity" (John Berger, *Ways of Seeing*, 1972). Photographic Image, Environmental Activist, Central London, August 2016.

Interviewer: What were the local community doing?
Interviewee: *So they formed a group about five months before me called Thames Central Open Spaces [@TCOSLondon], you might have seen them on Twitter as well? TCOS [www.tcos.org]. And they have a very different strategy; and I think it is quite important to, when you are doing any activism, to different points of attack. So for instance, they [TCOS] were very much focusing at that point on the local issue; the park which will be destroyed; the livelihood and the community aspects that would be destroyed. The fact that there were no questions asked and it was great ... The trees especially yeah. But what often, was the case at that point, was the developers behind it the Garden Bridge Trust would simply say: oh there is some opposition, but it's just a few local Nimbys. And anybody that was following the story knew that it wasn't like there were [saying]. But they also had connections to all over the place, to the architectural community and engineering and all sorts of things. But [criticism] was easily shut down. So as soon as I did something from the side, and I wasn't part of them, so I could pretend that I was connected or an off-shoot of them. And it was coming through the architectural community, it was coming through Architects' Journal and Building Design; and the Guardian and stuff. Suddenly they couldn't use that .... Will Hurst in particular has been really, really good, yeah! So as soon as it was coming from these other angles they couldn't use that line of defence anymore: saying oh it's just a few angry local people.*

Interviewer: Who's they?
Interviewee: *The Garden Bridge Trust, who are on the front of it; a lovely little charity ...*

(Semi-Structured, Qualitative Interview: Architecture Political Activist, Central London, August 2017) *got through planning and as an engaged architecturally political person, if I didn't know about it, I thought: who the hell does know about it? Anyway so, I had a few drinks because it was our private view. And I said: oh you should do something like a joke architectural competition, where instead of asking for serious solutions you are asking for dystopian solutions. So anyone can enter; cos for the Garden Bridge there was never an architectural competition. They just got Thomas Heatherwick in through the side door. So, I said you should do this joke one, where you are asking for like, if anyone that can design something as aggressive and obnoxious and bad for the environment; as blocks historic views and destroys a park. And see if anyone could come up with something as stupid as a Garden Bridge? And then, I went home and then she phoned me up a few days later and said: "Have you started yet?". And I said: "What?". I had to go through my head cos I had, had a few drinks. And I thought if any, ... certainly if you're creative; if you have an idea and someone else thinks of something rather than you, you think that there is something up? So I set up this little competition thinking if some local people ... it might be quite fun. And it just got a little bit bigger, and eventually entries came in from Japan, America and South Africa and all sorts of places and Russia. And through doing that I suddenly learnt a lot more. So I learnt, ok it [i.e. the Garden Bridge] is not only the few things she told me; and it started ticking all these boxes about things I had issues with. So the privately owned public space, like you mentioned. My background was working in conservation architecture; and my first look into it was that view of Waterloo Bridge, which I don't like every little bit of it; but I like the openness. And the fact that, that changing view; it has been there for two hundred years. So that was my look into it, and I thought, oh ... that's being blocked and effectively privatised; because it won't suddenly be free in 24 hours access. And that view, which is for me one of the richest ones in London is suddenly going to be owned by this corporate being. But there was also the Green Wash, pretending that it is good for the environment but it's not. How did this thing get, exist? ... So all these things, that for me, like we just said, were symbolic about so many things which are wrong with London, politics architecture at the moment, the community. Kind a was, tick, tick, tick it [Garden Bridge] became all of them. Yes, I really hated the thing itself [the Garden Bridge], I also hated what it represented as well. We were a society and politics in architecture; so it was one of those things, if you find out too much you can't stop; you can't think oh that was a fun little project, I will not sit back and do something else. Because like I was angry, as were the local community and they were already doing their things.*

Figure P.xvii.: "The inherent contradiction in perspective was that it structured all images of reality to address a single spectator who, unlike God, could only be in one place at a time" (John Berger, *Ways of Seeing*, 1972). Photographic Image, South Bank, Central London, August 2016.

Figure P.xviii.: "Adults and children sometimes have boards in their bedrooms or living-rooms on which they pin pieces of paper: letters, snapshots, reproductions of paintings, newspaper cuttings, original drawings, postcards. On each board all the images belong to the same language and all are more or less equal within it, because they have been chosen in a highly personal way to match and express the experience of the room's inhabitant. Logically, these boards should replace museums" (John Berger, *Ways of Seeing*, 1972). Photographic Image, South Bank, Central London, August 2016.

Prologue

By Composition of Forces

Figure Pro.i.: "One may remember or forget these messages but briefly one takes them in, and for a moment they stimulate the imagination by way of either memory or expectation" (John Berger, *Ways of Seeing*, 1972). Photographic Image, South Bank, Central London, August 2016.

Theoretical Framework: By Composition of Forces

[T]hat discipline creates out of the bodies it controls four types of individuality, or rather an individuality that is endowed with four characteristics: it is cellular (by the play of spatial distribution), it is organic (by the coding of activities), it is genetic (by the accumulation of time), it is combinatory (*by composition of forces*). And, in doing so, it operates four great techniques: it draws up tables; it prescribes movements; it imposes exercises; lastly, in order to obtain the combination of forces, it arranges 'tactics'. Tactics, the art of constructing, with located bodies, coded activities and trained aptitudes, mechanisms in which the product of the various forces is increased by their calculated combination are no doubt the highest form of disciplinary practice. In this knowledge, the eighteenth-century theoreticians saw the general foundation of all military practice, from the control and exercise of individual bodies to the use of forces specific to the most complex multiplicities. (Foucault 1991: 167, *my emphasis*)

Michel Foucault's (1988: 18) *Technologies of the Self* defines "technologies of sign systems" as one of four "specific techniques that human beings use to understand themselves". It has been my consistent contention that technologies of the sign have gained ascendency as they extend further, and further, into the financialised governing of everyday life. Conversely, Michel Foucault emphasises the operation of "technologies of power" and "technologies of the self" (ibid.). Foucault (ibid. 19) accentuates this latter trajectory thus: "I am more and more interested in the interaction between oneself and others and in the technologies of individual domination, the history of how an individual acts upon himself, in the technology of self". The apparent marginalisation of technologies of the sign, in this latter trajectory of Foucault's oeuvre, raises epochal issues; surely the complex networked assemblages of technologies of the sign that are pervading everyday life have equal significance to the technologies of power and self? However, neither Foucault (1988) nor prominent Foucauldian translations and analyses of Foucault's lectures and speeches on the archaeologies of knowledge (e.g., Gordon 1980, Sheridan 1994, Isin and Wood 1999) prioritises technologies of the sign. Conversely, it is my contention that "technologies of sign systems" as defined by Foucault (1988: 18) provide radically revelatory knowledge into the biopolitical processes of marketisation, financialisation, and informationalisation of everyday life. Integral to my assertion here is an appreciation of the contrasting orders of the sign and the complex formulations by which the interplay of "sign systems" operates to communicate and inscribe. Thus, central to the notion of adsensory technologies expressed here is a conception of advertising as inscriptive; this is premised on a definition of Foucault's (ibid.) sign technologies, which utilises an asyndeton to emphasise a complex interplay between differing orders of the sign: "Technologies of sign systems, which permit us to use signs, meanings, symbols, signification" (ibid. 18).

I have utilised a plethora of postmodern discourses in conjunction with Actor Network Theory so as to reconfigure advertising as an inscriptive technology, apposite for the deconstruction of marketing discourse and practice; and from this prioritising of sign technology (as opposed to technology of the self), I have critiqued the subjectivity of marketing segmentation practitioners and the objects of their gaze. Suffice to say, in reconfiguring advertising as an inscriptive technology, I have developed a valuable conceptual resource that provides a critical bridge and radical intervention into advertising and marketing practice. Indeed, John Berger (1972/1977: 60) in *Ways of Seeing* might concur that the feminism of my conception of advertising inscriptive technologies serves "as a bridge between two intense imaginative states". Nevertheless, neither *Adsensory Urban Ecology* nor *Adsensory Financialisation* are advocating the nudist feminist protesting of radical feminism or its contemporary concoction as pseudo-individualistic celebrity feminist exhibitionism. Indeed, in recent times Victoria Bateman's disrobing anti-Brexit radio and television media cliché protest antics have garnered a mixture of distain and puerile voyeuristic attention. Neo-Conservative feminist economists adopting bare-chested stunts so as to propagate a neoliberal economised welfare insurance, albeit wrapped in a #FBPE anti-Brexit guise, fail to recognise that their philosophically unsound meditation on the Emperor's New Clothes is merely nudity i.e., an objectification of nakedness in a patriarchal gendered culture industry. As Berger (1972/1977: 47) expresses it: "The surveyor of woman in herself is male: the surveyed female. Thus she turns herself into an object – and most particularly an object of vision: a sight". Given Victoria Bateman's reductive solipsistic bare-chested neo-Conservative feminism, it is unsurprising that she wrote "Welfare Reform: Why Subsidising Other People's Kids Must Have Limits" (Bateman 2015) and published this in CapX (2019) which describes itself as "founded to make the case for popular capitalism". What is surprising is the extent to which Bateman (2015) is misguided in her crude neo-Conservative assertion that the "bloated welfare state" operates "like buying insurance, but through the government rather than through an insurance company"; and furthermore the astonishing British imperialist resonance in her assertion that: "If the West is to maintain its position in the world economy, it needs to hold on to what made it great to begin with ... Pulling back welfare support, such as by limiting payments to two children or implementing a welfare cap, might seem ruthless, but it is the only way of making sure that we do not dispose of the foundations that have helped us to build economic success". Such, imperialist neo-Conservative feminist economics necessitates a post-colonial feminist riposte; for the "economic success" of the British empire was built through the enslavement, colonisation and international labour exploitation of the developing world. Furthermore, and with regards to my insistence that the concept of adsensory in respect to feminism is advanced beyond the solipsism of neo-Conservative economist nude protestations. It is my thesis, in this adsensory series, that adsensory financialisation involves the informationalisation of the body as object and subject of the advertising inscriptive technologies that are integral to the financialisation of health and wellbeing in western capitalist societies. Moreover, in accordance with my doctorate primary research interviews with single parents, National and Provincial building society marketing managers and end of contract exit qualitative interviews with consumer researchers, the transportation of commercial insurance and insurantial technologies onto state welfare provision and child maintenance involves the temporal negation of an ethics of care; whereby present wellbeing is displaced by a disembodied actuarial future.

Premised on the notion of advertising technologies as inscriptive, it has been my observation that the positivistic epistemologies that informed the marketing and advertising technologies of a Women's Market for insurance, from its inception, have been integral to the creation of this market. Reductive advertising technologies and spurious actuarial pseudo-science coalesce in the marketing of the incongruously designed (given the phenomenology of gendered time to reproductive domestic labour) Women's Market for insurantial products. Following this argument through, my recent book (Odih 2016) entitled *Adsensory Financialisation* details empirically an insidious regime of capital accumulation predicated on the expropriation of the human body as both object and subject of advertising technology relevant to the financialisation of health and social well-being. Several aspects of this book consider the extension of adsensory technologies into the culture industry. Bio-sensing festival soundscapes, digitally bio-mapping shared augmented realties, building local ethico-synoptic communities into international viewing audiences – these advances in biotechnologies present radical challenges to the simple application of critical theory to the contemporary culture industry. Indeed, the extension into touristic gentrification of audio-sensing tracking devices parallels the ascendency of the *Adsensory Financialisation* (Odih 2016) of health and well-being within the leisure industry. In the bio-sensing biotechnology of the body-tracking monitors now pervading commercial and healthcare leisure provision, the body is both object and subject of the inscriptive advertising technologies that are integral to the financialisation of health and well-being. Thus, adsensory financialisation refers to the centrality of the human body as a mediation and fabrication of the informationalising advertising technologies that are integral to the knowing of populations of bodies for it renders them increasingly subject to finance capital in the private insurance of our health and well-being.

Adsensory Financialisation situates wearable bio-technologies within the marketing healthcare management programmes currently aligning National Health Service neoliberal reengineering with consumer citizenship and the healthcare of populations. Furthermore, in their endeavour to network virtual communities, adsensory wearable technologies escalate the conditions of neoliberal healthcare entrepreneurialism and self-regulation. *Adsensory Financialisation* provides empirical evidence of a new mode of capital accumulation in which the advertising of the human body has become both the object and subject of financialisation. An integral feature of capital accumulation through adsensory financialisation is the emergence of levels of surveillance that exceed conception in terms of bio-politics disciplinary panoptics (Foucault 1991) for they embrace situations in which the many-are-watching the few, i.e., synoptics (Mathiesen 1997) and the many-are-watching the many in the ethico-synoptics of adsensory technological times.

Developing further my theme of adsensory technologies of the sign in conjunction with Daniel Bell's (1999) theory of the codification of knowledge as an axial feature of the structuring of post-industrial society, this book is entitled *Adsensory Urban Ecology* (Volume One) and case-studies the gentrification in the post-industrial urban spaces: London's Grenfell Tower, building refurbishment (2013–2017) and London's Garden Bridge River Thames project, speculative regeneration (2014 – 2017). These case studies illustrate, empirically, the extent to which advertising sensory (adsensory) technologies have become integral to the gentrification of post-industrial urban spaces. Specifically, adsensory refers to the significance of a sensory codification of the body, to the market-based urban ecology codification of knowledge relevant to the gentrification of post-industrial urban spaces. With regard to the research question that has guided my critical ethnography, it is thus: **What form of capital accumulation is emerging from the integration of adsensory technology into the gentrification of post-industrial urban spaces?**

Methodology; Live Streaming Critical Ethnography

Critical ethnography defines the methodological logic informing the method of application of ethnographic technique in this research. Committed to engaging with inequalities, critical ethnography focuses on the social structures which mediate articulations and demonstrations of reality. Axiomatic with its incisive critical investigative praxis is an "ethical responsibility geared towards addressing processes of unfairness or injustice within a particular lived domain" (Madison 2011: 5). Compassion effectively expresses critical ethnographic agenda; compassion through allowing oneself to identify with research subjects and their conditions of existence. Critical ethnographic empathy is not voyeuristic showcasing; rather there is a commitment not only to gaze but also to intervene in powerful signifying processes and disrupt their claims to truth. Thus the critical ethnographer interrogates "beneath surface appearances, disrupts the status quo, and unsettles both neutrality and taken-for-granted assumptions by bringing to light underlying and obscure operations of power and control" (ibid.). Such sentiment motivates the critical ethnographer to explore complexity, eschewing easily accessible pre-packaged research topics and actively seeking out the subjugated voices of minority groups. In so doing, the critical ethnography methodological logic applies and utilises research technologies "to penetrate the borders and break through the confines in defence of ... the voices and experiences of subjects whose stories are otherwise restrained and out of reach" (ibid.). Reaching out to these voices requires honesty and truth lest we as critical ethnographers become inveigled in the structured inequalities we are intent on delimiting and challenging. Thus, positionality frames approaches intent on reconfiguring the subject-object divide into a subject-to-subject relationality. Positionality bears some relation to reflexivity; although the former intends through self-reflection to self-declare one's own position. In so doing, we "turn back" on our own situation within structured relations of power; "we are accountable for our own research paradigms, our own positions of authority, and our own moral responsibility relative to representation and interpretation" (ibid. 8).

Ethnography refers to procedures and iterative practices designed to ascertain the culture, values and meaningful activities of a group, community or collection of networked individuals. Ethnography is invariably linked with symbolic meaning and the interpretation of social action in terms of symbolic interactionism (Blumer 1969). This conventional ethnographic fascination with the inter-subjective interpretation of occasions is complemented by analyses of our experiential capacity to apprehend sequences of social action as part of the phenomenology of everyday life (Berger and Luckmann 1966). Such an endeavour often posits a polarised differentiation between the ethnographer and the subject of analysis; and in so doing presupposes a focus on ascertaining descriptive accounts of contiguous experiences. Thus, conventional ethnographers document descriptively nuanced "realist tales", which adhere to the rigorous substantiation of "the comings and goings of members of the culture" and make claim to "the authenticity of the cultural representation" (Van Maanen 1988: 45). Realist tales are intimately concerned to "speak for their subjects, usually to an audience of other researchers" (Thomas 1993: 4). Axiomatic to authentically describing the subject is an adherence to neutrality; i.e., the suppression of the ethnographer's predisposition and biases. Cognizant of the vulnerability of such representational claims in the context of an epistemic alienation of positive social theory, realist ethnography tends toward a privileging of "naturalistic" enquiry. According to Norman Denzin (1989: 71), "naturalistic interactionism" methodology proposes "that humans engage in 'minded', self-reflexive behaviour. Humans act in ways that reflect their unfolding and emergent definitions of themselves and the social situations they confront".

When naturalism is integrated within the Research Act, the social scientist is entrusted to observe, listen and visually ascertain the first-person symbolic meanings through which group members align "on-going patterns of interaction" (ibid. 11). Consequently, naturalistic enquiry has an emphasis on "adopting the perspective...of the acting other" and in so doing realistically (Van Maanen 1988) documenting the group's social behaviour. Suffice to say, realist tales "decry the abstract and celebrate the concrete reference" (ibid. 48). Problematically, this quid pro quo is invariably at the expense of the analysis of the effects of structural inequalities and regulatory practices. Motivated by the immediacy of capturing the symbolic interaction of the group and conveying this in unbiased knowledgeable prose, realist ethnographic tales tend toward "parochial, romantic and limited vision" (ibid. 127). Conversely, in "critical tales" there is a redefinition of the application of ethnographic research, i.e., a progression beyond the mere production of knowledge toward foregrounding politics so as to "serve the needs of the culture being studied" (Tricoglus 2001: 139). Critical ethnographic tales recount the life-world of a group in terms of the articulation, enactment and embodiment of "historically structured social forms that organise, regulate, and legitimate specific ways of being, communicating and acting" (Simon and Dippo 1986: 197). Central to critical ethnography is, therefore, the simultaneous focus on hermeneutic reading of meaning and the necessity to encounter social research as an emancipatory agenda (Thomas 1993: 5). From this perspective of encounter, I came to discern that the critical ethnographic methodological approach that had accompanied the commencement of my recent ethnographic studies was morphing towards a phenomenon I had previously described as "live streaming ethnography".

Chance encounters in the live streaming offline ethnography occurred with regards to the case study of Brick Lane, London (detailed in Volume Two). Initially, this research was motivated by an empirical presupposition that some theoretical association can be formulated, linking the post-industrial gentrification of the urban spaces within the Spitalfields vicinity of London, with the area covered by the Whitechapel Gallery's, Janet Cardiff (1999) *Artangel* audio walk. Consequently, this empirical research case study commenced with my participative ethnographic partaking in the Whitechapel Gallery's Janet Cardiff audio walk. Images derived from the commencement of this audio walk provide a visual-scape and led into the wondrous street art gallery sporadically curated along Brick Lane, London. Here and elsewhere, my commitment to the time and space location of agents within the empirical field guided my development of live streaming ethnographic research. The Classical Greek philosopher Heraclitus (circa535 – circa475 BC.) espoused the idea that the universe is in perpetual fluctuation; continuity and motion epitomise the ebb and flow of social life. Flux is an apposite visual metaphor for the field of ethnographic research. Fluctuation also highlights the uniqueness of insight provided by entering into the stream of actions and being embedded within the moment of the live event. The metaphor of the stream resonates with Heraclitus' famous aphorism that we never step into the same river twice: "The river where you set your foot just now is gone – those waters giving way to this, now this" (Heraclitus 2003: 27). Live streaming ethnography is about engaging in the moment of the movement; observing, listening and learning while embedded in the rivulet of the event; flowing with the rhythm of meaningful engagement. Live streaming empirical ethnography requires an appreciation of social identities as constructed in and through time and space; an idea incisively advanced by Heraclitus (ibid. 51): "Just as the river where I step is not the same, and is, so I am as I am not". Methodologically, my formulation of live streaming interpretative structuralism involves the design of ethnographic techniques that enable observations and interviews to be embedded in the ebb and flow of meaning-making. In total, over twenty empirical interviews were carried out between February 2017 – December 2018; the ethnography observations of the Trafalgar Square, London busking community (Volume Two) in December 2017-December 2018; data triangulated January-February 2019.

Figure Pro.ii.: "If the new language of images were used differently, it would, through its use, confer a new kind of power. Within it we could begin to define our experiences more precisely in areas where words are inadequate. (Seeing comes before words)" (John Berger, *Ways of Seeing*, 1972). Photographic Image, Brick Lane, London, May 2017.

Figure Pro.iii.: "The way the painter has painted her includes her will and her intentions in the very structure of the image, in the very expression of her body and her face" (John Berger, *Ways of Seeing*, 1972). Photographic Image, Proximity Brick Lane, London, May 2017.

Live-streaming critical ethnography encapsulated Computer Mediated Communication (CMC) technologies linking video transcriptions of interviews/performances/activities and other material realities in the ethnographic spaces of my cases studies, with online virtual communities and social media idiosyncratic streams of *talk*. The latter methodological focus was of particular significance to the analysis of *talk* generated in online social media around the heart-rending subject of the Grenfell Tower tragedy; a key case study that features significantly in this book.

Ethnographic Offline, Qualitative Interview Method; Research Career and Data Analysis

Multiple portfolios of critical ethnographic methods and qualitative interview method form: Ethnographic observation, as well as social science interviews, management sciences interviews, which have as their focus the management of personal conduct, management of interpersonal behaviour, the management of organisations and consumer markets. Additionally, as necessitated by a focus on organisational care ethics, the portfolio of qualitative methods constitutive of Volume One and Two included exit interviews, conducted: (1) at the end of a contract/project (e.g. Brick Lane street artist); (2) at the culmination of conservation activism (e.g., Bath Heritage Watchdog); and (3) the dénouement of environmental activism (e.g., Thames Central Open Spaces).

Methodologically the exit interview endeavours to review and evaluate individual performance, within the context of the culmination of a formally ascribed period of activity, through a dialogic interplay of verbatim speech, petitioned evidence-based evaluation (e.g., photo-elicitation, petitioning respondents, dialogic real-time discussion of audio/visual recordings of personal conduct, actions and activities) and a reflexive practice-based impact assessment of withdrawal. Needless, to say, exit interview methodology is diametrically opposed to forensic architecture. This is because the exit interview does not seek to forensically excavate a linear past; but rather it endeavours to render visible the dialogic positioning of the self and subjectivity in a shifting narrative formulation of a past in which the subject is present. All five case studies (Volume One and Volume Two) are informed by primary interviews and ethnographic observations of purposively sampled individuals, groups, local government politicians, political activists, environmental activists, practitioners, and management consultations.

With specific regards to my professional experience research expertise and biographical acumen. Habitus and diaspora ingeniously entangle cultivated academic perspective with an embodied deeply entrenched critical insight into the perilous contradictions and conflicts inherent in the extension of a financialisation of social welfare into the domestic sphere. Nigerian Biafra diaspora, with respect to British colonial governance of West Africa, is uniquely emblematic of the exploitative extent to which colonisation, in actuality, manifests as an acculturated imposition of the financialisation of the domestic sphere. Indeed, up until its independence in 1960 the nation's currency, the Nigerian pound sterling exchange rate, was constantly paired to the British pound sterling. Consequently, for the first generation of Nigerian Biafra diaspora economic migrant communities settled in the city of London, the colonial legacy of British pound sterling mendaciously prowled their habitus. Inscribed into familial memory through the practice of my bilingual habitus, the legacy of British colonial financial governance precipitated my cultivation of a critical consciousness of financialisation; and an incisive realisation that this finance capital is primarily motivated by a future orientated profit maximum in disregard of present concerns for the health and well-being of its subjects.

The post-colonial family and children's social care financial arrangements of first generation Nigerian immigrants, settled in London from the 1967-1970 Biafra diaspora, precipitated my biographical, auto-ethnographical focus into the extension of financial services consumer markets into the household and the domestic sphere. Nigerian Biafra diaspora migrants, form a pertinent cohort of British colonial diaspora, as their family structures tenuously tethered after the ravages of civil war, coupled with a colonised acculturation into the finance capital of British colonial masters, constitute this particular Nigerian diaspora as experientially insightful and intuitively critical of the UK's financialising mode of social security. I am a second generation daughter of the Nigerian Biafra diaspora (i.e., 1967-1970), born in London into a habitus proficiently knowledgeable of British colonial finance capital and yet irreconcilably conflicted in their parental obligation and its translation into the UK's financialising of children's social care; with these conflicted contradictions tragically presciently, in recent years, leading to further empirical confirmation that black minority ethnic female headed households were disproportionately casualties of the UK's 2007-2013 subprime mortgage finance market crash. Indeed, the ramifications of my parent's Nigerian experience of British colonially imposed finance capital, coupled with their conflicted translation of the remnants of this legacy, as settled migrants in London from the Nigerian

Biafra diaspora, provided for a habitus imbued with knowledge of British colonial finance capital and its inherent contradictions.

Moreover, cognizance at the level of memory and habitus, of the injurious outcomes of British colonial financialisation penetrating into the domestic sphere of its Nigerian colony, coupled with my awareness of the conflictual translation (by the British settled Nigerian diaspora) of this mode of finance capital into childcare and social welfare, motivates within me a persistent critical introjection and refinement of academic acumen to make viable a feminist cultural political intervention into achieving an equality and diversity, fundamentality challenging market-based capitalist managerialism inequity in financial services consumer markets and the market-based management of voluntary sector care provision. Axiomatic to this is my heartfelt belief and intellectual academic principal that:

> Gendered time and financial services consumption, determines that wherever, child maintenance is financialised through a corrosion of the Beveridge social insurance state welfare model, by the arbitrary imposition of commercial insurance, nobody should be paid to profit for the abandonment to financialisation, of the financial maintenance of a child. (Odih 1990-2019)

My research career curriculum vitae, provides for a substantive level of empirical experience:

Dr. Pamela Geraldine Odih BSoc.Sc. (Keele University: Sociology and Politics), PhD. (University of Manchester, Institute of Science and Technology: School of Management Science)

1980s, Inner London Education Authority, Greenwich Borough interviews;
1990s, National and Provincial Building Society interviews;
1990s, Manchester voluntary sector organisations interviews;
2000s, London mentoring charities interviews;
2000s, London Kids Company interviews;
2011-2012, London Occupy LSX St Paul's Cathedral piazza ethnography and interviews;
2013-2014 London River Thames ecology river foreshore ethnography and interviews;
2016-2017 London Garden Bridge interviews;
2017-2018 Bath city conservationist activists Bath Press interviews;
2017 London Grenfell Tower local government interviews;
2017-2018 London Trafalgar Square busking community ethnography and interviews.

Prologue

Data analysis for my offline qualitative empirical interviews has continued to be informed by the interpretative qualitative data analytics of Grounded Theory and, specifically, Strauss and Corbin's (1990) *Basics of Qualitative Research* whereby the Strauss and Corbin (1990: 58) coding system of "open code" (thematic categorising), "axial code" (dimensions of thematic categories) and "selective code" (conceptual themes emerging from axial coding) was diligently and carefully applied to the qualitative transcripts or, for expediency, directly applied to the audio recording. The emerging empirical themes were developed through "theoretical sampling" (coding and analysing data concurrently so as to ascertain individuals, groups, human and nonhuman agents to next research), directed by a semblance of the pursuit of "theoretical saturation" (empirical situation in which no new conceptual directions appear relevant) as a basis of the construction of the theoretical concepts and formulations that form the primary conclusions of this book's original contribution, entitled *Adsensory Urban Ecology*.

ACKNOWLEDGEMENTS

I would like to express a heartfelt thank you to Professor David Knights who continues to inspire my academic development. Professor Barbara Adam's prolific contribution to the study of time and society has been inspirational, and I would like to pay tribute to her work. Genuine appreciation to Camilla Harding (Commissioning Editor), Amanda Millar (Editorial) at Cambridge Scholars Publishing. My colleagues at Department of Sociology, Goldsmiths University of London have been supportive: Dr. Brian Alleyne, Prof. Vikki Bell, Prof. Vic Seidler and Prof. Bev Skeggs. Big thank you to my friends Andrea Reay and Ivalee Harris. Special heartfelt thank you to my friend Andy and the enchanting cultural delights of the Edinburgh Festival 2018. Love and best wishes to my family.

Introduction

Post-Industrial Urban Ecology

Figure I.1.: "A people or a class which is cut off from its own past is far less free to choose and to act as a people or class than one that has been able to situate itself in history" (John Berger, *Ways of Seeing*, 1972). Photographic Image, Vicinity of Grenfell Tower; Lancaster West Estate, North Kensington, London, June 2017.

Technologies of the Sign

In the writings of Michel Foucault, we are challenged to interrogate liberal humanist ethical virtues. For more than twenty years of his academic career, Foucault was concerned to trace a history of the manifold ways in Western culture "that humans develop knowledge about themselves" (1988: 18). In a text entitled *Technologies of the Self*, Foucault clarifies very important conceptual tools necessary for decoding liberal humanism and rendering it intelligible as a system of knowledge with "specific 'truth games' related to specific techniques that human beings use to understand themselves" (ibid.). These techniques assume four major forms of "technologies", and each mode constitutes a vehicle of practical reason. The first, "technologies of production", permits the transformation of natural objects into resources for the mobilisation of human interests. Foucault recognises synergies here with dialectical materialism, "for instance one sees the relation between manipulating things and domination in Karl Marx's Capital, where every technique of production requires modification of individual conduct – not only skills but also attitudes" (ibid.). The theme of transformation is evident in "technologies of sign systems", the second mode of technology that humans use to organise social life and develop knowledge. Foucault describes this technology as modes of discourse and discursive practice "which permit us to use signs, meanings, symbols, signification" (ibid.). In Foucault's book, *Discipline and Punish*, technologies of sign systems enter a matrix of practical reasoning that functions in a manner that exceeds a positivistic ontology of the image as representing a mirror of the world that merely needs decoding. Instead, technologies of sign systems are integrated into the practice of organising and managing people and, in so doing, operate as modes of administration, regulation, and discipline.

Technologies of sign systems work in conjunction with the third specific technique that human beings have created to know themselves, i.e., "technologies of power". Foucault's focus here is premised on elucidating technologies that "determine the conduct of individuals and submit them to certain ends or domination, an objectivizing of the subject" (ibid.). These objectifying technologies form a recurrent theme in *Discipline and Punish* and in Foucault's (1998, 1992, 1990) later work, technologies of power are detailed in conjunction with the fourth of Foucault's technologies, i.e., "technologies of ... self". These permit individuals to voluntarily carry out practices "on their own bodies and souls, thoughts, conduct, and way of being, so as to transform themselves in order to attain a certain state of happiness, purity, wisdom, perfection, or immortality"

(Foucault 1988: 18). It is my contention that the codification of knowledge that is axiomatic to the urban regenerated post-industrial society demonstrates the extent to which Foucault's four technologies of modern governance increasingly translate into sign technologies. I appreciate that this conclusion is in contrast with the conceptual and theoretical change that can be deduced from Foucault's lectures in the late 1970s and early 1980s, during which time a theoretical focus on domination through the sign spectacle was displaced by a focus on "technology of self", as is evident in the following statement:

> Perhaps I've insisted too much on the technology of domination and power. I am more and more interested in the interaction between oneself and others and in the technologies of individual domination, the history of how an individual acts upon himself, in the technology of self. (Foucault 1988: 19)

The central objective of this book is to detail empirically the centrality of adsensory technologies to the codification of urban ecology as part of the gentrification of post-industrial heritage sites. Following Daniel Bell's (1999) theory of the codification of knowledge as an axial feature of the structuring of post-industrial society, this book's first case study focuses on the regeneration of the Grenfell Tower – once situated in North Kensington, London. Much attention has been drawn to the polyethylene-insulated cladding tiles in terms of insufficient building regulation in their installation on the Grenfell Tower building; and less attention has focused on the external cladding as part of a wider project of energy efficiency and aesthetic gentrification.

During the early hours of June 14th, 2017, Grenfell Tower was tragically engulfed by fire and this heart-breaking incident precipitated a justifiably angry chorus of condemnation directed initially at North Kensington's administration then spiralled to include an exploitative political economy of urban regeneration. Political economy makes apparent policies and practices that, in their rapacious scurrying for exploitative profit, are divested of any consciousness of apprehending the obvious negligence of covering decades-old buildings in polyethylene combustible cladding materials. Neoliberal re-engineered social housing façades provide the focus of this book's first case study. The concept of adsensory features, in terms of an aesthetically driven coding of urban regeneration knowledge, into which an urban ecological coding of the human body has become integral.

The second case study focuses on speculative capitalist investment and regeneration. "It's my duty to ensure taxpayers' money is spent responsibly" (Khan 2017) is the first line of the terse *Statement from the Mayor on the Closure of the Garden Bridge Trust,* issued Monday, 14th August 2017. Precipitately citing Dame Margaret Hodge's independent cost evaluation of the Garden Bridge, London mayor Sadiq Khan's statement provides a scathing indictment of Boris Johnson's irresponsibly commissioned Garden Bridge project (ibid.). Khan's incendiary statement of closure accentuates an astonishing revelation elucidated by *The Garden Bridge* report – the project had an irreconcilable "funding gap of over £70 million, potentially unlimited costs to London taxpayers to fund the bridge in the future, systemic failing in the procurement process" compounded by "decisions not being driven by value for money" (Khan 2017). Clearly exasperated by the lavish, improvident extravagance of the Garden Bridge project, Khan's (ibid.) statement heroically exclaims "I could not permit a single penny more of London taxpayers' money being spent on it". In response, the Garden Bridge Trust issued a contrite resignation establishing that the charity's intention to build what amounted to an artificial green park space across the River Thames had ceased to be a viable proposition and that they were "winding up the project" (Garden Bridge Trust 2017).

Barely able to camouflage its disaccord, the Garden Bridge Trust nonchalantly personalises the root incongruity thus: "On 28 April, Sadiq Khan wrote to Lord Mervyn Davies, Chairman of the Garden Bridge Trust, stating that he was not prepared to sign the guarantee for the annual maintenance costs of the Bridge, a condition of planning consent, despite previous assurances given about his support for the project". The aphoristic displacement of the unviability of the project is also endured by the syndicate of financiers: "Unfortunately, the benefactor concerned and the Trustees have all concluded that they cannot proceed with what was always designed to be a public project in the heart of the capital without the support of the Mayor of London" (ibid.). In full retreat from any hint of assigning self-blame and culpability, the statement concludes: "The Garden Bridge project will now be formally closed. This includes terminating contracts, and concluding donor funding agreements. The Trust itself will then be wound up in accordance with the Companies Acts" (ibid.). The central objective of this second case study i.e., the Garden Bridge project, is to ascertain critically the significance of adsensory financialisation to the privatisation of the urban ecology of riverside recreational spaces. Specifically, in this book's Garden Bridge case study, I reconfigure Karl Marx's conception of rentier capitalism as part of a techno-Prometheus ecofeminist critical analysis of the privatisation of public recreational urban river space.

In summary, the case studies of gentrification detailed in this book are thus: Aesthetics and the exterior fabrication of the Royal Borough of Kensington and the Chelsea Grenfell Tower 2014–2017 and the fatuous extravaganza of the Garden Bridge. These empirical case studies illustrate the extent to which advertising sensory (adsensory) technologies has become integral to the gentrification of post-industrial urban spaces. Specifically, adsensory refers to the significance of a sensory codification of the body, to the market-based urban ecology codification of knowledge relevant to the gentrification of post-industrial urban spaces. With regard to the research question that has guided my critical ethnography, it is thus: **What form of capital accumulation is emerging from the integration of adsensory technology into the gentrification of post-industrial urban spaces?**

PART ONE

ADSENSORY DIMENSIONS OF URBAN ECOLOGY

Figure P.I.: "Yet this seeing which comes before words, and can never be quite covered by them, is not a question of mechanically reacting to stimuli" (John Berger, *Ways of Seeing*, 1972). Photographic Image, North Kensington, London, June 2017.

Chapter One

Post-industrial Society and the Aestheticisation of Urban Ecology

Figure 1.1.: "Publicity is addressed to those who constitute the market, to the spectator-buyer who is also the consumer-producer from whom profits are made twice over — as worker and then as buyer. The only places relatively free of publicity are the quarters of the very rich; their money is theirs to keep" (John Berger, *Ways of Seeing*, 1972). Photographic Image, North Kensington, London, June 2017.

Photo Realistic Quality. Highly realistic and exact Exterior Visualization – including lights, shadows, street traffic, municipal facilities, plants and finally the building itself – all combined create a photo-realistic feeling, as if the picture is an actual photo, thus allowing [you] to imagine the plan as if [it] already existed in reality. (Triple D 2018)

Architectural visualisations, in application with 3D virtual reality, "are 3D renderings that virtualize the architectural programs … in a unique and precise quality, that resembles reality" (Triple D 2018). Precision of photo-realist simulacra is an ambition of architectural visualisation; illustrated by service provision proffering: "We can 'plant' the visualization in real surrounding of the project. Obtaining the surrounding photo can be done by a photographer or using a drone" (ibid.). Virtual tours, de rigueur to this architectural assemblage, provide 360-degree panoramic aspects "moving between points in a property or tour using the WebGL method"; the latter has similarities with kinetic computer gaming technology (ibid.). Convergent smartphone technology capacitates virtual reality viewing when used in conjunction with "WebGL cutting edge technology", enabling "you to walk inside an entire building or project" (ibid.). Marketing videos of architectural projects frequently apply virtual reality visualisation; effective exemplifications of which include "dynamic 3D rendering, combined with visual and audio elements, including narration …sound effects, music and visual effects" (ibid.). Convergence in tablet technology and sensory kinetic Apps technology is precipitative of augmented reality, architectural visualisation, as exemplified by "Augmented Reality Apps that upgrade the [classical 2D plan] visualizations and floor place, by adding 3D effects that blend with your printed plans, using a smartphone or a tablet" (ibid.).

Integral to this new generation of architectural visualisation are the sensory faculties and kinetic properties of the human body; and this observation constitutes a principal conjecture of this book, i.e., axiomatic with advances in urban ecology design technology is occurring an expropriation of the body as subject and object of advertising inscriptive technologies, as exemplified by innovations in 3D architectural visualisation whereby urban ecology increasingly provides configurations for the urban design of the regeneration of post-industrial urban spaces. Urban ecology logicises that: "The conventions and rules of aesthetic values have validity only when in context with underlying bio-physical determinants" (Hough 2004: 25). Geared towards the formulation of a new design language, urban ecology gains inspiration from architectural initiative that "re-establishes the concept of multi-functional, productive and working landscapes that integrate ecology, people and economy" (ibid.).

Developing more critically the concept of urban ecology while advancing the theme of adsensory technologies of the sign in conjunction with Daniel Bell's (1999) theory of the codification of knowledge as an axial feature of the structuring of post-industrial society, this book *Adsensory Urban Ecology* (Volume One) case studies gentrification in heterotopic (Foucault 1986) post-industrial urban spaces. Foucault's (1986) *Of Other Spaces* renders complex a delineation of the pre-modern ("space of emplacement") juxtaposed against a perspectivist cartography of the modern era for the latter displaces a sense of place in terms of an embodied relation between, for example, self and the natural world, replacing this with an insistence on the codified classification of space in terms of "the site", which "is defined by relations of proximity between points or elements; formally, we can describe these relations as series, trees, or grids" (ibid. 23). Classification of space in accordance with the grid properties of a perspectivist nomenclature enables an interchangeability by which is meant "the identification of marked or coded elements inside a set that may be randomly distributed, or may be arranged according to single or to multiple classifications" (ibid.).

While located in post-industrial urban spaces, the case studies that form the empirical basis of *Adsensory Urban Ecology* (Volume One and Volume Two) exhibit the complexity of multiple embedded spaces with echoes of "space of emplacement" existing in conjunction with the linear perspectivism of "the site". For example, the case study of the Trafalgar Square busking community (Volume Two) details the characteristically codified design of Foster and Partners' regeneration of the North Terrace into a pedestrianised piazza while also identifying, as part of my empirical ethnographic research data, a technical capital proficiency evident in the handicraft social labour of the busking community and situating the integral habitus of this technical capital as resistant to the music tourism commodity-form perspectivism of the Trafalgar Square ad hoc busking space. Foucault's conception of *Other* space is emblematic of the complexity of the post-industrial urban regeneration encountered and observed as part of my study of adsensory urban ecology for, in the concept of heterotopia, Foucault appreciates a precedence in phenomenology in which we are encouraged to recognise "that we do not live in a homogeneous empty space, but on the contrary in a space thoroughly imbued with quantities and perhaps thoroughly fantasmatic as well" (ibid.). Methodologically, the ethnographic case study of the Trafalgar Square busking community sort traces of connectivity between on-line and off-line gentrification; in actuality, the aleatory materialism of social media hyper-individualised exchanges revealed complexity albeit ultimately decipherable with the assiduous application of time, care and dexterity. Foucault's (1986: 24) account of assemblage and contestation has relevance to my conception of adsensory urban ecology in the sense that this mode of gentrification is helpfully comprehended "As a sort of simultaneously mythic and real contestation of the space in which we live".

The empirical case studies that form the basis of this volume: London's Grenfell Tower, perilous façadism refurbishment; and London's Garden Bridge project, speculative capital regeneration illustrate, empirically, the extent to which advertising adsensory technologies have become integral to the gentrification of post-industrial urban spaces. For example, case studies engage critically with the empirical observation that, in the post-industrial urban ecology of inner-city regeneration, adsensory technologies extend avariciously into the infrastructure of neoliberal managerialist audit-cultured "best value" gentrification. More specifically, adsensory refers to the significance of a sensory codification of the body to the market-based urban ecological codification of knowledge relevance in the managerialist gentrification of post-industrial urban spaces.

Indeed, one gains from the empirical case studies featured: firstly, perspective into the global scope of inscriptive advertising analogues in their capacity to link local communities with globally dispersed momentary affinities. Secondly, with adsensory accumulation the body is both subject and object of the advertising inscriptives that are integral to the financialisation of health, well-being and domicile in advanced Western capitalist societies. For an integral element of adsensory financialisation concerns informationalism. Castells (1996/2010: 99) defines informationalism in terms of an "informational economy" evident in advanced internationally networked capitalism which is experiencing a "shift toward a technological paradigm based on information technologies". Castells (ibid. 100) recognises that much of the informational mode of production mirrors its predecessor and replicates the historical rifts between capital and labour. Indeed, what distinguishes informationalism from significant aspects of the mode of production of recent eras is described by Castells (ibid.) thus: "What has changed is not the kind of activities humankind is engaged in, but its technological ability to use as a direct productive force what distinguishes our species as a biological oddity: its superior capacity to process symbols". It is indeed the advertising creation of "likes" in social media, "steps" derived from fitness trackers or 3D visualisations of e-architecture that forms the metric analogues, that are the basis of the inscriptive advertising sign technologies of the informational economy. Jean Baudrillard's (2003:129) *Consumer Society* is polemical in its provocative distillation of "the finest consumer object", in advanced capitalist society, "the body". Integral to Baudrillard's polemic is the emergence of a dualistic practice precipitative of the current mode of capitalist production; and this is "linked to a split ... representation of his/her own body: the representation of the body as capital and as fetish (or consumer object)" (ibid.). Baudrillard accentuates a caesura in the Cartesian mind/body dualism's privileging of cognitive capital, and a sacrilegious contravene in the "object of salvation", whereby the body "has literally taken over that moral and ideological function from the soul" (ibid.). Indeed, it is Baudrillard's (ibid.) contention "that, far from the body being denied or left out of account, there is deliberate investment in it (in the two senses, economic and psychical, of the term)". While agreeing in principle with Baudrillard, there are limitations in the dualistic separation of the economic and psychical practices of the body; for the reliquiae of Cartesian cognitive privilege assails in an uncontended diagrammatic schematic of the mind, body dualism. Conversely, axiomatic to my contention of an adsensory fourth-order of simulacra is an appreciation of bio-sensing advertising technologies as inscriptive in their rendering of both the economic body, and the psychical body, as knowable and amenable to regulatory intervention.

Advertising technologies in the informational economy are no longer either first or second-order sign-systems depicting a cultural economy of time in modernist reality (Odih 2007b); nor are they third-order simulacra making up and feigning to exist in postmodern times (ibid.). In the informational economy, analogues of advertising inscriptive sign technologies are no longer replica or hyper-real or simulation. Indeed, all three orders of the sign are now (dis)entangled elements (i.e., never transmuting in entirety, into real or hyper-real sign-systems or making believe, feigning existence as simulation) of capital accumulation for they have informationally codified the places, spaces, values, and material and immaterial capital of which they were once mere simulacra.

Indeed, my poststructuralist approach to postmodern sign-systems is far in advance of a reductive cultural theory that constructs postmodern signs as hyper-stimuli, triggers and determinants of behaviour. I am consistently critical of Gabriel and Lang's (1995, 2006, 2015) stimulus and response behavioural model, and its prognosis that postmodern simulation conflates with hyper-reality; for simulations feign existence and conversely hyper-reality refers to a heightened reality in which e.g., advertising practices seek (without guarantee) to fabricate signs that feign their existence. As Baudrillard (1983: 4) expresses it: "A hyperreal henceforth sheltered from the imaginary, and from any distinction between the real and the imaginary, leaving room only for the orbital recurrence of models and the simulated generation of difference". Consequently, I fundamentally disagree with Gabriel and Lang's (2006: 60) assertion that: the hyper-real and simulation are conflated into one "world". I also disagree with Gabriel and Lang's (ibid.) misguiding theory that: "In this hyper-real world, the consumer is no longer a communicator, nor are commodities sign-values. The consumer becomes a Pavlovian dog salivating mechanically at the sight of simple images, his or her emotions are conditioned responses to the sight of brands". It is not my intention to affront or disrepute their cultural theory, but rather to respectfully identify a conceptual misconception. For it is evident that, according to Baudrillard (1983) third- order simulacra, (i.c., simulations) feign their existence; they do not exist. As Baudrillard (ibid. 5) states: "To simulate is to feign to have what one hasn't". Consequently, there is no trigger; there is no transformation of the consumer into a passive receptacle of meaningless postmodern signs; simulatory signs feign their existence and their influence on sentience. Signs are unable to reduce the postmodern consumer into a retched Pavlovian salivating dog and this is because simulatory signs do not exist!

Suffice to say, in the informational economy a fourth-order of simulacra is establishing vital prominence whereby the sign has become adsensory and is subject to a polymerous financialisation in which assemblages of sign technologies avariciously (dis)entangle simulation from the opaque realities of sign-systems in which the body is both subject and object.

The research question that has guided my critical ethnography is thus: **What form of capital accumulation is emerging from the integration of adsensory technology into the gentrification of post-industrial urban spaces?** The empirical ethnographic case studies identify disruptive encounters between adsensory gentrification and embodied urban ecology. In so doing, this book examines empirically a new form of capital accumulation in inner-city gentrification, predicated on the (de)generative integrity of adsensory financialisation.

Figure 1.2.: "Publicity speaks in the future tense and yet the achievement of this future is endlessly deferred. How then does publicity remain credible - or credible enough to exert the influence it does? It remains credible because the truthfulness of publicity is judged, not by the real fulfilment of its promises, but by the relevance of its fantasies to those of the spectator- buyer. Its essential application is not to reality but to day-dreams" (John Berger, *Ways of Seeing*, 1972). Photographic Image, North Kensington, London, June 2017.

Post-industrial Society and the Aestheticisation of Urban Ecology 15

Figure 1.3.: "The entire world becomes a setting for the fulfilment of publicity's promise of the good life. The world smiles at us. It offers itself to us. And because *everywhere* is imagined as offering itself to us, *everywhere* is more or less the same" (John Berger, *Ways of Seeing*, 1972). Photographic Image, Vicinity of Grenfell Tower; Lancaster West Estate, North Kensington, London, June 2017.

Figure 1.4.: "Capitalism survives by forcing the majority, whom it exploits, to define their own interests as narrowly as possible. This was once achieved by extensive deprivation. Today in the developed countries it is being achieved by imposing a false standard of what is and what is not desirable" (John Berger, *Ways of Seeing*, 1972). Photographic Image, Vicinity of Grenfell Tower; Lancaster West Estate, North Kensington, London, June 2017.

Post-industrial Society and the Aestheticisation of Urban Ecology 17

Figure 1.5.: "We never look at just one thing; we are always looking at the relation between things and ourselves. Our vision is continually active, continually moving, continually holding things in a circle around itself, constituting what is present to us as we are" (John Berger, *Ways of Seeing*, 1972). Photographic Image, Vicinity of Grenfell Tower; Lancaster West Estate, North Kensington, London, June 2017.

Figure 1.6.: "A people or a class which is cut off from its own past is far less free to choose and to act as a people or class than one that has been able to situate itself in history" (John Berger, *Ways of Seeing*, 1972). Photographic Image, Vicinity of Grenfell Tower; Lancaster West Estate, North Kensington, London, June 2017.

PART TWO

ADSENSORY FAÇADES IN POST-INDUSTRIAL URBAN SPACE

Figure P.II.: "We only see what we look at. To look is an act of choice. As a result of this act, what we see is brought within our reach – though not necessarily within arm's reach. To touch something is to situate oneself in relation to it" (John Berger, *Ways of Seeing*, 1972). Photographic Image, Vicinity of Grenfell Tower; Lancaster West Estate, North Kensington, London, June 2017.

CHAPTER TWO

FAÇADE AS THE GENTRIFICATION OF POST-INDUSTRIAL URBAN SPACE

Figure 2.1.: "The inherent contradiction in perspective was that it structured all images of reality to address a single spectator who, unlike God, could only be in one place at a time" (John Berger, *Ways of Seeing*, 1972). Photographic Image, North Kensington, London, June 2017.

At least 79 people are dead. It is both a tragedy and an outrage, because every single one of those deaths could and should have been avoided. The Grenfell Tower residents themselves had raised concerns about the lack of fire safety in the block. The Grenfell Action Group had warned: 'It is a truly terrifying thought but the Grenfell Action Group firmly believe that only a catastrophic event will expose the ineptitude and incompetence of our landlord,' the Kensington and Chelsea Tenant Management Organisation. (Jeremy Corbyn, Islington North, Labour MP, 22nd June, Hansard 2017)

In the small hours before dawn, Wednesday 14th June 2017, a tragedy of unparalleled magnitude in the United Kingdom's contemporary peacetime history, materialised in North Kensington, London. Grenfell Tower, established in the 1970s as a magnificent twenty-four storey social-housing edifice, caught fire; within hours a pyramid of rapacious flames had engulfed the building's refurbished exterior. The right honourable MP for Islington North and leader of the Labour Party, Jeremy Corbyn in response to the 22nd June 2017 House of Commons statement by Prime Minister Theresa May, seethed with indignation at the failure of Kensington and Chelsea Tenant Management Organisation to heed the erudite and foreboding warnings articulated by the Grenfell Action Group (ibid.). As the immensity of the tragedy became apparent, the astonishing ineptitude of the Kensington and Chelsea Tenant Management Organisation grew exponentially with the inadequacy of its emergency response. Residents were instructed to comply with an anachronistic "stay in your homes" fire regulation that was oblivious to the extent the internal and external building refurbishment had breached the building's capacity to contain a fire (ibid.). The integrity of the building's fire safety, as with "4,000 other tower blocks", was undermined by the failure of successive governments to implement Frances Kirkham's 2013 Lakanal House fire coroner's recommendations and legislate for the retrofitting of sprinklers in all residential social housing tower blocks (ibid.). Disaffection and public anger at the brutal reality of compromised fire safety swiftly coalesced with that of the 2014 appointed chief executive officer (Nicholas Holgate) of the Royal Borough of Kensington and Chelsea and rapidly precipitated Nicholas Holgate's resignation, which was publicly welcomed by the Prime Minister Theresa May.

In the maelstrom of the tragedy and the ensuing crisis in housing the dispossessed survivors, Kensington and Chelsea Council's floundering created a political vacuum, comprehensive, coherent leadership was urgently sought. Operationally, the newly elected Labour Party Member of

Parliament for Kensington, Emma Dent Coad, amongst others, responded to the local governance void, receiving praise "for the tireless and diligent way she has stood up for her constituents in the very short time since she was thankfully elected to the House" (ibid.). Prime Minister Theresa May's 22nd June 2017 Grenfell Tower statement announced measures to substrate the deteriorating competency of the Conservative-run council alongside the establishment of an independent public inquiry. In response to the latter, the leader of the opposition, Jeremy Corbyn, insisted, amongst other interventions, that the appalling dereliction of the fire alarm system be investigated: "Many residents reported that they were only alerted to the fire by the screams of their neighbours ... Something went catastrophically wrong which lost life" (ibid.). In the immediate aftermath of the initial shock and devastation, public scrutiny of health and safety concerns over the fire-resistance of the exterior wall cladding, newly installed by the building refurbishment company Harley Facades Limited, intensified. Echoing this anxiety, and in response to the Prime Minister's statement, Jeremy Corbyn insisted that the public inquiry "must also address ... whether the cladding used was illegal, as the Chancellor has suggested, and whether it should be banned entirely; and what wider changes must be urgently made to building regulations" (ibid.). Set within the "strapped for cash" context of the neoliberal competitively tendered contractual culture of local authority service provision, it seems apposite and justified for one to voice "suspicion" "that many local authorities – strapped for cash after seven years of cuts – have cut back on fire testing and cut back on inspections because they simply have not got the staff to do it anymore" (ibid.). Similarly charged were the issues of financing the inspection of suspect tower blocks in the UK, the removal of highly inflammable external wall cladding systems and the retrofitting of sprinklers. With specific regard to the latter:

> Lessons must be learned in the public inquiry, and a disaster that should never have happened must never happen again. The Government must delay no longer, and must now implement the recommendations of the 2013 inquiry report into the Lakanal House fire. The public inquiry into Grenfell Tower must also establish whether lives could have been saved if those recommendations had been implemented in full, and if the recommendations of the all-party group on fire safety and rescue had been heeded by the Government. (Jeremy Corbyn, Islington North, Labour MP, 22nd June, Hansard 2017)

Following Daniel Bell's (1999) theory of the codification of knowledge as an axial feature of the structuring of post-industrial society, this chapter's

Façade as the Gentrification of Post-industrial Urban Space 23

case study focuses on the regeneration of the Grenfell Tower – once situated in North Kensington, London. The principal objective of this chapter is to explore critically the 2014–2016 exterior fabrication of the fateful Grenfell Tower and identify this as axiomatic with an adsensory aestheticisation of urban regeneration; for much attention has been drawn to the polyethylene-insulated cladding tiles installed onto the Grenfell Tower building as part of a wider project of energy efficiency and aesthetic gentrification.

Figure 2.2.: "Alternatively the anxiety on which publicity plays is the fear that having nothing you will be nothing" (John Berger, *Ways of Seeing*, 1972). Photographic Image, North Kensington, London, June 2017.

During the early hours of June 14th, 2017, Grenfell Tower was tragically engulfed by fire and this heart-breaking incident precipitated a justifiably angry chorus of condemnation directed initially at North Kensington's administration; and then spiralled to encapsulate an exploitative political economy of urban regeneration. Political economy makes apparent policies and practices that in their rapacious scurrying for exploitative profit are divested of all consciousness necessary to apprehend the obvious negligence of encapsulating decades-old buildings in glittering highly combustible cladding materials. Neoliberal re-engineered social housing façades provide the focus of this chapter's case study. The concept of adsensory features here in terms of an aesthetically driven coding of urban regeneration knowledge, is one in which the aspiration of best value is no longer a sign of value; rather, the pursuit of value for money has become its primary goal. In this respect consider the following product specification:

> Grenfell Tower Exterior Refurbishment
> Update – Friday 23rd June [2017]
> Grenfell Tower: Celotext is to stop the supply of RS5000 for use in rainscreen cladding systems in buildings over 18m tall
>
> Celotex is shocked by the tragic events of the Grenfell Tower. Our thoughts are with everyone affected by this devastating human tragedy. We have been supplying building products for over forty years and as a business our focus has always been to supply safe insulation products to make better buildings.
> …
> Celotex notes the comments made by Scotland Yard at this morning's briefing in respect of the insulation used in Grenfell Tower. In view of the focus on rainscreen cladding systems and the insulation forming part of them, Celotex believes that the right thing to do is to stop the supply of Celotex RS5000 for rainscreen cladding systems in buildings over 18m tall with immediate effect (including in respect of ongoing projects), pending further clarity.
>
> (Celotex 2017)
>
> Important: On 23 June 2017, in view of the focus on components of rainscreen cladding systems, Celotex stopped the supply of Celotex RS5000, pending further clarity. Material about the product is for information only. Celotex do not currently supply a solution for buildings over 18 metres.
>
> (Celotex 2017c)

Within the miasma of devastation and despair in the immediate aftermath of the Grenfell Tower fire tragedy, a maelstrom of despondency and disarray rapidly identified, as catalyst, the building's exterior wall cladding. The company called Celotex precipitately trailed speculation over retrenched local council refurbishment expenditure. Established in the 1920s, Celotex's London base was premised on the importation of insulation from the parent Celotex manufacturing company in the United States (Celotex 2017a). In 2012, Saint-Gobain, the premier world leader in "habitat and construction markets" (ibid.) purchased Celotex, establishing Celotex Saint-Gobain as "The leading UK PIR thermal insulation provider for the building and construction market" (Celotex 2017). In an effort to seize corporate social responsibility and circumvent denigration of its product's integrity, Celotex Saint-Gobain began in June 2017 to issue statements on its website's home screen. The first, posted on Thursday, 15th June 2017, expressed appropriate condolences for the losses at Grenfell Tower, swiftly followed by a declaration of proprietary with regards to the insulation used to clad the building: "Our thoughts are with those affected by the terrible fire at Grenfell Tower in London. Our records show a Celotex product (RS5000) was purchased for use in refurbishing the building" (ibid.). The Celotex RS5000 product features in a brochure available from the Celotex Saint-Gobain website. Described as "developed specifically to enhance the thermal performance of external façade constructions", the Celotex RS5000 product is advertised as "the first PIR insulation board to meet the performance criteria in BR 135 for insulated rainscreen cladding systems"; furthermore, it confirmed that the product is suitable "for use in buildings above 18 meters in height" (Celotex 2017b). Product specifications outline the RS5000 fire resistance properties as follows:

> Featuring a premium lambda performance of 0.021 W/mk and textured aluminium foil facings, Celotex RS5000 offers enhanced thermal performance, an A+ rating when compared to the BRE Green Guide and Class 0 fire performance. With Celotex RS5000 you are specifying an insulation board that: Features a super low lambda value of 0.021W/mk offering enhanced thermal performance; Is the first PIR insulation board to successfully test to BS 8414-2:2005, meet the criteria set out in BR 135 and therefore can be considered for use in buildings above 18 meters in height; Has Class 0 fire performance throughout the entire product in accordance with BS 476; Achieves an A+ rating when compared to the BRE Green Guide; Is supported by LABC approval. (Celotex 2017b)

At the time of writing, Celotex Saint-Gobain's habitat technical director is Mark Allen. In early July 2017, news media journalists revelled (O'Neill

2017) in their having made connections between Mark Allen, the habitat technical director of Celotex Saint-Gobain, and a key member of the UK government Building Regulations Advisory Committee (BRAC). Indeed, and according to current GOV.UK publications, current membership of the BRAC includes Mark Allen, cited as "Technical Director Saint-Gobain Delegation UK and Ireland" (BRAC 2017). The remit of the BRAC is to provide an advisory role to the Secretary of State for the Department of Communities and Local Government (DCLG); the current communities secretary is the Rt. Hon. Sajid Javid MP. In accordance with government protocol, members of BRAC are appointed by the Secretary of State for the DCLG; although appointed "on an independent voluntary basis to represent particular areas of expertise or experience", members appointed to BRAC usually tenure for two to three years (BRAC 2017). In early July 2017, amidst the news furore over the Grenfell Tower tragedy, journalists insinuated a conflict of interest, credibility and impartiality arising from Celotex Saint-Gobain's habitat technical director assuming membership of BRAC and potentially advising government building regulations on the product at the centre of the public inquiry, Celotex RS5000. Indeed, the product specification of Celotex RS5000 was already central to a sensational revelation by the British Broadcasting Corporation (BBC) on Friday, the 30th of June, 2017.

BBC journalists Symonds and De Simone (2017) claimed that "documents obtained by the BBC suggest" that "cladding fitted to Grenfell Tower during its refurbishment was changed to a cheaper version". Grenfell Tower was refurbished with the RS5000 cladding product sourced from Celotex Saint-Gobain; however, it is claimed that the cladding specified in the original building design refurbishment specification was of a higher fire grade standard for documents shown to the BBC journalists indicate that "zinc cladding originally proposed was replaced with an aluminium type, which was less fire resistant, saving nearly £300,000" (ibid.). BBC journalists Symonds and De Simone (ibid.) insist that the documentation made available (partially revealed in the BBC broadcast news item) indicates that the contractors to whom the refurbishment of the Grenfell Tower was designated "were asked in 2014 to replace zinc cladding with a more economical aluminium version" (ibid.). It is estimated that by installing "aluminium cladding in lieu of zinc cladding" the sum of "£293,368" was shaved off the project costing (ibid.). The exchange enabled an alternative colour scheme to be introduced into the cladding system, but Symonds and De Simone (2017) are resolute in the belief that economising was the primary motivation for the exchange. Quoting documents sourced from journalists at *The Times*, BBC News journalists Symonds and De Simone (2017) advance the accusation that the Grenfell Tower contractors received emails prompting them to observe effective costing "on cladding that could be shown to the councillor overseeing the work".

The notion that pressure was indirectly levied on the Grenfell Tower contractors to opt against the use of "zinc cladding with a fire-retardant core" (ibid.) is an issue duly delegated to the public inquiry on Grenfell Tower to elucidate, but it will be a disconcerting truth of the political economy of Grenfell Tower's refurbishment if it is indeed proven that "Council minutes from 2013 show dissatisfaction with the initially-preferred contractor for not keeping the scheme within budget" and that "Further bids were invited, and this led to the appointment of a different contractor in 2014 which was then asked to make savings including on the cladding" (ibid.).

Some evidence in support of the BBC journalists' (ibid.) claim is available in a Royal Borough of Kensington and Chelsea TMO (KCTMO) planning permission public consultation document dated "29th May 2012 at 19:00pm" and entitled "Notes from Grenfell Tower Evening Meeting". Present at the meeting was Studio E Architects; the initial Grenfell Tower building refurbishment architect. According to minutes taken, the meeting opened with a presentation from Studio E Architects in which the intended ideas and project proposal for cladding Grenfell Tower were delivered to the TMO resident members (KCTMO 2012). In minutes derived from a 12th July 2012 meeting of the KCTMO located at the Lancaster West Estate Office, it was noted that the Studio E Architects representative had stated that "we were looking to relocate the nursery and boxing club" (KCTMO 2012a:21). Noted further was the Studio E Architects representative's declaration: "We will be spending 6-8 million pounds on the tower, full re-clad, heating, windows and … we are looking to create 4 new family size units" (ibid.). The explanation for the relocation of the nursery was given thus: "The reason being to facilitate the re-modelling of [the] Tower to accommodate new residential units and to provide more space for both boxing and nursery clubs" (ibid.). Furthermore, the relocation of the nursery "down a level" is justified by the architect's proposal "to try and provide the nursery with new external play area by taking out footpaths and access ramp to deck level" (ibid. 21-22). Both the latter features appear relevant to public inquiry queries regarding emergency service access to Grenfell Tower. Notes and minutes for the

KCTMO 19th July 2012 state that the "Pre-Application meeting" for the Grenfell Tower regeneration project received a presentation from Studio E Architects in which it was stated: "It is to be a complete overclad project with consolidation at lower floors and extending the building envelope to the ground floor" (KCTMO 2012b: 24). Significantly, a clear statement of Studio E Architects' preference for a zinc exterior membrane cladding is minuted thus:

> BS [Bruce Sounes Studio E Architects] explained that an overclad and rainscreen system is being proposed Zinc or eternity particle board are being investigated (OK with EG [Edward George Planning Officer RBKC] but suggested that colour choice should avoid grey).
>
> Considering Aluminium windows but still talking to residents about design considering safety etc. Considering ribbon approach to window design but depends on 'infill' panels.
>
> Canopy – EG would prefer to see amount reduced but to avoid creating darker areas under canopy. MW [Marc Watterson Taylor Young] suggested transparent material could avoid this but may have maintenance issues.
>
> Lower levels are likely to need brick finish for robustness, to match cladding at upper levels.
>
> (KCTMO 2012b)

KCTMO (2012c) collated the minutes and evidence of public engagement in a document entitled *Grenfell Tower Regeneration Project, Engagement Statement; Planning Application October 2012*. Principal within this document are minutes from a series of consultations concerning the design proposals, conducted during February 2012 – August 2012. It was intended that these talks, involving the Royal Borough of Kensington and Chelsea in affiliation with KCTMO, would be "based on building positive engagement with local communities and stakeholders through consultation prior to Planning submission" (ibid. 3). Furthermore, in accordance with public planning consultation rhetoric, tenant participation is an integral performative capital, enabling the presumption of advocacy from residents. Operative features of the public engagement discourse are deployed in the statement: "The focus was to continue to provide opportunities for local residents to understand, and influence the development of the design proposals for the Grenfell Tower Regeneration Project before the application was submitted" (ibid.). Operationalised in a range of consultation meetings and quantitative methods, the KCTMO (ibid.) document announces success in having achieved advocacy from residents and stakeholders: "In analysing the responses, there is clear evidence of support for the project". Minor detraction appears in the concession that "during the early stages of the consultation there were some concerns over elements of design" (ibid.). The document reconciles these detractions in its paradigmatic public consultation consensus discourse, proverbially:

> Whilst we recognise that not everyone will support the proposals, many of these concerns have now been addressed and are reflected in the proposal development. It also meets the guidance set out in the Localism Act (2011) which sets out a requirement for community engagement in advance of the submission of major planning applications. (KCTMO 2012c: 3)

Speculation about performed public engagement is not intended; rather, the process of consultation comes into focus when the processes of operationalising engagement are critically reviewed. Key among these is the process of operationalising the regeneration project's intention to refurbish the building's exterior. In a section of KCTMO (2012c:7) entitled "Questionnaires" are questions about the residents' preference for exterior refurbishment: "Do you think Grenfell Tower would benefit from thermal insulation cladding?". Elsewhere, it is minuted that on 26/07/2012 a "discussion with design proposals" resulted in the following recommendations and requests from the residents: "External Canopy: residents would like to see a new canopy which offers protection and shelter around the block. External cladding proposal favourable to residents seem to be for profiled Zinc. Although we seem to have some feedback on type of cladding it's still undecided on their preferred colour for the cladding" (ibid. 15). By January 2014, these issues appear to have achieved sufficient resolution for in a document dated 10//01/2014 and in accordance with the Town and Planning Act 1990, the Royal Borough of Kensington and Chelsea (2015:1) granted permission for the "Refurbishment of existing Grenfell Tower including new external cladding and fenestration, alterations to plant room, reconfiguration of lower 4 levels to provide 7 new residential units (use class C3), replacement nursery (use class D1) and boxing club (use class D2) facilities, external public realm works, redevelopment and change of use of existing garages to refuse collection area". While this initial planning permission document had little detailed reference to the specification of the building material, one assumes that it would have been in accordance with Studio E Architects' preferences. Evidence to the contrary is proffered by a Royal Borough of Kensington and Chelsea (2015) document agreeing that "the requirements of the conditions(s) … have been discharged, in accordance with the plans submitted". The condition referred to is described as "details required by condition 3 (materials)" (ibid.). Drilling further down into the document it becomes apparent that the specification for zinc exterior cladding has been altered for amidst the planning legal repertoire is the following clear statement: "Main building panels: Reyondbond/reynolux, in Smoke Silver Metallic (colour No. E9107S) attached with concealed fixings" (ibid.). A cursory perusal reveals that Reyondbond is an "aluminium composite panel" and Reynolux "prepainted aluminium coil or sheet manufactured through coil coating" (Arconic 2017).

Façade features in both product descriptions – Reyonbond: "rain screen cladding systems (ventilated facades)" and Reynolux: "prepainted aluminium is a tremendously versatile product. It is suitable for roofs, facade cladding … can be used in new construction as well as for refurbishment" (ibid.). Product specifications for Reynolux include the statement: "It can also resist strong windloads as well as extreme climatic conditions and temperature deviations (-50 °C to +80 °C)" (ibid.). Arconic's coated aluminium sheet cladding with Celotex RS5000 insulation core was very early in the public inquiry depicted as an accelerant to the spread of the apartment fire that engulfed Grenfell Tower. On 6th July, *The Guardian* (2017), in an article provocatively entitled "Grenfell Tower: Fire-proof Cladding Specified by Architects Used Only on Ground Floor", argued that the "glass reinforced concrete (GRC) panels" evidently used on the lower parts of the Grenfell Tower were not used higher in the building. And, more specifically, Robert Booth of *The Guardian* (ibid.) identifies that in 2012 the KCTMO "had balked at estimates from the contractor Leadbitter rating the project in 2012 at a cost of £11.3m", its replacement being the appointment of Rydon "on a tighter budget of £8.7m" (ibid.). It appears that the replacement of the contractor was a result of a "value engineering process" according to the "Kensington and Chelsea's housing and property scrutiny committee" (ibid.). The managerial language of "value engineering" is in contradiction with the discourse of resident engagement articulated in the Grenfell Tower Regeneration reports that KCTMO regularly provided residents during the refurbishment period 2013 – 2016. For example, in an 11th September 2013 report, the KCTMO (2013) included a statement of reassurance regarding tenant participation in the selection of Grenfell Tower contractors; specifically the: "Selection of contractor … is proceeding as per the European procurement regulations (OJEU). Resident involvement will be an important part of contractor selection …" (ibid.). Further to the 11th September 2013 report, in

November 2013 the KCTMO (2013a) newsletter announced that tender notice for Grenfell Tower contractors "was published on the OJEU (Office of the European Journal) for transparency and audit". It was confirmed that the closing date for the expression of interest in the tendered Grenfell Tower refurbishment contract closed on the 20th September and five contractors had been shortlisted (KCTMO 2013a). An operationalisation of resident participation in terms of a rhetorical discourse of user engagement is proffered in the following statement: "The TMO would like to take the opportunity to thank residents who helped us to assess the contractors in terms of their responses to questions about how they coordinate with residents, and their suitability and experience in carrying out similar works" (ibid.). An exuberantly sub-titled "It's all systems go!" KCTMO (2014) April newsletter announced to Grenfell Tower residents that the contractors had been selected: "a company called Rydon and the total cost almost £10m". Rydon is publicised in the newsletter as "a construction, development, maintenance and management group" with a decade of "experience in the refurbishment of tower blocks" KCTMO 2014). Rydon's decade of experience was highlighted as including the refurbishment and modernisation of a twenty-three storey tower block located in Newham, London, with emphasis being placed on how Rydon's "projects have involved work to the building's façade, as well as replacement of rain screen cladding and communal heating systems, whilst residents were in occupation" (ibid.).

In an October KCTMO (2014a) newsletter, intriguingly sub-titled "What's been happening?", residents were informed: "Cladding: the Council has selected a smoke silver metallic (grey) colour for the cladding". Viewing of a sample of the cladding placed in the Grenfell Tower building's main entrance was encouraged. Prophetically, given our tragic vista of hindsight, residents were given the following instructions in reference to the disturbance caused by the erection of an external frame on Grenfell Tower outer wall so the insulation cladding could be hung: "This will cause the external walls to vibrate, so please remove all valuable items away from walls connected to the outside of the building. If you need to escape the noise, please use the available quiet spaces" (ibid.).

Figure 2.3.: "Publicity helps to mask and compensate for all that is undemocratic within society. And it also masks what is happening in the rest of the world" (John Berger, *Ways of Seeing*, 1972). Photographic Image, Vicinity of Grenfell Tower; Lancaster West Estate, North Kensington, London, June 2017.

Façade as the Gentrification of Post-industrial Urban Space

Figure 2.4.: *Love Assisst(f)*: "One may remember or forget these messages but briefly one takes them in, and for a moment they stimulate the imagination by way of either memory or expectation" (John Berger, *Ways of Seeing*, 1972). Photographic Image, Vicinity of Grenfell Tower; Lancaster West Estate, North Kensington, London, June 2017.

Dialogic Resistance to the Simulacra of Façade – Introducing the Grenfell Action Group

> Noise from strong winds: on the morning of 15 January several of you reported a loud vibrating noise coming from the building exterior the night before. Rydon's sub-contractor checked if any of the cladding support equipment on the building was loose. In fact it was strong winds which caused the cladding support frames to vibrate, so there's nothing to worry about! Once the cladding is installed this will not happen. (KCTMO 2015: 1-2)

> The demolition of the top of the external staircase has now been completed … Cladding angles being installed from the mast climber. (KCTMO 2015a: 2)

KCHPSC's (2013) Kensington and Chelsea Housing and Property Scrutiny Community 16th July 2013 update report on the Grenfell Tower refurbishment provides highly significant insights into critically prophetic tensions, evident at the inception of the public consultation process. Conceding to awareness of "a number of communications from a small number of residents in the form of blogs and open 'round robin' e-mails", the KCHPSC (ibid. 1) report aimed to clarify the planned refurbishment of the Grenfell Tower "located on Lancaster West Estate, adjacent to the site of the KALC project". In a move towards budgetary transparency, the KCHPSC (ibid.) report declared that the Royal Borough of Kensington and Chelsea cabinet had on 2nd May 2012 approved a financial "budget of £6m to deliver major improvements to the fabric of Grenfell Tower" (ibid.). It was stated that the refurbishment was to be financed from income propagated "from the sale of basement spaces in Elm Park Gardens" (ibid.). The initial budget of £6m, according to KCHPSC (ibid.), was increased to accommodate "additional investment" in the renewal of the communal heating system, intended to "complement the proposed investment in the building fabric" (ibid. 1-2). KCHPSC (ibid. 2) reported that a budget increase to £9.7m would be proposed to the July meeting of the Royal Borough of Kensington and Chelsea cabinet meeting. Central to the proposal was an intention to advance the thermal insulation of the building through the "thermal external cladding of the building"; in conjunction with enhancing the building's residential capacity through the renovation, into additional living spaces, of "underused lower levels of the building" (ibid.). Of further significance is the KCHPSC (ibid.) report's account of the contrary contractual decision-making that appears to substrate the proposed £9.7m budget. It is stated that "Since January, the design team has been working with Leadbitter (the proposed contractor) to bring the scheme within budget and to ensure that the project will deliver value for money" (ibid. 3). The KCHPSC (ibid.) report's accusation of an adagio in the "progress" with Leadbitter appears to have been a euphemism for a recalcitrance on the part of Leadbitter to present a reduced budget costing. Indeed, KCHPSC (ibid.) reports: "Leadbitter currently estimate the cost of works to be £11.278m (inclusive of fees), which is £1.6m above the current, proposed budget".

Unable to bring Leadbitter "within budget", the KCHPSC (ibid.) report determinedly announces competitively tendering the contract, a process described as follows: "It is now proposed to market test the works through an open OJEU tender to ensure that the best contractor is selected and value for money is achieved" (ibid). Competitive tendering is also presented as providing for a more expedient commencement date: "The process will result in a start on site in Quarter 4 of 2013-2014. By comparison, the IESI procurement process with Leadbitter would have resulted in a start on site at the end of Quarter 3" (ibid.). Significantly, the KCHPSC (ibid.) report declares that in conjunction with the competitive tendering procurement process, the budget evaluation will also involve the design team undertaking a process of "value engineering" intended "to maximize the delivery of key project outputs within the proposed budget" (ibid.). Further detail regarding the market-based machinations and decision-making on the regeneration budget is available in a KCCM (2014) report entitled: *Cabinet Meeting – 19 June 2014 Report by the Director of Housing Grenfell Tower Major Works and Hidden Homes Project*. The central intention of this report was to seek agreement on an increase of the Grenfell Tower regeneration budget to £10.3 million.

Having briefed the Royal Borough of Kensington and Chelsea cabinet on the outcome of the December 2011 KCTMO exercise that identified Grenfell Tower was in need of substantial investment, the report reaffirms that following a presentation to cabinet on 2nd May 2012, agreement had been achieved for a £6 million allocation towards the regeneration scheme (KCCM 2014). The £6 million budget was to be drawn from net capital receipts of £13 million obtained from the sale of apartments in Elm Park Gardens (ibid. 1). It was stated that the initial programme of works (external cladding, etc.) was expanded to include the upgrade and renewal of Grenfell Tower's communal heating system; necessitating that "On July 2013, Cabinet agreed a revised budget for the whole Grenfell Tower project of £9.7 million" (ibid. 2).

KCCM (2014: 2) provides further details as to the change of contractors and organisational reasoning that appears to have led to these decisions. Of significance is the revelation that the KCTMO intended "that the Kensington Academy and Leisure Centre (KALC) and Grenfell Tower projects would work closely together with the same design team, consultants and contractor to deliver continuity in design and development process". This aspiration for a seamless aesthetic branding was disrupted, momentarily for "as negotiations progressed it became apparent that it would not be possible to agree a contract price with the agreed budget with Bouygues UK" (ibid. 2). Consequently, KCTMO, in consultation with Kensington and Chelsea Council, agreed to procure a new contractor "through an OJEU competitive tender process" (ibid.). According to the KCCM (2014: 2) report, sixteen prospective contractors submitted to the OJEU tender process the required pre-qualification questionnaires, and five of these contractors were selected to enter the Invitation to Tender (ITT) stage. The outcome of ITT was that on 27th March 2014 the KCTMO board agreed the selection of the maintenance management group Rydon Property Services Ltd as the approved contractor for the overhaul refurbishment and renovation of Grenfell Tower; as the KCCM (2014: 5) report expresses it: "Rydon submitted the most economically advantageous tender, scoring highest on both price and quality" (ibid.). Rydon had agreed to bring the scheme within a budget of £9.7 million and the cabinet sought to "increase the capital provision for the scheme to £10.3 million, enabling a contingency of approximately 6% to be established" (ibid. 8).

Furthermore, it was announced that cost savings would be extracted once "a clear cost base" could be discerned and "applied when the exact scope of works is defined in negotiation with Bouygues, the contractor for the KALC project" (ibid. 5). The issue appears, here, to have been ambiguity over the boundaries between the KALC project and the regeneration of the Grenfell Tower. This observation is confirmed by the following statement: "Discussions are underway between all parties to agree the boundary between the two projects and to agree how to manage the interface. When this is resolved, there should be cost savings in the Rydon tender" (ibid.). Other attempts to "reduce the net expenditure on the scheme" related to "a requirement of the tender" that Rydon "secure 'ECO' grant funding from energy suppliers to support the project" (ibid.). While it was uncertain in 2014 whether Rydon could secure this form of grant, the KCCM (2014:5) report expressed a capital interest thus: "We would therefore recommend in the budget that we plan not to receive any ECO grant funding and if we actually manage to receive some funding, then this can be used to reduce the net expenditure on the scheme".

Rydon's remit included responsibility for "design, construction and resident liaison work" with contract administration duties provided by the consultants Artelia "and Max Fordham as specialist mechanical and electrical consultants" (KCHPSC 2016:1). In an 11th May 2016 report by the director of housing to the Kensington and Chelsea Housing and Property Scrutiny Committee, it was affirmed that financing for the Grenfell Tower regeneration scheme was illuminated by a "stock condition information" inquiry, which had also provided justification for the nearby Kensington Academy and Leisure Centre programmes (ibid.). The suggestion here and elsewhere is that oversight of these programmes was retained by KCTMO; indeed, KCHPSC (2016: 1-2) attempts to affirm this in the statement that: "Rydon were responsible for design, construction and resident liaison work. The TMO worked with all partners and were responsible for the overall project management". Nevertheless, one discerns from the emulously labyrinthine contractual agreements and market-based competitive certification of value that a culture of contracts mediated the KCTMO's oversight of the Grenfell Tower regeneration scheme.

Figure 2.5.: "This has the effect of closing the distance in time between the painting of the picture and one's own act of looking at it. In this special sense all paintings are contemporary. Hence the immediacy of their testimony. Their historical moment is literally there before our eyes" (John Berger, *Ways of Seeing*, 1972). Photographic Image, Vicinity of Grenfell Tower; Lancaster West Estate, North Kensington, London, June 2017.

Façade as the Gentrification of Post-industrial Urban Space 39

Figure 2.6.: "To great Omnipotence a debt can owe? Or owing, can repay it? Would'st thou dare Barter upon equality!" (Ann Yearsley, *On Jephthah's Vow, Taken in a Literal Sense*, 1787). Photographic Image, Vicinity of Grenfell Tower; Lancaster West Estate, North Kensington, London, June 2017.

Case Study, Interview Transcription – Grenfell Tower, North Kensington London 2017

Interviewer: *Do you live around here?*
Interviewee (i): *Yes, I live behind there [gesturing to flats in proximity of Grenfell Tower].*

Interviewer: *So you were woken up?*
Interviewee (i): *We were woken up, well I was still awake; I was sitting in the kitchen and I was about to go to my bed. And my son's bedroom is on this side, mine is on the other; and he saw the flames. I couldn't see the flames. And my son said something's happening. And when I came towards the door, we heard the screaming of the children: "Help, help, help!". We came out on the balcony and erhm ... Probably they wanted somebody to help them get out of the windows. There was a lady, right on the top. I don't know which floor, she was flashing the light; and she was screaming hysterically. So some people here, said they were woken up by the explosion, the noise of the explosion I didn't hear that. But I could hear the children. That was just by ten past one; twenty, twenty seven past one I called the 999 and it took about five minutes before they answered. And so I came running around here, there [Grenfell Tower] to see what was happening. And I said to the police: "Where are the people? How are you evacuating them?".*

[Pause: A woman overcome with tears approaches myself and the interviewee]

Interviewee (i): *You know people?*

Interviewer: *I'm so sorry, I'm so sorry [acknowledging her visible distress and tears]. I teach at Goldsmiths and I have been watching the television and the news as well; and this lady was trying to tell me.*
Interviewee (i): *I am sort of shock in my brain. So I said to the police: "Where are the people? Where is the evacuation?" And they said: "In the other corner". So I knew it wasn't here so I went further up and they said: "No it is further down". So basically, I went from that side [gesturing direction] near the sports centre; Kensington sports centre. There were about thirty people who managed to come out; they came out before the fire brigade arrived. They also said that the fire brigade people said to the people: "Go to your flats until we come to rescue you". So there were a lot of people with families; ... another boy who was screaming: my*

grandfather who's locked in the toilet – because all the rooms are on fire, we called him again and there is no answer. So everybody had something to say. They sort of were hopeful some of them; because this inside of the building was not on fire yet [gesturing direction]. That side [gesturing direction] was up to the top. And I know it was burning in that corner [gesturing direction]. It moved across like that [gesturing accelerated speed of travel] and a little bit this way. And we knew it was a disaster when it came to the middle... It was just after three o'clock the fire came from this side to the front ... People were hopeful their loved ones would be alive ... The fire it went so fast. You know so fast. Some people fainted. They wouldn't take water because they were fasting. And I think this problem continues a lot of them in the Latimer Centre? They are on the brink of fainting and they won't take water because they are fasting. Where is their religious leaders to explain to them? So basically, probably in Westway these are the people who are directly, they have close family; and the ones who have distant family and friends they are in Latimer Road, sorry, Latimer Christian Centre ...

Interviewee (i) to Interviewee (ii): *Have you got family and friends?*

Interviewee (ii): *People are coming out that I know from the neighbourhood; you know that you've seen around, you know you've seen that you know them. But there's a couple that were on the 13th floor and they were told to go back to the flat.*

Interviewee (i): *I am angry because that is the management. This building was refurbished, not many years ago. They changed the lifts; they had more security systems, they had security men downstairs; it was painted on the outside. It looked beautiful. But they were too greedy to give them the ten million. We couldn't get even a chunk of it, to get our windows double glazed. I was for an entire year, attending the meetings and I was fighting to get a chunk to get double glazing. They wouldn't give it to us because they wanted to do this fancy [Grenfell Tower]. They took the whole lot, ten million pounds.*

Interviewer: What do you think about the cladding?
Interviewee (i): *It's deadly. It's a combustible material.*
Interviewee (ii): *I think the horrible thing is that the people in the building had been complaining about it. Even in the reception, even in the reception, there was apparently a sprinkler and an alarm; they lowered the, they had a false ceiling, and so the alarm and the sprinkler were above.*
Interviewee (i): *The fact that they built Aldridge Academy in front of the tower block, it means the fire brigades could not access it, in case of fire.*

All these things; at the meetings; all together; at the meetings we kept telling them, telling them. But they were too ambitious ...
Interviewee (ii): *But isn't that different material? Aldridge Academy?*
Interviewee (i): *And the material, it's the same thing.*
Interviewee (ii): *Isn't it cladding? Is it the same?*
Interviewee (i): *But this one is flat. That one had a gap which allowed the air, the oxygen. So it made it very combustible ... All the buildings in Westfield they have the same material.*

Interviewer: And it [cladding] lets in air so, so the fire spread into the cladding.
Interviewee (i): *And it spread from side to side. And of course inside the flats you have furniture you have curtains, you have bedding. And then the smoke. The lady who was screaming, right there [gesturing direction] she was later leaning out of the window; because of the fumes, she fainted and fell over. People were saying they would jump. They were not jumping; they were fainting from the smoke; and they were falling from the windows.*

Interviewer: Did they try and tell people? Were there meetings to try and say the building wasn't?
Interviewee (i): *There was, we are very concerned about the first security.*

Interviewer: Why do you think they ignored it?
Interviewee (i): *This is what appears. The council, this is the council building. The council had an organisation which started with the name TMO, Tenant Management Organisation. I was a member from the start of this organisation. So what it meant is residents were involved. They discussed with the officers, this officer the TMO who managed the buildings of the council. But the residents had a say, so nothing would go ahead unless the residents agree to the go-ahead. Many years later, and I feel guilty about that, because we convinced all the residents to vote. They wanted to become, from TMO to ALMO. By becoming ALMO {**Interviewer:** "What's ALMO?" [Arms- Length Management Organisation]}. I can't remember now. All it meant, it would get, the council would get millions of pounds from the government to carry out projects like new kitchens and bathrooms. So we encouraged people to vote, unless we voted; we encouraged people to vote in the hope we would, they would have a new kitchen and bathroom. But we didn't know all of the rest of the story. So by becoming ALMO the TMO becoming ALMO: what it meant was that they*

were making the decisions; they were inviting the residents just to let them know what decisions they had made.

Interviewer: Who are they?
Interviewee (i): The TMO

Interviewer: The TMO?
Interviewee (i): The ALMO. The TMO had become ALMO so all the people say TMO, but it is not TMO it is an ALMO it is Kensington and Chelsea ALMO. So this is what happens when people have the same, continue with the same spirit; with the same, what is it called? Ethics, mentality? That they are going to get together and they are going to negotiate what they are going to do in their area. But it is the wrong route. It doesn't work anymore. I don't know what we need to do? We need a lot of things here. I don't know how we can go about, so that we can convince them to give us what we need for our security; for our health and safety. And at the moment, they are talking about demolishing everything; and rebuilding hundreds more flats; so they can sell them in the private sector. So all they are thinking is: money, money, money, money! People are saying they had a profits [focus]; it is because things are not working in the same way as they used to work when it was a TMO. Because it was a Tenant Management Organisation, the tenants had a say. But with the ALMO this doesn't work; they make all the decisions but they have to consult us. That this is what they have decided to go ahead and do. But we have no effect.

Interviewer: When you were in consultation; so you were in consultation as part of the ALMO; and the ALMO was looking after all the flats round here?
Interviewee (i): They are still looking after all the flats.

Interviewer: And so when you were at meetings, did they not listen? Did they not listen to you? How did you know you weren't listened to?
Interviewee (i): They listen but they don't; it was what they want to do.

Interviewer: What did you want that they didn't listen to?
Interviewee (i): Well, we need double glazing. We don't have double glazing. Some of the flats, I don't know about these flats, along, alongside of the block: You've got the entrance, it's a corridor with a boiler, combination boiler with a pilot, and then the kitchen. So if there is ever going to be a fire in a flat over there, it is more likely it can happen from

cigarettes in another room; it is more likely it will happen in that spot because you have the gas on, the boiler. Which means you cannot use the entrance or the exit to get out. You are jammed and there is no entrance from the back, no exit from the back. There is no other staircase, and I have been inviting the, you know when it was still TMO, have been inviting them; telling them. Told the fire brigade, nobody's listening. So unless an accident happens.

Interviewer: And what about the gas? Had they fitted a gas pipe in the building?
Interviewee (i): *I don't know, the gas was exploding, on fire. You could hear, explosions, explosions.*

Interviewer: And there was only one fire exit?
Interviewee (i): *Only one; this is the building, this is the centre of the building [gesturing]. There are two lifts on this side and then the staircase. The fire started from there [gesturing] it was going upwards.*

Interviewer: On which floor did it start?
Interviewee (i): *I think third or fourth something like that? So it spread this way, and inside. The lifts collapsed, there was a vacuum there, this is what people say – and the staircase in flames. The fire brigade couldn't get in and people couldn't get out. So only those people who used their common sense, their instinct, they dashed out of the building.*

Interviewer: People were told to stay in the building?
Interviewee (i): *All of them were as you say. I have only seen about thirty people who came out, before the fire brigade arrived.*

Interviewer: Thirty? So how many people were in that building?
Interviewee (i): *They say four hundred, five hundred people, but I say six hundred, maybe more?*

Interviewer: How many people came out?
Interviewee (i): *I have seen, around thirty people. You can go to the Westfield and find out how many people have come out; and erhm they will tell you. But I have seen about twenty, thirty people maximum; maximum thirty people. When the fire brigade came, they told people to go back in flats in safety, until we come and evacuate you. This was their plan to evacuate. Nobody imagined that the fire was going to spread all around the building and inside. Don't forget that a while ago there was a fire in*

Shepard's Bush in a flat. They controlled it ... But they learned a lesson from that; because a lot of people run in different directions; and they had accidents, because they didn't follow instructions. So the policy changed and everybody went to the meetings and we were all advised; in the situation of a fire this is a procedure. And it was from there we were told that you have to stay where you are until you are evacuated. So people, most of the people followed instructions; they went back into their staircase and if some of them tried to come out they found it very difficult because it was dark – this is what I hear from people there was no lighting in the staircase; and it was full of suitcases. Because people started packing up and they were ready to go out when they were told, go back to the flat. Like the lady, she was coming out with six children and she ended up with four, she doesn't know where the other two are. The smoke came; it was dark; it was children{s} ... [pause: grieving]. (**Interviewer:** "Sorry"). You know I cannot believe it that these huge buildings, they use only one, you know they have this erhm, huge tapes in the corners of the building. And all you see is just two {**Interviewer:** "Fire hoses"} fire hoses ... There is water on the side of this building [gesturing to the adjacent building]. Why they didn't connect to ...

Interviewer: Why do you think so many things went wrong?
Interviewee (i): ... Say it was a forest, they would have to put out the fire; they would have to contain the fire with all sorts of materials to put out the fire. [Grenfell Tower] ... nothing! I'm telling you I was standing at the other side until four o'clock and all the fire engines they were all in large groups, they didn't move ... maybe there were some of them on this side ... Filipinos, Eritreans, of course, I know some other people like Ukrainians; they came out, they didn't listen to anybody. They didn't listen to the TMO; they didn't listen to the fire brigade. They were ethnic minorities there all of them. I think they should put a monument there. There should be a monument there; there should be a monument there. So many lives. So many children; you know the cries of the children ... People were saying don't worry, don't worry the fire brigade are coming. I have never seen police officers so grim, so red, so sad ... People are going to protest. So now we have to wait and see who is going to accept any responsibility. With one putting the blame on the other.

Interviewer: The ALMO, do you think they will take responsibility?
Interviewee (i): It's a very big project ... This is a regeneration programme. It is a regeneration which comes from the government. It's bigger than regeneration because the money was from the charity. Even if

you blame the contractors, you know they did all the checks and everything they say. These big companies they subcontract and subcontract smaller companies. So one person will be trying to put the responsibility on the other. And it will never end. This story will never end; because those mostly responsible will have to advance money for compensation; and it is going to be very ugly, it is going to be embracing for them. People who have family lost their life. I don't know what's going to happen ... It's terrible. I don't know if you understand the feeling, it's just disappointment. And there were no more voices. When the voices stopped, what do we do?

Interviewer: *There is nothing you could have done.*
Interviewee (i): *They were asking for help and there was nobody to help them ... It was one of the strongest buildings. It was beautiful when they painted the outside, there was no need to put this other stuff.*

(Unstructured Qualitative Interview: Resident, Vicinity of Grenfell Tower; Lancaster West Estate, North Kensington, London, June 2017)

Figure 2.7.: "But there is the evidence of the paintings themselves: the evidence of a group of men and a group of women as seen by another man, the painter. Study this evidence and judge for yourself" (John Berger, *Ways of Seeing*, 1972). Photographic Image, Vicinity of Grenfell Tower; Lancaster West Estate, North Kensington, London, June 2017.

Figure 2.8.: "These relations between conqueror and colonized tended to be self-perpetuating" (John Berger, *Ways of Seeing*, 1972). Photographic Image, vicinity of Grenfell Tower; Lancaster West Estate, North Kensington, London, June 2017.

Façade as the Gentrification of Post-industrial Urban Space 49

Figure 2.9.: "The artificiality is deep within its own terms of seeing, because the subject has to be seen simultaneously from close-to and from afar" (John Berger, *Ways of Seeing*, 1972). Photographic Image, Vicinity of Grenfell Tower; Lancaster West Estate, North Kensington, London, June 2017.

Figure 2.10.: *Love Assisst(f)*: "One may remember or forget these messages but briefly one takes them in, and for a moment they stimulate the imagination by way of either memory or expectation" (John Berger, *Ways of Seeing*, 1972). Photographic Image, Vicinity of Grenfell Tower; Lancaster West Estate, North Kensington, London, June 2017.

Chapter Three

Cladding Façade, Red Herring? Market-Based Managerialism and the Gentrification of Post-Industrial Space

Figure 3.1.: "No other kind of relic or text from the past can offer such a direct testimony about the world" (John Berger, *Ways of Seeing*, 1972). Photographic Image, vicinity of Grenfell Tower; Lancaster West Estate, North Kensington, London, June 2017.

"Grenfell insulation passed fire safety tests after being covered in boarding" (Sky News 14/06/2018)

Thursday 14th June 2018 commemorated the first anniversary of the Grenfell Tower tragedy. News broadcast media, while reverential in their condolences, persevered unabated with their vociferous pursuit of the external refurbishment as the prime culprit in the Grenfell Tower fire tragedy. Sky News (2018) published a scathing commentary on the deficient safety tests carried out on "the combustible insulation" that formed the external refurbishment of the tower. Scientific credibility and factual incredulity elide in the Sky News article's revelation that "a layer of magnesium oxide boards", apparently marketed as entirely non-flammable, "were added to some of the cement-based panels that Celotex claimed were the only product covering its combustible insulation" (ibid.). Celotex, in the moral dramaturgy of the Grenfell Tower cladding, featured persistently as the corporate villain and rapacious capitalist wrangler, incautiously obviating safety regulations and motivated solely by the unscrupulous profit maxim of corporate capitalism. Undeviating from this castigation of Celotex, Sky News reliably informs that: "The combustible insulation that was fitted to the outside of Grenfell Tower passed its official fire safety test after being partially covered by fireproof boarding that no one was told about" (ibid.).

According to Sky News (ibid.), the "plastic foam insulation" product Celotex RS5000 was adhered to the exterior of the Grenfell Tower block "without the magnesium oxide boards"; evidence to substantiate this incrimination is presented by Sky News in the form of evasive omissions carried out by Celotex, for Celotex "did not publicise it had used them [fireproofing, magnesium oxide boards] to pass the test and they were not mentioned in safety certificates based on BRE's reports of the materials tested" (ibid.). The imbrication of Celotex as key miscreant becomes ever more resolute with the revelation that the Building Research Establishment, ascribed principal responsibility to conduct fire safety tests at government headquarters, had said that "it relied on Celotex to give them the correct information" (ibid.). Sky News reports this as having been revealed during the Grenfell Tower inquiry "which is investigating the tragedy that killed 72 people in June 2017 when combustible insulation and combustible cladding panels helped to spread a fire that had started in a fourth floor flat" (ibid.). Consistent with the article's vilification of Celotex as the offender, Celotex's subsequent attempts to legitimise the efficaciousness of its product were repudiated, as is evident in the following Sky News (ibid.) extract: "In April 2018, weeks after admitting its actions in correspondence to the Grenfell Tower Inquiry, Celotex paid to have the 2014 test conducted again without the fire-proof boards and passed". And yet skulduggery pervades the rhetorical framing of Celotex for despite Celotex announcing "We commissioned a further test ... which aimed to mirror, as closely as possible, the system as described in the August 2014 report" and proffering that "The test results show that the rainscreen cladding system tested (which included RS5000) met the performance criteria", the Sky News article persists in its vilification of Celotex, stating that: "The discrepancies in the 2014 RS5000 test were revealed in a report by fire engineer Dr Barbara Lane commissioned by the Grenfell Tower inquiry" (ibid.). My concern here is not to adjudicate whether the Sky News article is equitable and just in its admonishment of Celotex as the conceivable perpetrator of corporate malpractice for therein resides the purpose of the Grenfell Tower fire inquiry. Rather, my concern pertains to the sociological issue in which questions need to be asked of the dramaturgy and the public hysteria that participated in the configuration of Celotex as a folk devil.

In *Folk Devils and Moral Panics*, Stanley Cohen (1972/2002) identifies that the formulation of "folk devils" is a recurring feature of Western societies whereby "societies appear to be subject, every now and then, to periods of moral panic" (ibid. 1). During these episodes, marginal groups are centre-staged in a spectacular media maelstrom in which they "become defined as a threat to societal values and interests" (ibid.). Correlations can be evidenced between the roles ascribed in Cohen's (ibid.) dramaturgy of moral panic and those adopted by the broadcast media in the aftermath of the Grenfell Tower tragedy. For example, the apparent socially evasive villainy of Celotex is as Cohen described moral panic more generally "presented in a stylized and stereotypical fashion by the mass media; the moral barricades are manned by editors, bishops, politicians and other right-thinking people" (ibid.). Even the most cursory perusal through media broadcasts in the immediate aftermath of the Grenfell Tower fire reveals the evolution of Celotex bearing significant corporate responsibility for the tragedy, and this frequently took the form of Cohen's (ibid.) characterisation of moral panics in terms of "socially accredited experts pronounce their diagnoses and solutions; ways of coping are evolved or (more often) resorted to; the condition then disappears, submerges or deteriorates and becomes more visible". It is the latter repercussions of moral panics that are cause for concern in this chapter for it is a dire misconception to conceive resolutely the exterior cladding and its installation as the primary miscreants in this tragedy; in so doing, one facilitates moral conditions for Celotex and its cladding emporium to be hurled into the limelight, obfuscating more complex perpetrations and accelerating this ready-made folk devil's descent into moral panic obscurity. As Cohen (ibid.) describes moral panics more generally, "Sometimes the panic passes over and is forgotten, except in folklore and collective memory; at other times it has more serious and long-lasting repercussions and might produce such changes as those in legal and social policy or even in the way the society conceives itself". It is imperative that the spectacular media focus on the Celotex cladding emporium dimension of the Grenfell Tower fire tragedy should not be accepted unreservedly in the collective recesses of contemporary moral panics. Rather, it is essential that questions are raised not only of the deviating irregularities of the exterior refurbishment cladding of Grenfell Tower but also we need to enquire as robustly about the emerging simulacra of the Celotex cladding emporium as a pervasive dimension of present and future inquiries. It is only by questioning what resides in the midst of the emerging spectacular simulacra that one might commence revealing the labyrinthine complexity of the local governance mismanagement seditiously skulking in the shadows of the conveniently fabricated cladding folk devil. Conversely, in the immediate aftermath of the Grenfell Tower fire tragedy, across broadcast newspaper media and characteristic of the London centric speech radio broadcasting, there was a chorus of castigation and incrimination directed at the Grenfell Tower refurbishment cladding as the prime suspect in the impromptu court of clickbait popular news media. Indeed, from Cohen's (1972/2002) critical conceptual framework of *Folk Devils and Moral Panics*, consider the following transcription extract derived from my interview with a journalist reporting in June 2017 in the vicinity of the Grenfell Tower:

Interviewer: *... I am just a researcher at the University [of London].*
Interviewee: *The materials used here have been linked with fires across the country in different tower blocks over the last fifteen years. And they still used it. Because, they are allowed to. That's the only reason they used it, is because they are allowed to.*

Interviewer: Wasn't there a choice between two different ...?
Interviewee: *There's something funny about the way they fitted it. They fitted it; there must have been a gap between the cladding and the wall ... Ten minutes, twelve minutes; top to the bottom in flames ...*

Interviewer: You said that partly it was issues around the cladding?
Interviewee: My fire engine chief, who I speak to quite regularly, said he had never seen a fire like this ... Remember that building in 2009, Lackanal House? That [fire] was taken over two flats. This took over ... This building, they seem to make it beautiful from the outside.

Interviewer: What do you think about the sprinklers?
Interviewee: The alarm system did go off. You could stand next to it and go: Oh yeah it's going off ... It's a central one but it was so quiet nobody could hear it. The guy whose fire went off, whose fridge exploded, the fire was small at that stage. He put some stuff into a bag ... And had the time to do that. And then he knocked up his neighbours. And I wonder why is there not fire extinguisher access on each floor?

(Unstructured Qualitative Interview: Reporter, Vicinity of Grenfell Tower; Lancaster West Estate, North Kensington, London, June 2017)

Market-based Managerialist Gentrification – Grenfell Tower, London (2012-17)

Grenfell Tower is located on Lancaster West Estate, adjacent to the site of the KALC project which is currently on site. On 2nd May 2012, RBKC Cabinet approved a budget of £6m to deliver major improvements to the fabric of Grenfell Tower ... As part of the quarterly monitoring process, Cabinet will be asked at its meeting in July to increase the budget for the scheme to 9.7m ... Since January, the design team has been working with Leadbitter (the proposed contractor) to bring the scheme within budget and to ensure that the project will deliver value for money. Progress has been slow and Leadbitter currently estimate the cost of works to be £11.278m (inclusive of fees), which is £1.6m above the current, proposed budget ... It is now proposed to market test the works through an open OJEU tender to ensure that the best contractor is selected and value for money achieved ... In tandem with this procurement process, the design team will undertake a 'Value Engineering' process to maximize the delivery of key project outputs within the proposed budget ... The refurbishment of Grenfell Tower is a large and complex project and time and careful planning has been required to ensure that the proposals and design of the scheme meet the requirements of residents, RBKC and Planners. Particular focus has been required to ensure that the project representing value for money and can be successfully delivered to the satisfaction of residents.

(Kensington and Chelsea Housing and Property Scrutiny Committee, KCHPSC 2013: 1-4)

Market-based managerialism pervades the language of the "engineering" determinant of "value"; and this, if left unchecked, would challenge the participatory public engagement model that the KCHPSC (2013) report's pleonexia for managerialist value avariciously intended to cultivate. Consequently, the report invests detail in operationalising public engagement: "Resident engagement in the refurbishment of Grenfell Tower has been reviewed and actions agreed to ensure that all residents have clear information about the current status of the scheme and are clear about how they can influence the proposals" (ibid. 3-4). The circulation of newsletters was a method of communication much favoured by Kensington and Chelsea Tenant Management Organisation (KCTMO), and the KCHPSC (ibid. 4) report details the use of newsletters to reach out to the Grenfell Tower resident community, as is evident in the following statement: "Next steps involve a further newsletter which will be sent to Grenfell Tower residents giving feedback and responding to the issues raised at the public meeting". As indicated, public meetings were utilised in conjunction with the newsletter as a mode of public engagement; their joint deployment is assumed sufficient to achieve and demonstrate "that all residents have an opportunity to engage in finalizing the scope of works; be consulted on the designs submitted to planning and be involved in the selection of the contractor for the works". Seemingly cognizant of the ease of disengagement precipitated by managerial approaches to public engagement, the KCHPSC (ibid.) report places some emphasis on how "particular focus will be given to face to face contact with residents to ensure the widest possible engagement".

However, this managerial engineering of the public consultation process continuously struggled to contain the critical voices expressed by Grenfell Tower residents whose lived experience of the refurbishment provided for an embodied resistant knowledge. Some indication of this tension is provided in the KCHPSC (2016) report in which it was documented that "A group of residents living in Grenfell Tower formed a resident compact halfway through the project in June 2015" (ibid. 2). Apparently, "The TMO worked with the compact to address issues that were raised relating to the regeneration project" (ibid.). The KCHPSC (2016: 2) report reluctantly concedes that liaison had fallen short of ameliorating the compact group's concerns for "At full Council on 2nd December 2015 a petition signed by 51 residents was tabled at the meeting". Unable to reconcile the compact group's concerns, KCTMO referred "the matter to the Housing and Property Scrutiny committee", which received a speech by a member of the compact group at a meeting on the 6, January 2016.

Prior to the delivery of this speech "At the Board meeting of the 5th January the KCTMO Board members were made aware of the petition and agreed that a delegated group of board members would review the issues raised" (ibid.). The KCHPSC (2016: 2) report proceeds to state that "The Scrutiny committee was then informed that the Board would review the project and respond to the matters raised in the speech by the compact. The Board has previously been emailed a full copy of this speech". This sequencing of events suggests that a decision concerning the strategy of public relations engagement had been made prior to the compact group member's speech, irrespective of the speech's content. Grenfell Action Group (2016) made available the *Grenfell Tower Residents Address RBKC Scrutiny Committee* and thus it is possible to gain a comprehensive insight into the contention. Indeed, the discursive composition of the speech from its onset provides a powerful oratory of discontent, immortalised for generations of local authority officials to contemplate:

> Thank you for allowing the residents of Grenfell Tower the opportunity to inform the Scrutiny Committee of the ill treatment, incompetence and plain abuse that we have experienced at the hands of the TMO during the Grenfell Tower Improvement Works. I am speaking to you in my capacity as a Lead Representative of the Grenfell Tower Resident Association, that has formed through adversity, in the summer of 2015 with the support and encouragement of our local MP, Lady Victoria Borwick. (Grenfell Action Group 2016)

Established in 2015, the Grenfell Tower Resident Association displays knowledgeable aptitude in its substantial complaint about "ill treatment" by the KCTMO and the latter's failure to heed multiple expressions of risk of endangerment concerning the refurbishment of the Grenfell Tower. Substantiation and quantification weigh heavily in favour of a contract in which the invidious tournament of contractual competition has become a substitute for democratic and representative local governance. As Berger (1972/1977: 149) observes with regards to capitalist sign-systems, "publicity turns consumption into a substitute for democracy". Seemingly cognizant of the powerful sign of quantified representation, the Grenfell Tower Resident Association, prior to its 2016 speech to the Housing and Property Scrutiny Committee, gathered quantitative survey data from Grenfell Tower leaseholders and tenants. Survey instruments were designed "to measure levels of resident satisfaction/dissatisfaction as a result of the TMO's handling of the improvement works" (Grenfell Action Group 2016: 1)). The survey results are revelatory for "90% of Grenfell Tower residents have reported that they are dissatisfied with the way in which the TMO has conducted the Improvement Works … 58% of residents who have had the Heating Interface Unit (HIU) fitted in their hallways would like them to be moved to a more practical and safe location" (ibid.).

Apparently, KCTMO "without any prior consultation" determined that the HIU for each refurbished apartment should be located in the hallway (ibid.). Residents adversely reacted to this determination; "so incensed by this oppressive and unfair action of the TMO that they came together to deny access to their properties to TMO contractors" (ibid. 3). Conceding to a groundswell of resistance, KCTMO eventually agreed to place the remainder of the HIUs in the kitchen of each apartment. Residents with the HIU fitted in the hallway expressed concern about health and safety and this was compellingly represented by the Grenfell Tower Resident Association thus: "However, many residents are currently lumbered with the HIU being located in their hallways which they believe is a health and safety issue, not least because the HIU is positioned directly above the electrical fuse box at the entrance to their properties and the fact that the sharp edges of the boxing protrude to cause a live danger to small children" (ibid.). Further to these issues of "poor workmanship and site management", the Grenfell Tower Resident Association insisted on "an independent investigation into the awful quality of individual works and the general poor management of the Improvement Works project" (ibid.). These legitimate concerns were continuously ignored, it is argued, leading to a call for an inquiry.

> In conclusion, the Grenfell Tower RA are asking the Chairman of the Housing and Property Scrutiny Committee to undertake an urgent scrutiny of the TMO management of the Improvement Works at Grenfell Tower and commission an independent investigation into the issues we have just raised. Time and again residents' views have been ignored or downplayed. Despite interventions from our MP, Victoria Borwick, and our ward councillors, our day-to-day concerns have been belittled and side-lined and we have had to endure living conditions that, at times, have been intolerable. (Grenfell Action Group 2016: 6-7)

On November 20th, 2016, the Grenfell Action Group (2016a) blogged a devastating premonition entitled: *KCTMO – Playing with fire!* It was stated that, in 2013, Grenfell Tower residents were besieged by "a period of terrifying power surges that were subsequently found to have been caused by faulty wiring"; as a result, the KCTMO, it is argued, "narrowly averted a major fire disaster at Grenfell Tower" (ibid. 1). In a nuanced and prophetically compelling conclusion, the blog posting makes the following admonishment:

> In the last twenty years and despite the terrifying power surge incident in 2013 and recent fire at Adair Tower, the residents of Grenfell Tower have received no proper fire safety instructions from the KCTMO. Residents were informed by a temporary notice stuck in the lift and one announcement in a recent regeneration newsletter that they should remain in their flats in the event of fire. There are not and never have been any instructions posted in the Grenfell Tower noticeboard or on individual floors as to how residents should act in event of a fire. Anyone who witnessed the recent tower block fire at Shepherds Court, in nearby Shepherd's Bush, will know that the advice to remain in our properties would have led to certain fatalities and we are calling on our landlord to reconsider the advice that they have so badly circulated. The Grenfell Action Group predict that it won't be long before the words of this blog come back to haunt the KCTMO management and we will do everything in our power to ensure that those in authority know how long and how appallingly our landlord has ignored their responsibility to ensure the health and safety of their tenants and leaseholders. They can't say that they haven't been warned! (Grenfell Action Group 2016a: 2)

Figure 3.2.: "The compositional unity of a painting contributes fundamentally to the power of its image. It is reasonable to consider a painting's composition. But here the composition is written about as though it were in itself the emotional charge of the painting" (John Berger, *Ways of Seeing*, 1972). Photographic Image, Vicinity of Grenfell Tower; Lancaster West Estate, North Kensington, London, June 2017.

Cladding, Red Herring? Deconstructing Local Council Political Discourse of Grenfell Tower Façade

"The Prime Minister is deeply saddened by the tragic loss of life in the Grenfell Tower ... The Prime Minister's thoughts are with all of those affected by this terrible incident and the emergency services, who are working tirelessly in very difficult circumstances" (Prime Minister's Office 2017). In the fledgling hours of Wednesday 14th June 2017, the unimaginable tragedy, forewarned sadly in the Grenfell Action Group prognostications, was realised in unparalleled corporeality. Chaotic scenes of distressed, traumatic consternation saturated news media; spectacles only exceeded by the devastating reality of the Kensington and Chelsea Council's paralysis of ineptitude. Indeed, the Prime Minister was moved to openly rebuke the Conservative council in a 22nd June 2017 Grenfell Tower House of Commons debate; as follows:

> We already know that many children are among the dead and that in some cases whole families perished. Those who survived have lost loved ones, friends, neighbours and, in many cases, everything they own. It should never have happened ... I shall say how we will discover why it did, but as I said yesterday, that initial failure was then compounded by the fact that the support on the ground in the initial hours was not good enough. As Prime Minister, I have apologised for that second failure and taken responsibility for doing what we can to put it right ... What became clear very quickly was that the Royal Borough of Kensington and Chelsea could not cope, and it is right that the chief executive officer has now resigned. It is also why I set up the Grenfell Tower recovery taskforce, which I have been chairing personally. (Hansard 2017, Vol. 626)

At a minimum the Royal Borough of Kensington and Chelsea illuminated the scale of its ineptitude as it floundered in the maelstrom of an unprecedented crisis of emergency response but at worst the Grenfell Tower tragedy coalesced an insidious malaise afflicting the culture of local governance within the Royal Borough of Kensington and Chelsea. Politicians, previously tentative and circumspect, were, in the aftermath of the Grenfell Tower fire, castigating in their disapproving articulation of the organisational culture of the KCTMO. Most pertinently edifying are the retrospective insights into the culture of KCTMO provided by the Member of Parliament for Kensington, Emma Dent Coad. Elected in the June 2017 general election by a slim difference of 16,333 to the Conservative Party candidate's 16,313 (RBKC 2018), Emma Dent Coad became the Labour Party's premier Kensington MP. In a powerful and provocative parliamentary maiden speech commencing with the acerbic promise never to emulate the "organising skills" of her "immediate predecessor Victoria Borwick", she delivered a tremendously affecting trenchant account of the trauma of the Grenfell Tower fire (Coad 2017). Implicitly recognised class divides were blazed through as the MP "for both Harrods and Notting Hill Carnival" described how "the good people of South Kensington have had their eyes opened in the past week and are asking the same questions that we're asking in North Kensington" (ibid.). The speech's attempt to straddle communities was frequently audibly supported by corroborative cries of "hear, hear"; Coad continued the discursive strategy of syntagmatically aligning belonging with class when she pronounced: "The horror and fear of this man-made catastrophe will be etched on all our hearts forever" (ibid.). The speech here takes a paradigmatic turn to express lamentation: "The tears may never stop. I know this from the grief etched on faces of people in Ladbroke Grove, total strangers approaching me for comfort, reassurance, a question, a hug to share their fears and disbelief that such horror could be visited upon our neighbourhood". The latter statement achieves what Fairclough (2001: 240) defines as "local social structurings of semiotic difference" for nuanced and embodied empathy is clearly the intended outcome of this syntagmatic discursive strategy. Proceeding then, Coad (2017) deftly mobilises semiotics, imbuing metaphor into description: "the burnt-out carcass of Grenfell Tower and all it represents, lowers over us". The grimacing, scowling imagery of a darkened menacing cascade drives the paradigmatic selection of the word "lowers". According to the sociolinguistics of Fairclough (2001: 240): "The paradigmatic aspect of language, in accordance with the usual grammatical sense of 'paradigm', concerns the range of alterative possibilities available, and the choices that are made amongst them in particular texts". Paradigmatically, Emma Dent Coad's description of the inordinately monumental relic of Grenfell Tower makes conscious linguistic turns so as to build contiguity with the foreboding semiosis of the vengefully scowling indignant sepulchre; the towering carcass of Grenfell Tower. As the speech progresses, it becomes apparent that the deftly accomplished semiosis of the spectacle of a fire-ridden Grenfell Tower is intended to pave the way for a critical pronouncement of the social realities of discordance and hierarchical inequities pervading the Royal Borough of Kensington and Chelsea: "the Red Cross managing a relief program in [pause] Kensington" (Coad 2017). The pause operates effectively as a rhetorical device, leaning back to provoke the hypocrisy of the wealthiest borough in London relying upon charitable emergency relief. In a statement of reiteration to the many neglected voices, Coad recontextualises into politics the problematic local governance by the

Kensington and Chelsea Council: "Tenants of Grenfell and other housing association properties have been voicing their very serious and evidenced concerns about poor and diminishing housing standards, and how appeals, complaints and petitions had been ignored and discredited" (Coad 2017). Suggestion here of the discrediting of personal experience even when articulated into quantitative measurement techniques places emphasis on the extent to which "the order of discourse" (Fairclough 2001: 235) powerfully mobilised to include contiguities and exclude dissenting voices. To "recontextualise other practices" refers to the process by which an agent incorporates "other practices ... into their own practice, and different social actors will represent them differently according to how they are positioned within the practice" (ibid. 234-235). A recontextualising of other practice is evident as and where Coad (2017) gives an eyewitness account: "I've witnessed over the years the deterioration and perhaps even deliberate managed decline of social housing. The frustration of a minority party councillor is huge". Emma Dent Coad progresses to provide crucial insights into the political machinations of a local council that had become oligarchical in tenure:

> Eleven Labour councillors in Kensington and Chelsea Council listened to the concerns and put them forward and shouted out for their residents but they are a minority. Decisions are made in Cabinet where Labour have no representation. In my eleven years as a councillor in the community where I was born and bred, I have seen housing conditions that are shocking ... Child poverty in Kensington is the same as child poverty in Lanark and Hamilton East: 25% in Kensington ... All these issues and more occurred in Grenfell Tower, including power surges that blew all the electrical devices. And yet, the residents' protestations were ignored and so-called 'frequent complainers' were blacklisted. By what process of de-regulation and the bonfire of red tape was this disaster allowed to happen? Some people think that social tenants have no right to live in an area like 'desirable' Kensington. Some people demonstrate a total lack of empathy or even respect for those not born to a world where basic human comforts and a good education are given. Some people think social tenants should simply move away if they don't like what they have been given and that housing people on low incomes in the inner city which they serve through their labour is not a public good but some kind of privilege to which they are not really entitled. So we have heard, after this disaster, that voluntary groups and charities have 'stepped up' to deal with this and [that] they are wonderful – and indeed they are. But I want to live in a world where charities don't exist and where volunteers aren't needed to fill yawning gaps where local services have been cut or withdrawn to be replaced, as it is in Kensington, by prep schools. People of all backgrounds should be safe in their beds, have food in the fridge and shoes that are the right size on

their children's feet; the basic human needs cannot be met in a world of charities, food banks and handouts. In a council with a third of a billion pounds in reserves, I don't understand how that can be. The burnt carcass of Grenfell Tower speaks for itself and has revealed the true face of Kensington. The mask has dropped. We have poverty, malnutrition, overcrowding, poor maintenance and underlining this a lack of care. The people who have been failed want justice accountability and an honest and transparent process to achieve it. We all now have to step up and ensure that we live in a world where a terrible and avoidable tragedy like the fire at Grenfell Tower never happens again. South Kensington has stood with North Kensington and we will work together to achieve this, as first Labour MP for Kensington. (Coad 2017)

Wednesday 19th July 2017 witnessed the first quorum since the Grenfell Tower fire tragedy, a full council meeting of the Royal Borough of Kensington and Chelsea Council, during which Cllr. Elizabeth Campbell was appointed as council leader following the resignation of Cllr. Paget-Brown. In accordance with council and democracy compliance, the Council meeting's agenda was made available; and agenda RBKC (2017) revealed that several petitions were scheduled to be discussed, one of which is entitled: *Petition on the Cabinet, Grenfell Tower and Regeneration*. Further inspection yields the petition as actually entitled: *Petition in Respect of the Cabinet, Grenfell Tower and Regeneration*. Petition RBKC (2017a) is understandably intemperate, pungent and also persuasively tenacious in its condemnation of the Cabinet of the Royal Borough of Kensington and Chelsea; as is evident in the following extract:

> We, the undersigned, who live or work in the Royal Borough of Kensington and Chelsea, demand the immediate resignation of the full cabinet of RBKC. The Cabinet's decisions across a series of departments have culminated in the horrifying and completely avoidable loss of life in the catastrophic fire at Grenfell Tower on the 14th of June 2017. Given the Council's failure to respond to the litany of safety and fire concerns raised by Grenfell Tower residents, we have no confidence in this Council's ability to manage or build public buildings and therefore demand the immediate cessation of all regeneration projects, particularly the construction of new buildings, but including the demolition, or 'improvement' of current buildings stock – projects of the kind that the current cabinet have shown themselves grossly incapable of managing.
>
> Our demands:

- The immediate resignation of the full cabinet of the Council
- An immediate halt of all building projects managed by the Council and associated demolition/transfer of buildings
- An urgent review of all major planning decisions
- A full suspension of all 'regeneration' projects and local masterplans, including estates
- New community co-designed masterplans for key North Kensington areas, including Latimer, Westway and Earl's Court.

(RBKC 2017a: 1)

In accordance with the Council's petition regulation scheme, the Grenfell petition, having achieved "in excess of 1,500 signatures" (ibid.), was awarded an item on the 19th July 2017 Council agenda. This and other scheduled items precipitated highly invigorating, emotional and passionate speeches. Poignant amongst these was a speech delivered by Cllr. Elizabeth Campbell, the newly appointed Council leader.

Figure 3.3.: "On each board all the images belong to the same language and all are more or less equal within it, because they have been chosen in a highly personal way to match and express the experience of the room's inhabitant" (John Berger, *Ways of Seeing*, 1972). Photographic Image, Vicinity of Grenfell Tower; Lancaster West Estate, North Kensington, London, June 2017.

Cladding, Red Herring? Deconstructing the Hyper-Mediated Performativity of Façade Public Accountability: "Medium is the Message" (McLuhan)

In *Understanding Media: The Extensions of Man*, McLuhan (1964: 23) challenges, directly, a positivistic epistemological tradition which insists on the existence of a correspondence between the medium and the objective world. As McLuhan expresses it, "In a culture like ours, long accustomed to splitting and dividing all things as a means of control, it is sometimes a bit of a shock to be reminded that, in operational and practical fact, the medium is the message" (ibid.). By this McLuhan means that the message broadcast is largely an outcome of its mediation: "This is merely to say that the personal and social consequences of any medium – that is, of any extension of ourselves – result from the new scale that is introduced into our affairs by each extension of ourselves of by any new technology" (ibid.). McLuhan (ibid.), in this respect, provides an enlightening account of the electric light. Beginning from the premise that "the electric light is pure information. It is a medium without a message, as it were, unless it is used to spell out some verbal ad or name" (ibid.), McLuhan proceeds to, very convincingly, argue "that the 'content' of any medium is always another medium" (ibid.). For example, the content of a book is the medium of written text, and the content medium of written text is the alphabet. While this stands to reason, if we now consider this application in regard to the media broadcasting of local council meetings and the circulation in the manner evident in Royal Borough of Kensington and Chelsea (RBKC) council public meetings in the aftermath of the Grenfell Tower tragedy, our attention is drawn to what McLuhan (ibid. 24) describes as "the psychic and social consequences of the designs or patterns as they amplify or accelerate existing processes". The message of contemporary digital media networked communication is axiomatic with "the change of scale or pace or pattern that it introduces into human affairs" (ibid.). Facebook, Twitter and the vast array of social media that now punctuate our everyday communications did not introduce networking into social life but rather have accelerated beyond, and compressed into, new morphologies existing in social intercourse. Returning to the analogy of the electric light, the Grenfell Tower RBKC council meeting video recordings produced in the aftermath of the tragedy, conceived as electronic encasing, are not the determinants of the message; as with the electric light, "Whether the light is being used for brain surgery or night baseball is a matter of indifference. It could be argued that these activities are in some way the 'content' of the electric light, since they could not exist without the electric light" (ibid.). Similarly, in many respects, the use of broadcast media to scale-up the circulation and transmission of RBKC council meeting webcam video recordings conforms to McLuhan's observation "that 'the medium is the message' because it is the medium that shapes and controls the scale and form of human association and action" (ibid.). It is from this theoretical framework that I now proceed to deconstruct several key video-recorded and broadcast media-circulated RBKC council meetings that took place in the aftermath of the Grenfell Tower tragedy. The featured episode in which the Kensington and Chelsea Tenant Management Organisation (KCTMO) was subject to extensive scrutiny was portrayed through mainstream broadcast media channels as a rabble-rousing, hostile blame culture emanating from the survivor community and local residents.

Royal Borough of Kensington and Chelsea, Council Meeting Webcast (2017) of 19th July 2017

Kensington and Chelsea Council's (2017) press release entitled *Council Leader Pledges Hundreds of New Social Housing Units and a Reformed Council "Changed Forever" by the Grenfell Fire* provides extracts of Cllr. Campbell's speech, which express an assurance to "create a future for this borough together with our residents". In a balanced and circumspect series of extracts, the press release is at pains to promote common sense and moderation in Cllr. Campbell's strategic management of what is described as "the Grenfell fire" (ibid.). The latter unfortunate phrase appears in contradiction to the said intention to cultivate a new organisational culture; as the press release states: "Unveiling a refreshed leadership team, the Council leader pledged there would be a new culture at Kensington and Chelsea with local consultation at its heart" (ibid.). Indeed, the press release's one-dimensional thought (Marcuse 1964) technologically rational iteration of the meeting is artificially frictionless for, as with many aspects of the aftermath of the Grenfell Tower tragedy, the Wednesday 19th July 2017 meeting attracted the broadcast news media, which rapidly channelled bite-sized media click-economy dramatic sensations. In the expeditiously disseminating fluvial of social media, Cllr. Campbell's speech achieves a less successful dramaturgy. Prior to the empirical deconstruction of this speech, it is necessary to outline briefly the theoretical framework that forms the basis of this analysis of the Kensington and Chelsea Council meeting webcast, transmitted in the immediate aftermath of the Grenfell Tower tragedy.

Baudrillard's (1968/2005: 212) *System of Objects* eloquently details a process of Othering that is a feature of the Council meeting webcast. It is evident that the Council meeting webcasts that were produced and circulated in the immediate aftermath of the Grenfell Tower tragedy functioned as publicity, apparently intended to assure the immediate community of survivors and the wider press, public, and political observers that consultative action was being taken. However, it is also evident that the webcasts generated unprecedented levels of spectacle as their "first-order simulacra" (where an image merely replicates reality) (Baudrillard 1968/2005) dramatically degenerated into "second-order simulacra" (where an image becomes largely indistinguishable from the reality it represents and thus begins to challenge the authenticity of the original representation; but where the reality, embattled form, continues to exist as an original reality) (ibid.) that threatened to destabilise the credibility of the Kensington and Chelsea Council consultative meetings, making it appear that the Council was in crisis and hurtling towards a vote of no confidence in its capacity to manage the crisis. Baudrillard, *System of Objects*, identifies "A Universal Code: Status" in which "The objects-cum-advertising system therefore constitutes less a language, whose living syntax it lacks, than a set of significations" (ibid.). The Kensington and Chelsea Council meeting webcast programmes were clearly a matrix of significations with varying accreditations of value ascription. In their obsessive calibrating of actions into binary digital form, the webcast programmes epitomise an "impoverished yet efficient" system that "is basically a code" (ibid.). And yet it is not an arbitrary reductive stimulus for "it does not structure the personality, but designates and classifies it" (ibid.); a process that might be described as follows:

> What is more, the fact that a system of identification is now in place which is clearly legible to all, that the signs of value are entirely socialized and objectivized, by no means implies any true 'democratization'. On the contrary, it would appear that the insistence on univocal reference merely exacerbates the desire to discriminate: within the very framework of this homogeneous system, a perpetually renewed obsession with hierarchies and distinctions is to be observed. Even though barriers of morality, social convention and language have been overturned, new barriers and exclusions have arisen in the realm of objects: a new class or caste morality is thus enabled to colonize the most material and hitherto unchallengeable of spheres. (Baudrillard 1968/2005: 214)

Similarly, the Council Meeting Webcast (2017) of 19th July 2017, originating from the Royal Borough of Kensington and Chelsea website, provides a compelling insight into a Council deteriorating into a second-order simulacra of its decentring reality, faltering in its response to a crisis for which it was increasingly blamed. The full video is 3.40:44 in duration and at position 0.18:05/3:40:44, Emma Dent Coad MP provides the following powerful oration, uninterrupted by the audience members:

> Thank you, Madame Mayor. It doesn't matter if you leave in the morning from an overcrowded, damp ridden flat in the Grove, or from a six million pound five-bedroom house in Chelsea, if you have humanity you deserve respect. I have lived over half my life in North Kensington and I am proud to be part of the community that has been so spectacularly betrayed and which has risen up in response. Grenfell survivors don't want apologies; they don't want charity; they don't want pity! They want respect, justice and a permanent home to replace what has been taken from them so cruelly and unnecessarily. This Council has let down Grenfell people, not just in the first few hours, not just the first few days; but every day for five weeks. Rearranging the deck chairs on the top deck of the Titanic that this Council represents will not deal with this atrocity. We need fundamental change and this cannot come about under the supposedly new regime offered to us tonight. If you cannot understand this, then you understand nothing. To borrow a much-abused phrase, this Council is not fit for purpose. The world is watching, do the right thing, admit your failures, bring in the commissioners before it gets any worse for those you failed. Thank you [sound of an extended long, jubilant applause]. (Webcast Observation: Council Meeting Webcast 2017, RBKC Meeting Recording:19th July 2017)

The RBKC Council Meeting Webcast (2017) proceeds after the rapturous applause achieved by Emma Dent Coad to record the Madame Mayor at 0.19:10/3:30:44 making the following request: "Are there any other nominations?" As this was received in silence, Madame Mayor follows the request with the statement: "Would all those in favour of Elizabeth Campbell please show". As Madame Mayor surveys the audience seeking votes in favour of the candidate, the Cllr. adjacent puts up his hand and this is met with a raucous resounding chorus of "boo" sounds. As the camera's focus moves from Madame Mayor and deeply spans the audience, from member galleries can be heard the words "Shame on you" and then less audibly discernible rebukes. The Madame Mayor enquires "And those against?", at which time the audience's heckles reach a crescendo. Madame Mayor seeks assurance from an adjacent colleague, who is heard to say "Carry on"; but this is on microphone and heard by the audience, a member of which sarcastically shouts: "Just carry on like before!" Madame Mayor, now more assertively in repose, then states at 0:19:51/3:40:44: "I can announce that the election of Councillor Elizabeth Campbell as leader is carried". The audience gallery delivers an even louder and resolute chorus of "Shame", "Shame on you". Madame Mayor, now clearly operating procedurally, says: "Councillor Campbell, would you like to address the chamber?". The audience gallery erupts with cries of "Shame on you", "Shame on you!" and shouts of "Boo". The Council Meeting Webcast (2017) video now pans outwards to reveal Cllr. Elizabeth Campbell preparing to address the chamber; and she commences with the statement: "Madame Mayor, I would normally address my speech to you and members of the chamber [pause]"; there occurs a sharp interruption here as a member in the audience gallery shouts "Resign" (RBKC Council Meeting Webcast 2017, author's annotations).

A significant feature apparent from the Council Meeting Webcast (2017) of Cllr. Campbell's speech is the consistency of the audience interruptions for they are far from random raucous heckles; rather, the areas of the speech that appear to incite disaffection from the audience relate to references made to the Council's public management prior to the Grenfell Tower fire and its subsequent attempts to reach out to the community. This audience response was no mere pantomime drama; rather, the cries of "lies", "negligence" and "resign" were profoundly expressed and one gains audibly and visually a sense of a deeply disaffected constituency harbouring endemic levels of mistrust. Indeed, a widely circulated impromptu speech delivered by a resident of Grenfell, and also made available on the Council Meeting Webcast (2017), powerfully captures the exasperation of a disenchanted community. Cllr. Campbell had promised to provide the Grenfell residents with the opportunity to make ordered speeches in the council chamber. The following is a transcription of the fervid, affecting impromptu speech at duration 1:14:10/3:40:44:

> Resign, resign, resign [Madame Mayor says: 'Can we have one person at a time addressing the meeting'] Resign! Resign! You ain't listening! I propose to you, you let my wife and kids down, so resign! You murdered my friend's wife and kids, you are not going to murder my wife and kids. Resign! I don't trust you, I don't trust your party! Resign! [Madam Mayor says: could we please calm down] … You have to kill me, kill me [applause from the public gallery]. You'll have to kill me and then you can take the power. No, honestly, kill me and then you can take the power. Because I don't see why you can't listen to all those people who came through the fire! Listen to them folks, they don't want you! They want Emma [MP Emma Dent Coad], [pause, sounds of support], they want Jeremy [MP Jeremy Corbyn], [pause, a loud enthusiastic supporting applause]. I don't want you, I don't want you [said emphatically and passionately beats against his chest]. My son doesn't want you, my daughter doesn't want you, my wife doesn't want you, the dead doesn't

want you. You let the dead down, now you wanna come for the living? Are you having a laugh? You are not in power ... the people must choose you. And we have not chosen you. So Madame [directed at Cllr. Elizabeth Campbell], please Madame, step down and resign! [Received with a resounding applause]. (Webcast Observation: RBKC, Council Meeting Webcast 2017, RBKC Meeting Recording:19th July 2017)

This powerful oration galvanised tremendous social media coverage; it was retweeted 7,500 times and "liked" 9,100 times (19th – 24th July 2017) from the Sky News (2017) @SkyNews platform. Impassioned and vehement in its articulation, the speech reveals insights into a reality of public management diametrically contrary to the dialogically conferred image of a brand of public management so falteringly conveyed in Cllr. Elizabeth Campbell's speech. Cognizant that the meaning of social media messages is mediated by the medium, plausible comparisons can be made for the social media edited/crafted/meme-circulated impromptu speech of the irate Grenfell resident, alongside similar incidents I witnessed on the 15th and 16th June 2017, suggests the issue of folk devil blame, in terms of highly combustible building cladding, is actually accomplishing a deflection from a deeper malaise of marketised public management in which cladding a tower in combustible insulation is in actuality a sign of the marketised times of the Kensington and Chelsea Tenant Management Organisation (KCTMO). The following section explores the practice of public management with an emphasis on marketisation; and in so doing, begins to make links between the culture and practice of the façade of post-industrial regeneration and the tragedy of Grenfell Tower.

Cladding Façade, Red Herring? 71

Figure 3.4.: "A people or a class which is cut off from its own past is far less free to choose and to act as a people or class than one that has been able to situate itself in history" (John Berger, *Ways of Seeing*, 1972). Photographic Image, Vicinity of Grenfell Tower; Lancaster West Estate, North Kensington, London, June 2017.

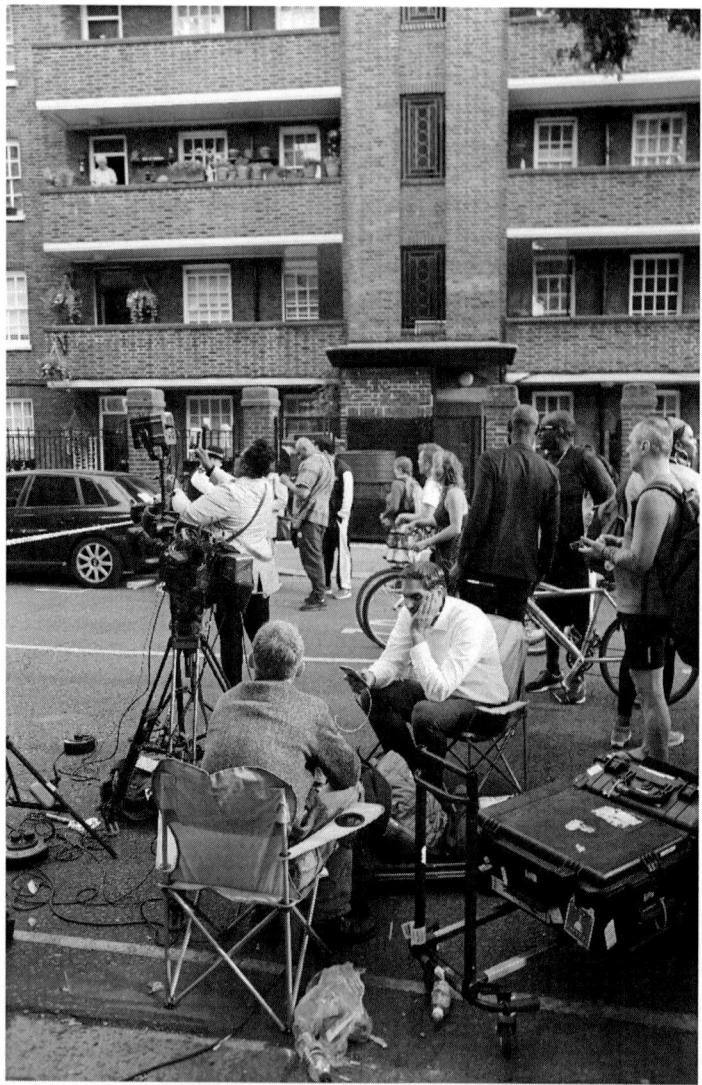

Figure 3.5.: "A people or a class which is cut off from its own past is far less free to choose and to act as a people or class than one that has been able to situate itself in history. This is why – and this is the only reason why – the entire art of the past has now become a political issue" (John Berger, *Ways of Seeing*, 1972). Photographic Image, Vicinity of Grenfell Tower; Lancaster West Estate, North Kensington, London, June 2017.

Cladding, Red Herring? Dialectics of "Best Value" Façade in a Managerial, Public Sector Contract Culture

Cllr. Elizabeth Campbell's Kensington and Chelsea Council leadership speech of 19th July 2017 pledged that "the culture of this Council will change; in practical terms that means we will create a future for this borough together with you, our residents" (Council Meeting Webcast 2017). The integrity of the pledge is of course unquestionable; rather it is necessary to apprehend the management ideas that adminiculate the KCTMO and the delivery of the cultural change collaterally pledged by Cllr. Elizabeth Campbell. Public sector critical management theory provides resourceful insights that are relevant to a comprehensive apprehension of KCTMO's organisational culture and the issue of aesthetics in the regeneration of Grenfell Tower. Of particular relevance is the concept of "new public management", developed to ascertain a pervasion of managerialism in the public sector in the 1980s (Ferlie et al. 1997: 1). Amidst the rise of the New Right's neoclassical liberal Thatcherism public sector philosophy, policy and practice became subject to a sustained ideological challenge. It was no longer considered appurtenant to advocate "the well-established organizational paradigms of the public corporation and of the large-scale, standardized, and professionalized Welfare State agency" (ibid.). Rather, the discourse of "new public management" prioritises market-led efficiency and managerial organisational structures to facilitate "a convergence of technological innovation and cost-drivers" in the delivery of increasingly privatised public sector services (ibid. 3). Infused by the conflicts and contradictions of its New Right neoclassical liberal antecedents, this new form of public sector management pursues an achievement of value through the "doing more with less" (ibid. 6) whereby the 1980's pursuit of compulsory competitive tendering (CCT) continued into New Labour's regime of Best Value (BV) and pursued a quasi-market outsourcing into the private sector or public sector services. The local governance iteration of this model of privatisation was, in the 1980s, driven by a proliferation of New Right neoclassical liberal initiatives intent on privatising nationalised industries; and in so doing cultivating workers into a constituency of shareowners. It is increasingly evident that social policy faculties that endure in the public sector are subjected to the categorical performance measurement processes "of manageralization and marketization" (ibid. 3). Given that public sector services are indirectly transactional, funded through taxes as opposed to at the point of use, it is difficult to create orthodox market dynamics, thus neoclassical liberal policy attempts to cultivate quasi-markets "whereby previously line-managed organizations disaggregate into purchasing and providing wings, with relations between them governed by contract rather than hierarchy" (ibid. 6). Funding for the proliferating quasi-market structures is increasingly shifting from an onus on the public expenditure to that of private competition whereby a "number of independent providers may compete for contracts" (ibid.).

In the discourse of neoclassical liberal public management, competitively resourced quasi-markets provide improved scrutiny as a quest for analogues of market processes produces an obsession with audits, market-testing, service-user insights and competition-based market corrections. Consumer sovereignty and consumer-led choice become the pinnacle rhetorical orchestration of public services that are no longer public. Indeed, in the declining presence of direct line management, market analogues operate regulatory structures advertising the successful transition of neoclassical liberal rhetoric into market-based managerial practice. With regards to the latter, the introduction into the public sector of streamlined Total Quality Management (TQM) and Business Process Reengineering (BPR) systems are designed to alleviate the burdensome weight of vertically hierarchical bureaucratic management structures. But herein reveals some of the tensions and contradictions of the new neoclassical liberal public sector management regime for it seeks to retain "direct management control" and yet it also strives towards "downsizing and decentralization" (ibid. 12). Ferlie et al. (1997) attempt to address these contradictions by modelling four variants of new public management. The first, referred to by Ferlie et al., (1997: 10–11) as "NPM Model 1: The Efficiency Drive", having bestridden the 1980s with its less potent influence, continues to encourage in public sector management: (1) an aggrandised ministration to "financial control"; (2) hierarchical, quantifiably monitored performance; (3) use of standardised audit techniques and their extension into assessing both operational and professional services; (4) emphasis on user-engagement responsiveness, informational services provision and consumer citizenship; (5) compulsory competitive tendering as part of a deregulated labour-market and use of public private partnership – enabling the accruement of – "individually agreed reward packages at a senior level"; (6) predominance of management intervention in the directorship of the practice of professionals; (7) engineering of an entrepreneurial culture of professional conduct and enterprising management; and a (8) shift in corporate governance away from a powerful apex of "elected representatives and trade-unionists" towards "moves to a board of directors model". Ferlie et al. (1997: 12) construct a second model of neoliberal management within the public sector entitled "NPM Model 2: Downsizing and Decentralisation"; the distinctive feature being an amplification of "market-mindedness to more elaborate and developed quasi-markets; a (still ambiguous) shift from planning to quasi-markets as the mechanism for allocating resources within the public sector" (ibid. 13). In the third, entitled "NPM Model 3: In Search of Excellence", Ferlie et al. (1997: 14) identify a "bottom-up form" in which excellence is pursued through "radical decentralisation" and a "top-down form" in which excellence is predicated on change management directed by "a more assertive and strategic human resource management function" and "top-down" management of organisational change driven by charismatic leadership roles "seen as personal rather than team-based". Ferlie et al. (1997: 14-15) define "NPM Model 4: Public Service Orientation" as the fourth neoliberal model of public sector management, with its main distinction being "a major concern with service quality" coupled with an emphasis "on securing participation and accountability as legitimate concerns of management in the public sector". Ferlie et al. (1997:15) discern in "NPM Model 4" a "scepticism as to the role of markets in public services".

While in some agreement with many of the neoliberal features of new public management critically identified by Ferlie et al. (1997), an alternative observation, reflective of my own empirical research, is that public sector management is currently beset by the contradictions and conflicts of market-based managerialism, marketisation and the quasi-market transactional culture of the contract. Returning to the Kensington and Chelsea Tenant Management Organisation (KCTMO), it is clear that markets approximate characterised public service delivery, prioritising market-based relations, and in so doing distancing engagement with service users. Indeed, even the most cursory perusal through the strategic management documents issued by KCTMO discloses a service commitment suffuse with market-based mechanisms. For example, the KCTMO (2017a) document entitled *Value for Money Strategy 2014-17* identifies Value for Money (VfM) as a prominent mode of local government strategy arising early within the context of the establishment of the Audit Commission in the 1980s (ibid. 3). The KCTMO document divulges that during this period of inauguration of the Audit Commission: "Councils were introduced to the 'three Es' – economy, efficiency and effectiveness – as key concepts in the assessment of VfM"; retaining, to the present day, a centrality of government policy on VfM. Indeed, the KCTMO document claims that: "The National Audit Office, inheritor of the Audit Commission's responsibilities for setting VfM policy for local government, uses the same set of concepts virtually unchanged in 30 years". The document attempts to effectively situate itself within a history of New Right, New Labour regimes, referring further to the recent political ventures of the Conservative and Liberal Democrat coalition. Thus we are presented with an uncritical litany of three decades' worth of neoliberal reverberations of VfM: "Government has been, by turns, more or less directive as to how councils should approach VfM, with new initiatives succeeding each other: compulsory competitive tendering, Best Value, housing inspections, comprehensive performance assessment, comprehensive area assessment, and the establishment – and then abolition – of the TSA as housing regulator" (ibid.). Contiguous with the KCTMO (2017a) document's affirmation of neoliberal VfM strategy, an uncontentious account of decentralised market-based regulation of local governance is presented thus:

> Current arrangements under the Coalition government largely remove external regulation and avoid prescription; these leave councils with full responsibility of deciding how best to make drastic reductions in spending demanded by the government's austerity measures. The introduction of self-financing has partially exempted council housing from these pressures and enabled LAHOs to take a more strategic and longer term view of their housing assets. Although TMOs, ALMOs and local authorities are not held to account by the HCA, the governance and VfM standards should be used as self-regulating tools. The TMO receives a management fee under the terms of the modular management agreement (MMA) with RBKC from the Housing Revenue Account (HRA). The recent freedom in HRA Finance, whereby RBKC is now receiving all its rents and has in place a strategy, and the HRA business plan, which is projecting a proposed surplus of £33m by 2020. The management fee for 2015-16 is £10.7m; this is £890K lower in absolute terms than the fee for 2005-06 and £4.04m lower after adjusting for inflation. This represents a saving of 28.4% on the management fee. (ibid. 3)

The picture we obtain from the KCTMO (2017a) VfM strategy is that of contradiction and tension arising from clashes between market-based transactional dynamics and long-term planning. Indeed, it is an often-recognised feature of the application of market mechanisms to the public sector that: "Markets and planning constitute alternative approaches to coordinating economic activities" (Walsh 1995: 32). The former involves an exchange relationship mediated by "the price mechanism" whereby price enables comparative indices, enabling assumptions to be made about quality, value and market-sector pricing (ibid. 32-33) for it is assumed that actors "will adjust their actions in the market depending on the information that they get through the price system, and those actions, in turn, will contribute to price adjustments" (ibid. 33). Furthermore, the market is assumed to be self-regulating; as Walsh's (ibid.) *Public Services and Market Mechanisms* observes: "The market produces coordinated results without conscious coordinating processes". Thus, when the KCTMO (2017a: 3) document makes reference to "government largely remove external regulation and avoid prescription; these leave councils with full responsibility of deciding how best to make drastic reductions in spending demanded by the government's austerity measures", it is featuring a market-based government strategy that is a condition and consequence of KCTMO's management strategy. And this is in contrast with the process and practices of planning as indicated in the following KCTMO *Value for Money Strategy* document: "The introduction of self-financing has partially exempted council housing from these pressures and enabled LAHOs to take a more strategic and longer term view of their housing assets" (ibid.). Planning management strategy involving the authoritarian application of resources based on a formulated processes of systematisation is evident in the latter statement. That the KCTMO *Value for Money Strategy* manifests market and planning strategies is emblematic of how, as Walsh (1995:33) observes, "all political systems are a mixture of market principles and organised, authority-based planning, but the mix can vary greatly". Evident in the KCTMO (2017a: 3) *Value for Money Strategy* is an extension of market-based mechanisms into transactional relations and planning decisions; this is particularly apparent when one considers the KCTMO's self-stated VfM-mediated list of strategic priorities:

1. Understanding the costs and how we compare to others.
2. Achieve VfM through effective procurement.
3. Efficiency in service delivery.
4. Promote and embed VfM.

(KCTMO 2017a: 3)

It might help here to revisit the KCTMO (2017a: 2) document's definition of VfM: "The TMO is committed to providing high quality value for money services for our customers. VfM involves making the best use of its finite resources (both physical and human) to deliver the highest levels of satisfaction and value added services to our customers". In the area of procurement, VfM is an integral feature of the KCTMO's strategy; as the KCTMO (2017a: 3) document expresses it: "Procurement forms an integral part of the value for money strategy and has the potential through modern methods to deliver service improvements". As one may have already discerned, VfM will therefore have been an integral part of the procurement contracts through which the Grenfell Tower refurbishment was accomplished and thus it is necessary to investigate how VfM provided the condition and consequence of the Grenfell Tower refurbishment programme. Firstly, VfM mediated the KCTMO's framework of procurement agreements, indicated thus:

> The Board has agreed to the establishment of a framework agreement for four years to carry out the capital work and decorations. The total value of the framework agreement could exceed £90m. The first year's contracts have been awarded, but are subject to leaseholder challenge. With the agreement of RBKC the TMO is taking the framework agreement to the Upper Tribunal to get a determination binding on all parties and which will also set a binding precedent for the whole sector. The hearing is expected in summer 2015. VfM was included as part of the procurement matrix and is embedded in the contracts. (KCTMO 2017a: 3)

Early in this chapter, I explored tensions that had arisen between the initial management contractor of the Grenfell Tower refurbishment programme Leadbitter and their subsequent replacement by the refurbishment-centred Rydon Construction, Development, Maintenance and Management. The discussion, thus far, of the KCTMO's VfM strategic approach to procurement illuminates how the rhetorical capital of cost comparison can in actuality manifest perturbingly austere stringent decisions. The latter is particularly evident in terms of the integration of VfM in the operational matrix of the KCTMO's framework for contract management and related procurement skills. In this respect, the KCTMO (2017a: 3) *Value for Money Strategy* states the following about contract management:

> As a part of the service reviews the TMO has recruited staff with an emphasis on contract management skills in the asset management sector in place of staff with the traditional direct engineering skills. The contracts let in 2014-15 have all included VfM in the tender process and have detailed provision to allow contract monitoring. (ibid.)

According to Walsh (1995: 40), the focus of classical contract theory is "discrete contracts", short-term and existing for a limited period only whereby the concept of "discrete" refers to "contracts in which there is an instantaneous exchange of rights and duties, and in which the parties to the contract do not have a continuing relationship" (ibid.). Walsh (ibid.) argues that the concept of "discrete contracts" does not reflect the complexity of modern organisations and thus contracts this with "contract forms in circumstances where there are to be repeated exchanges within a continuing relationship". While supportive of a notion of adopting complexity in organisational analysis, it is apparent that several key features of the "continuing relationship" contract model are also apparent in the "discrete contact" form. Firstly, Walsh (1995: 41) identifies how contracts are "a means of 'making the future present'". The notion of a contract speculating about a future that is not knowable in its totality is acutely relevant to the "discrete" short-term contract. And thus Walsh's (1995) suggestion that the unknowability of the future precipitates the development of institutional structures "that allow the postponement of choice" (ibid. 41) is of particular significance to the "discrete contract". It is evident that the short-term contracts are the preference of the KCTMO and its three-year strategic planning i.e., 2014 – 2017. Following Walsh (1995: 41), it would appear that these "discrete contracts" are able to make "future decisions more tractable" by embedding the "postponement of choice" within the retrenchment rhetoric of market-based VfM for the "making of the future present" aligns with a rhetoric of VfM, which is also a self-validating sign. Although Walsh (1995: 41) does not explicitly refer to poststructuralist sign-systems, one can build from several of Walsh's reflections a contract culture in which the contract begins to determine the very substance of its being. For example, Walsh (ibid.) states the following about contracts in modern organisations: "The different forms of contract will depend upon what can be observed and how much the observation of performance will cost. For example, if it is difficult to assess objectively whether or not the contractor has performed, then it may be necessary to build contract forms that incorporate trust and reputation". Here again Walsh refers to the necessity to embed the contract into a "supporting institutional social framework of norms and relationships"; but again Walsh assumes that this is the predisposition of long-term contracts for "anonymity and one-off relationships make contracting difficult" (ibid.). However, this presents limitations to an understanding of short-term contracts of three-year strategic planning, such as that evidently practised by KCTMO.

Walsh (ibid. 41-42) argues that successful contractual conditions require that "the contractual system needs an institutional framework that provides for stability of relations" and that "it is unlikely that the formal legal framework will be an adequate institution for ensuring that contract obligations are met, for it is likely to be slow, inflexible and costly". It is my contention that in the short-term culture of procurement outlined in the

KCTMO (2017a) *Value for Money Strategy* there is consistent evidence that the contract culture is supported by the structures, processes and practices of VfM, but more specifically by VfM operating as a sign-system. Inferred by Walsh (1995: 42), a culture of the contract is evident where "the contract then becomes the basis on which continuing relations are negotiated, rather than a detailed statement of the nature of the relationship". But the latter features of the contract culture, for Walsh (ibid.) refers to extended contracts: "The extended nature of complex contractual relationships influences the way that contracts are monitored, the way that failure to meet responsibilities is dealt with, and the way that disagreements between the parties to the contact resolved". Furthermore, Walsh (ibid. 42-43) argues that "the longer the contractual relationship is to last, the more likely it is to be self-enforcing since the parties will value the relationship. Cooperation is easier the stronger a shadow the future casts on the present". Conversely, it is my contention that these conditions are met in the short-term contract through the mobilising of self-validating sign-systems of value, such as VfM in respect to the KCTMO (2017a: 3) *Value for Money Strategy*.

Elsewhere, the notion that public management is predicated on marketing knowledge is evident in the writing of Ian Greener (2009). According to Greener (ibid.), the postmodern turn in management theory arose in the 1970s, its principal ambition being to reveal contradictions in the modernist meta-narrative of rationality pervading the field of management studies. Greener (2009: 61) argues: "In the post-modern view, traditional public administration failed because of its dependence on the meta-narratives of rationalistic decision-making and democratic accountability, both of which might be interesting theoretically, but cannot be supported by their practice in reality. Public administration is portrayed as a modernistic project that is no longer sustainable". Engaging with key advocates for a decentring theoretical approach to policymaking within the public sector management, Greener (ibid.) presents an alternative view to the replacement of rational decision-making models of public participation with an emphasis on "greater public deliberation and involvement in public services" (ibid.). Greener's alternative model, presented within the context of the postmodern turn in management theory, advocates a resurrection in public involvement in public sector service provision, achieved through "a 'politics for amateurs'" (ibid.). The latter refers to a situation "in which the public are able to engage with service change and direction on more straightforward terms" (ibid. 61-62). Of significance is that Greener's account of postmodern management theory is focused on "the analysis of power and power relationships" for "it has become as common to ask 'who gains' from reform programmes as 'what happened' as a result of their interaction" (ibid. 62). When exploring the limitations of this postmodern public management approach, Greener (ibid.) focuses on the extent to which theory can alienate practising managers thus supporting the idea that: "Academics, in turn, have a great deal to gain by engaging in the problems of public management not only in terms of generating new empirical (case) material, but also in attempting to test out some of their ideas in practice" (ibid.). By emphasising the opportunity to "test out" a postmodern management theory, the limitations of existing management theory and Greener's postmodern approach are revealed. In my previous book, entitled *Adsensory Financialisation*, critical interventions were made into the postmodern management science, cultural theory for Gabriel and Lang (1995, 2006, 2015) and numerous other prominent cultural theorists within the management sciences miscomprehend Baudrillard's (1983) conception of *simulations*; they struggle to comprehend that simulation feigns existence i.e., simulatory signs are not stimulants or triggers as they have no basis in reality other than to feign existence. Nor is simulation solely the preserve of algorithmic programmes. Rather, it is evident that, firstly, Baudrillard (1983) makes a distinction between hyperreality and simulation as is evident in the statement that "Los Angeles and the America surrounding it are no longer real, but of the order of the hyperreal and of simulation" (ibid. 25), the latter clarified as "Disneyland is presented as imaginary in order to make us believe that the rest is real, whereas all of Los Angeles and the America that surrounds it are no longer real, but belong to the hyperreal order and to the order of simulation" (Baudrillard 1994: 12). Secondly, it is my comprehension that Baudrillard envisaged situations whereby simulation is emerging from hyperreality in terms of the integration into reality, through e.g., postmodern advertising practice, of "models of a real without origin or reality" (Baudrillard 1983: 2). Axiomatic with this, is that neither simulation or hyperreality are conflated into each other. Adsensory financialisation identifies how, in their appeal to the cultivation of the soul via hyperreal aesthetics of bodily health and well-being, adsensory biotechnologies (e.g., bio-metric smart watches) are generating hyperreal metrics that through e.g., postmodern advertising practice, are formulated intermittently into simulatory signs without substantial basis in reality; for these simulatory signs feign their existence (Odih 2016).

In many respects, Greener (2009) mirrors the shortcomings in Gabriel and Lang's (1995, 2006, 2015) management science cultural theory for

Greener's (2009: 61-62) advocacy for a postmodern management theory that can be tested implicitly assumes the existence of a substance that can be substantively tested; and in so doing fails to appreciate that according to Baudrillard (1983) third-order simulacra do not exist. Consequently, it is not my intention to present as postmodern the concept of VfM detailed in the KCTMO's (2017a) *Value for Money Strategy*. Rather, it is my contention that the matrix of VfM and KCTMO strategy has increasingly operated as a second-order simulacra, perpetually engaged in the replication of sign-systems that mirror its purchase on reality while succeeding in distorting and blurring it; nevertheless the simulacra of value is unable to entirely negate reality of the existence of value. Following this analogy it is proposed here that the original purpose of VfM as an indicator of value in the KCTMO business strategy over time came to be dramatically transformed into the epitome of value such that, as Berger (1972/1977: 21) might say: "This new status of the original work is the perfectly rational consequence of the new means of reproduction". But as objective measures of value enter into the symbolic realm of sign-value, the conception of VfM in the KCTMO business strategy, unbeknown to the KCTMO organisational practice, engages with mystification and the cultivation of legitimation. In so doing, as Berger (ibid.) might say: "The meaning of the original work no longer lies in what it uniquely says but in what it uniquely is". VfM in the KCTMO business strategy becomes redefined as sacred, born of an efficiently prosperous market-led organisational culture. As Berger (ibid.) might say: "This value is affirmed and gauged by the price it fetches on the market". But given that VfM is supposed to be an objective measure of value, and thus detached from the propaganda of market-based relations, its descent into neoliberal commerce denatures its original non-market-based meaning. As Berger (ibid.) might say, "its market price is said to be a reflection of its spiritual value".

Figure 3.6.: "This value is affirmed and gauged by the price it fetches on the market" (John Berger, *Ways of Seeing*, 1972). Photographic Image, Vicinity of Grenfell Tower; Lancaster West Estate, North Kensington, London, June 2017.

Figure 3.7.: "Yet the spiritual value of an object, as distinct from a message or an example, can only be explained in terms of magic or religion" (John Berger, *Ways of Seeing*, 1972). Photographic Image, Vicinity of Grenfell Tower; Lancaster West Estate, North Kensington, London, June 2017.

Figure 3.8.: "It is the final empty claim for the continuing values of an oligarchic, undemocratic culture" (John Berger, *Ways of Seeing*, 1972). Photographic Image, Vicinity of Grenfell Tower, North Kensington, London, June 2017.

Adsensory Gentrification – Politically Mobilising Façade as the Miscreant of Grenfell Tower

In the aftermath of the Grenfell Tower fire (14th June 2017), the Department for Communities and Local Government (DCLG) commissioned the Building Research Establishment (BRE) to conduct a broad-scale test to evaluate the combustibility of aluminium composite material (ACM) panels in combination with different foam insulation cores and to ascertain how different combinations of these cladding materials operate in a fire (DCLG 2017). DCLG was acting here under the auspices of Community Secretary Sajid Javid's 27th June 2017 establishment of an Independent Expert Advisory Panel, tasked with providing critical guidance on immediate building safety measures deemed necessary following the Grenfell Tower fire. According to DCLG (2017), the independent Expert Advisory Panel on 6th July 2017 recommended that a comprehensive scale test, defined as BS 8414, be conducted so as to provide clarification and guidelines for immediate action for building owners. The text consisted of a comparative analysis of the combustibility and behaviour in a fire of six combinations of aluminium composite material panel and polyethylene insulation core (ibid.). The first cladding system tested was formed "using ACM panels with an unmodified polyethylene core and a rigid polyisocyanurate foam" (ibid.) similar to the cladding system used to refurbish the exterior of Grenfell Tower. According to DCLG (ibid.): "The test results show that this system failed to meet the criteria set out in building regulations guidance BR 135".

On 30th August 2017, the DCLG (2017a), in conjunction with Community Secretary Sajid Javid MP, published "the terms of reference for the independent Review of Building Regulations and Fire Safety", previously commissioned in the immediate aftermath of the Grenfell Tower. These terms of reference speak directly to "the system failures" made manifest in the large-scale testing, carried out by BRE, of the aluminium composite material (ACM) panel and polyethylene core cladding system fitted onto the Grenfell Tower and on tower blocks across London (ibid.). The purpose of the Independent Review of Building Regulations and Fire Safety is twofold: firstly, "to make recommendations that will ensure we have a sufficiently robust regulatory system for the future"; and secondly, "to provide further assistance to residents that the complete system is working to ensure the buildings they live in are safe and remain so" (ibid. 1). Led by Dame Judith Hackitt, the review, in addition to other objectives, is concerned to "consider the competencies, duties and balance of responsibilities of key individuals within the system in ensuring that fire safety standards are adhered to" (ibid.). By the time of the establishment of the review in August 2017, the statutory inquiry into the Grenfell Tower fire, led by Sir Martin Moore-Bick, had started and the review led by Dame Judith Hackitt confirmed that it would co-operate extensively with the public inquiry (ibid.). On 26th July 2017, the Communities Secretary Sajid Javid established a task pronounced as providing "support" for the beleaguered Royal Borough of Kensington and Chelsea (RBKC), which from the onset of the public enquiry was flying haphazardly against the deluge of public criticism (DCLG 2017c). Evidence of the spiralling descent of central government confidence in the capacity of the KCTMO to self-govern was transparently evident in the DCLG (ibid.) statement declaring that: "The Taskforce will provide assurance to the Secretary of State that RBKC has the capacity and capability to deliver an effective long-term recovery plan for its residents taking into account their views". Further evidence of the crisis in confidence looming over the KCTMO was revealed in a scoop by *Guardian* journalists Mason and Sherwood (2017). It was reported that Prime Minister Theresa May had conceded during a private recent visit to survivors of the Grenfell Tower tragedy that the Kensington and Chelsea Council's response to the fire emergency had been inexplicably inadequate; and according to the reported residents' accounts, Theresa May "assured them that the tenant management organisation (TMO) would no longer be responsible for the rest of the [Lancaster West] estate" (Mason and Sherwood 2017). The Prime Minister's pledge that the Conservative-led KCTMO would be divested of its oversight of the Lancaster West housing estate was, according to Mason and Sherwood (ibid.), confirmed in a letter from the Council leader Elizabeth Campbell, which allegedly stated: "We wrote to the TMO yesterday and said that we didn't think the most viable option was to work with them going forward". The removal of TMO's oversight authority by central government of an estate within the TMO's jurisdiction is seemingly unprecedented but it seems in accordance with central government's desperate attempts to stem the descent into a total crisis of its Conservative-led Kensington and Chelsea Council. Thus, it is entirely plausible that, as reported by Mason and Sherwood (2017), Downing Street would reveal the Prime Minister had "confirmed that the TMO will be removed from the management of the Lancaster West [Grenfell Tower] estate and she recognised that the council did not respond quickly enough". But what is far less plausible is the ability of the Conservative central government to obfuscate the management ineptitude of the KCTMO if in months or years to come, the Metropolitan Police decided to move forward in pursuit of corporate manslaughter chargers. In respect to the latter, consider the following extract from a letter received in July 2017 by selected residents of the Lancaster West estate:

> After an initial assessment of that information, the officer leading the investigation has today notified Royal Borough of Kensington and Chelsea and the Kensington and Chelsea Tenant Management Organisation that there are reasonable grounds to suspect that each organisation may have committed the offence of corporate manslaughter under the Corporate Manslaughter and Corporate Homicide Act 2007. (Metropolitan Police 2017 in Construction Manager 2017)

In September 2017, I secured an interview with a Labour councillor (Cllr.) within Kensington and Chelsea Council. The Cllr's eloquently pensive, detailed and earnest account of the management culture of Kensington and Chelsea council and its KCTMO provided for an unparalleled introspection of the issues I have raised in this chapter concerning the aestheticisation of urban regeneration in the context of neoliberal public management culture. Indeed, nuances in the materiality of the Kensington and Chelsea's Council's management culture – described in this chapter as a management culture mediated by the pursuit of contracts and the second-order simulacra of Value for Money (VfM) – were all the more disconcerting when relayed in their complex and nuanced actuality by Cllr., during our interview. Two particular issues need to be outlined here as part of this chapter's conclusion. Firstly, of concern is the extent to which Kensington and Chelsea Council's wholesale adoption of neoliberal public management practices cultivated a contractual culture predicated on property development; indeed, the Cllr., referred similarly to a property development culture at Kensington and Chelsea Council, evident in the practices of its KCTMO. Leaving the speculation of this property development culture yielding direct rewards in terms of company directorships to one side, more compelling are the revelations regarding a property development culture in which the reneging by property developers on commitments to ensure mixed accommodation was systematic. Two aspects of this practice are particularly disconcerting. Firstly, as described by the Cllr., around "twelve years ago" the management culture of Kensington and Chelsea transformed markedly into what the Cllr. poignantly describes as "Thatcherite". The transformation in organisational culture involved the displacement of a culture described as based on "patrician" that infantilised the social housing tenants with self-righteous indignation. Apparently the appointment of highly entrepreneurial council leaders supplicated by a rise of neoliberal public management-led policies directed at the local government loosened the hold of the culture of "patrician" and fuelled it with the high octane pursuit of property development. And thus arose the first of two contractual culture-fuelled abnegations of equitable responsibility with regards to the social housing tenants under the charge of the KCTMO for it is suggested that inroads made during the Greater London Council years towards ensuring parks and public spaces surrounded social housing tower blocks and other residencies were deliberately – although legally – eroded. In the albeit modest public spaces, the recreational spaces available to social housing tenants were systematically being used to build additional housing. While this might be observed as a noble intention, the primary destination of these new properties was, apparently, not as priority social housing but rather the lucrative private sector. The following extract from my interview with Cllr., provides further details about the transformation of the organisational culture of the KCTMO from "patrician" to a competitively rapacious contract culture geared to property development:

***Interviewer:** Hmm by far ... So the culture of the actual Council you think was?*

***Interviewee:** As I say, I have been a councillor for a very long time; and when I've, and I have checked this with people who have been around for as long as me just to make sure that I am not seeing everything through rose-tinted spectacles, but other people who have been around, said that the culture of the Council at one stage was very old-fashioned patrician, erhm, patrician approach of: We are a wealthy local authority with a number of poorer people and we will do the best we can for them; because we can, because we are a very wealthy local authority. Kensington and Chelsea decided to become Thatcherite just at the point when everybody else decided that, erhm. And so they then sort of started to want to redevelop the area, and to pay for the, {**Interviewer:** "So when was this?" "When did they decide this?"}.*

Oh I would say about twelve years ago: there was a change in the leadership of the Council; there was certainly a change [in culture] and Rock Feilding-Mellen holds a lot of responsibility for this, cos his background, whilst he's posh, he reckons he's very good, he reckons he's a property developer. He's been a very successful property developer but he certainly sort to uses the portfolio of the Council and his idea was that we would redevelop the large estates, making them more "socially balanced", by which he meant he would move in private owners. Yeah, and there is an argument, I mean, we all in theory believe in mixed tenancies. But he wasn't offering to move council tenants into private estates, he was offering to move, to sell, to sell off, or to build new properties within the Council, within existing estates and to sell them off. It was moving rich people in to share the space that was available on the estate, rather than, as I say there was no suggestion that poorer people would, they would provide properties for poorer people in the wealthy areas of the borough. So they started to sort of, and Grenfell Tower was supposed to be one of the, no, no, I am getting ahead of myself now. There are other estates, where they had been built properly according to Parker, Parker ...: what's the standard? Anyway, the old GLC which specified the size of rooms and Parker – oh I'll think about it and go and look it up later. And so they had, they had sort of gardens; they'd had open public spaces [referring to the Kensington and Chelsea social housing that were built during the era of the Greater London Council (GLC) and incorporated Lord Justice Parker's housing design proposals].

 So our estates, our existing estates built at that time do have open public spaces around them, they saw this as an opportunity to squeeze in, to build into the estates more properties. Now, given that we are the most built-up local authority in the country, there's an argument in favour of that; erhm but the key being that they wanted to sell them off rather than use them for social housing. His theory was: we'll sell off a certain amount and erhm make some money and we'll use that to pay for the upgrading of what was left. But actually they were flogging stuff off as quickly as possible. So when they are accused of "social cleansing", there's a lot to be said for that. I forget, we are going slightly in circles, but that's why the tenants were reluctant to leave Grenfell Tower and put up with all this shit of the way they were treated [referring to the inconvenience of the refurbishment and KCTMO actions].

They thought that, at least at the end of the day: I will still be occupying my flat, which will have been updated. And contrary to sort of popular belief, the flats inside were very good; were built to a high standard. You see some of the national press report that these, there was a slum property or whatever. A slum property full of immigrants is what the tabloid newspaper would like you to believe. That's not true; it was property built to a very high standard and the majority of tenants had been there for a very long time. In fact, I have got figures that the average length of tenancy of that block was twelve-and-a-half, was getting onto thirteen years. And I know myself some people who have been there for more than thirty years. So it was a stable balanced, balanced community.

(Semi-Structured Qualitative Interview: Labour Cllr., Kensington and Chelsea Council, London, September 2017)

Cllr., although not directly stating such, provides reasonable indication of the Conservative-led council as presiding over a woeful abnegation of commitment to a balanced mix-model of social and private residential housing. Nevertheless, the attribution of castigation should not be reserved directly as an issue of Council accountability. Rather, one should consider as the prime culprit the amendments made to the social housing obligations that came into being in 2013 as part of adjustments to Section 106. Section 106 is the obligation for residential housing developers to provide for a proportion of any new building to be dedicated to affordable housing. Specifically,

> S106 Obligations Overview
> Legislation
> Planning obligations under Section 106 of the Town and Country Planning Act 1990 (as amended), commonly known as s106 agreements, are a mechanism which make a development proposal acceptable in planning terms, that would not otherwise be acceptable. They are focused on site specific mitigation of the impact of development. S106 agreements are often referred to as 'developer contributions' along with highway contributions and the Community Infrastructure Levy … The common uses of planning obligations are to secure affordable housing, and to specify the type and timing of this housing; and to secure financial contributions to provide infrastructure or affordable housing.

(Planning Advisory Service 2018)

The Department for Communities and Local Government's (2013) *Section 106 Affordable Housing Requirements; Review and Appeal* details amendments to this section of the Town and Country Planning Act 1990 so as to address a supposed situation in which "Unrealistic Section 106 agreements negotiated in differing economic conditions can be an obstacle to house building" (ibid. 2). It is alleged that a situation had arisen in which "stalled schemes due to economically unviable affordable housing requirements result in no development, no regeneration and no community benefit" (ibid.). So as to address this apparent disruption to the market economy of social housing planning obligation, additional sections were inserted into the existing Section 106 provision whereby "the Growth and

Infrastructure Act inserts a new Section 106BA, BB and BC into the 1990 Town and Country Planning Act" (ibid.). It is intended that "these sections introduce a new application and appeal procedure for the review of planning obligations on planning permissions which relate to the provision of affordable housing" (ibid.). It is evident that under these revised conditions of social housing provision obligation, developers are provided with the opportunity to challenge the economic viability of social housing provision as part of their new development. One is able to discern that a subtle de-regulation of Section 106 social housing obligation has, indeed occurred, as indicated in the following statement:

> An application may be made to the local planning authority for a revised affordable housing obligation. This application should contain a revised affordable housing proposal, based on prevailing viability, and should be supported by relevant viability evidence. The local planning authority may prepare its own viability evidence or provide commentary on the evidence submitted in support of the application ... Where the local planning authority does not agree with the developer's revised proposal for affordable housing, or does not determine the application, Section 106BC provides a right of appeal to the Secretary of State. The viability evidence supporting the application should be submitted with the appeal to support the developer's assessment of a viable affordable housing requirement. The local planning authority may also submit evidence ... If allowed, the outcome of a successful appeal would be a revised affordable housing requirement in the Section 106 agreement for three years, starting on the date when the appellant is notified of the appeal decision.
>
> (Department for Communities and Local Government 2013: 2-3)

It is my contention that the 2013 amendments to Section106 of the Town and Country Planning Act of 1990 within the context of Kensington and Chelsea Council's legitimately legal evolving property development organisational culture fuelled the managerially orientated business contract culture.

Furthermore, based on my primary empirical research and document analyses, it is apparent that the contract culture of property development, fuelled by a neoliberal performance-driven metric of Value for Money (VfM), enabled or presented little challenge to property developers who were willingly shirking the commitment to the integration of social housing into their building programmes. More specifically, property developers were apparently consistently defaulting on their planning permission promises to provide a percentage of development as social housing. Rather than confront this, it is suggested that Kensington and Chelsea Council would adopt a retrospective approach, favouring the reasoning put forward by the property developer and seeking compensation through the reallocation of funds to other infrastructure projects. Of significance was the suggestion that property developers offering to provide social housing amongst their builds outside of Royal Borough of Kensington and Chelsea was often a favoured proposition in discussions of compensation; and this generated the accusation of "social cleansing". Furthermore, the KCTMO regeneration projects were said to be subject to a wider contract culture of underspending within the Kensington and Chelsea Council. It was suggested that in addition to the vast sums accrued through the selling of its very lucrative housing stock, Kensington and Chelsea Council accrued large amounts of its £300 million reserve through underspending on its infrastructure projects. Echoes of this were discussed earlier, in this chapter, with regards to procurement and issues raised by Rydon's commissioning in terms of Value for Money. A further manifestation of the contract culture of property development, said to have been evident at Kensington and Chelsea Council, was a systematic undermining of the role of the "expert". The Cllr., described the displacement of a previous culture of expertise and specialisation which focused on "pride in the service they provided". In the neoliberal market-led property development culture of Kensington and Chelsea's Conservative-led council expertise came to be associated with inflexible bureaucratisation and ascribed negative connotations that suggested its obstruction of a more dynamic contract culture of "certification". According to the Cllr., the ultimate perils of this displacement meant that those councillors that would ordinarily specialise in, for example, fire regulation had long since been displaced by a self-certifying contract culture in which the contractor was an integral feature of the certification of their service provision. The Cllr., pronounced poignantly that Grenfell Tower is an outcome of this self-certifying contract culture of property development. The very detailed qualitative semi-structured interview I conducted with the Cllr., is located in the epilogue; entitled *Timely Reflections*, it contains the full transcription of the 7th September 2017 interview with the Cllr.

The Cllr's benevolence of spirit infused the interview with a heartfelt integrity and a genuine care; indeed, the attention to detail and ethics of care bestowed on each interview question inspired a sense of confidence in the empirical direction and its focus on organisational culture. Obviously, degenerate organisational cultures are symptomatic of a more complex and insidious malaise, providing only modest insights into labyrinthine factors necessitates a public enquiry with regards to the Grenfell Tower fire tragedy. Nevertheless, the disturbing frequency with which degenerate organisational cultures, in various guises, can be observed as having operated within the KCTMO indicates that a neglect of neoliberal contract-led organisational cultures and their apotheosis into pernicious sign-objects furnish the latter with more surreptitious arbitrary power. Acknowledging this, one may appreciate my apprehension and solicitude, having read through Sir Martin Moore-Bick's (2017) formal opening statement for the Grenfell Tower inquiry in despondent realisation that the culture of the Kensington and Chelsea Council's organisation and that of its KCTMO was conspicuously absent from the terms of reference and all feature themes of the inquiry. Rather, what did feature in the Thursday 14th September *Chairman's Opening Statement* was a disconcerting affirmation that a procedural justice, devoid of emotional entanglement, would pervade the inquiry. Granted, the "period of silence" at the commencement of the statement displayed affecting poignancy and sensitivity. Sentimentality and vehemence are abundantly evident Sir Martin Moore-Bick's (2017) account of the anguished period (immediately after the Grenfell Tower fire) on June 28th when Prime Minister Theresa May appointed Moore-Bick (ibid. 2) "to chair a public inquiry into the disaster", with the originally constructed purpose of the inquiry "to find out what had happened and why it had happened, with a view to ensuring that a similar catastrophe could never occur again". We are informed that the public consultation to determine the inquiry's terms and reference was launched on 5th July 2017 and this involved engaging with "over 550 responses", many from the residents of Grenfell Tower and the residents located within the proximity of the Lancaster West estate (ibid.). In its reception of "over 550 responses" and the distillation into a terms of reference presented to the Prime Minister on 10th August 2017, the public inquiry consultation process demonstrates an eager intention to be seen to be listening. However, the limits to an empathetic engagement are replete in the text of the opening statement. Of general concern is the adamant and perilously procedurally authoritarian refusal of Sir Martin Moore-Bick to commensurately involve the surviving residents of Grenfell Tower, as evidenced in the following extract from the Statement:

> I know that many of the survivors would like me to appoint someone from among their number, or perhaps another local resident, as one of my assessors. Many of them can, of course, provide valuable evidence and I shall ensure that all their evidence is heard and carefully considered, but to appoint as an assessor someone who had direct involvement in the fire

would risk undermining my impartiality in the eyes of others who are deeply involved in the Inquiry. I have therefore come to the conclusion that I cannot take that course. As a result, I have approached a number of people, all completely independent of those whose conduct may have to be investigated, who have expertise of a social and administrative nature that enables them to provide me with the assistance I need to carry out my task.

(Moore-Bick 2017: 2-3)

Without being considered too bedevilled by poststructuralism, I'd like to draw your attention to an intriguing feature in the etymology of the word "assist". Numerous nineteenth-century editions of *Nouveau Dictionnaire Classique de la Française* (1875: 71) identify trajectories in the etymology of the word that link it to the classical French masculine word *assis, (assist (m))*, in conscious opposition to the feminine French word: *assise (assisst(f))*. Assuming a plausible basis in this hypothetico-deductive reasoning of the gendered etymology of the word *assist(m)*, it is reasonable to assume that this word is embedded in a technically purposively goal-oriented masculine rationalisation of providing support as opposed to an ethics of care (c.f. Gilligan 1993) involving embodied, experiential ethical judgement and a relationality in memory and time (Odih 2014). Moore-Bick's (2017) resolute adherence to an objectively rational and detached "ethic of judgement" (Gilligan 1993) is disconcertedly resonant with an epistemology of a rationalist linear time of memory through which neoliberal public sector management theory and practice emerge.

On 28th September 2017 it was announced, unsurprisingly, that the Kensington and Chelsea Tenant Management Organisation (KCTMO) had lost its contract with respect to the management of the Council's housing stock. In actuality, the repudiation of the KCTMO's responsibility had been singled out earlier (as described above) and detailed in the Notice of Meeting for the Royal Borough of Kensington and Chelsea Council dated 27 September 2017 and issued on 19 September 2017. In the RBKC's (2017b) 27 September 2017 *Council Public A*genda document, one of the main no-confidence motions directed against the KCTMO was entitled Motions for Debate (i) KCTMO, proposed by Cllr. Taylor-Smith, seconded by Cllr. Hargreaves; it stated the following:

> This Council recognises the breakdown of trust between the KCTMO and its tenants and leaseholders. It calls on the Executive to terminate the current contract and establish a new management structure for the Council's social housing stock.

Chapter Three

> The Council acknowledges that this is a complex issue and calls on the Executive to ensure that it fully works with tenants, leaseholders, residents' associations and other interested parties in developing and agreeing a workable management structure for the future.

(RBKC 2017b: 3-4)

The 27 September 2017 RBKC's (2017b) *Council Public Agenda* additional item of motion of no-confidence in the KCTMO was entitled Motions for Debate (ii) KCTMO, proposed by Cllr. Press and seconded by Cllr. Dent Coad. This second KCTMO no-confidence motion commenced by registering support for the Kensington and Chelsea Council leadership and its chief executive in their repudiation of the KCTMO and endorsing the galvanising consensus that the KCTMO "is no longer tenable and that the organisation needs to be dismantled and replaced" (RBKC 2017b). In addition to this reiteration of endorsement, the second motion of repudiation referred to an open letter that had been received by Council leaders, having been constructed by "14 KCTMO Residents' Associations" insisting, in essence, that all confidence in the KCTMO's capability to manage effectively and fairly the Kensington and Chelsea Council's social housing on behalf of the Royal Borough of Kensington and Chelsea had dissipated. Appropriately realising these seismic shifts in the tectonic plates of KCTMO power, the (ii) KCTMO motion seized the opportunity to propose a new model of Tenant Management Organisation; as they expressed it: "The position of the KCTMO is no longer tenable and there is an urgent need to adopt a different, resident-focused model of managing council housing in our borough" (RBKC 2017b: 4). Some indication of how this alternative model might operate is inferred by the statement in the motion about phasing the termination of the KCTMO and the making of "calls on the Executive to take immediate action to end its contract with KCTMO" (ibid.). The motion entitled (ii) KCTMO proposed "a staged transition and closure" which would be more inclusive of the residents in its actively participatory democratic engagement, whereby it was proposed that:

> This Council also undertakes to ensure that everyone subject to the TMO's management – Council tenants and leaseholders, absentee leaseholders and the tenants of leaseholders – are not only consulted but can fully participate from the onset in the process of deciding and co-designing how their homes and estates are managed in the future. (RBKC 2017b)

Interestingly, and according to the RBKC (2017c) webcast of the full Council Meeting on Wednesday 27 September 2017, the (i) KCTMO no-confidence motion proposed by Cllr. Taylor-Smith made a circumstance of incorporating the participatory democracy features proposed in (ii) KCTMO by the Cllr. and seconded by Cllr. Dent Coad, but it did so punctuated by a chorus of heckles from the public gallery directly challenging the legitimacy and authority of the Conservative councillors, as indicated in the following brief transcription of the webcast:

Madame Mayor: There are three motions: Motion one, an amendment has been tabled, Cllr. Taylor-Smith, would you move and Cllr Hargreaves to second.

Cllr. Taylor-Smith: I beg to move, Madame Mayor.

Madame Mayor: Cllr. Taylor-Smith, do you wish to speak?

Cllr. Taylor-Smith: Yes, I do, thank you. [heckles from the public gallery]. The Council has listened to residents across the Borough and changes will be made. We are looking at the options for the future management of housing and we will work closely with tenants, leaseholders, residents' associations and other groups to develop and agree a way forward. Residents of the Council, the government and the TMO itself have come to the conclusion that after the tragedy of June 14, the TMO no longer has the trust of residents in the Borough. In light of this, we are working with the TMO to terminate the contract with the Council. In coming to this view, I draw reference to the open letter to Council leaders from 14 CTMO residents' associations stating that they have no confidence in the TMO's abilities to manage council housing on behalf of the Council. Drawing particular attention to issues of fire safety as well as meeting with 25 residents' association leaders, where a unanimous vote of no confidence in KCTMO was taken. The key issue for us all is to draw the relations with the TMO to a close in an orderly fashion to ensure that the TMO's management of the Borough's estates can continue as we move towards a resolution. Let me be clear what resolution looks like: it means listening to residents; engaging with them; consulting and understanding, how they want their homes and neighbourhoods to be managed in the future. We will go back to the first principles and discuss all possible options: Who should manage your homes? What kind of organisation should partner us? And how should this happen? And we want you to be leading us, not the other way round. Residents working in partnership with the Council hold the key to how their communities will run; and how we hope you will fully engage with us. I know we need to earn your trust for this to happen and my colleagues in the chamber and I are determined to do that. As I said, the TMO appreciates that it must withdraw; to do this in an orderly fashion we must go through the correct and prescribed legal process that means securing the vote of a majority of the TMO membership to allow this to happen. This in turn will allow the TMO with guidance to provide services for residents across the Borough and to finalise and deliver fire risk assessments while we go through the consultation and transition process. We are already moving forward with the Lancaster Estate; Steve Jacobs, who many of you know and may be family with from RBKC, is now on the ground at Lancaster West effectively fronting the TMO starting to resolve issues raised by residents. I would also emphasise that ensuring our residents get improved services and that their requests are responded to quickly will be our priority throughout the process. But this will take time. Both sides of the chamber share this same objective [heckles from the public gallery]. If I may finish [Madame Mayor: 'Can you allow Cllr. Taylor-Smith to finish']. If I may [interrupted by heckles from the public gallery]. [Members of the public gallery begin to applaud the heckler's challenge to the Cllr.]. If I may finish [further heckling from the public gallery]. Just to finish: Both sides of the chamber share the same objective of creating a different resident-focused model of managing council housing in the Borough and I am pleased to support the spirit of the labour amendment and would like to recommend that we vote for it. However, for legal reasons of employment law, I would ask the proposer of an amendment to remove the reference to guaranteed employment rights … [Cllr. Thompson: 'I proposed the amendment and we are prepared to accept the amendment to the amendment that Cllr. Taylor-Smith has indicated']. Thank you very much. Thank you; and with that minuted, Madame Mayor, I am most happy to support the amendment.

Madame Mayor: OK, I would now like to put the amendment to the vote. Would all those in favour please show [counting in favour]. I declare the amendment carried. Would you like to sum up or we just go to the vote? I now put the motion as amended to the vote. Will those in favour please show [counting in favour]. I declare the motion as amended carried.

(RBKC 2017c, Webcast of 27th September 2017 Council meeting)

This extract of the webcast of the full 27th September 2017 Council meeting of Kensington and Chelsea Council provides further features confirming the neoliberal public management contract culture that appears to have consumed the KCTMO. Of particular significance is Cllr. Taylor-Smiths' statement that the KCTMO would be invited to vote on its withdrawal; and this is despite the Conservative councillors having agreed that the KCTMO is "no longer tenable". The issue of dissolving the KCTMO provides further insight into the autocratic, self-serving imperative and values that came to define the KCTMO. Indeed, the KCTMO's degenerating organisational culture became increasingly transparent as it unashamedly clung onto power in the somewhat chaotic period of "transition" instituted by the Royal Borough of Kensington and Chelsea Council. RBKC (2017d) published on 11 October 2017 a newsroom press release entitled: "KCTMO and Council working together to secure orderly transition". RBKC (ibid.) stated that the Kensington and Chelsea Council and the KCTMO had agreed to collaborate in the "transition to new management arrangements for the Council's housing stock". In a rather confused and contradictory manoeuvre, the Royal Borough of Kensington and Chelsea Council insisted that the dissolution of the KCTMO is fundamentally the obligation of the KCTMO, as is evident in the following statement: "The decision to terminate the agreement between the Council and KCTMO is for the resident members of KCTMO to consider at its Annual General meeting on 17 October 2017" (ibid.). We are informed that the Chair of the KCTMO Board sent postal communications to KCTMO resident members advocating "them to take the decision to terminate the agreement" (ibid.). The press release then progresses to detail the following disconcerting proposal:

> Once the agreement between the Council and KCTMO ultimately comes to an end, there will no longer be resident members of KCTMO. As they are the only members of KCTMO at the moment, it is proposed that at this point the Council becomes the sole member of KCTMO to ensure that the company continues to exist so it can answer questions of the Public Inquiry and any police investigation in respect of the Grenfell Tower tragedy. KCTMO's Annual General Meeting will also consider this proposal. (ibid.)

The RBKC (ibid.) proposal to replace the remaining resident members of the KCTMO, and in so doing make the Conservative majority-led Kensington and Chelsea Council "the sole member of KCTMO", was a provocative proposal as it was clearly intent on centralising control of the KCTMO and doing so through the expropriation of resident member democratic advocacy. The Grenfell Action Group (2017) promptly published a rebuff to the proposal and its staged authenticity of democratic participation; and did so in a well-crafted posting briefed by solicitors, the following extract of which is illuminating:

> In light of the fire at Grenfell earlier this year, RBK&C has resolved to end the TMO's role in managing properties in the Borough. It has, as a result, indicated an intention to terminate the Modular Management Agreement by which the TMO fulfils its functions. On termination of the Management Agreement, the TMO will cease to have any 'Members' as defined in the Articles. RBK&C has therefore proposed that, on termination, it should become the sole member of the TMO.

> ...
> There is no evidence before us that RBK&C has any malicious intent in seeking to take over the TMO in this way. At the same time, it is likely to be advisable that adequate checks are imposed on it. If it became the sole member of the TMO, there would be no company law mechanism for victims and former residents to exert influence over the TMO's behaviour, such as there is at present. Although RBK&C's letter of 16 October 2017 refers to the role of the Board in ensuring accountability, all Board members will (is the Resolutions are passed) be appointed by the RBK&C.
>
> (ibid.)

It is indeed disconcerting that a management organisation routinely now admonished by its own Kensington and Chelsea Council as "untenable" be invited to veto its own withdrawal. And the October 2017 proposal issued by Royal Borough of Kensington and Chelsea Council prescribing that it should become the sole member of the KCTMO is yet another dismaying insight into the dictatorial power of the contract culture that clearly consumed and degenerated the VfM principles of the KCTMO and its Conservative led-Council.

Timely Reminders

Suffice to say, it is my contention that if the Grenfell Tower fire enquiry, and for that matter any future enquiry, pursues resolutely and unwaveringly a procedural judgement ethics of disembodied, disengaged objectivity, it will struggle to connect not only in terms of emotion, empathy and consideration but also of understanding the tremendous centrifugal propensity of the technologies of the sign that are condition and consequence of the mediated epistemology through which we are coming to know the Grenfell Tower fire tragedy. Indeed, one might responsibly and confidently conjecture, as this chapter has ventured to systematically argue, that a critical engagement with organisational culture and the neoliberal managerialist technologies of the sign that took hold of and denatured the KCTMO's business strategy of VfM need also feature in Sir Martin Moore-Bick's Grenfell Tower Enquiry and all further enquiries into the Grenfell Tower fire tragedy.

Furthermore, when considering the Grenfell Tower Enquiry's colossal task, my thoughts are directed toward a fable by Borges that features frequently in the poststructural cultural theory of Jean Baudrillard. In *Simulations*, Baudrillard (1983) perceptively recounts a tale by Borges as an allegory of an irksome second-order simulacra that aggravates the very reality that it is intended to represent. In the Borges tale, cartographers commissioned to map an empire become so obsessed with the task of charting the territory that they produce a colossal map that physically stretches over the territory that it is originally intended to map; thus creating a simulacra of the second-order for, in contrast to the intention of first-order simulacra to represent reality, second-order simulacra are intricately connected to that which they strive to represent, to such an extent that they blur the distinction between the real and representation. Baudrillard (1983) eloquently mobilises visual metaphors to convey the blurring of the real and representation in the second-order simulacra and the extent to which this form of representation begins to corrode and to change the substance of its reality. As Baudrillard (1983: 1) envisages:

> If we were able to take as the finest allegory ... the Borges tale where the cartographers of the Empire draw up a map so detailed that it ends up exactly covering the territory (but where the decline of the Empire sees this map become frayed and finally ruined, a few shreds still discernible in the deserts – the metaphysical beauty of this ruined abstraction, bearing witness to an Imperial pride and rotting like a carcass, returning to the substance of the soil, rather as an aging double ends up being confused with the real thing) – then this fable has come full circle for us, and now has nothing but the discrete charm of second-order simulacra.

Baudrillard's (ibid.) imagery of "an Imperial pride ... rotting like a carcass" hauntingly imagines the burnt-out carcass of the Grenfell Tower, its coruscated glare, unedifying and disenchanted. The Grenfell Tower refurbishment was obsessed with the cartography of a uniform aesthetic; replete in the planning and design of the refurbishment and manifest in the VfM cladding of the building's exterior. VfM operates here as a corrupted second-order simulacra that symbolically and literally denatured the reality it was initially designed to represent. Baudrillard's (1968/2005) *The System of Objects* provides a theoretical framework pertaining to second-order sign-systems comparable with the transmutation of VfM from a sign of value to a determination of value, and progressing into a metaphorical degradation of value. Prior to applying this form of poststructuralism, consider the following extract from the KCTMO's (2017a: 5) *Value for Money Strategy*:

> 9. Promote and embed VfM culture
> The Board of the TMO has overall responsibility for direction and governance and agrees the VfM strategy. The responsibility for delivery of the strategy and the action plan is through the senior management teams.

They will ensure that the VfM Strategy and action plan are put in place, reviewed on a regular basis and make any suggestions for changes to the Board as appropriate. Managers are responsible for ensuring VfM in the day-to-day management of their service and in helping to consider VfM in any new proposals or reviews of their service area. They will also need to work with the senior management teams to ensure that VfM is understood by all staff who are encouraged to contribute ideas to support this agenda.

10. Promote and embed VfM vulture
This strategy will be delivered within existing budgets and no additional resources are required.

11. Monitoring
The actions contained in the plan will be monitored and evaluated by the Board. Action plans will be updated and reviewed on a quarterly basis and refreshed annually as necessary.

12. Supporting policies and plan
The VfM strategy underpins all other strategies.

(KCTMO 2017a: 5)

It is my contention that the matrix of the VfM and KCTMO procurement strategy transformed from VfM providing a means to the achievement of value (a measure of value) to VfM becoming a determinant of value; and in so doing, VfM became a corrupted second-order simulacra. In a passage of *The System of Objects* entitled "A Universal Code", Baudrillard (1968/2005: 212) describes how "the objects-cum-advertising system" is "less a language, whose living systems it lacks, than a set of significations". Similarly, VfM, as documented by the KCTMO (2017a), materialises far in advance of a generic management and reveals itself to be a complex lexicon of signification; it is, as Baudrillard (1968/2005: 212) might observe, "basically a code". In the above extracts of the KCTMO's (2017a: 5) *Value for Money Strategy* is evident not a structuring of organisational personnel and culture but rather a classification and placing into a hierarchy the categories of VfM implementation. Baudrillard (1968/2005: 212) observes that "the objects-cum-advertising system ... does not structure social relationships, but breaks them down into a hierarchical repertoire. In its formal expression it constitutes a universal system for the identification of social rank: the code of 'status'". Consider in this respect the following extract from the original 2014 planning permission document that secured the refurbishment of the Grenfell Tower:

Proposal: Refurbishment of existing Grenfell Tower including new external cladding and fenestration, alterations to plant room, reconfiguration of lower 4 levels to provide 7 new residential units (use class C3), replacement nursery (use class D1) and boxing club (use class D2) facilities, external public realm works, redevelopment and change of use of existing garages to refuse collection area.

Site Address:
Grenfell Tower, Grenfell Road, London, W11 1TH

…

Materials to be used on the external faces of the building(s);
Reason - To accord with the development plan by ensuring that the character and appearance of the area are preserved and living conditions of those living near the development suitably protected.

(RBKC 2014a: 1-2)

To reiterate, it is my contention that the matrix of the VfM and KCTMO procurement strategy for 2014 – 2017 transformed from a means of achieving value (a measure of value) to a determinant of value; and in so doing VfM became a corrupted second-order simulacra. In the above extract, the 2014 planning permission document repeats on frequent occasions the statement: "To accord with the development plan by ensuring that the character and appearance of the area are preserved and living conditions of those living near the development suitably protected" (ibid.). One might speculate that in these utterances, VfM appears to have been translated into an aesthetic; a second-order simulacra incessantly determining value in its own sign-system image. Indeed, Baudrillard (1968/2005: 212-213) identifies how "the objects-cum-advertising system … offers a universal system of decipherable signs for the first time in history". Considered as an objects-cum-advertising system, the VfM procurement strategy mediation on the management decision-making for the external façade of the Grenfell Tower clearly responded to an aesthetic code committed to preserving the "appearance" of the area. In so doing, it swathed the Grenfell Tower in what Baudrillard (1968/2005: 213) might describe as a "code" that in its universality "is usurping the place of all other codes". KCTMO demonstrably swathed Grenfell Tower with a universally communicable code, saturated with symbolic value and decipherable across VfM-audited determinants of value. Baudrillard (1968/2005: 214) observes an insidious paradox in the universal code status, and this relates to a deterioration of democratic influence as a correlate of the extension of the universal code. As Baudrillard (1968/2005: 214) expresses it:

> What is more, the fact that a system of identification is now in place which is clearly legible to all, that the signs of value are entirely socialized and objectivized, by no means implies any true 'democratization'. On the contrary, it would appear that the insistence on univocal reference merely exacerbates the desire to discriminate within the very framework of this homogeneous system, a perpetually renewed obsession with hierarchies and distinctions is to be observed. Even though barriers of morality, social convention and language have been overturned, new barriers and exclusions have arisen in the realm of objects: a new class or caste morality is thus enabled to colonize the most material and hitherto unchallengeable of spheres.

Similarly, it is discernible from the earnest committed resistance of the Grenfell Action Group that the insistence on a universal code of aesthetics for Grenfell Tower in keeping with the regeneration of the area and preserving its "appearance" evidenced a perilous attrition of democracy. Value for Money (VfM) evolved from a first-order simulacra of value into a corrupted second-order simulacra, ravenously and narcissistically producing images of value mirrored in its own vanquished commodity-sign. In this sense, cladding becomes an allegory, a tabula rasa saturated with the sign-value of market-based avaricious capitalism; a glistening beacon of fated venture capitalism. The Kensington and Chelsea Tenant Management Organisation's VfM business strategy started as a measure of a reality of value only to spiral uncontrollably into a determinant of a reality of value that intends narcissistically to shroud and displace all other realities of value. In the culture and governance of the Kensington and Chelsea Tenant Management Organisation, VfM rapaciously descended into a corrupted second-order simulacra; a form of universal objects-cum-advertising system that privatised the spoils of marketised VfM and democratised the inequities of a marketised mode of public management democracy in which the commodity-sign of value became a thoroughly corrupted second-order simulacra.

Figure 3.9.: *Love Assisst(f)*: Volunteering my time at the Grenfell Tower tragedy site. Heartbreaking and, according to my interviews, there were much higher losses. PamxXx (15 Jun 2017). "Today the attitudes and values which informed that tradition are expressed through other more widely diffused media – advertising, journalism, television" (John Berger, *Ways of Seeing*, 1972).
https://twitter.com/geraldi23591291/status/875385080717463552

Chapter Three

◀ Back to Fitbit   18:57   ≯ 100%
mobile.twitter.com

←   Tweet

Pam xXx
@geraldi23591291

Love Assisst(f): Words cannot express the devastating imagery of Grenfell Tower. JC is right ... we need to know why so many lives lost xXx

Figure 3.10.: *Love Assisst(f)*: Words cannot express the devastating imagery of Grenfell Tower. JC is right ... we need to know why so many lives lost xXx (15 June 2017); @Robert_W_Nelson: "So true". "Every image embodies a way of seeing" (John Berger, *Ways of Seeing*, 1972).
https://twitter.com/geraldi23591291/status/875410180296585218

Figure 3.11.: *Love Assisst(f)*: (16 June 2017): "One may remember or forget these messages but briefly takes them in & for a moment they stimulate the imagination" (John Berger, *Ways of Seeing*, 1972).
https://twitter.com/geraldi23591291/status/875782215577239552

Figure 3.12.: *Love Assisst(f)*: (16 Jun 2017): "One may remember or forget these messages but briefly takes them in & for a moment they stimulate the imagination" (John Berger, *Ways of Seeing*, 1972).
https://twitter.com/geraldi23591291/status/875787769729220609

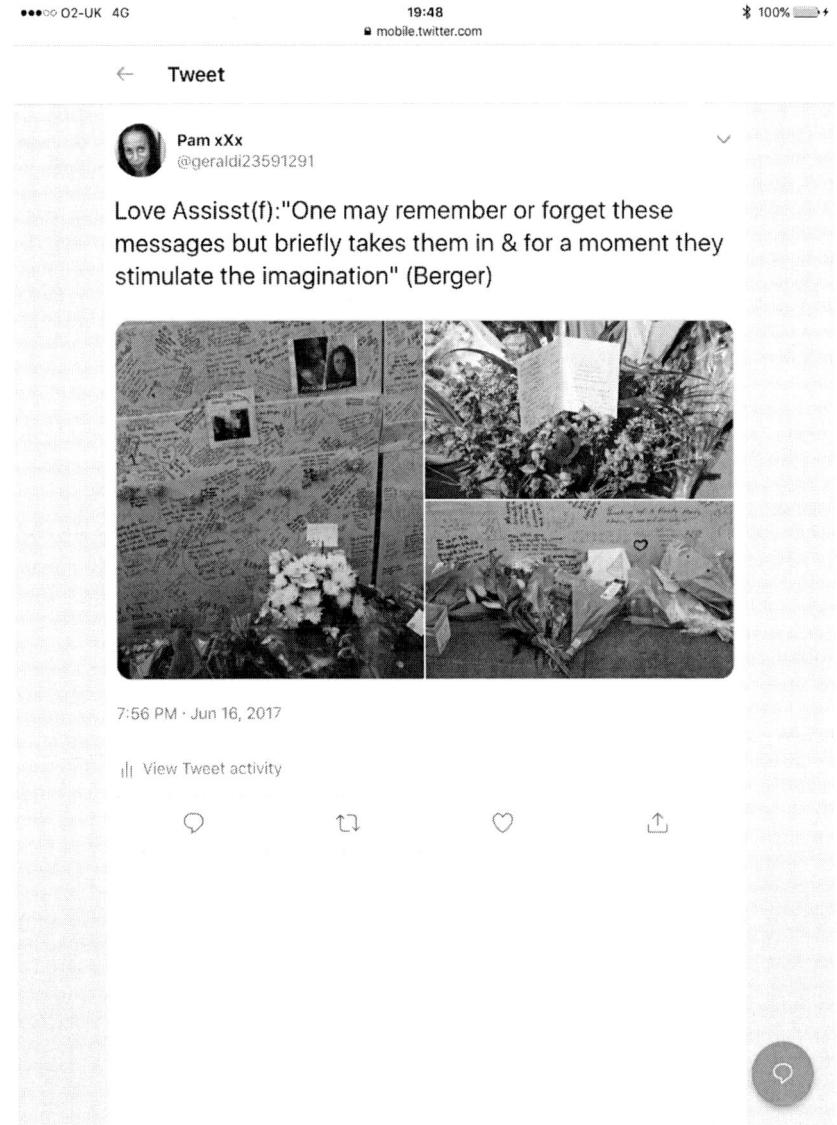

Figure 3.13.: *Love Assisst(f)*: (16 Jun 2017): "One may remember or forget these messages but briefly takes them in & for a moment they stimulate the imagination"; "What is a love of art?" (John Berger, *Ways of Seeing*, 1972). https://twitter.com/geraldi23591291/status/875789312465526785

Figure 3.14.: *Love Assisst(f)*: (20 Jun 2017): "One may remember or forget these messages but briefly one takes them in, & for a moment they stimulate the imagination"; "What is a love of art? ... What does it show?" (John Berger, *Ways of Seeing*, 1972). https://twitter.com/geraldi23591291/status/877184335681662980

Figure 3.15.: *Love Assisst(f)*: (20 Jun 2017): "One may remember or forget these messages but briefly one takes them in, & for a moment they stimulate the imagination"; "Not only personal experience, but also the essential historical experience of our relation to the past: that is to say the experience of seeking to give meaning to our lives, of trying to understand the history of which we can become the active agents" (John Berger, *Ways of Seeing*, 1972).
https://twitter.com/geraldi23591291/status/877185458333245440

112 Chapter Three

Figure 3.16.: *Love Assisst(f)*: (21 Jun 2017): "One may remember or forget these messages but briefly takes them in & for a moment they stimulate the imagination"; "The compositional unity of a painting contributes fundamentally to the power of its image. It is reasonable to consider a painting's composition" (John Berger, *Ways of Seeing*, 1972).
https://twitter.com/geraldi23591291/status/877592798291251210

Figure 3.17.: *Love Assisst(f)*: (21 Jun 2017): "One may remember or forget these messages but briefly takes them in & for a moment they stimulate the imagination"; "A people or a class which is cut off from its own past is far less free to choose and to act as a people or class than one that has been able to situate itself in history" (John Berger, *Ways of Seeing*, 1972).
https://twitter.com/geraldi23591291/status/877594903974465536

Figure 3.18.: *Love Assisst(f)*: (23 Jun 2017): "One may remember or forget these messages but briefly takes them in & for a moment they stimulate the imagination"; "This has the effect of closing the distance in time between the painting of the picture and one's own act of looking at it. In this special sense all paintings are contemporary. Hence the immediacy of their testimony. Their historical moment is literally there before our eyes" (John Berger, *Ways of Seeing*, 1972).
https://twitter.com/geraldi23591291/status/878257462322880512

CHAPTER FOUR

URBAN ECOLOGICAL FAÇADE AS AN ADSENSORY GENTRIFICATION OF POST-INDUSTRIAL SPACE

Figure 4.1.: "Both media use similar, highly tactile means to play upon the spectator's sense of acquiring the real thing which the image shows. In both cases his feeling that he can almost touch what is in the image reminds him how he might or does possess the real thing" (John Berger, *Ways of Seeing*, 1972). Photographic Image, Vicinity of Grenfell Tower; Lancaster West Estate, North Kensington, London, June 2017.

Grenfell Tower Refurbishment: Problematisation and Displacement of Environmental Ethics

Interviewer: I just came down to see the, this [gesturing to the handfuls of charcoal remnants of the Grenfell Tower exterior wall cladding scattered on the pavement] and erhm [pause].
Interviewee (1): [Standing in gateway of flats in proximity to Grenfell Tower]. This was the outside.
Interviewer: What is this? [referring to charcoal debris remnants of the exterior cladding of the Grenfell Tower]
Interviewee (1): This is the outside cladding of the building. And this is the foam that was behind. So what you see when you look at the building is that [places the different textured charcoaled material adjacent, so as to reconstruct their positioning in relation to each other], and they're different colours [material is charcoal-coloured fire-burnt cladding from the exterior wall of Grenfell Tower]. They inject it with expanded foam. So what happened, you see, the foam burnt.
Interviewee (2): You understand what he is saying? [prompted by my silence].
Interviewee (1): This was, look; if you look at that, that was like that [places the different-textured charcoaled material adjacent to reconstruct their positioning in relation to each other]. This was against the concrete; and it's like this, like that. The fire was travelling here [gestures a funnel effect propelling fire up through the core of the sandwiched layers of the cladding], that's why the building burnt. Here, we have chicken foil; it's aluminium! It's bloody chicken foil! Look [effortlessly tears into strips the charcoal-coloured aluminium]. That's what they covered the building with; with that [gesturing to two differently textured charcoal-coloured materials] and that! It's aluminium foil with what you cook your turkey! It's aluminium!
Interviewee (2): That's ten million?
Interviewee (1): It's aluminium!
Interviewee (2): Is that ten million?
Interviewee (1): Look, it's aluminium, chicken foil, what you cook your chicken or turkey ... This is the expanded foam and that's the aluminium foil; here, put them together. Now that's after burn, the foam when it burnt. It's very, very light ... you cover a building with these two materials! ... They didn't cook the turkey, they cooked the bloody building!
(Participant Observation and Unstructured Group Interview: Impromptu group gathering, speaking within the vicinity and close proximity of Grenfell Tower, North Kensington London, Thursday 15th June 2017)

Urban Ecological Façade as an Adsensory Gentrification of Post-industrial Space

In the early hours of Wednesday 14th June 2017, there occurred in Grenfell Tower a heartbreaking tragedy unparalleled in peacetime Britain. In the immediate aftermath of the Grenfell Tower fire, media speculation feverously agitated the seemingly maniacal cladding of the exterior building. Amidst the frenetic audio-visual media dramaturgy pursuing villains and maligning culprits, a complex imputation and critical derogation of the colossal visual spectacle is reluctantly being heard. This chapter goes beyond the media obsession with the façade per se, being primarily motivated by a critical knowledge of the limitations in the wholesale application of apolitical façadism to explain the gentrification of post-industrial urban spaces. Part one of this chapter engages with the market-based construction of sustainability and energy efficiency preeminent in Royal Borough of Kensington and Chelsea's (RBKC 2012d) planning permission application entitled: Grenfell Tower Regeneration Project; Sustainability and Energy Statement. Section 2.0 of RBKC's (2012d: 6) Sustainability and Energy Statement planning application is entitled "Refurbishment Response to Existing Energy and Environmental Issues"; so entitled, it lends itself to the application of actor network theory (ANT) as an instrument of critical engagement. In the sociological application of ANT, we are encouraged to scrutinise a social phenomenon in terms of the heterogeneous entities of actors and networks engaged in its being (Callon 1986a). In respect to a critical analysis of the claims to environmental energy efficiency proclaimed of the Grenfell Tower refurbishment, the application of ANT to the scrutiny of KCTMO and RBKC environmental documents (as accomplished in this chapter) reveals the Grenfell Tower refurbishment as constituted through the translation of disparate agenda, conflated within an opportunistic programme of environmental energy efficiency; the latter being ruefully undermined by the property development culture of the KCTMO. In so far as the KCTMO's property development culture pursued maximum exchange value through least investment in monetary cost, any problematisation of the Grenfell Tower refurbishment, in terms of energy-efficient ecological solutions, would inevitably be determinately compromised.

Part two of this chapter identifies as condescending and ruefully supercilious the presumption that the external refurbishment of the Grenfell Tower would rejuvenate and modernise the building. The leader of RBKC, Cllr Nick Paget-Brown, apparently made such a proclamation on 11 May 2016 after a delegation of RBKC councillors visited the Grenfell Tower on completion of its £10 million refurbishment. Cllr

Paget-Brown is reported to have said: "It is remarkable to see first-hand how the cladding has lifted the external appearance of the tower and how the improvements inside people's homes will make a big difference to their day-to-day lives" (RBKC 2016). Part two of this chapter is keen to engage critically with an aesthetics of façadism in urban regeneration and the adsensory urban ecology that is increasingly pervading this regime of aestheticisation. In so doing, part two attempts to make contemporary the classic, seminal semiotician architectural work by Venturi, R., Scott Brown, D., and Izenour, S., (1977) entitled *Learning from Las Vegas: The Forgotten Symbolism of Architectural Form*. Perri 6 and Jeremy Kendall's (1997) *The Contract Culture in Public Services* provides an additional trajectory of critical engagement. Indeed, my principal concern is to examine critically a political economy of the sign in urban ecology, integral to the expropriation of environmentalism in the regeneration of post-industrial urban spaces. In this respect, consider the following RBKC (2012: 4) statement:

> Climate Change. Alongside all the other London Local Authorities, the Council is looking at the potential opportunities from the forthcoming national Green Deal/Energy Company Obligation (ECO) scheme to address carbon emissions reduction in the Borough and other benefits such as tackling fuel poverty. By the end of 2012, the Council will have to agree a position in the delivery of this scheme. The Scrutiny Committee would be consulted before the report is submitted to the Cabinet for decision.

(RBKC 2012: 4)

RBKC (2012), alongside documents detailing the Energy Company Obligation (ECO) scheme and empirical data challenging the market-based transactional implementation of ECO, provides for the primary basis of this chapter's part one and part two critical engagement with the refurbishment of Grenfell Tower. This chapter identifies inherent inequities in the market-based transactional dynamics of ECO-funding schemes; and in so doing raises concerns about the Grenfell Tower refurbishment in terms of an expropriation of market-based urban ecology.

Grenfell Tower Fire, the Complexities of Researching Urban Ecology in Brexit Times

"The Grenfell Tower fire would not have happened without the EU and global warming" is the title of a rather provocative and hyperbolic article written by Christopher Booker and published in the *Telegraph*, 08 July

2017. In his article, Booker, often described as pro-Brexit, provides for an original, albeit extrapolated, insight into a contextual perspective on the international ecological politics that may have precipitated aspects of the Grenfell Tower refurbishment procurement. The article commences with a journalistic peremptory characteristic of subscription articles, intended to enthral the would-be subscriber, for we are informed that: "The cause of the conflagration was less to do with the 'rainscreen' cladding: it was the combination of 6in of combustible Celotex insulation foam behind it with a void creating a 'chimney' effect, sending the flames roaring up the building" (ibid.). According to Booker (ibid.), an eleven-floor residential apartment block fire at Knowsley Heights Liverpool, in "1989 [1991]" prompted the Building Research Establishment to excogitate preventative safeguarding measures. Similar case study material is cited by Nathan White and Michael Delichatsios (2015), as is evident in the following extract from *Fire Hazards of Exterior Wall Assemblies Containing Combustible Components*:

> Knowsley Heights, UK, 1991
>
> Knowsley Heights is an 11-floor apartment building located in Liverpool, UK. Prior to the fire the building was recently fitted with a rain screen cladding installed with a 90 mm air gap behind and rubberised pain coating over the external surface of the concrete wall behind. No fire barriers were provided to the air cavity behind. The rain screen and cavity without barriers covered the building from ground floor to the top of the 11th floor. The rain screen material was a Class O (limited combustibility) rated product using BS 476 parts 6 and 7 (BSL, 1981; BSL, 1987).
>
> A fire started in a rubbish compound outside the building rapidly spread vertically through the 90mm air cavity. The fire destroyed the rubbish compound and severely damaged the ground floor lobby and the outer walls and windows of all the upper floors. No smoke or fire spread to the interior of the building.
>
> BRE has cited this fire incident as a motivator for subsequent building code changes and development of a large scale façade fire test.
>
> (White and Delichatsios 2015: 40)

It is a significant revelation, provided by White and Delichatsios' (2015: 40) case study, that the fire at Knowsley Heights did not "spread to the interior of the building" for this should inform the enquiry that the almighty devastation of the Grenfell Tower fire was catalysed by a combination of exterior and interior refurbishment errors. Complex oversight and an interrogation into the Grenfell Tower refurbishment procurement are, however, of little interest to Christopher Booker's self-determined pursuit of pro-Brexit and anti-EU blame for the Grenfell Tower fire. Thus we are informed that an outcome of the consultation was, as described by Booker (2017), the British Standards advisory that fireproofing tests on the external façade of a high rise building needed to be revised for "it found that this should be a new 'whole system test' covering all the materials used on the outside of buildings to see how they interacted when installed together" (ibid.). The crucial issue of contention, as expressed by Booker (ibid.), is European Commission legislation introduced in 1994 inaugurating a European Union (EU) regulation fire test "which was exactly what the BRE had found so inadequate with existing practice a 'single burn' test applied only to each material separately" (ibid.). Following the House of Commons investigation of a tower block fire in Scotland in 2000, it was, according to Booker (ibid.), "recommended that the BRE's 'whole system test' should be adopted as the British Standard, BS8414". Booker (ibid.) is insistent that the EU's 2002 regulation on fire resistance test measures overrode the Building Research Establishment's preference for a "whole system test" and therein resides part of the problem with regards to the substandard exterior refurbishment of the Grenfell Tower; as the following extract argues:

> By 2002, however, the EU had adopted its inadequate test, incorporating it in a European standard using EN 13501. Under EU law, this became mandatory, leaving the UK's BS 8414 as only a voluntary option. (ibid.)

> The EU had also become obsessed with the need for better insulation of buildings to combat global warming, which became its only priority. All that mattered was the 'thermal efficiency' of materials used for insulation, for which none was to prove better than the polyisocyanurate used in Celotex chosen in 2014 for Grenfell. (ibid.)

In keeping with the inflationary anti-EU language of Booker's (ibid.) article, it is promulgated that "fire experts across Europe" have expressed disparaging disquiet at the EU's preference for single-element rather than whole-composition fire resistance testing of building exterior cladding. In particular, it is argued that "fire experts across Europe" have attempted to alert the EU "that the lack of a proper whole system test was ignoring the risk of insulation fires, not least in Germany where there have been more than 100" (ibid.). The anti-EU rhetorical framework of Booker's (ibid.) argument, however, struggles to explain how it was that the planning permission of the domestic refurbishment of the Grenfell Tower achieved a rating of "Good" from the very same evaluation establishment that Booker preferences over the EU's fire resistance testing measures, the Building Research Establishment Environmental Assessment Method (BREEAM). Indeed, BREEAM (2012: 4) stated the following as part of its "Good" accreditation of the Grenfell Tower refurbishment:

> The Pre-Assessment Estimate shows that by achieving the minimum standard requirements together with assumptions of good sustainable design practice the proposed refurbishment project could achieve a BREEAM rating of 'Good'. (BREEAM 2012: 4)

Returning to Booker's (2017) article and its assertion of a connection between EU environmental regulation and the Grenfell Tower as "precisely the point" and the extraordinary statement that "without these two factors, ['EU and global warming'] the fire could never have happened" (ibid.), Booker (2017) dismisses the inconsistency and contradiction evident in the article's argument with regards to the BREEAM "Good" rating. But the strength of the anti-EU environmental regulation theory presented by Booker (2017) doesn't really recover from the contradictory evidence of the BREEAM "Good" rating, as is evident in the article's recourse to myth-making and the insinuation of conspiracy expressed in the following extract:

> Strangely, the maker of Celotex has stated on its website that the material used in Grenfell has been tested by the BRE as meeting fire safety requirements. But the BRE has tartly responded that this test referred to a different installation; and that 'Celotex should not be claiming that their insulation product can be used generically in any other cladding system'.
>
> Had the Grenfell installation been properly tested under BS 8414 it would not have met the standard, and thus the fire could not have happened. The ultimate irony is that China and Dubai are now adopting mandatory systems based on BS 8414. They can do this because they are not in the EU. But, because Britain is still in the EU, it cannot legally enforce the very standard which would have prevented that disaster.

(Booker 2017)

Contradictions and conflicts pervade Booker's (2017) article and it is deeply problematic to force a pro-Brexit stance into the highly complex circumstances that caused the Grenfell Tower fire. It is also highly reductive and deterministic to presume that EU laws are dictated to organisations and imposed on their regulatory conduct. Conspicuously absent from Booker's (ibid.) argument is any evidence of empirically based organisational research into councils, local government and public sector management. Moreover, it is perilously naïve to build a simplistic adoption model of EU environmental law for the sole purpose of promoting a pro-Brexit explanation of the Grenfell Tower fire. Cognizant of this problem, it is not my intention in this chapter to build an anti-Brexit model of environmental urban ecology as a nemesis. Rather, it is my intention to theorise the problematisation of the Grenfell Tower refurbishment in terms of energy-efficient urban ecology.

Sustainability and Energy Statement: Translating the Regeneration of Grenfell Tower into a Programme of Energy Efficiency

"[A]s part of the Grenfell Tower refurbishment scheme, the current energy and environment comfort problems can be addressed … within the London Plan's aim to bring existing housing stock up to the Mayor's standards on sustainable design and construction" states the enterprising and highly ambitious commitment of RBKC's (2012d: 4) planning document "Grenfell Tower Regeneration Project … Sustainability and Energy Statement". Energy efficiency improvements are identified in RBKC's planning document as a primary motivation for the refurbishment; indeed, it is stated: "The poor insulation levels and air tightness of both the walls and the windows at Grenfell Tower result in excessive heat loss during the winter months. Addressing this issue is the primary driver behind the refurbishment" (ibid.). The aperture of the windows at Grenfell Tower is targeted as one of several priority areas for energy efficiency improvement; as is evident in the following statement:

> Due to valid safety concerns the windows at Grenfell Tower are restricted to open no more than 100 mm. This restriction causes chronic overheating in the summer months. It is essential that the renovation works do not make the overheating problems any worse and where possible we will strive to reduce overheating in line with current guidelines. (ibid.)

The refurbishment concern of "overheating" consequent of the reduced aperture of the windows at Grenfell Tower was expeditiously linked to the heating system; and these concerns were linked to the exterior cladding works to justify their concurrent undertaking. One example of RBKC's (2012d: 4) opportunistic formulation of the existing Grenfell Tower improvement problems into a triad of energy efficiency problems is evident as follows:

The heating system exacerbates the overheating problem due to its high uncontrolled heat losses throughout the year (including summer) and is also reaching the end of its design life. The client wishes to update the heating system at this point. Updating the heating system allows the disruptive works to 'piggy back' on the recladding works. (ibid.)

RBKC's opportunistic enrolment of Grenfell Tower's building predicament into a programme of energy efficiency and environmental benefits is further evident in the following RBKC (2012d: 5) extract, which refers to the issue of overheating:

Overheating

Grenfell Tower currently suffers from chronic overheating in the summer. Presently the south facing flats experience the highest temperatures. The current climate change predictions for London over the next 30 to 50 years predict that peak summertime temperatures will rise. Doing nothing to improve the overheating now will result in further problems to all flat orientations in the future.

Ventilation to the flats is via single glazed horizontal sliding windows. These units are poorly sealed compared to modern standards and offer no solar control. There is also a desire to restrict the opening of the windows for safety reasons; both to mitigate the risk of falls and to combat the problem of residents throwing objects from the windows.

By providing constant ventilation the existing poorly sealed windows are helping to reduce overheating. Increasing the air tightness and insulation levels alone without thinking about the flat cooling would result in a worse overheating problem than that currently being experienced.

In its attempt to contextualise the predicament of "overheating" within London-centric climate change predictions, RBKC (2012d) paradigmatically enrols the Grenfell Tower Regeneration Project into the equally London-centric myopic conception of climate change that defined the then-mayor of London's plan for energy conservation; the latter is also referenced in RBKC (ibid. 4):

'The London Plan July 2011' aims to conserve energy. A defined energy hierarchy should be followed. This hierarchy is as follows:
1. Be lean: use less energy, in particular by adopting sustainable design and construction measures
2. Be clean: supply energy efficiently
3. Be green: use renewable energy

The tendency for the RBKC (2012d) *Sustainability and Energy Statement* planning application to localise Grenfell Tower's ecological predicament, rendering the refurbishment amenable to lowest-cost, scaled-down construction projects, is apparent in the following extract:

> Heating System
>
> The residential units are heated by a single loop ladder arrangement which also provides domestic hot water (DHW) via a hot water cylinder in each flat. The pipework serves the flats via six rises (1 per flat on each floor) and from there runs within the flats to radiators through pipework cast into the screed floors. The pre-existing problem with summertime overheating of the flats is in part caused by the floor and ceiling slabs radiating heat due to the hot pipework within. There is also currently no individual control of the heating system within each flat beyond the ability to turn off a radiator manually.
>
> The summertime overheating is a symptom of the greater problem of heat loss and therefore energy waste due to the insufficient method of heat distribution throughout the building. The heating system is now 30 years old and is coming to the end of its design life. Occurrences of leaks in this heating system are beginning to increase.
>
> (ibid. 5)

Section 2.0 of RBKC's (2012d: 6) *Sustainability and Energy Statement* planning application is entitled "Refurbishment response to existing energy and environmental issues", and so lends itself to the application of Actor Network Theory (ANT) as an instrument of critical engagement. In the sociological application of ANT, we are encouraged to scrutinise a social phenomenon in terms of the heterogeneous entities of actors and networks engaged in its being. In respect to a critical analysis of the claims to ecology made of the Grenfell Tower refurbishment, the application of ANT would presuppose that the tower's refurbishment is a social phenomenon constituted through the translation of separate agenda conflated within an opportunistic programme of environmental energy efficiency. The latter, from an ANT perspective, does not relate to a prefabricated construction for in ANT: "Once an actor-world comes into being, it does not draw its entities from previously established stock" (Callon 1986a: 24). With respect to the configuration of environmental energy efficiency utilised in justification of the programme of refurbishment of the Grenfell Tower, from an ANT perspective the phenomenon has no equivalence: "it is not constituted in the way of a shopping cart is filled. In short, there is no world, or worlds from which pre-existing elements can be extracted" (ibid.). Nor is it presumed that the representation of the environment and its energy efficient conservation as pronounced in RBKC (2012d) are realistic for as Callon (19986a: 24) observes: "Actors may construct a plurality of different and incommensurate worlds". Indeed, in the process of translation into a programme of environmental energy efficiency, the refurbishment of Grenfell Tower, actors and networks from a plurality of contrasting agenda can be observed. The reconciliation of these incommensurate agenda can be traced to the contract culture of property development but this is certainly not a sole determinant of the incommensurate alliance of corporate and public management agenda.

The inclination of translation is apposite with regards to the Grenfell Tower because it emphasises the enrolment of heterogeneous entities of actors into a programme of refurbishment collectively identified as an expedient resolution to the contrasting agenda of the separate actors. According to Michel Callon (1986a: 26): "Translation is a definition of roles, a distribution of roles and the delineation of a scenario. It speaks for others but in its own language". In this respect, consider the following extracts of RBKC's (2012d) Sustainability and Energy Statement planning application:

Insulation and Energy

The wall construction of Grenfell Tower is a solid concrete construction. Insulation is provided by a 12 mm layer of insulation bonded to the rear of the integral plaster board lining. The resulting U-value of the existing wall is 1.5 W/m^2.K. This is five times higher than current Building Regulations would allow on a new flat.

The existing windows are now coming to the end of their design life and require replacing. The existing window U-value is in the order of 5.5 W/m^2.K or about three times that above the level required by current Building Regulations. In addition to the poor thermal performance these windows also leak heavily which contributes to excessive heat loss, drafts and noise penetration.

Grenfell Tower has a communal bathroom extract system. The system extracts air at a rate of 1.8m^3/s, 24 hours a day, 365 days a year. This warm air extracted from the bathrooms represents a significant wasted energy stream out of the building.

(RBKC 2012d:4)

> Insulation
>
> Improving the insulation levels of the walls, roof and windows is the top priority of this refurbishment.
>
> Improving the insulation levels on a solid wall construction is always best done from the outside of the wall. This solves several issues with thermal bridging and interstitial condensation. Thermal bridging will be kept to a minimum by insulation window reveals and using thermal breaks on all fixings that link the new rain screen cladding to the existing concrete structure.
>
> The chosen strategy is to wrap the building in a thick layer of insulation and then over-clad with a rain screen to protect the insulation from the weather and from physical damage.
>
> … The proposed insulation levels far exceed those required by Building Regulations. Insulation improvements may only happen once or twice in a building's lifetime due to the complexity and disruption caused. For this reason we are going over and above current Building Regulations to make sure the building continues to perform well into the future.
>
> (RBKC 2012d. 6)

According to Michel Callon (1986a: 26), axiomatic with the accomplishment of translation is moderation derived from the enrolment of oppositional ideas: "Successful translation depends upon the capacity of the actor-world to define and enrol entities which might challenge these definitions and enrolments". It is an interesting feature of RBKC's (2012d: 6) account of the Grenfell Tower insulation improvements that it attempts to enrol several oppositional elements into its proposal: (1) alleviation of disruption experienced by tenant; and (2) a dire record of building improvements to Grenfell Tower. Success in this translation is achieved by presenting a third element as the solution to the problems encountered by the enrolled elements. Callon (1986a: 26) writes that the third element "becomes a passageway through which all the other entities that make up its world must pass". It is my contention that in the Grenfell Tower refurbishment, environmental energy efficiency became the third element through which existing ordinarily oppositional agenda were translated. According to Callon (ibid.): "To translate, then, is to oblige an entity to consent to detour". Indeed, it is evident that the oppositional political agenda of RBKC, alongside its neoliberal public management KCTMO, and the voices of resistance emanating from the tenants of Grenfell Tower were partially detoured into the proposal of a programme of refurbishment premised on environmental energy efficiency. In ANT the process of "detour" is more formally described as "problematisation" and involves a situation whereby "the translation thus maps out a geography of necessary points of passage for those elements who wish to continue to exist and develop" (ibid.). It is my contention that the energy efficiency environmental premise of the Grenfell Tower refurbishment programme was a detour in order to enrol incommensurate alliances and irreconcilable oppositional agenda. Axiomatic with this process of translation is "displacement". According to Callon (1986a: 27), the act of translation involves navigation in order for the incommensurate alliances to concede to the proposed problematisation as a resolution to their respective problems. As Callon (ibid.) expresses it: "While translation determines where the points of obligator passage will be located, this does not exhaust the action. The translator-spokesman and the translator-strategist who impose certain itineraries are bringing about movement". Thus the enrolled elements require a connection to facilitate the acceptance of direction towards conceding the problematisation presented to them.

In Callon's (1986a: 27) account of an automobile innovation, in displacement "entities are converted into inscriptions: reports, memoranda, documents, survey results, scientific papers. These are set out and received back, acted upon and reacted to". Callon traces agencies that coordinate "the circulation of inscriptions, as well as the movement of people". The establishment of knowledge and expertise-based markers to guide and direct the enrolled into accepting a problematisation is therefore crucial to a successful translation. As Callon (ibid.) states: "Translation cannot be effective, i.e. lead to stable constructions, if it is not anchored to such movements, to physical and social displacements". Thus, integral to Callon's study of translation is displacement and the locating of centres of translation that "organise and structure movements". This accumulation of expertise, knowledge and information provides an effective guide for the enrolled in informing their concession to the proposed problematisation; and in so doing "the actor-world accumulates materials that render it durable" (ibid. 28). Callon (ibid.) summarises these elements of translation thus: "To translate is to speak for, to be indispensable, and to displace. All translation works to solidify actor-worlds. Successful translation quickly makes us forget its history". With respect to the process of displacement, it is my observation that part of the circulation of knowledge and expertise integral to aligning the enrolled oppositional positions in concession with an energy-efficient-premised refurbishment required the introduction into the proposal process a body of knowledge and expertise deemed to be credible accreditation to the pursuit of an energy efficiency problematisation of oppositional agenda with regards to Grenfell Tower's refurbishment. Through interviews and document analysis, it became apparent to me that an integral feature of the process of displacement was the Energy Company Obligation (ECO) funding application secured by Rydon Construction in conjunction with the KCTMO. Indeed, the market-based competition structure of ECO funding coupled with its government basis position ECO funding as an effective displacement through which to align the contested factions of the Grenfell Tower refurbishment. Prior to detailing the ECO-funding programme and analysing the KCTMO's engagement with it, consider the following concluding reflections on translation: "The notion of translation recalls all the work and the consent that was granted, that was needed in order to achieve the seemingly natural order, where each element relates with the others" (Callon 1986a: 28).

Energy Company Obligation Funding: Translation, Problematisation, Displacement

> The Energy Company Obligation (ECO) is a government energy efficiency scheme in Great Britain to help reduce carbon emissions and tackle fuel poverty. The scheme began in April 2013, and over time it has been amended ... [The scheme has two main categories of obligation: CERO and HHCRO]. Carbon Emissions Reduction Obligation (CERO): Under CERO, obligated suppliers must promote 'primary measures', including roof and wall insulation and connections to district heating systems. Some CERO must also be delivered in rural areas. Home Heating Cost Reduction Obligation (HHCRO): Under HHCRO, obligated suppliers must promote measures which improve the ability of low income and vulnerable household to heat their homes. This includes actions that result in heating savings, such as the replacement or repair of a boiler ... Under ECO2, which ran from April 2015 to March 2017, suppliers also delivered against a further obligation called the Carbon Saving Community Obligation (CSCO). Suppliers were required to meet their CSCO targets by 31 March 2017.
>
> (Ofgem 2018)

The Energy Company Obligation (ECO) programme enrols each of the largest energy suppliers into a mandate, by the Department of Energy and Climate Change, to furnish energy-efficient home improvements proportionate to each energy company's respective share of the energy market (Which 2017). The obligated energy suppliers are mandated to contribute, proportionately, to home improvements "that will cumulatively reduce

CO_2 emissions by a certain amount" (National Audit Office 2016: 5). Energy companies that renege on this commitment are served penalties. The obligated energy suppliers can install energy-efficiency measures directly (e.g., loft insulation, replacement boilers, wall insulation) or contract an energy-efficient home improvements installer "either directly or through public auctions over a 'brokerage platform'" (ibid.).

In a Commons Briefing paper entitled "ECO, the Energy Company Obligation", authored by David Hough (2017: 3), the Conservative Government's ECO programme is detailed and described as providing "funding for energy efficiency measures for difficult to treat homes and the homes of 'those most in need'". The ECO programme provisions funding to upgrade energy efficiency in complicated, difficult-to-refurbish housing and the residence of low-income households. The programme's first ECO scheme premiered on 1st January 2013 in Great Britain (ibid.). Indeed, the United Kingdom has pioneered the policy of energy supplier obligations as an instrument for achieving energy efficiency in the reduction of household greenhouse gas emissions; in 1994, the UK was first, among the European countries, in its inauguration of energy suppliers into a programme of Energy Savings Obligations (ibid. 5). Thereafter, energy efficiency policies assigning obligations on energy suppliers have become "the principal instrument to deliver energy savings in the housing stock" (ibid.). Consequently, in 2008, the Labour Government launched its mechanism for securing reductions in household greenhouse gas emissions, the Carbon Emission Reduction Target (CERT) scheme. CERT's inauguration was closely followed, in 2009, by the Community Energy Saving Programme (CESP) scheme. CERT and CESP progressed until December 2012 and within this duration designated a substantial "increase in the scale of GB supplier obligation schemes with some 8.5 million insulation and heating measures delivered through the schemes" (ibid.).

The Energy Bill 2011, introduced by the Conservative and Liberal Democrat coalition, pioneered the programme of Energy Company Obligation (ECO), commencing from 2012 and replacing the previous energy efficiency schemes CERT and CESP. The ECO scheme initially substrated the Coalition's Green Deal for it prioritised low-income households unable to independently accomplish energy savings and those residencies unsuitable to qualify for Green Deal finance (ibid. 7). The ECO scheme gained priority in the political aftermath of the 2015 general election whereby the Department for Energy and Climate Change (DECC) promptly announced an end to the Coalition's flagship Green Deal scheme, citing "low take-up and controversy surrounding standards of delivery" (ibid. 7). Conversely, DECC evaluated positively the ECO scheme based on its achievements and "positive impact" in addressing the energy efficiency needs of low income households (ibid. 8). The Spending Review and Autumn Statement 2015 established a "third phase for ECO ('ECO 3')" (ibid. 8). In a section entitled "Lower energy bills", the Government details its intention to reduce the estimated impact cost of green policies "on the average annual household energy bill"; and the magnitude of this saving is envisaged to derive from a reform of the ECO programme. Specifically, it is stated: "The new scheme will upgrade the energy efficiency of over 200,000 homes per year, saving those homes up to £300 off their annual energy bill, tackling the root cause of fuel poverty …" (HM Treasury 2015: 39). In 2017, the Government announced further reforms to the ECO programme, emphasising its focus on low-income families and redirecting its refurbishment scheme towards fewer low-cost measures "towards energy efficiency gains in non-gas homes" (Hough (2017: 8). Specifically, in a parliamentary question directed to the Secretary of State for Business, Energy and Industrial Strategy and answered 23rd February 2017, it was stated that:

> The Government recently confirmed plans for the Energy Company Obligation (ECO) policy for 2017-18. In 2017-18, 70% of the support under the scheme will be directed at low income households. This represents an increase from £310m to £450m of funding per year, under the Affordable Warmth Obligation. The policy also includes elements designed to incentivise delivery to non-gas homes, such as an uplift of 35% to 45% (depending on the measure) for delivery to such homes under the Affordable Warmth element of ECO, and limiting the deployment of gas replacement boilers to enable a more diverse mix of measures to be delivered.
>
> As a result, the Impact Assessment for the policy estimates that 16% of the delivery under Affordable Warmth will be to homes not heated by main gas. This represents a significant increase on delivery to this group to date, which is below 2%.

(House of Commons 2017)

In October 2017 the Conservative Government's Department for Business, Energy and Industrial Strategy (BEIS) published its energy efficiency strategy entitled "The Clean Growth Strategy Leading the Way to a Low Carbon Future". BEIS (2017: 5) defines clean growth as the strategy's conceptual axiom, which "means growing our national income while cutting greenhouse gas emissions". BEIS (ibid.) describes the Clean Growth Strategy as in accord with the intention of the Climate Change Act 2008 and its commitment to establish a target year of 2050 for the reduction of specified greenhouse gas emissions "by at least 80 per cent ... when compared to 1990 levels" to be achieved partly "through a process of setting five-year caps on greenhouse gas emissions termed 'Carbon Budgets'" (ibid.). Central to the Climate Change Act 2008 is the commitment to "confer powers to establish trading schemes for the purpose of limiting greenhouse gas emissions or encouraging activities that reduce such emissions or remove greenhouse gas from the atmosphere" (Gov.UK 2017). The Energy Company Obligation (ECO) programme is utilised to this effect; as detailed in BEIS (2017), a feature of the Clean Growth Strategy is "support around £3.6 billion of investment to upgrade around a million homes through the Energy Company Obligation (ECO), and extend support for home energy efficiency improvements until 2028 at the current level of ECO funding" (ibid. 13).

BEIS (2017: 132) sets out ambitious future objectives for the reduction of greenhouse gas emissions with the Department for Business, Energy and Industrial Strategy and features the ECO programme; for example, a 2017 target commits to "explore ways in which we could make it easier for innovative approaches or products to be installed under our consumer-facing schemes such as the Energy Company Obligation". The inference here is that ECO schemes exhibit a paucity of creative innovation in their convergence toward lowest-cost energy efficiency measures. Indeed, it is insufficiently recognised that "initially supplier obligation schemes took a market based approach, allowing suppliers to install the lowest-cost measures such as insulation of lofts or delivery in urban areas" (Hough 2017: 3). For example, Fu et al. (2016) provides for a micro-analysis of "community engagement in tackling fuel poverty" which case-studies Kensington and Chelsea; but its micro-analysis neglects a critical engagement with the market-based dynamics of the ECO-funding programme. Conversely, this chapter focuses on the market-based dynamics of ECO as part of a broader critique of the Kensington and Chelsea Tenant Management Organisation (KCTMO) in terms of its expropriating contract culture; ultimately, part one of this chapter is concerned with establishing that the Rydon construction commissioning of the Grenfell Tower refurbishment was keen to capitalise on the accreditation of ECO-funding so as to further placate oppositional agenda within the local council, its KCTMO and resistance from tenant communities within the Grenfell Tower. Returning to my previous discussion of Actor Network Theory (ANT), the translation of oppositional agenda into an albeit tenuous concession towards a mutually application problematisation requires displacement. This is because, as Callon (1986a: 27) observes, "while translation determines where the points of obligatory passage will be located, this does not exhaust the action". Axiomatic to which proposition is that the enrolment of actors and networks into the concession of a detour, a problematisation, requires the on-going negotiation of legitimation of the conceded detour. Callon (ibid.) describes this situation thus: "The translator-spokesman and the translator-strategist who impose certain itineraries are bringing about movement". Integral to this "movement" is the negotiation of intellectual boundaries establishing expertise and providing justification for a direction of "movement". Consequently, Callon (ibid.) identifies that a component "of translation is displacement, in a literal sense". Connections, guides and parameters are formulated as part of the process of displacement for "some link is necessary to make entities accept certain spokesmen and certain points of passage" (ibid.). In Callon's (ibid.) account of an automobile innovation, displacement protuberance is exemplified by entities that are "converted into inscriptions" whereby the latter take the form of report dossiers and scientific articles, survey results, etc., Returning to my discussion of Rydon construction and the KCTMO's ECO-funding application and security, it is my contention that enrolling ECO-funding into Grenfell Tower's refurbishment provided a displacement through which oppositional factions, within the RBKC Council and Grenfell Tower residents, could be reassured that an environmental energy-efficiency problematisation of the Grenfell Tower refurbishment would reconcile their disparate oppositional agenda.

The ECO-funding proposal co-produced by Rydon construction and the KCTMO exemplified how in the process of displacement "entities are converted into inscriptions ... These are sent out and received back, acted upon and reacted to" (Callon 1986a: 27). ECO-funding operates as an effective displacement because its market-based competition and energy efficiency knowledge-based accreditation ascribe to its affiliated refurbishment programmes environmentalist legitimacy and acumen. It is Callon's (ibid.) primary observation that "translation cannot be effective, i.e. lead to stable constructions, if it is not anchored to such movements, to physical; and social displacement". In respect to the Grenfell Tower refurbishment, securing ECO-funding provided substantiation to the environmental principles that the KCTMO were keen to displace onto the problematisation that is the Sustainability and Energy Statement (RBKC

2012d) of the Grenfell Tower planning application. The governmental protocol and regulation of ECO-funding provided further credence to Grenfell Tower refurbishment's genuine commitment to environmental issues. Callon (1986a: 27) similarly observes how in displacement the conversion of entities into densely bureaucratic knowledge-based structures "extends the future of its actor-world ... The actor-world accumulates materials that render it durable" (ibid. 27-28). It is evident that comparisons exist in this process with ECO-funding and the government's Energy Company Obligation programme. However, there are also inherent contradictions embedded within the structures of the government's ECO programme that limit its claim to equitable environmental sustainability; and in so doing present limitations to the KCTMO's legitimacy in insisting that the Grenfell Tower refurbishment was premised on environmental principles.

Displacement Contradictions: Limitations of Energy Company Obligation as a Displacement Signifying Equitable Environmental Sustainability

Introduced in January 2013, the Energy Company Obligation (ECO) programme seeks "to reduce Britain's energy consumption and support people living in fuel poverty by funding energy efficiency improvements in homes" (Gov.UK 2017). It is a political intention that ECO is foremost in the reduction of "carbon emissions from Britain's domestic building stock, which is an essential part of the UK's plan to meet its statutory domestic carbon emission reduction targets by 2050" (ibid.). Energy suppliers with in excess of a quarter of a million customers or deliver more than 400 gigawatt hours of electricity or over 2,000 gigawatt hours of gas have legally set obligations to install energy efficiency improvement measures (Ofgem 2017). The extent of an energy supplier's legal obligation is calculated in accordance with its market share of the gas and electricity energy supply market (Gov.UK 2017). ECO is funded by legally obligated gas and electricity energy suppliers and the Office for Gas and Electricity Markets (Ofgem) administers the programme. Market-based trading is also a feature of the ECO programme, especially at its delivery interface. Firstly, ECO facilitates energy suppliers to deliver directly or indirectly set energy efficiency obligations. With regards to the latter, the energy supplier enters into competitively tendered contractual agreements with partners such as local authorities and installation contractors. Delivery measures directly require energy suppliers to utilise in-house installation service provisions. Competition enters into the direct delivery route with respect to facility, for energy suppliers choose domestic building stock for the company to comply with its legal obligation. Specifically, "Energy suppliers obligated under the scheme decide how they meet their obligations, including which homes to treat and how much subsidy they provide to each heating or insulation measure" (Gov.UK 2017). Officially it is presumed that criteria for this selection prioritise low-income, vulnerable to energy inefficiency households, as is evident in the following statement: "This may depend on size and type of the property, the consumers' individual circumstances and whether other finance is also being used, for example Green Deal finance". However, as discussed later, it is argued that energy suppliers favour the selection of domestic building stock deemed more easily amenable for the energy company to comply with their legal obligation. A second feature of the market-based dynamic of the ECO programme is the brokerage of a mechanism that facilitates "open and competitive delivery of ECO" (ibid.). Specifically, "brokerage operates through fortnightly, anonymous auctions where ECO providers can sell 'lots' of tonnes of carbon savings or bill savings to energy companies in return for ECO subsidy" (ibid.). The market-based trading features of ECO have been accentuated by the introduction, in 2017, of the facility for "obligated suppliers to trade their obligations with other obligated energy suppliers" (Ofgem 2017).

In 2017, the National Energy Action (NEA) published its response to the Mayor of London's (2016) "A City for all Londoners". Under the heading "Environment, Transport and Public Space", the Mayor details an aspiration that by 2050 "London to be zero carbon"; vehicles for achieving this include "introducing measures for cleaner, more efficient energy production and use" (ibid.). In response to the Mayor's (2016) consultation, NEA (2017) identifies several problems evident in the current Energy Company Obligation (ECO) that have particular relevance to London. Of significance to this discussion of ECO-funding and the Grenfell Tower refurbishment are NEA's concerns that:

> Despite their efforts and signs that local authorities may have a greater role in the delivery of the future ECO scheme, deep cuts to council funding continues to make it more challenging than ever (and in some cases impossible) to commit resources to tackle fuel poverty locally. (NEA 2017: 10)

Of particular further significance is NEA's (2017) critique of the opportunities available in the ECO programme for legally obligated energy suppliers to cherry-pick domestic building stock considered more easily amenable to the installation of energy efficiency measures. An indication of this concern is evident thus: "The Mayor should use his convening powers to help take advantage of the 'eligibility flexibility' options within ECO and ensure that if councils do not intend to use the new eligibility flexibility powers, a relevant body must be declared with the 'delegated responsibility' to refer households" (ibid. 21). As an outcome of enquiries I made to Ofgem to ascertain the degree to which energy suppliers within ECO schemes could prioritise certain refurbishments over others, I received the following emailed interview response from an assistant manager within Ofgem's ECO department:

Interviewer: Is the extent to which, in the Energy Company Obligation (ECO) programme, energy suppliers can choose domestic building stock deemed more easily amenable for the company to comply with their legal obligation?
Interviewee: *ECO places obligations on suppliers to deliver measure[s] to domestic premises. It focuses on insulation and heating measures and supports vulnerable consumer groups. It is up to the energy companies to determine which measures they choose to fund, the level of funding they provide (including if they offer measures for free) and the installer they choose to work with. Whilst Ofgem administers ECO, we do not have sight of, nor are involved in, contractual arrangements between the energy companies, installers and consumers. Energy companies work with third party installers to deliver their obligations.*

Interviewer: What is ECO-funding as per the parameters of the Energy Company Obligation programme?
Interviewee: *The funding of measures and contractual decisions are not within Ofgem's administrative remit. As detailed above, it is the responsibility of the energy companies to determine which measures they choose to fund and the level of funding they provide. The Energy Company Obligation (ECO) is not a grant scheme and as such different energy companies or installers may provide different levels or types of support towards the installation of energy efficiency or heating measures. Consumers may be asked to contribute towards the cost of the installation of a measure. However, we do not comment on scale or cost of customer contributions.*

Suppliers can also use ECO Brokerage to buy forward contracts for the delivery of carbon or cost savings by participating authorised sellers.

Installers can sell 'lots' of savings which they then have to deliver for the energy company who successfully bids for the lot. Ofgem does not have a role in administering the ECO Brokerage, which is operated by the Government Procurement Service. For further information on the ECO Brokerage mechanism, please refer to the government website here[1].

Interviewer: Description of the process by which a local authority can apply for ECO-funding and insights as to what form that ECO-funding will take.

Interviewee: *It is the responsibility of the obligated energy companies to arrange delivery of energy efficient measures to meet their obligations. In the case of LA (Local Authority) Flexible Eligibility (further details below), it is up to the energy companies to determine the local authority they choose to work with.*

To provide you with some context, under the Home Heating Cost Reduction Obligation (HHCRO), suppliers must deliver measures that reduce home heating costs for low income, fuel poor and vulnerable people. HHCRO measures can be delivered to:
a) private domestic premises occupied by someone in receipt of specific benefits (the help to heat group)
b) private domestic premises listed in a local authority (LA) declaration, and
c) social housing with an EPC [energy performance certificate] energy efficiency rating of E, F or G.

To make LA declarations, LA's must produce a statement of intent (SoI) regarding its delivery of the ECO flexible eligibility provision. This SoI should be publicly available (for example published on an LA's website) so that it can be easily accessed by interested parties. Ofgem does not approve LA Flexible eligibility schemes. For further guidance on LA Flexible Eligibility, please refer to the Department for Business, Energy and Industrial Strategy's (BEIS) Guidance Note, which can be found here[2]. You can also refer to sections 5.63-5.91 of our ECO2t Guidance:

---

[1] Gov.UK (2018); *Energy Companies Obligation: Brokerage, Department for Business, Energy and Industrial Strategy and Ofgem, Gov.UK.* Available at: https://www.gov.uk/guidance/energy-companies-obligation-brokerage

[2] DBEIS (2017); *Energy Company Obligation – Flexible Eligibility*, Department for Business, Energy and Industrial Strategy. Available at:

Delivery³.

Interviewer: *What criteria would make a local authority's ECO-funding application more competitive and likely to be successful in the process of ECO-funding competition?*
Interviewer: *Does the securing of ECO-funding, by a local authority, provide a level of accreditation, certification and or regulatory award?*
Interviewer: *Does the securing of ECO-funding, by a local authority, provide it recognition by national/international organisations specialising in environmental sustainability?*
Interviewee: *As above, it is up to the energy companies to determine the local authority they choose to work with. Ofgem do not have sight of, nor are involved in, contractual arrangements between the energy companies, installers, consumers and local authorities.*
Interviewee: *I hope this information is helpful. Our Frequently Asked Questions which you can find here and Delivery Guidance (as listed above) may also be of interest to you. If you have any further questions regarding the ECO scheme, please contact us at eco@ofgem.gov.uk.*

Kind regards,[name redacted]
EESP Assistant Manager
Energy Efficiency and Social Programmes
9 Millbank, London
SW1P 3GE
[www.ofgem.gov.uk]www.ofgem.gov.uk

(Structured Qualitative Open Question Format Emailed Questionnaire, Bespoke Organisation/Management Specifically Designed, Self-Administered Questionnaire: EESP Assistant Manager, Energy Efficiency and Social Programmes, Ofgem, 3rd November 2017, London)
In September 2017, during an interview with an "energy expert", the issue of energy suppliers cherry picking preferable domestic property for ECO energy efficiency installations yielded some important implications

---

https://assets.publishing.service.gov.uk/government/uploads/system/uploads/attachment_data/file/608042/ECO_Help_to_Heat_flexible_eligibility_guidance_for_LAs.pdf
³ Ofgem (2017a); *Energy Company Obligation 2017 – 18 (ECO2t) Guidance*: Delivery; 12th April 2017; Information Type: Guidance; Policy Areas: Environmental Programmes ECO., Ofgem. Available at:
https://www.ofgem.gov.uk/publications-and-updates/energy-company-obligation-2017-18-eco2t-guidance-delivery

relevant to the Rydon construction and KCTMO ECO funding application. Of initial significance, and in accordance with the concerns raised in chapter two, regarding the KCTMO's devalorising of in-house established expertise, government cuts in local authority funding have precipitated a shortfall of professional local authority personnel specialising in energy efficiency. And, according to the "energy expert" I consulted, the following situation is arising across many local authorities:

***Interviewee:** There used to be a lot of local energy programmes in place historically; but those have fallen off with a decline in national funding for energy efficiency overall. And the fact that there has been a decline in local authority energy officers working on this stuff. So typically local authorities have had a local authority energy officer in their area and that's no longer the case. (**Interviewer:** "Local authority energy officers?") Yes, that would try and provide assistance for vulnerable households on a range of matters; help advance any local commitments that the local authority had made to local efficiency, erhm, to sort of tackle fuel poverty or climate change ... Just energy in the round so they might be looking at decentralised energy; they might be looking at a range of initiatives that might be there to not only help on the environmental side but also the social dimension. Typically, their role was to, some of them still exist, but invariably they don't anymore because they are seen as a luxury. Their role was leveraging in local, national funding; help try and advance local projects; galvanise and inform local politicians about a portfolio about what energy efficiency are taking place in an area; could take place in an area to help government processes at a local authority level ... There are a few local authorities where they still exist but, obviously, given the wider austerity measures; the fact that the national reporting requirements that were in place as part of communities and local government were removed; there was an indicators set and progress on these issues was monitored centrally for a while, but when Eric Pickles took over in communities and local government, they took out those reporting, need for those national reporting mechanisms and there's been a consolidation, local authorities just fund statutory duties and although local authorities retain certain responsibilities around housing standards, particularly enforcement of the private rented sector, it is often seen as a nice-to-have rather than an essential activity. So that resource has gone ... I am sure you are aware with local authorities; they have been under extreme financial pressures to reduce their capital and revenue budgets through successive comprehensive spending reviews. I think that they are receiving sixty percent less from central government than they were; their* *ability to raise council tax has obviously been inhibited through the council tax freeze; and just the politically contentious nature of doing that anyway, business rates have been frozen so there is very little revenue coming into local authorities to sustain that kind of activity. We would see it as a great shame, local authorities are well placed to kind of galvanise activity that wouldn't happen naturally.*

Interviewer: How might this relate to the ECO assistance?
Interviewee: *Well, previously, in the heyday, in the kind of heyday, I guess, there was decent homes funding available from central government. It was not only there to support energy efficiency, it was equally there to provide capital revenue for improving social housing because there was a large backlog of social housing that was extremely poor quality, again, not just in the energy efficiency side but in general and so the Decent Homes Programme was established to try and address that backlog of properties without suitable capital investments. So there was that scheme and, at the same time, private tenure properties benefited nationally from something called Warm Front, which is a grant-based programme again funded from central government that was there to install insulation and heating measures; and at the same time as that, you had supplier obligations of which the Energy Company Obligation is a successor; and previously those supplier obligations were much larger in scale. So there was something called the Carbon Emission Reduction Target, CERT, and Community Energy Saving Programme (CESP). And both of those schemes were funded through consumers' bills and weren't funded through general taxation, like those other two programmes were. But all in all that was kind of a war chest in terms of focused resources on energy efficiency. So a lot of those local authority [energy] officers would have tried to use those funding schemes, plus others at a local or national level to try and improve the situation of poor people living in the worst housing conditions. Back then, in 2012/13, changed when the government, erhm, stopped funding the Decent Homes Programme, stopped funding the Warm Front programme and reduced the previous two obligations, CERT and CESP to a single supplier obligation – which is called the Energy Company Obligation ... The impact of the latter was quite significant because previously CERT had been providing support for very basic insulation measures, cavity wall insulation ... and CESP had been doing a bit more heavy lifting in terms of funding boiler replacements, internal external solid wall insulation. So it moved from a situation where they were treating supplier obligations and tax funded polices as the same, to approximately one and a half billion a year going into energy efficiency*

measures and that went down to just under one point one billion pounds. But the supplier obligation was then left to do everything. The Energy Company Obligation was there to do two things, primarily. It was there to support fuel poverty and it was largely focused from 2013-2015 on funding gas boilers essentially, or that's what it ended up achieving. And it was also there to provide some assistance for wall insulation. And initially it was conceived that it was to do more of the latter, i.e. treat more extensive measures through something called the Green Deal ... Which was a mechanism designed to put a charge on the energy meter to pay back the cost of the energy efficiency measures through the savings on people's bills and the idea was to provide some subsidy through ECO to make that on the energy meter work more effectively to reduce the payback period centrally ... The supplier obligation is a very different proposition. Because it is essentially, it is led by the energy companies, in order to pay for the policy charge their customers a certain amount and they deliver what targets the Government sets them. In order to do that most cost effectively and rightly so they should deliver cost effectively, in order to do that cost effectively, they cherry-pick essentially from whoever is eligible to see the cheapest way that they can meet their target. And as a result of that .. concern that the most vulnerable households don't benefit to such an extent because vulnerable people tend to live in poorer conditions and therefore before you can think about doing any energy efficiency work, you might have a lot more supplementary work you need to do before those energy efficiency measures can be installed. We often find in our work that people living cluttered lives and cluttered houses, essentially, and it is very difficult to fund that work through any other way. So as a result the poorest households don't benefit from a policy they need most benefit from ... So when energy suppliers try to meet those targets cost effectively, they or their contractors try to meet those targets in properties [in a way] that is most cost effective to meet those targets.

(Semi-structured, Qualitative Interview: Energy Expert, London, 29th September 2017)

The latter issue concerning "cherry picking" households for the application of Energy Company Obligation measures by energy suppliers has significance to the Rydon and KCTMO ECO-funding application in the sense that the successful application, while unquestionably achieved on merit, might also be construed as an outcome of ECO energy suppliers "cherry picking" refurbishment properties that are easily amenable to the expedient installation of energy efficiency measures.

Rydon Construction and the Grenfell Tower, Energy Company Obligation (ECO); Perils of Market-based Energy Efficiency

Fay Edwards, Chair of KCTMO, which manages the tower on behalf of the borough, said: 'I'm delighted that we have been successful in appointing Rydon. I sat on the tender panel and was involved in the interview process. Residents of the tower have long had to put up with a sub-standard heating system and poor insulation and this has affected the quality of their lives. The new heating system will mean they can adjust the heating to their own needs for the first time'. (RBKC 2014a)

RBKC (2016) published a press release on 13th May 2016 featuring a visit made by the leader (Cllr Nick Paget-Brown) and deputy leader (Cllr Rock Feilding-Mellen) of the Royal Borough of Kensington and Chelsea to Grenfell Tower subsequent to the £10 million refurbishment. Further confirmation is provided in RBKC (ibid.) that Grenfell Tower's refurbishment was funded by the Council's £67 million capacious regeneration investment in the district. Energy efficiency features continually in the press release, with emphasis placed on enhancement achieved through "the installation of insulated exterior cladding, new double-glazed windows and a new communal heating system", all of which, we are assured, "will greatly enhance the energy efficiency of the tower and help reduce residents' living costs" (ibid.). RBKC (ibid.) provides some partial insights into Rydon Construction's successful commissioning, albeit disclosed and entangled in the rhetoric of energy efficiency, for we are informed that the two-year project designed and delivered by KCTMO in partnership with Rydon Construction was complicated "as it took place with all 120 flats occupied throughout" (ibid.). Evidently, "logistics had to be carefully managed to minimise disruption" and that "essential to the progress of the project was close consultation with residents ensuring that access to their homes was possible at all key stages"; but even the most cursory of perusals through the Grenfell Action Group blog posts provides disquieting evidence to the contrary. Indeed, the RBKC (ibid.) press release, with the benefit of hindsight, was riddled with contradictions in its emphasis, on the one hand, on lowest-cost property occupied improvement and, on the other, assiduous energy efficiency refurbishment of the property. Nevertheless, self-convinced of their success in squaring this circle, the leader of Kensington and Chelsea Council (Cllr Nick Paget-Brown) is quoted as saying: "It is remarkable to see first-hand how the cladding has lifted the external appearance of the tower and how the improvements inside people's homes will make a big difference to their day-to-day lives" (ibid.). The KCTMO's Chief Executive (Robert Black), similarly enamoured with self-congratulations, is quoted thus:

> We're delighted to have worked in partnership with the Council to deliver this major regeneration of the tower. This has improved the homes overall and residents can now have the benefits of living in energy-efficient homes, all in a vastly improved environment. I am especially pleased with the nine new homes, which cost £878,000 to deliver, and add much-needed family homes for the Royal Borough. The whole project was done within budget too. (RBKC 2016)

"The whole project was done within budget too" (ibid.) triumphantly vaunts the KCTMO's Chief Executive. Viewed from within the prism of hindsight, this rodomontade of accomplishment is chilling and tragically disenchanting for less than a year later, the Grenfell Tower was ablaze, destroyed in a horrendous fire. It is no doubt injudicious to denounce the RBKC's (2016) boastful self-accolade merely in terms of the tragedy unless it can be plausibly argued that the objective to achieve the lowest-cost property improvements was irreconcilably in contradiction with the objective to retrofit energy efficiency refurbishments to the entirely occupied property. One is driven to enquire whether naivety or avarice motivated the RBKC officials, oblivious to the irreconcilable contradictions inherent in their energy efficiency-branded refurbishment of the Grenfell Tower. Indeed, we need to map more effectively the energy efficiency agenda against the lowest-cost improvement objectives so as to reveal discontinuities in the former and the powerful overriding motivations of the latter.

"Grenfell Tower refurbishment contract agreed. A major milestone in the £10m refurbishment of the Royal Borough's Grenfell Tower in North Kensington has been reached with the appointment of the construction company Rydon to carry out work" assuredly announces the Royal Borough of Kensington and Chelsea's 9 April 2014 press release (RBKC 2014a). We are informed further that the Grenfell Tower refurbishment was funded by the RBKC as an integral part of the wider £57 million regeneration of the borough, "which will see it transformed by 2016" (ibid.). The Rydon refurbishment management contract was awarded by KCTMO, accredited as managing the tower block on behalf of Kensington Council (ibid.). The press release accentuates a commitment to energy efficiency as steering the selection of Rydon in the competitive tendering process: "The large scale works will include an upgrade to the cladding to the exterior of the building, new windows and a totally new heating system. All of this will greatly enhance the energy efficiency of the tower" (ibid.). RBKC (2014a) is insistent that Rydon demonstrated the capacity to provide an exceptional standard of resident consultation in the retrofitting into local council housing stock of energy efficiency appliances. Thus we are reliably informed that "Rydon was appointed under strict OJEU (Official Journal of the European Journal) guidelines. KCTMO required a contractor that could demonstrate outstanding resident engagement in similar tower block refurbishment" (ibid.). Less evident in the RBKC (ibid.) notification is the self-evident fact that where energy efficiency refurbishment translates into occupied property refurbishment, the possibilities of lowest-cost savings are highly attractive to a property development contractual culture rapaciously intent on cutting costs, as is evident in the actions of the KCTMO.

In its 2017 website advertising, Rydon promotes its commitment "to preserving and enhancing the environment" through the registration of all its projects under the auspices of "the nationally recognised Considerate Construction scheme" (Rydon 2017b). Elsewhere on its website, Rydon details its Residents 4 Low Impact Sustainable Homes (Relish) project, promoted as a "response to the pressing necessity to find sustainable ways to reduce carbon emissions in the home, and eliminate the existence of fuel poverty" (ibid.). The Relish project is apparently committed to low carbon solutions through adopting "a pragmatic and cost effective approach to retrofitting homes, alongside a stakeholder education programme" and the combined effect of these initiatives to "reduce carbon emissions and energy costs for residents" (ibid.). Rydon's (ibid.) "pragmatic and cost effective approach" is clearly a commissioning advantage, especially when this translates into "retrofitting homes" without having to incur the immensely expensive liability of temporarily rehousing residents. Furthermore, one might initially concede that Rydon's programmes of low carbon emission solutions to building stock refurbishment provided the primary incentive to commission its services in the refurbishment of the Grenfell Tower. However, even a cursory perusal into the market-based dynamic of ECO-funding makes evident endemic inequities in the pursuit of contracts for the refurbishment of local council social housing building stock.

Prior to promulgating its removal of all reference to Grenfell Tower from its website "as a mark of respect", Rydon Construction (2017) avidly promoted announcements of the completion of its management of the £8.6 million refurbishment of Grenfell Tower, which constituted a component of a £57 million borough-wide urban regeneration of Kensington and Chelsea, London (Rydon Construction 2017a). Indeed, its now archived rodomontade web-advertising unabashedly vaunted: Grenfell Tower (contract name) refurbishment was contracted at the "Contract Value" of "£8.7m" and delivered at "£8.6m" during a "Contract Period" of "66 weeks" and for the "Client: KCTMO Limited" (ibid.). Rydon Construction, keen to bounce new business from its web-advertising, placed emphasis on its management of the refurbishment "with residents still in occupation" (ibid.). Such economies of scale are attractive to cash-strapped local authorities, eager to avoid the expense of temporarily rehousing council tenants during prolonged refurbishment programmes. Further, features of interest with regards to the Rydon Construction (2017a) web-advertising notice relate to its accentuation of the project as an urban regeneration: "Located in the Lancaster West Estate"; "the project on the 1970s-built tower". Of particular significance are the poignant references made to improving the "energy efficiency of the building" (ibid.) for the Rydon Construction web-advertising material coheres the external rainscreen cladding refurbishment of Grenfell Tower with the intentioned achievement of improved energy efficiency: "Externally, rain screen cladding, curtain wall façade and replacement windows were fitted, improving thermal insulation and modernising the exterior of the building" (ibid.). Later in this chapter, the issue of aesthetics will be explored critically; however, the concern of this discussion is the mediation, in terms of neoliberal market-led public management, of the modernising of the exterior of the Grenfell Tower building. In this respect, the construct of a contract culture of public management is particularly pertinent for the energy efficiency dimension of the exterior refurbishment of the Grenfell Tower was partly secured through the rapacious market-based dynamics of the Energy Company Obligation (ECO) funding scheme as is evident in the following Rydon Construction (2017a) statement: "Rydon achieved a BREEAM rating and secured eco funding from KCTMO".

The "eco funding" to which Rydon Construction's (2017a) web-advertising refers is detailed more extensively in an earlier RBKC (2012a) document entitled: Energy Efficiency, Fuel Poverty and Environmental Health. Information and Advice for Private Sector Landlords. RBKC (2012a) appropriately identifies the programme of Energy Company Obligation (ECO) as having replaced two schemes of energy supplier obligation that ended in 2012: Launched in 2008 the Carbon Emissions Reduction Target (CERT); and launched in 2009 the Community Energy

Saving Programme (CESP). The CERT scheme necessitated that all energy suppliers with a customer base in excess of 50,000 actively provide initiatives such as loft insulation, etc., designed to reduce household greenhouse gas emissions (RBKC 2012a). CERT-financed energy efficiency schemes, it is said, focused "on providing the most cost effective measures such as cavity wall and loft insulation", with some CERT schemes having progressed to providing advanced "measures such as solid wall insulation" (ibid. 8). In conjunction with CERT, CESP is an energy supplier obligation scheme directed at improving "energy efficiency standards and reduce fuel bills in low income areas" (ibid. 9). In contrast with CERT, CESP espoused a community-based "whole house" approach in which local authorities operated in partnerships with energy suppliers, local authorities and community groups (ibid.). RBKC (2012a: 9) states clearly that for the duration of the existence of CESP, no energy efficiency projects were undertaken within the CESP programme. Specifically, it pronounced that:

> Although parts of the Royal Borough have been declared as CESP eligible areas, lack of match funding has meant that no works have been undertaken in the public or private sector. (RBKC 2012a: 9)

In December 2012, both the CERT and CESP energy efficiency programmes were discontinued, ostensibly replaced by the ECO programme; phase one and thus the first ECO scheme commenced on 1st January 2013 (Hough 2017: 3). The official remit of ECO states that it "provides funding to improve energy efficiency in difficult to treat housing and the homes of 'those most in need'" (ibid.). Initially, ECO paralleled concurrently the Green Deal, which was designed to provide loans for energy efficiency augmentations but then the latter was discontinued. In its current incarnation, ECO has three dimensions: "Affordable Warmth"; "Carbon Saving Obligation"; and "Carbon Saving Communities Obligation" (ibid.). ECO schemes commenced in phase one of the programme coincided with the time-frame of Rydon construction's collaboration with KCTMO to secure ECO-funding as phase one ran from 1st January 2013 to March 2015. On initial perusal, one might argue that Rydon's track record in securing ECO-funding coupled with its successful navigation of the government's ECO market-based brokerage mechanism confirmed the KCTMO's commitment to low carbon emission energy efficiency. However, even the most cursory perusal through the archives of the Grenfell Action Group discloses evidence of questionable practice by Rydon in their management of the installation of the energy efficiency improvements to the Grenfell Tower. Indeed, there is much to suggest that

Rydon's commitment to ECO-funded energy efficiency was more in principle than in practice for in its pursuit of lowest-cost refurbishment of the Grenfell Tower, ecology trailed far behind the race to the bottom in cost savings.

In March 2015, the Grenfell Action Group (2015) posted a blog entitled Grenfell Residents Resist TMO Intransigence. According to the blog posting, the residents of Grenfell Tower had reached a point of exasperation with the KCTMO and Rydon's incautious installation of the energy efficient home improvements. With regards to the latter, residents were particularly aggrieved "with the TMO/Rydon's intention of giving residents no choice over where the new boilers will be positioned inside their properties and favouring the cheapest and most unsightly option" (ibid.). The blog, posted 11th March 2015, provides in some detail evidence of its frustrated attempts to engage the Grenfell Tower project management within the KCTMO; a detailed extract of the KCTMO project manager Claire Williams response is provided thus:

> The TMO has consulted residents on the heating proposal, in group sessions and also individually. Rydon are discussing the heating layout with each household as works progress, as there are some options for pipework layouts where furniture or practicality demands.
>
> There is a misunderstanding on the HIU location – the proposed position was not determined by cost. The location is determined by technical regulations (it needs to be close to a drainage point); and now we have accessed more homes it is clear that the existing pipework ducts behind the bathroom ... are not easily accessible. So this is the best technical solution for plumbers working in occupied properties – i.e. cause less disruption to the building fabric, which will also mean we will not need to be in homes for longer than necessary. It has been noted in every newsletter since October 2014 that works would be undertaken within the flats in the New Year, so this should not be a surprise.
>
> I note that working in residents' homes when they are fully occupied and furnished is not simple. This is why we looked to a contractor with this type of experience with Resident Liaison Officers to work with residents. The existing layout of Grenfell meant that the solution was never going to be easy – but the TMO could not afford to wait for the heating system to fail before it undertook works. Please ask any residents with queries to either talk to Rydon's RLOs or they can contact me [Claire Williams] direct.

(Grenfell Action Group 2015)

The KCTMO project manager Claire Williams' response provides further crucial evidence of contradictions and conflicts between the KCTMO's ECO-funded energy efficiency improvement drive on the one hand and the KCTMO's lowest-cost determination to conduct, in occupied properties, an incautious refurbishment on the other. Furthermore, Claire Williams admits a lack of planning by Rydon in its determination of an accessible location for the installation of the energy efficient improvements to the heating system. Here and elsewhere there is evidence that KCTMO's commitment to an energy efficiency-premised refurbishment was perilously compromised by the property development contract culture that priorities lowest-cost profit gains. An issue I shall explore in part two of this chapter is whether the refurbishment of the exterior façade perilously deteriorated the external aesthetic integrity of the Grenfell Tower.

Grenfell Tower Refurbishment: "Heroic and Original, or Ugly and Ordinary[?]" (Venturi et al. 1977)

By now it almost goes without saying that a catalogue of failures and criminal negligence contributed to the Grenfell Fire disaster. The criminally negligent decision to replace the external cladding and insulation with inferior alternatives that were highly toxic and highly combustible was of course chief among these. But there were many other factors that contributed to this catastrophe: the gross overdevelopment of the adjacent area that badly compromised emergency access, the gross underfunding of the fire service over recent years that left them ill-equipped to deal with the enormity of the challenge they were faced with, the smoke detection and extraction system and the fire alarms, all of which appear to have failed, the botched installation of the windows and the decision to fix gas pipes for the new heating and hot water system to the walls of the stairwell and lobbies. All these factors appear likely to have contributed significantly to the disaster. (Grenfell Action Group 2017a)

RBKC's (2012b) Design and Access Statement for the October 2012 planning application of the Grenfell Tower refurbishment provides some detail into the history of the building. Grenfell Tower is described as settled at the northern region of the Lancaster West 1 Estate, situated in the Notting Barns Ward of North Kensington. The Lancaster West Estate was once heralded as a beacon of housing regeneration for it was built in the twilight years of the 1970s, eradicating previous slum housing properties that were blighted by an absence of internal plumbing and reconfiguring previous street planning (ibid. 2). RBKC (ibid.) describes how in the

1970's reconfigured street pattern of the Lancaster Estate, "the streets – referred to as Walkways – are linked together into a single network at the northern end and the connection to Grenfell Tower is via a bridge at its south-west corner". In the 1990s, further street patterning of the Lancaster Estate intentionally limited "the use of the streets as thoroughfares", a consequence of which was "whereas Grenfell Tower once had more than one point of access, including at Walkway level, it is now only accessible via a small reception at ground level on the south side of the tower" (ibid.). Design and access planning permission focused significantly on the "elevated street" features of the front access and were concerned to address the apparently unsightly service yard area and lower ground parking which in the original 1970's architectural plan were "intended to be out of sight", achieved through lowering the ground level (ibid.). Apparently, and according to RBKC (ibid.), the service yard was an intrusive site: "For the residents of Grenfell tower the yard is very much in view, not tidily concealed" (ibid.). (Re)constituted through the aesthetic economy of the KCTMO's property development contract culture, the service yard is described as "a hostile environment for pedestrians and a dark unpleasant space to be in" (ibid.). Intent on homogenising the branded aesthetic economy of the Lancaster West Estate, RBKC (ibid.) details that "the TMO intend reducing the amount of traffic in this area" and that the "application proposes transforming it into a pedestrian priority zone" (ibid.). Grenfell Action Group (2017a) raise important questions as to the suitability of the access routes to the Grenfell Tower. With regards to the Grenfell Tower building, its pre-refurbishment structure comprised of twenty storeys of residential apartments above four storeys of community facilities/office spaces situated at podium level (RBKC 2012b: 4). Architecturally, the pre-refurbishment building was square in plan: "The north and south elevations are almost identical, as are the east and west" (ibid.). The exterior facing structure of the pre-refurbished Grenfell Tower is described thus:

> The structural frame: columns, core stairs and floor plates are in-situ poured concrete. Pre-cast concrete panels form the cladding to the residential floors: one panel type serves as a horizontal structural spandrel, spanning column to column and the other is a facing to the columns, each panel a full storey height. (RBKC 2012b: 4)

In *Learning from Las Vegas, Part II*, entitled "Ugly Ordinary Architecture, or the Decorated Shed", Venturi et al. (1977: 85) identify confutation in modern architecture's co-existent emphasis on symbolism, aesthetics, subjective emotional perception, use-value and structural functionality.

The latter suggests that architectural design contends with contradictory preoccupations with "symbolic and representational elements" (ibid. 87). Venturi et al. (ibid.) are concerned to methodologically compare contradictory elements in their case-studied primary architectural manifestations for "architecture depends in its perception and creation on past experience and emotional association and ... these symbolic and representational elements may often be contradictory to the form, structure and program with which they combine in the same building". Placing contradiction at the epicentre of their analysis enables Venturi et al. (ibid.) to construct a complex case for criticising a manifestation of architecture fixated with symbolic aesthetic "where the architectural systems of space, structure, and program are submerged and distorted by an overall symbolic form" (ibid.). Euphemistically defined as a "duck", Venturi et al. (ibid.) explain that "This kind of building-becoming sculpture we call the duck in honour of the duck-shaped drive-in, 'The Long Island Duckling,' illustrated in God's Own Junkyard by Peter Blake". Venturi et al. (ibid.) contrast the application of symbolism in architecture in "duck" form with architectural design in which symbolism is secondary to the functional programmatic utility of the building. The latter is euphemistically defined as "the decorated shed" for this is "where systems of space and structure are directly at the service of program, and ornament is added independently of them" (ibid.). Both forms of symbolism have their reality in actual architectural structures; as Venturi et al. (ibid.) express it: "The duck is the special building that is a symbol; the decorated shed is the conventional shelter that applies symbols ...We maintain that both kinds of architecture are valid – Chartres is a duck (although it is a decorated shed as well), and the Palazzo Farnese is a decorated shed – but we think that the duck is seldom relevant today, although it pervades Modern architecture". In a discussion entitled "Is Boring Architecture Interesting?", Venturi et al. (ibid. 101) discuss their comparative analysis of Paul Rudolph's Crawford Manor (built between 1962–1966, New Haven USA) with Venturi and Raunch, Cope and Lippincott Associates' Guild House, Friends' Housing for the Elderly (built between 1960–1963, Philadelphia USA). Prior to relaying their analysis, Venturi et al. (ibid. 90) provide concise analytics pertaining to the overall ambition of their theoretical framework, and this has relevance to a comparative critical formulation of architectural symbolism and Grenfell Tower. Indeed, Venturi et al. (ibid. 90) affirm that they "argue for the symbolism of the ugly and ordinary in architecture and for the particular significance of the decorated shed with a rhetorical front and conventional behind: for architecture as shelter with symbols on it".

Remaining with the methodological insights provided by Venturi et al. (ibid. 90) in their "Duck and the Decorated Shed" comparison of Paul Rudolph's Crawford Manor with their architectural project Guild House, they are unapologetically committed to the intellectual value of analysing buildings at the level of symbolism and this provides inspiration to the value of analysing Grenfell Tower's refurbishment in terms of semiosis, aesthetics and organisational culture. As Venturi et al. (ibid. 90-91) express it:

> [P]lease do not criticize us for primarily analyzing image: We are doing so simply because image is pertinent to our argument, not because we wish to deny an interest in or the importance of process, program, and structure or, indeed, social issues in architecture or in these two buildings. Along with most architects, we probably spend 90 percent of our design time on these other important subjects and less than 10 percent on the questions we are addressing here; they are merely not the direct subject of this inquiry.

Progressing with the Venturi et al. (ibid.) comparison method of analysis provides further depths of analytics applicable to a critical engagement with the exterior refurbishment of Grenfell Tower. Venturi et al. (ibid. 91) describe how "Guild House has ornament on it; Crawford Manor does not … The ornament on Guild House is explicit. It both reinforces and contradicts the form of the building it adorns. And it is to some extent symbolic". In contrast, Crawford Manor rejects, as with "most orthodox Modern architecture … ornament and association in the perception of forms" (ibid. 92). Their preference for Guild House becomes evident as one begins to discern the form and distinction of the decorated shed. Returning to the section of their book entitled "Heroic and Original, or Ugly and Ordinary?", Crawford Manor's architectural symbolism provides nuanced levels of comparison with the refurbishment of Grenfell Tower's exterior. And this might come as some surprise for, according to Venturi et al. (ibid. 93), the symbolism of Crawford Manor "is what we call 'heroic and original'". Although the poured concrete formulaic substance of Crawford Manor "is conventional and ordinary", its pretensions aspire to "the image [of] heroic and original" (ibid.). It is surprising that the symbolism of their much-favoured Guild House is defined as "ugly and ordinary" for in contrast to the pouring of formulaic design into fabricated heroic moulds evident in the Crawford Manor building, Guild House is brutally honest in its undisguised "technologically unadvanced brick, the old-fashioned, double-hung windows, the pretty materials around the entrance, and the ugly antenna not hidden behind the parapet in the accepted fashion, all are distinctly conventional in image as well as substance or, rather, ugly and ordinary". Complexity is introduced by their suggestion that features evident in the façade of Guild House that pertain to "pretensions of the 'giant order' on the front" are evidence of how the decoration of construction, through the "juxtaposition of contrasting symbols – the application of one order of symbolism on another" – provides illustration of "the decorated shed" (ibid. 91-100). This complex weaving between styles imposed onto a functional constructed form of a building "is what makes Guild House an architect's decorated shed – not architecture without architects" (ibid. 100). In describing a close approximation to the ultimate form of the conceptual model of the decorated shed, Venturi et al. (ibid.) argue:

> The purest decorated shed would be some form of conventional systems-building shelter that corresponds closely to the space, structure, and program requirements of the architecture, and upon which is laid a contrasting – and, if in the nature of the circumstances, contradictory – decoration. In Guild House the ornamental-symbolic elements are more or less literally appliqué ... The symbolism of the decoration happens to be ugly and ordinary with a dash of ironic heroic and original, and the shed is straight ugly and ordinary, though in its brick and windows it is symbolic too.

The Venturi et al. (ibid.) position is complex for while the muted symbolism and aesthetic modesty of Crawford Manor prompt the praiseworthy exclamation "Unadmitted decoration by the articulation of integral elements ... Heroic ... Pretty (or at least unified) all around", Venturi et al. (ibid. 101) describe Crawford Manor as having "impoverished itself by rejecting denotative ornament and the rich tradition of iconography in historical architecture and by ignoring – or rather using unawares – the connotative expression it [modern architecture] substituted for decoration". Complexity emerges here in respect to tensions within the discipline of architecture in the 1970s in which conservative prudent orthodoxy was successfully subduing movements favouring form over function. Indeed, Venturi et al. (ibid. 101) state, "When it cast out eclecticism, Modern architecture submerged symbolism". In so doing, Modern architecture "promoted expressionism, concentrating on the expression of architectural elements themselves: on the expression of structure and function" (ibid. 101-103). Of significance to the application of an analysis of the architectural design of Grenfell Tower refurbished exterior cladding aesthetic, Venturi et al. (ibid. 103) argue that in the Modern architecture of the 1960s and 1970s can be observed a mediation of the political and economic context; for as is the case of the Crawford Manor, "It suggested, through the image of the building, reformist-progressive social and industrial aims that it could seldom achieve in reality". Ironically, although our initial response is to pronounce the aesthetic of the refurbished Grenfell Tower a duck, there are consistent elements evident of a standardised impoverished corporate aesthetic reminiscent of what Venturi et al. (ibid. 87) describe as "the decorated shed"; but this can easily be explained in terms of the pouring into corporate moulds a standardised aesthetic reminiscent of a decorated construction but in actuality a pseudo-decorated shed; equivalent ultimately to a duck. Instead of photographic imagery of the 2016-completed exterior of Grenfell Tower, the following description provided, in 2016, by the refurbishment management company Rydon, provides an important illustration of a semiosis in the discourse of pretentious heroic, reformist-progressive ecological urban regeneration.

> Rydon has completed the refurbishment to Grenfell Tower for Kensington & Chelsea Tenant Management Organisation (KCTMO), upgrading the 24-storey 1970s building as part of a £67m borough-wide regeneration.
>
> The £10m project included extensive remodelling of the bottom four floors creating nine additional new homes, improved communal facilities for the residents, and improved spaces for two local businesses. Externally, rain screen cladding, replacement windows and curtain wall façades have been fitted giving the building a fresher, modern look. All of the remodelling & refurbishment works were completed with residents still in occupation on the upper twenty floors.
>
> Dale Youth Boxing Club, which had produced some of the UK's best boxing talent including Olympic Gold medallist James DeGale and former European, British and Commonwealth super-middleweight champion George Groves, is based within Grenfell Tower. The work has provided the club with improved facilities that will hopefully produce many more champions of the future.
>
> Grenfell nursery was relocated to a larger and more convenient space on the ground floor next to a new outside play area.
>
> Internally, a new, more efficient communal heating system and bespoke smoke extract and ventilation system were fitted. The works achieved a BREEAM Good rating and Rydon helped the client secure eco funding grants.
>
> Cllr Nick Paget-Brown, the leader of the Royal Borough of Kensington and Chelsea, visited the site in May and said:

'It is remarkable to see first-hand how the cladding has lifted the external appearance of the tower and how the improvements inside people's homes will make a big difference to their day-to-day lives'.

'As well as this investment, in a relatively short space of time Grenfell Tower residents have benefitted from a brand new academy and leisure centre, which represents our ongoing commitment to North Kensington'.

(Rydon 2016/2017)

In this aftermath of the Grenfell Tower fire tragedy, one gains clarity in the critical interpretation of Rydon's (ibid.) July 2016 statement; for Rydon's oblivious self-consciousness of its dialogue is at best incongruous with its pronounced management expertise and at worst cliché descending rapidly into a parody of formulaic corporate neoliberal urban regeneration. Indeed, proclamations of the cladding providing "a fresher, modern look" and lifting the building's exterior appearance all seem oblivious to the extent to which such publicity corporate-washes the specific and particular urban vernacular of the architecture. Berger's (1972/1977: 149) *Ways of Seeing* describes how "publicity adds up to a kind of philosophical system. It explains everything in its own terms. It interprets the world". Rydon's publicity statement of completion, in retrospect, was prophetic for it precipitated a way of seeing Grenfell Tower in its own image and yet it appears eerily oblivious to its self-parody. Berger's (ibid. 150) insight into the totalising aspirations of publicity is critically toying with the hyperbole of second-order advertising publicity simulacra; the following exquisite Berger epithet resonates with Rydon's completion statement for the statement is bereft of reflexive intuition and self-conscious efficacy of its limitations, and descends perilously into a nonchalant parody of itself:

> The entire world becomes a setting for the fulfilment of publicity's promise of the good life. The world smiles at us. It offers itself to us. And because *everywhere* is imagined as offering itself to us, *everywhere* is more or less the same. (Berger 1972/1977: 150)

In the publicity, articulation and actuality of Grenfell Tower's refurbished exterior aesthetic is evident many of the limitations of Modern architecture; whereby the latter has been observed by Venturi et al. (1977: 103) thus: "By limiting itself to strident articulation of the pure architectural elements of space, structure and program, Modern architecture's expression has become a dry expressionism, empty and boring – and in the end irresponsible". Indeed, Venturi et al. (ibid. 103) identify an irony in which the architecture of the 1970s expressed a pedantic reverence in terms of function, which limits challenging innovation and leans towards decorative standardisation, resulting in excessively banal monuments to mediocre symbolic aesthetic. More specifically:

> Ironically, the Modern architecture of today, while rejecting explicit symbolism and frivolous appliqué ornament, has distorted the whole building into one big ornament. In substituting 'articulation' for decoration, it has become a duck. (Venturi et al. 1977: 103)

Following Venturi et al. (ibid.) in their critical conceptualisation of substituting "articulation" for decoration in Modern architecture, consider again the following statements derived from the refurbishment of the Grenfell Tower planning permission document:

> Materials to be used on the external faces of the building(s);
>
> *Reason* – To accord with the development plan by ensuring that the character and appearance of the area are preserved and living conditions of those living near the development suitably protected.
>
> (Kensington and Chelsea 2014)

If the refurbished external cladding of the Grenfell Tower is, retrospectively, to be considered a duck, one is provoked to wonder whether this state of existence was a transition from a prior form as an architecturally decorated shed. Venturi et al. (1977) provide a detailed genealogy tracing the emergence of, in recent times, an architectural form predicated on excessive banal decoration. In reference to their observation of the architectural form they define as a duck, Venturi et al. (1977: 129) identify "how heroic and original (H&O) architecture derives dramatic expression from the connotative meanings of its 'original' elements: It gives off abstract meanings – or rather, expressions – recognizable in the physiognomic character of the architectural elements". Referring once again to the statement of refurbishment completion provided by Rydon (2016/2017), the discourse of façade is replete with the modernist aspiration of ecologically efficient exterior mirroring efficiently ecologically designed interior living spaces whereby heroism pertains to the application of science and Modern architecture to construct, from the banal and ordinary 1970s' tower block architecture, a building far removed from the archaic, the bygone, unrequited 1970s' utopia of social housing. In the 2016-completed Grenfell Tower refurbished exterior can also be discerned aspects of what Venturi et al. (1977: 129) describe as "ugly and ordinary (U & O) architecture". They describe how designing a feature of a building often involves beginning with similar features that you recognise from other buildings, and they argue, "This approach is symbolically and functionally conventional, but it promotes an architecture of meaning, broader and richer if less dramatic than the architecture of expression" (ibid.). Furthermore, "ugly and ordinary (U&O) architecture ... includes denotative meanings as well, derived from its familiar elements; that is, it suggests more or less concrete meanings via association and past experience". Reflecting on the visual aesthetics of the 2016 refurbished Grenfell Tower building, one can discern a corporate veneer of standardised Fordist production in the aluminium skin of the composite panels used to clad the exterior of the building. The rain screen exterior cladding and accompanying corporate windows appear resonant with an ordinariness of application concerned more with function than aesthetic design and thus initially appear reminiscent of "ugly and ordinary" in that "they are not merely ordinary but represent ordinariness symbolically and stylistically; they are enriching as well, because they add a layer of literary meaning" (ibid.). "Ugly and ordinary" in this sense has value and integrity in its prioritising of function over form; however, Grenfell Tower's external refurbishment provides for a second-order simulacra of "ugly and ordinary" for its denotation as a standardised form mimics the reality of ordinary without exceeding beyond the superior value of "ugly and ordinary" architecture.

Indeed, "ugly and ordinary (U&O) architecture" denotes, in standardised form, elements from previous rationalising architectural traditions; it is apparent that the Grenfell Tower's "civic monumentality" refurbished aesthetic was a grandiose expression of the neoliberal managerialism structure and program that pervaded KCTMO. Grenfell Tower's coruscate aluminium composite panels sandwiched a highly flammable polyethylene core; its ensemble architectural aesthetic conveyed in abstract forms the KCTMO's neoliberal corporatized public management and imposed on the civic deposition of the Grenfell refurbishment project a decorative façade of accomplished neoliberal marketised public management. Through the standardised banality of aluminium panels, a familiarity shone through, radiating a conspicuous sign of managerialist corporate capitalism. A sign language of post-industrial architecture is clearly evident in the formulaic panelling aesthetic of the refurbished Grenfell Tower, this having displaced the transparently industrial savoir-fare of the building's 1970's tower block utility-orientated simple architectural form. Venturi et al. (1977: 162) describe Modern architecture to be bestridden by a "progressive, technological, vernacular, process-orientated, superficially socially concerned, heroic ... content". In attempting to source the emergence of this Modern architectural tradition, they argue, "Our point is that this content did not flow inevitably from the solving of functional problems but arose from Modern architects' unexplicated iconographic preferences and was manifest through a language – several languages – of form, and that formal languages and associated systems are inevitable and good, becoming tyrannies only when we are unconscious of them" (ibid.). Following on from the proposition of the unexplored architectural language, Venturi et al. (1977: 162) emphasise that in Modern architecture there is a propensity to obfuscate that "the content of the unacknowledged symbolism of current Modern architecture is silly. We have been designing dead ducks". Furthermore, and more specifically, they argue:

> When Modern architects righteously abandoned ornament on buildings, they unconsciously designed buildings that were ornament. In promoting Space and Articulation over symbolism and ornament, they distorted the whole building into a duck. They substituted for innocent and inexpensive practice of applied decoration on a conventional shed the rather cynical and expensive distortion of program and structure to promote a duck; minimegastructures are mostly ducks. It is now time to reevaluate the once-horrifying statement of John Ruskin that architecture is the decoration of construction, but we should append the warning of Pugin: It is all right to decorate construction but never construct decoration. (Venturi et al. 1977: 163)

Schumacher's (2010) article "Façadism Returns, or the Advent of the 'Duck-orated Shed'" provides contemporary engagement with the duck Vs decorated shed debate, and in so doing engages even a cursory perusal into the subject area of urban façades with deterrent foreboding. According to Schumacher (ibid. 128), the embedded culture of contemporary architecture is implicitly directed by the ordinance "that a façade ought to fit tightly around its building, like a well-fitting suit"; architectural deviations from this directive risk the derisive acclaim of being "false façades". Postmodernism, according to Schumacher (ibid.), disrupted this rigid modernist aesthetic "so that façades relatively independent of their interiors were encouraged"; and this paradigm shift laid the foundation for the rise "of the neo-modernism of the last two decades [which] has integrated this 'disconnected' façade into the practice of what otherwise is a revival of the system of the heroic period of the movement". Following previous architectural debates "between the 'Duck' and the 'Decorated Shed'", we are informed by Schumacher (ibid. 137) that in contrast to the functionalist banality of the "decorated shed" designed "to take an ordinary, functionally designed building and make it appear more important than its part might imply", the architectural artifice of the "duck", it is said, "goes beyond symbol; it also involves plasticity, and the idea that important spaces, structural relationships and interior hierarchy are projected to the outside and made visible". Schumacher's (ibid.) insights, however, have limited application to the study of Grenfell Tower for they lack a focus on the political and technological context of the architectural façade. Conversely, Esperdy's (2005) analysis of 1930s' USA architectural building practices emphasises "that modernisation embodied a nexus of social, economic, and technological factors that transformed the interaction of architects, manufacturers, and clients, as well as the buildings they produced" (ibid. 25). Esperdy's theoretical framework provides for original insights into a matrix of economic and political themes that propagated the installation of façades rather than new renovation as a response to demands for urban regeneration of residential property during the 1930s Great Depression in the USA. Modernisation provided the construction industry with an expedient resort apposite for a construction industry beset by the short-term uncertainties of financial depression. As Esperdy (ibid. 27) observes: "The onset of the depression ... by the early 1930s modernization was repositioned as a crucial building industry activity, one that would produce jobs, increase demand for materials, and generate economic revival". Expediency appears to have been a particularly attractive feature as "the advantage of modernisation over waiting for the uncertain revival of new construction was that it could accomplish ... goals in the short term because modernization projects typically required less capital, planning, and preparation than new construction – both on the drafting boards and at the building site" (ibid.).

In conjunction with these economic and expedient features, it is the observation of Esperdy (ibid. 36) that the appeal of modernisation as opposed to new constructions during the Great Depression gained traction from a paradigm shift in the discipline of architecture, which became less resistant to modernisation programmes predicated on projects that "consisted principally of exterior work, the replacement or renovation of storefronts and building façades". And this required overcoming hierarchical distinctions concerning the lesser substantive architectural dexterity and proficiency required of modernisation. The derision and lesser acclaim attributed to modernisation supposed that "this was, namely, work that was more visual than spatial in its impact, more ephemeral than permanent in its intentions, and more in tune with the marketplace than the canons of tradition" (ibid.). Consequently, the shift to modernisation required a corollary paradigm shift in architecture. Esperdy (ibid. 38) has documented the political and academic manifestations of the new modernisation paradigm, arguing, "While architects may have initially accepted small-scale commercial modernization projects simply to mitigate the immediate impact of the depression, their work on U.S. Main Street produced something far more consequential – a modernist architecture that, however superficial and ephemeral, was also widespread and accessible". Indeed, Esperdy's (2005) account of 1930s' USA and the preference for modernisation as an antidote for economically insecure short-termism in the construction industry has some comparison with the conditions of urban regeneration in the context of the neoliberal public management contract culture of the Kensington and Chelsea Tenant Management Organisation in 2014-2017 London. As per the conclusions of Venturi et al. (1977: 162), the corporate commerciality of urban gentrified architecture is pervaded by "progressive, technological, vernacular, process-orientated, superficially socially concerned" heroism. It has been a consistent theme of this chapter that the exterior refurbishment of the Grenfell Tower did not primarily inductively derive to address a specific issue of functionality but, rather, as Venturi et al. (ibid.) might similarly have argued, "that this content did not flow inevitably from the solving of functional problems but arose from Modern architects' unexplicated iconographic preferences and was manifest through a language – several languages – of form, and that formal languages and associational systems are inevitable and good, becoming tyrannies only when we are unconscious of them".

Given the vast array of possibilities available to one of London's wealthiest boroughs, how was it ever conceivable to clad the Grenfell Tower in aluminium panels with a highly flammable polyethylene core? Put differently, to what extent did the value for money (VfM) aesthetics of the cladding of the Grenfell Tower become a determinant of value as opposed to an indicator of value? It has been my intention to discern and define the public management culture of the Kensington and Chelsea Tenant Management Organisation's (KCTMO) regeneration of the Grenfell Tower. Through analysis of the KCTMO's planning permission and procurement documents relevant to the refurbishment of the Grenfell Tower, it is unequivocal that a marketised, contract culture perilously pervaded the public sector management of the 2014 procurement, design and refurbishment of the Grenfell Tower.

Timely Reflections

Heating System

The summertime overheating is a symptom of the greater problem of heat loss and therefore energy waste due to the inefficient method of heat distribution throughout the building. When the age/construction of the building façade and likely efficiency of the heating plant is taken into consideration, it is clear that there are significant carbon reductions to be made by refurbishing the façade and heating in a cohesive manner ... Keeping the system renewal confined to spaces that are currently only used for heating and hot water means that the installation of the new system will minimise the disruption to the flats. (RBKC 2012d: 11)

The emergence of neoliberal Conservativism in the late 1970s precipitated a seismic shift towards market-based managerialism in the procurement and delivery of public sector services. Perri 6 and Jeremy Kendall's (1997) *The Contract Culture in Public Services*, referring to the UK's voluntary sector, defines neoliberal public management as evidenced by a contract culture in which "contracting turns the relationship between the state and hundreds of thousands of private and once 'civic' associations from one of gift-giving and community development into a legal matter of service delivery at a price" (ibid. 1). In the market-based nexus of voluntary sector contracting culture, the purchaser-provider dyad reconfigures into quasi-markets relations between users (consumers) and service providers (procurers). As Perri 6 and Kendall (1997: 2) put it: "The power relationships between purchasers, professionals, volunteers and the wellsprings of private voluntary organisation have been reorganised fundamentally. For service users, securing access to services, redress or alternatives are processes that have been entirely transformed". The recurrent analytical conceptual theme of marketised consumerisation in third-sector provision has equivalent trajectories with the rise of neoliberal public management within the local governance of urban regeneration. Indeed, key themes raised by Perri 6 (1997: 181) with regards to the unobtainable goals of contracting policy, detailed in "The new politics of welfare contracting", have applicability to an analysis of the conflictual contradictions that beset the public management of Grenfell Tower's refurbishment. According to Perri 6 (ibid. 182), the most conflicted and discordant "policy goals that contract welfare might be thought to serve are efficiency, innovation, accountability and better targeted distribution of services". *Value for Money Strategy 2014-17* provides a detailed account of the KCTMO's (2017a) intention to achieve "efficiency in service delivery" as the key feature of its four "strategic priorities" (ibid. 3). The

KCTMO's prioritising efficiency is in keeping with neoliberal contractual discourse; indeed, as Perri 6 (1997: 182) observes about welfare contracting: "Economists sometimes like to think of contracting as a 'market-like' mechanism, and begin with a favourable disposition towards it on the grounds that it might promote efficiency". Market-based management discourse invariably aligns a valorisation of efficiency with the presumption that such conditions procreate creative innovative. Indeed, neoliberal managerialism promulgates an entrepreneurial spirit and thrives on belief in its possibilities. As Perri 6 (ibid.) observes with regards to social service provision: "The idea was that contracts would specify what was wanted from, for example, social services in terms of the impact or – in the purchases' jargon – 'outcomes' upon client lives. Then it would be up to contractors to work out the best was to deliver those outcomes". Innovation, it is thought, is stimulated further through the untethering of providers from "the detailed prescription of inputs that have dogged the administration within government" (ibid.). Inherent contradictions limit these aspirations in innovative creativity; first and foremost, political pressures require from government agencies detailed specification of inputs but "in fields such as social services where it is difficult to define the desired outcomes, the scale of the problem is redoubled" (ibid. 183).

When explored further, these incongruencies in a contract-culture mediated delivery of welfare services in terms of efficiency, accountability, innovation and service distribution raise pertinent issues concerning environmental urban ecology and the exterior refurbishment of Grenfell Tower. As stated in the Rydon (2016/2017) brochure, Kensington and Chelsea Tenant Management Organisation secured, with the assistance of Rydon, an "ECO-funding" grant to support ecological features of the refurbishment and regeneration programme. Given that the centrality of the contract culture within the KCTMO appears to have corrupted the integrity of the VfM strategy such that it became a second-order simulacra of its potential, it is evident that a culture of contract acquisition also impacted negatively on the commitment to the environmental principles of the Grenfell Tower refurbishment.

Urban Ecological Façade as an Adsensory Gentrification of Post-industrial Space

Figure 4.2.: "Capitalism survives by forcing the majority, whom it exploits, to define their own interests as narrowly as possible. This was once achieved by extensive deprivation. Today in the developed countries it is being achieved by imposing a false standard of what is and what is not desirable" (John Berger, *Ways of Seeing*, 1972). Photographic Image, Vicinity of Grenfell Tower; Lancaster West Estate, North Kensington, London, June 2017.

Figure 4.3.: "We only see what we look at. To look is an act of choice. As a result of this act, what we see is brought within our reach - though not necessarily within arm's reach. To touch something is to situate oneself in relation to it" (John Berger, *Ways of Seeing*, 1972). Photographic Image, Vicinity of Grenfell Tower; Lancaster West Estate, North Kensington, London, June 2017.

Urban Ecological Façade as an Adsensory Gentrification of Post-industrial Space 163

Figure 4.4.: "Not only personal experience, but also the essential historical experience of our relation to the past: that is to say the experience of seeking to give meaning to our lives, of trying to understand the history of which we can become the active agents" (John Berger, *Ways of Seeing*, 1972). Photographic Image, Vicinity of Grenfell Tower; Lancaster West Estate, North Kensington, London, June 2017.

Figure 4.5.: "A people or a class which is cut off from its own past is far less free to choose and to act as a people or class than one that has been able to situate itself in history" (John Berger, *Ways of Seeing*, 1972). Photographic Image, Vicinity of Grenfell Tower; Lancaster West Estate, North Kensington, London, June 2017.

Urban Ecological Façade as an Adsensory Gentrification of Post-industrial Space

Figure 4.6.: "One may remember or forget these messages but briefly one takes them in, and for a moment they stimulate the imagination by way of either memory or expectation" (John Berger, *Ways of Seeing*, 1972). Photographic Image, Vicinity of Grenfell Tower, Lancaster West Estate, North Kensington, London, June 2017.

Figure 4.7.: "One may remember or forget these messages but briefly one takes them in, and for a moment they stimulate the imagination by way of either memory or expectation" (John Berger, *Ways of Seeing*, 1972). Photographic Image, Vicinity of Grenfell Tower; Lancaster West Estate, North Kensington, London, June 2017.

Figure 4.8.: "One may remember or forget these messages but briefly one takes them in, and for a moment they stimulate the imagination by way of either memory or expectation" (John Berger, *Ways of Seeing*, 1972). Photographic Image, Vicinity of Grenfell Tower; Lancaster West Estate, North Kensington, London, June 2017.

Figure 4.9.: "One may remember or forget these messages but briefly one takes them in, and for a moment they stimulate the imagination by way of either memory or expectation" (John Berger, *Ways of Seeing*, 1972). Photographic Image, Vicinity of Grenfell Tower; Lancaster West Estate, North Kensington, London, June 2017.

Urban Ecological Façade as an Adsensory Gentrification of Post-industrial Space

Figure 4.10.: "One may remember or forget these messages but briefly one takes them in, and for a moment they stimulate the imagination by way of either memory or expectation" (John Berger, *Ways of Seeing*, 1972). Photographic Image, Vicinity of Grenfell Tower; Lancaster West Estate, North Kensington, London, June 2017.

PART THREE

ADSENSORY FINANCIALISATION OF ABSOLUTE BOARDER CONTROLS

Figure P.III.: "Yet this seeing which comes before words, and can never be quite covered by them, is not a question of mechanically reacting to stimuli" (John Berger, *Ways of Seeing*, 1972). Photographic Image, Environmental Activist, Central London, August 2016.

CHAPTER FIVE

GARDEN BRIDGE, RENTIER CAPITAL AS THE ADSENSORY FINANCIALISATION OF URBAN DECAY

Figure 5.1.: "Serving as a bridge between two intense imaginative states" (John Berger *Ways of Seeing*, 1972). Photographic Image, Environmental Activist, Central London, August 2016.

Londoners will, like me, be very angry that London taxpayers have now lost tens of millions of pounds – committed by the previous Mayor [Boris Johnson] on a project that has amounted to nothing. (Sadiq Khan 2017)

"It's my duty to ensure taxpayers' money is spent responsibly" (Khan 2017) commences the tersely charged *Statement from the Mayor on the Closure of the Garden Bridge Trust*, issued Monday 14th August 2017. Precipitately citing Dame Margaret Hodge's (2017) *The Garden Bridge* independent cost evaluation, Mayor of London Sadiq Khan's statement provides a scathing indictment of Boris Johnson's irresponsibly commissioned Garden Bridge project. Khan's incendiary statement of closure accentuates an astonishing revelation elucidated by *The Garden Bridge* report – the project had an irreconcilable "funding gap of over £70 million, potentially unlimited costs to London taxpayers to fund the bridge in the future, systemic failing in the procurement process" compounded by "decisions not being driven by value for money" (Khan 2017). Clearly exasperated by the lavish improvident extravagance of the Garden Bridge project, Khan's (ibid.) statement heroically exclaims "I could not permit a single penny more of London taxpayers' money being spent on it". In response, the Garden Bridge Trust issued a contrite resignation establishing that the charity's intention to build what amounted to an artificial green park space across the River Thames has ceased to be a viable proposition and that they were "winding up the project" (Garden Bridge Trust 2017). Barely able to camouflage its disaccord, the Garden Bridge Trust (ibid.) nonchalantly personalises the root incongruity thus: "On 28 April, Sadiq Khan wrote to Lord Mervyn Davies, Chairman of the Garden Bridge Trust, stating that he was not prepared to sign the guarantee for the annual maintenance costs of the Bridge, a condition of planning consent, despite previous assurances given about his support for the project". The aphoristic displacement of the unviability of project is also endured by the syndicate of financiers: "Unfortunately, the benefactor concerned and the Trustees have all concluded that they cannot proceed with what was always designed to be a public project in the heart of the capital without the support of the Mayor of London" (ibid.). In full retreat from any hint of harbouring blame, the statement concludes: "The Garden Bridge project will now be formally closed. This includes terminating contracts, and concluding donor funding agreements. The Trust itself will then be wound up in accordance with the Companies Acts" (ibid.). The central objective of this chapter's case study of the Garden Bridge project is to formulate an ecological framework so as to ascertain the significance of adsensory financialisation to the privatisation of the urban ecology of riverside recreational spaces.

Brief History of the Garden Bridge: Past, Present and Fated Future

Living Bridges (Murray and Stevens 1996) consummately curates 1996 Royal Academy exhibition competition entries for an animated bridge spanning the River Thames. The corrivalry was entitled: Thames Water Habitable Bridge Competition. Antoine Grumbach's Garden Bridge excelled with a stellar array of eminent pedigrees. *Living Bridges* provides a concise annotation of Grumbach's Garden Bridge in terms of its aesthetic, design and location. Emblematically situated "in the bend of the River Thames", Grumbach's portent Garden Bridge was designed to traverse "the two banks of the river with a series of gardens placed on either side of a covered arcade" (Murray and Stevens 1996: 140). Versatile flexibility pervades Grumbach's Garden Bridge architectural design; "conceived as a structure able to accommodate a variety of functions which can change over time" (ibid.). Closer inspection of the architectural design operationalises the principal features of "variety" and "change" for the proposed Garden Bridge was comprised of three elements. The southern reaches of the structure harboured a capacious canopy called the "World's Culture Greenhouse", a public space for dining, retailing and live music concerts, flexibly configured for any number of public activities (ibid.). The gateway to the bridge level is arrived at via interior and exterior staircases, an escalator and elevator vehicles. The garden composition themes the water level access for situated at either side of the greenhouse are "broad walks" which furnish connections between the garden bridge and the river foreshore/bank. Located between the World's Culture Greenhouse and the bridge's towers is the Garden Arcade; all three elements of the Garden Bridge structure effusively embody the en plein air design as they open directly onto the bridge's expanse of the river (ibid.). The envisioned residential space includes a hotel and apartments alongside restaurants and conclaves for the confluence of individuals; all pre-eminently crowned as greenhouses on the roof of the Hanging Gardens Towers, which sustain the cables reinforcing the suspended range of the Garden Bridge. Façades adorning the exterior of the towers "are covered with a double metal skin which supports the vertical garden" and "the crowns of the towers are adorned with two winged shapes which evoke flight toward the 3rd Millennium" (ibid.). To surmise the principal distinction of Antoine Grumbach's Garden Bridge, it comprises a triumvirate of habitat: World's Culture Greenhouse; Garden Arcade; and Hanging Garden Towers. Indeed, these structural elements provide much verification of the credence of originality ascribed to Thomas Heatherwick's 2014 Garden Bridge for in

2014, Lambeth Planning Applications Committee published an approved planning application submitted by the Garden Bridge Trust in which the following proposal application for a garden bridge was made:

Proposal Application(s)

Erection of a pedestrian bridge with incorporated garden, extending for a length of 366m over the River Thames from land adjacent to The Queen's Walk on South Bank (in the London Borough of Lambeth) to land above and in the vicinity of Temple London Underground Station on the North Bank (in the City of Westminster), the structure of the bridge having a maximum height of 14.3m above Mean High Water and a maximum width of 30m; the development also comprising the erection of 2 new piers in the River Thames; erection of a single-storey landing building (incorporating maintenance, management and welfare facilities and up to 410sqm A1, A3 and/or D1 floorspace with additional ancillary service and plant) on land adjacent to The Queen's Walk, opposite the ITV building; associated public realm works, works to trees (including the removal of trees); associated construction work (including laying out of a construction access from Upper Ground) and works sites; and works within the River Thames (including temporary and permanent scour protection, relocation of moorings and erection of temporary structures).
…

Recommendation(s)

Resolve to approve the application, subject to conditions and to any direction as may be received following, further referral to the Mayor of London and the Secretary of State.

(Lambeth Planning 2014: 2)

Planning applications are characteristically officious statements yet the compendium of the Garden Bridge Trust's application exudes the audacious grandiosity, seductive charm and impractical visionary that framed much of the Garden Bridge project. Thus, with an astonishing privation of pragmatism, the Executive Summary apprises: "The application proposes a 366m pedestrian bridge, with incorporated garden, spanning the River Thames, landing on the roof of Temple Underground station on the north side and on The Queen's Walk (in front of the ITV building) on the south side" (Lambeth Planning 2014: 5). Lavishing praise on the applicant (Garden Bridge Trust), we are informed that the planning application was successfully subject to a Planning Performance Agreement, which the applicant assailed. Less transparent in the Executive Summary is the fraction and contestation precipitated by the urban ecological threat presented by the proposed Garden Bridge; and the concern raised about financialised capital privatising yet another enclave of public recreation. Rather, the planning application executive summary nonchalantly self-satiated on the meagre instances of local community consultations; apparently "The planning application has been advertised by way of letters to local residents, site notices and a newspaper advert" (ibid.). Robust full consultation, as per statutory planning procedure, was obviously in evidence but here again the reportage lacked nuanced insights in its preference for a prefabricated narrative of local community acquiesces. Axiomatic with this lack of detailing is the rather blithe statement: "The Local Planning Authority (LPA) has received extensive response to the planning application, all of which has been given consideration prior to making this recommendation" (ibid.). The recourse to absolutes invariably infers the unviability of limits and thus prompts ambivalence. And even the most cursory of perusals in and around the proposed location of the Garden Bridge visually alerted the observer to a disquiet palpably simmering among the local community.

Nevertheless, the planning application executive summary endeavours to masquerade discontent, as is evident in the following rhetorical moderation: "Public responses (i.e., not from statutory consultees) have been largely mixed, with a large number supporting and a large number opposing the bridge for various reasons" (ibid.). Conspicuously less moderation is applied to the extraordinary aggrandisement of the urban ecological reassurance of the Garden Bridge. "Iconic nature of the design" brazenly reads the superlative invocation of equivalences rendering "new" as spectacularly modern, progressive and preferred. Modernism is indeed the blithe leitmotif pirouetting through such statements as: "The iconic nature of the design, the new viewpoints it will create and the inherent attractiveness of a high quality landscaped open space will create a popular visitor attraction that will support London's world city role" (ibid.). Modernist perspectivism, complete with its centralising apex, rationalisation and hierarchies of power, features incisively in John Berger's (1972/1977) *Ways of Seeing*. According to Berger (ibid. 16), perspective centralises space into series of gradients converging at an apex, point and/or absolute. Such aspiration is evident in propositions exalting that the Garden Bridge "will add to the existing network of cultural and tourist attractions on the South Bank as well as provide an alternative route to these facilities from the Underground network" (Lambeth Planning 2014: 5). The perspectivist methodology continues unabated in the following statement: "The proposal will enhance London's Green Grid, linking existing open spaces north and south of the River as well as improving options for walking in the City" (ibid.). Berger (1972/1977: 16) identifies how "perspective makes the single eye the centre of the visible world. Everything converges on to the eye as to the vanishing point of infinity". Axiomatic with the pursuit of absolute axes in space and time is the disregard for contextual embodied relational care for other and the environment. Only by assuming a disembodied perspective can one legitimately justify the spatial cleansing of heritage trees as a proportionate loss in a new urban ecological vista, as is evident in the following statement:

> The loss of open space on the South Bank and removal of a number of mature trees is outweighed by significant amount of new planting and urban greening. In each of these regards the development delivers against a number of objectives set out within the Development Plan and is supported in a number of policy terms. (Lambeth Planning 2014: 5)

Referring to Berger's (1972/1977: 16) *Ways of Seeing*, the philosophical perspective harbours earth-defying aspirations analogous to celestial heights for "The visible world is arranged for the spectator as the universe was once thought to be arranged for God". Herein resides a paradox because "According to the convention of perspective there is no visual reciprocity. There is no need for god to situate himself in relation to others: he is himself the situation" (ibid.). Absolutist in its erasing of the South Bank's heritage tree vista, the Garden Bridge proposal unashamedly assumed Providence, rationalised as urban regeneration, but the design falls foul of perspectivism's paradox, as defined by Berger (ibid.): "The inherent contradiction in perspective was that it structured all images of reality to address a single spectator who, unlike God, could only be in one place at a time".

Finance capital operates as a convivial obligato, fervently mediating capitalism's harnessing of visual perspective to its privatisation of public recreational space. Unsurprisingly, the executive summary of the Garden Bridge planning application interconnects gentrification with "economic benefits"; and in so doing reve'ls in finance capitalism's plethora of prepossessing local authority budgetary gains. Meagre offerings of compensation inevitably rally the chagrin of dispossessed communities; and thus pledges of "contribution towards the Waterloo Opportunity Area's development potential" (Lambeth Planning 2014: 5) in conjunction with short-term construction work opportunities paled into insignificance compared with the unashamed spectacle of private sector finance gains that would be realised by privatising the public recreational spaces north and south banks of the River Thames. Thus, unsurprisingly, the coruscating finance capital spectacle overshadowed the Garden Trust's woefully exiguous attempt at cultivating advocacy within the local community via a third sector volunteer programme described as follows: "The Garden Bridge Trust is also committed to a volunteer programme, which would provide local people with an opportunity to gain valuable skills and experience in horticulture" (Lambeth Planning 2014: 5). It remains a paradox as to why a project that alleged ecology as its principal distinction consistently disenchanted as it languished against sustaining the existing urban ecology of the north and south river banks.

Nevertheless, and seemingly oblivious to this latter scenario, the Garden Bridge Trust propelled its privatisation agenda through increasingly opaque façades of community-centred gentrification. Of particular interest are the eco-tourist elements of the proposed venture for these elements reverberate neoliberalist financialising intervention. Neoliberalism refers to socio-economic political agenda of marketised privatisation, philosophically substrated by possessive individualising home economicus rationality. Within the sociology of tourism, critical theorists have identified an increasing propensity for neoliberalist market relations to provision eco-touristic ventures, an exemplary is this critical theorist writing is West and Carrier (2004). The resulting "conjunction in ecotourism of the environment and the market" manifests a multitude of exploitative relations of capital and labour (ibid. 484). Particularly disconcerting is a form of land enclosure through the inscription and imposition of Eurocentric "virtualism" onto eco-touristic space (ibid. 485). Prior to defining this process, consider the following extracts of the Garden Bridge Trust planning application; the first derives from the executive summary and the second derives from the main body of the report:

> In the circumstances it is considered that the Garden Bridge would align neatly with Core Strategy Policy PN1 (Waterloo). The bridge would enhance the South Bank in its role as an international leisure centre and a London tourist destination. It would also deliver additional open space for public use as part of a network of pedestrian routes and spaces. The bridge would also: contribute positively to the leisure, recreation and tourist offer of the Central Activities Zone in accordance with Core Strategy Policy S3, promote walking in line with Core Strategy Policy S4; and increase the quantity, quality and accessibility to open space in accordance with Core Strategy Policy S5. (Lambeth Planning 2014: 5)

> The Garden Bridge would have economic benefits for both the south and north banks of the river. On the South Bank the increase in footfall would

benefit existing businesses. There would also be an associated increase in tourism revenues as a result of the Garden Bridge being a tourist attraction. There would also be a significant increase in footfall and pedestrian activity on the North Bank area as the Garden Bridge would complete a missing link between the South Bank and areas to the north such as Covent Garden and the Temple. The Garden Bridge could be a mayor catalyst for change that would lead to an increase in new business activity in the area. (Lambeth Planning 2014: 29-30)

Applying West and Carrier's (2004: 485) concept of "virtualism" makes evident limitations in the model of leisured eco-tourism proposed by the Garden Bridge venture. According to West and Carrier (ibid.), axiomatic with the intervention of neoliberal financialised capital into eco-tourism is a propensity to model the environment according to Western aesthetic ideas; extending beyond marketing and advertising this "virtualism" is a feature of institutional structures, policies, practices and governance (ibid.). Western Eurocentric "virtualism" is clearly in operation with regard to the Garden Bridge Trust's simulacra of a real (albeit discontinuous with the existing local biodiversity) leisure space modelled on the Western capitalist theme park; which might be described as confirming "to the virtual reality defined by important Western models of society and nature" (ibid.).

Concepts such as "virtual reality" as introduced by West and Carrier (ibid.) refer less to the computer-mediated experience of situating the spectator in a cinematic scene and more in this instance to the "reshaping" of landscapes to coincide with Western aesthetic environmental idealism. Acknowledging this, I concur with West and Carrier (ibid.) – where "virtualism" is evident in eco-tourism, this will inevitably undermine the prerequisite to prioritise nature. Specifically, "This reshaping underlies … an important contradiction in ecotourism: its tendency to lead not to the preservation of valued ecosystems but to the creation of landscapes that conform to important Western idealizations of nature through a market-oriented nature politics" (ibid.). Such sentiment aptly describes the intended leisure theme park modelling of the Garden Bridge and the framing of its use of its recreational space; for its Western leisure theme park proffered a distortion of a public recreational non-commercialised independently creative river bank space. But in order to circumvent mystifying the erstwhile of this river space, it is necessary to examine further the particular visual culture proffered by the Garden Bridge project against the historical vista of the South Bank for "if we can see the present clearly enough, we shall ask the right questions of the past" (Berger 1972/1977: 16). To its credit, the Garden Bridge planning application engaged consistently with the seismic reconfiguration of the South Bank river vista proposed. Detrimental to this strategy is its unwavering perspectivist virtualism and concomitant disregard for the local community and wider public commitment to the indigenous biodiversity of the south and north river bank; for example, consider the nonchalant deprecation of the historical riverbank vista evident in the following extract:

> The Bridge will undoubtedly occupy a conspicuous position in views up and down stream. It will become part of the setting of, and be visible in views from, a number of designated heritage assets. The Bridge, which is intended to be densely planted at a low level with some taller tree planting, would present as a picturesque incident in the riverscape – it's planting spilling out to the existing mature tree planting on both the North and South banks. Its low slung and restrained architecture and engineering will undoubtedly change the character of existing views, both from the river bank and buildings along the river bank and the varied planting will catch the eye in such views. However, the introduction of the bridge, the detailed design and the approaches to it from the river bank will change but will cause less than substantial harm to the setting of, and views to and from the riverscape and historic assets of identified importance – especially when considering that views from the bridge itself will enhance or better reveal the significance of highly significant heritage assets.
>
> (Lambeth Planning 2014: 5)

Seemingly oblivious of the incongruity of an obstruction to a heritage vista promising to "enhance or better reveal the significance of highly significant heritage assets", the planning application proceeds to presage a sensory experience equally flawed in its ahistorical abstract empiricism. Indeed, my concept of adsensory urban ecology is particularly apposite in application here for the body features as both object and subject of advertising technologies integral to the financialised privatisation of urban public recreation space. An illustration of this adsensory technology in practice is evident in the following extract:

> The planting strategy for the garden comprises five character areas; pioneer, wild glade, scarp, cultivated glade and leafy which transition across the bridge. The diverse colours, smells and textures of plants will provide visitors with a stimulating experience as they navigate through the garden. Overall it is considered that the layout, planting and materials used on the deck of the bridge would create an attractive and inspiring environment; a place people will want to visit and enjoy. (Lambeth Planning 2014: 5)

Incongruent paradoxes pervade this description of sensory experience and being for "it is seeing which establishes our place in the surrounding world; we explain that world with words, but words can never undo the fact that we are surrounded by it" (Berger 1972/1977: 7). It is because "the relation between what we see and what we know is never settled" (ibid.) that the Garden Bridge's arbitrary and absolutist imposition of aesthetic meaning and sensory experience is so irascible in its imperious pretensions. Fascinatingly, the local community, faced with an extraordinarily supercilious disdain for indigenous urban ecology, mobilised the immediacy of their experience of this pending corruption of the river bank's sensory ambience. In retrospect, civility in response to disruption of the body's manifestation of habitus (Bourdieu 1990/2017) and its sense of belonging in space, time and place is unsurprising, especially when we appreciate Berger's (1972/1977: 8) statement thus:

> Yet this seeing which comes before words, and can never be quite covered by them, is not a question of mechanically reacting to stimuli. (It can only be thought of in this way if one isolates the small part of the process which concerns the eye's retina.) We only see what we look at. To look is an act of choice. As a result of this act, what we see is brought within our reach – though not necessarily within arm's reach. To touch something is to situate oneself in relation to it. (Berger 1972/1977: 8)

The latter statement is particularly pertinent here for in its absolutist virtualism, the Garden Bridge was an inherently ahistorical, detached and disengaged imposition on the heritage of London's South Bank vista exacerbated by an intentioned privatised exclusive which would render it remote for local communities. Accepting that "to touch something is to situate oneself in relation to it" (ibid.), it is axiomatic that enclosure is also an affront on the sense of place of belonging. Indeed, the intention to spatially privatise the Garden Bridge sensory experience is evident in the following extract:

> The bridge would be open to the public all year with the exception of an agreed number of days where fundraising or community events may be held on the bridge. The Environment Assessment (EA) predicts 7 million visitors annually, with peak weekday demand of 4,000 people (between 5pm and 6pm) and 5,000 people on a Saturday (between 5pm and 6pm). Overall, both Lambeth and TFL Transport Planners consider the trip generation assessments to be generally sound. However, this is a unique proposal for which there is no precedent to make comparisons against. It is very clear therefore that a very robust, comprehensive and response Operational

> Management plan is going to be needed to ensure the project is a successful one in terms of visitor experience that maintains its attraction to all users.

(Lambeth Planning 2014: 6)

Despite suggestions seemingly to the contrary, the visual, olfactory, haptic sensory encounter proffered by the Garden Bridge, where privatised, would only afford a singularity of perspective for its artificial images were destined to be "a sight" in which, "recreated or reproduced", its "appearances or set of appearances" had become "detached from the place and time in which it first made its appearance and preserved" (Berger 1972/1977: 9-10). Indeed, "every image embodies a way of seeing" (ibid.) and this observation is particularly pertinent to the contrived urban ecology of the Garden Bridge. Yet, this is not to ascribe to visual culture an anarchic descent into chaotic relativism for "although every image embodies a way of seeing, our perception or appreciation of an image depends also upon our own way of seeing" (ibid. 10). Virtualist in its perspectivist aesthetic, the Garden Bridge offered "a direct testimony about the world" (ibid.) of financialised market capitalist real estate. Nowhere is this more evident than with regards to the privatisation of profit and democratisation of the Garden Bridge's maintenance. Indications of alleged subterfuge and devious machinations in the Garden Bridge planning permission document were in plain sight, whereby responsibility for maintenance was conspicuously obviated. For example, the document states:

> Subject to responsible and robust management and maintenance, there is no reason to suggest that the bridge will not be successful in terms of visitor experience that maintains its attraction to all users. A draft Operations Management Plan has been provided by the Trust. Through their commitment to consultative and collaborative working with key stakeholders and landowners, LBL, officers are confident that within the next three years before opening the Trust will be able to work up a final plan that suitably addresses the extensive visitor and operations management requirements of the bridge. The final Operations Management Plan will need to be formerly agreed by both Lambeth and Westminster before the bridge can open, at which point Lambeth can ensure it is fit for purpose – having full regard to the existing knowledge and expertise of Stakeholders on the South Bank.

(Lambeth Planning 2014: 6)

After inevitably achieving approval for its 2014 planning permission application, preconstruction costs rapidly initiated a domino effect of tumbling financial insecurities. Limited public records afford partial insight into the plummeting crevice into which public funding was lavishly cascaded. In a letter dated 25th May 2016, written by Rt. Hon. Patrick McLoughlin MP (2016), who was then the secretary of state for transport, highly questionable justifications were given to Philip Rutnam (permanent secretary, department for transport) "to increase the department's preconstruction commitment to the Garden Bridge by up to £15m". Judging from the letter, it was received wisdom that increases to the preconstruction costs of the Garden Bridge would expose the exchequer to a substantial amount of risk. It is also discernible from the letter that the secretary of state for transport had received analyses describing "the transport benefits of the Garden Bridge as quite limited" (ibid.). Swiftly dismissing these salutary forebodings, insistence is propagated on "the wider benefits to the government's agenda and to the London economy" of the Garden Bridge while admitting that these are "not fully captured by the department's assessment" (ibid.). Virtualism features opulently in the secretary of state's justification for the increased preconstruction commitment; threadbare clichéd facile stereotypes of the Garden Bridge as an "iconic tourist attraction right in the heart of our capital city", a catalyst "helping the UK tourism industry grow" while expeditiously contributing "to some of DfT's own policy objectives, including promoting walking and physical activity" (ibid.). Virtualism constitutes a dimension of the rhetorical structure of the argument for the substantive threat of non-compliance is manifest in the secretary of state's formidable declaration "that a failure to increase our preconstruction commitment to the Bridge will lead to a high risk of the project being cancelled by its Trustees" (ibid.). Sabre-rattling menacing forebodings of cancellation featured frequently as a rhetorical façade to obfuscate questions to the contrary as public funds were hurled into the preconstruction commitment for the Garden Bridge, some illustration of which is provided in the following extracts of correspondence between Philip Rutnam (permanent secretary/transport) and Patrick McLoughlin (secretary of state/transport) in which the former (PAC 2016: 12) is seeking ministerial guidance from the latter on the topic of Garden Bridge risk to taxpayers' money:

Department of Transport
From the Permanent Secretary
[To] Rt Hon Patrick McLoughlin MP
24 May 2016
Secretary of State
Department for Transport

Dear Secretary of State,

Commercially Sensitive – The Garden Bridge

...

As you will know, the Chancellor announced as part of the 2013 Autumn Statement on 5 December 2013 that the Government would commit £30m of funding to support the development and construction of the Garden Bridge. The funding was to be made available by this Department subject to there being a satisfactory business case for the project. After examining the business case for the project in summer 2014, my judgement was that the transport benefits of the project were limited and came with a relatively high level of risk to value for money. However, on the balance of probabilities I considered that this risk was acceptable, and therefore that the department's funding contribution to the project could be made (subject to appropriate controls) without needing to seek a direction from you.

One important control on the DfT's contribution is a cap on the amount that can be spent prior to construction. This was originally set at £8.2m, but it has since twice been agreed to increase the cap following requests from the Garden Bridge Trust, and it now stands at a little under £13.5m. The Trust has now asked for a further increase in its permitted preconstruction spending up to £15m (across DfT and TfL combined). This is to underwrite the potential cancellation liabilities that it now will face if the project does not proceed. The Trustees have been advised that under charity law they could become personally liable for the Trust's unmet financial obligations if they have failed to manage risk prudently.

Following recent discussions with the Mayor of London, DfT has been asked to increase its preconstruction exposure by up to £15m to underwrite the potential cancellation liabilities. The probability of these liabilities materialising is not negligible, as there remain a number of significant risks to the delivery of the project. These include long-standing difficulties in obtaining all the required land on the south bank of the Thames. At the time of writing these have not been resolved (and this letter is marked as Commercially Sensitive as its contents could weaken the Trust's position in the ongoing negotiations). The Trust also needs to raise more than £40m in new donations over and above those already paid or pledged in order to fund the bridge in full, and we cannot be certain that it will be able to do so.

...

For this reason, I am seeking a formal direction from you in order to approve a further increase in the Department's preconstruction commitment to the Garden Bridge. Although the preconstruction 'cap' has been increased in the past, I consider that it is right to seek a direction in this instance, as both the size and increase (15m) and the reason for it (underwriting potential cancellation liabilities, rather than funding ongoing development work) are materially different to what has gone before.

...

Yours Sincerely
Philip Rutnam

(PAC 2016: 12)

Department for Transport
[To] Philip Rutnam
Permanent Secretary
Department for Transport
33 Horseferry Road
25 May 2016
London
SW1P 4DR

Dear Philip,

Thank you for your letter. This is to confirm that I am formally directing you as Accounting Officer to increase the department's preconstruction commitment to the Garden Bridge by up to £15m.

...

Your letter described the transport benefits of the Garden Bridge as quite limited, but I consider that the wider benefits to the government's agenda and to the London economy are significant, and not fully captured by the department's assessment.

The Garden Bridge will become a key and iconic tourist attraction right in the heart of our capital city, helping the UK tourism industry to grow. It will also contribute to some of DfT's own policy objectives, including promoting walking and physical activity.

I also note that a failure to increase our preconstruction commitment to the Bridge will lead to a high risk of the project being cancelled by its Trustees. Cancellation would lead to the public sector's already committed contribution to the bridge (in excess of £35m) being effectively written-off. Providing the additional commitment requested will maximise the likelihood of the government securing value from the investment already made.

In light of these factors I believe there are sufficient reasons for issuing you with a direction to increase the department's preconstruction commitment to the Garden Bridge by up to £15m.

I note that you will copy our exchange of letters to the Comptroller and Auditor General, and to the Treasury Officer of Accounts.

Yours Sincerely,
Rt. Hon. Patrick McLoughlin MP

(PAC 2016: 13-14)

Evidently it was the opinion of senior politicians that revenue from tourism coupled with ample cost benefits derived from event hosting provided enough basis for substantive increases in public sector taxpayers' preconstruction financial investment in the Garden Bridge. Such confidence in tourism and recreational service provision revenue seems paradoxically naïve given Philip Rutnam's (PAC 2016: 12) commercially sensitive disclosure that the Garden Bridge Trust was struggling with "long-standing difficulties in obtaining all the required land on the south bank of the Thames".

Publicly Accounting for Touristic Virtualism; Garden Bridge Value for Money?

Principal to the objectives of the Dame Margaret Hodge (2017a) *Garden Bridge Review* was to interrogate the value for money of public investment in the Garden Bridge project. Reportedly, and according to the Public Accounts Committee (PAC), by October 2016, "£60 million of public money [had] been pledged to the proposed £185 million footbridge: £30 million from central government and £30 million from Transport for London" (Commons Select Committee, PAC 2016). Refusing to take a position on the merits of the Garden Bridge project yet expressing scepticism on its value for taxpayers' money, in October 2016, PAC collated ministerial correspondence, questions to relevant civil servants in the Garden Bridge decision-making process and other documents so as to present a Public Accounts Committee (PAC) dossier of the Garden Bridge project. A framework for the dossier is presented in the form of a timeline of PAC's official encounters with the Garden Bridge, "including correspondence regarding a ministerial direction to increase the Department for Transport's preconstruction commitment to the project" (ibid.). Described by Meg Hillier MP (Chair, Committee of Public Accounts) as a "chain of evidence we've considered around the project and the Department for Transport grant" (PAC 2016: 1), the dossier provides nuanced evidence of how prospects for tourism and private event hosting were repeatedly mobilised to persuade increased public sector funding and obfuscate liability for the mounting risk to taxpayers' money. Working through the dossier's transcripts of the PAC engagements with the Garden Bridge project during the 2015-2016 Parliament session, the following are prime instances of the latter issue whereby projected tourism and cultural attraction revenue was (at best) naively or (at worst) politically mobilised as justification for increased public sector taxpayers' preconstruction investment in the Garden Bridge project.

According to the PAC (2016: 5-8) committee meeting transcription, on 17th October 2016, Tom Scholar (permanent secretary at the Treasury) provided oral evidence to the Public Accounts Committee on the topic of value for money and the Garden Bridge project. Scholar was asked to outline the assurances received by the Treasury prior to promising £30 million of central government public sector money to the Garden Bridge project. In response, Tom Scholar refers to an obligation to fulfil prior established commitments made by a previous administration in 2013; having apparently undertaken a "thorough analysis of the business case by the Department for Transport" (ibid. 5). Furthermore, the 2013 business case presented "a range of benefits that could be delivered by this project" (ibid.). It is notable that Tom Scholar had only recently been appointed, in 2016, as permanent secretary of the Treasury and thus was beholden to relay second-hand retrospect accounts of decision-making. This becomes significant when he is asked to account for why the Garden Bridge project was assigned to the Department for Transport as this required (re)defining the principal remit of the Department. Thus it is significant that Tom Scholar replies: "I am not sure which way round that goes, but since it is a bridge, I think the decision was taken that its primary purpose is transport-related" (ibid. 6). The Chair's sleight-of-hand response confirms – and belittles – Tom Scholar's importune definition of the remit of the Department for Transport: "Okay. Note to everyone: bridges always come under the Department for Transport. I have to remember that for the future" (ibid.). Curiously, and prior to further discussion of the business case, the Chair enquires whether the maintenance cost for the Garden Bridge would be "funded by the taxpayer"; to which Tom Scholar categorically replies: "No. The commitment, as I understand it, is to the construction costs, with the guarantee that you referred to as well. That is the total public exposure, or the total Government exposure" (ibid.). Within a year, Tom Scholar's response would prove formidably prophetic as the Garden Bridge Trust would declare the cessation of the project on the basis that responsibility for the Garden Bridge's maintenance was in actuality an irreconcilable quandary. But, returning to the issue of tourism and its positioning as part of the business case for the Garden Bridge as value for money, the Chair of the Public Accounts Committee sitting in which Tom Scholar provided oral evidence on 17 October 2016 enquired about the principles of a costing model adapted from the tourism sector, used to cost cultural attractions, and applied to the prospecting of costs for the Garden Bridge. The Chair states:

> Q9 Chair: Going back to the business case, I appreciate that the Department for Transport was the sponsoring Department, but as the spending watchdog within Government the Treasury surely had some sight of this. In the business case, the Garden Bridge Trust said that about 70% of the cost would come from donations. I am referring to a report about the operational viability of the garden bridge – a review of the draft operations and maintenance business plan – from March 2016 by someone called Dan Anderson, a director at Fourth Street. It was published in July this year. I don't know whether you are aware of this document.
>
> Tom Scholar: I have not seen the document, no.
>
> Q19 Chair: Okay. I can pass a copy to you. Let me quote from the relevant part. It is talking about getting 70% of the benefit from donations from the private sector. On page 5 of the report, it says: 'All the same, it is worth noting that while voluntary income represents between 10% and 30% of total income at cultural attractions like Tate, V&A, Science Museum, Kew and the Royal Parks, it amounts to almost 70% of projected income for the Garden Bridge'. On the face of it, do you think that makes a good business case for the Government to let taxpayers' money be spent on?
>
> (Public Accounts Committee [PAC] 2016: 6)

While it is significant that the Garden Bridge's cost risk liability balance sheet was encumbered by a 70% reliance on "voluntary income" from the private sector, it is deeply troubling that the private sector investors pledged millions based on the uncertain conditionality of projective tourism and corporate event hosting with seemingly little regard for the simmering quarrel over maintaining the Garden Bridge. That the latter was becoming an issue of irreconcilable contention was evident in the later sections of Tom Scholar's oral testimony, at which point the Chair gave way to Kevin Foster as interviewer. Tom Scholar was asked:

> Q12 Kevin Foster: Mr Scholar, a moment ago in response to a question about maintenance you said that the taxpayer is only liable for the construction cost. Who is liable for the ongoing maintenance of this bridge, if it is built?
>
> Tom Scholar: Again, I can just tell you what my understanding is, and I will check the position afterwards.

Chair: We recognise that you are not the biggest expert on the Garden Bridge.

Tom Scholar: My understanding is that the trust is responsible for that.
Q13 Kevin Foster: Given that the likely length of time for bridge maintenance is in decades rather than years, what would happen if the trust was unable in future years to raise cash?

Tom Scholar: There is a guarantee, which the Chair referred to a few moments ago, that relates to the possible cancellation costs in the event that the project does not go ahead.

Q14 Kevin Foster: Let us assume it is built. It would then need ongoing maintenance. If the trust was not able to fund that, given that we are talking about decades of maintenance, who would the liability fall to for a bridge over the Thames?

Tom Scholar: I think in that case the responsibility would fall to Transport for London, as the authority with the responsibility for implementing this.

(Public Accounts Committee [PAC] 2016: 6)

In a letter, dated 22nd June 2016, from Ali Morgan (Private Secretary to the Comptroller and Auditor General) to Meg Hillier MP (Chair, Committee of Public Accounts) and entitled "Garden Bridge – Ministerial Direction", the issue of construction cost liabilities was more clearly established and some concern regarding the uncertainties of tourism revenue was expressed. Specifically, and with regards to construction costs, it was stated that:

> I know you are familiar with the Garden Bridge, a project led by the Garden Bridge Trust, a charity working with Transport for London (TfL). In his letter to the Secretary of State, Philip Rutnam sets out the brief history of the Department's commitment to the Garden Bridge project. In essence the Chancellor, through the Department, committed to provide funding of £30 million from TfL's budget. The remaining funding – to meet an expected total project cost of around £175 million – is due to be raised from private sources.

(Public Accounts Committee [PAC] 2016: 6)

Referring to an earlier correspondence between Rt Hon Patrick McLoughlin MP (Secretary of State Department of Transport) and Philip Rutnam (Permanent Secretary Department for Transport), Ali Morgan questions the former's assertion that projected tourism revenue realistically provided support or justification for agreement to increase the public sector's preconstruction investment in the Garden Bridge. Ali Morgan specifically states that:

> On 25 May 2016 the Secretary of State for Transport, Patrick McLoughlin MP formally directed … Philip Rutnam to increase the Department's preconstruction commitment to the Garden Bridge project by up to £15 million. In doing so, he cites 'wide reasons' for continuing to support the project, including tourism benefits. He also justifies the increase in the Department's commitment on the grounds that without it, there is a higher likelihood that the project would be cancelled by the trustees, leading to a write off of £35 million of public funds spent to date. From a value for money perspective, we would share the Accounting Officer's concerns about advancing further funds where there is diminishing confidence in the project proceeding, notwithstanding that there are sunk costs. It therefore is appropriate that in considering his responsibilities under *Managing Public Money* the Accounting officer did not consider sunk costs in his assessment of the risks to value for money presented by further financial commitment to the project.
>
> (Public Accounts Committee [PAC] 2016: 10)

In a document entitled "Key features and timeline of the Garden Bridge project", PAC (2016: 17) provides a detailed chronology of key public sector funding commitments made from the inception of the Garden Bridge project. At first sight the funding structure is reasonably straightforward. It had been agreed that the Garden Bridge funding was principally an undertaking of the charity The Garden Bridge Trust; to this was committed "contributions of £30m from TfL directly and £30m from the Department for Transport (via an increase in the TfL block grant)" (ibid.). It was forecast that the aggregate construction cost for the Garden Bridge was approximately £180m, which would mean that the £120m outstanding from the £60m public sector funding was "to be sourced from private financing (including donations)" (ibid.). Tracing back to the initial announcement of public sector funding for the project, it is documented that the government's earliest proclamation pledge of £30m funding to the Garden Bridge was "in December 2013 in HM Treasury's National Infrastructure Plan" (ibid.). Documented communication between the Chancellor of the Exchequer and the Mayor of London established confirmation that the funding was contingent on several circumstances; integral amongst these was, firstly, the construction of a business case in accordance with the "Government investment appraisal guidance"; and secondly "that the value for money requirements are met" (ibid.). In May 2014, TfL assembled a Strategic Outline Business Case with the authority of the Garden Bridge Trust –

which the TfL business plan sought to accurately represent. It is stated that the TfL Business Case "assessed a benefit/cost ratio (BCR) for the Garden Bridge of 5.8, assuming a public contribution limited to £60 million" (ibid.). In July 2014, the TfL Business Case progressed through to the Department for Transport's Board Investment and Commercial Committee (BICC) so as to achieve detailed evaluation. Scrutiny of the TfL Business Case yielded features of key concern: (1) "the uncertainty of the value for money case", with apprehension focusing acutely "on the point of the extent to which the benefits expected would be achieved"; (2) "the viability of the overall project" given its perilous dependency on receipt of suitably competitively tendered design and construction bids and this latter risk exacerbated by reliance, for a vast proportion of its construction funding, on private sector financing; and (3) "the narrow build window" (given that the bridge necessitated completion prior to the 2018 commencement of the Thames Tideway Tunnel project) (ibid.). According to PAC (2016: 17), the BICC acknowledged these concerns, with the outcome being that:

> Officials then briefed the Secretary of State for Transport on the concerns identified, and proposed to vary the grant to TfL in 2014-15 by the full £30m, enabling TfL to provide funding on a phased drawdown basis, subject to the Trust fulfilling milestones and conditions to be agreed in a future funding agreement. The Secretary of State then wrote to the Mayor in November 2014 to confirm that the TfL grant for 2014-15 had been re-determined to provide an additional £30m, subject to a number of conditions concerning controls over expenditure and project monitoring. A maximum of £8.2m was to be spent on pre-construction activities. The £30m was paid over the same month.
>
> In June 2015, the trust requested an increase of £3.5m on the portion of the funding available for pre-construction activities. As a result, the amount of the DfT grant earmarked for this work increased by the Department's share of the increase, from £8.2 to £10.0m.
>
> The funding agreement between TfL and the Trust for the full £60m was signed in July 2015, enabling drawdown of the grant following the completion of relevant milestones. The agreement explicitly states that the Trust is responsible for cost overruns and ongoing maintenance.
>
> PAC (2016: 17)

Concern about whether "benefits expected" were realisable and, indeed, realistic requires further discussion in relation to the positioning of tourism as a revenue stream for the Garden Bridge. On 14th December 2016, Meg Hillier MP wrote, in the capacity of Chair of the Committee of Public

Accounts, to Tom Scholar (Permanent Secretary HM Treasury). Meg Hillier commences the letter with specific insight into the state of play at the close of the 17th October PAC committee hearing thus: "Following the committee's hearing on 17th October where we questioned you about funding for the Garden Bridge, we asked you to provide us with an analysis of the Garden Bridge business case" (Hillier 2016). It is apparent that the Committee of Public Accounts was in recent receipt of "an analysis from a Treasury official by email [received] on 17th November [2016]" (ibid.). Hillier queried the lack of Parliamentary portal in issuing the Treasury's response on unheaded paper and with an insufficient indication that the Permanent Secretary had personally authorised its content. Appended to Hillier's letter to the Permanent Secretary HM Treasury is the "Text received from HM Treasury". Within the latter document the issue of tourism features significantly thus:

Text received from HM Treasury:

Analysis of the Garden Bridge business case:

The strategic outline business case was submitted to the Department for Transport (DfT) in July 2014. It was prepared by Transport for London (TfL) on behalf of the Garden Bridge Trust and followed the five case model, as outline in The Green Book.

The strategic case identified a number of problems with existing arrangements, for example, a 'missing' pedestrian link between Temple Station and the South Bank, which this project would address. It also identified a number of further opportunities that fitted with the wider policy context, such as the DCMS policy of helping the UK tourism industry to grow, and the DfT ambition to encourage walking as an alternative to other modes of transport. The Garden Bridge also supported the Mayor's Transport Strategy.

The economic case estimated that the Garden Bridge would generate benefits in a number of ways. For example, increased tourism revenues, increased construction sector exports, health benefits, journey time saving and increases in property values and rents. If all of these benefits were included, then the project had a BCR of 5.8. However, there was considerable uncertainty over the robustness of some of these benefits, such as whether increase in business rents and property values represented additional value to the UK economy and how much is displacement from other areas. A wide range of possible BCRs was therefore included to reflect this uncertainty.

…

The analysis contained in the business case was deemed sufficient to advise Ministers on. The view of DfT Ministers, based on the business case, was that although this was a highly unusual project with a very wide range of possible BCRs, there was a reasonable prospect of it delivering value for money, although this was dependent on two points. Firstly, the level of confidence in estimates of the impact on land values and overseas investment, and secondly the effective delivery of the project, as there were some significant deliverability risks. Ministers took the view that many of these uncertainties were always likely to be present at this stage in the project's development and were expected to be addressed as the scheme progressed. They concluded that the best way forward was for the GLA transport grant to be increased by £30m in 2014/15, with TfL then managing the flow of this funding to the Trust to enable the development and delivery of the bridge. HM Treasury Ministers agreed with this approach.

(HM Treasury quoted in Hillier 2016)

Hillier's 14th December response to the above 17th November "Text received from HM Treasury" expressed incredulity at the brevity and flimsy level of analysis provided by the HM Treasury in response to the request from the Committee of Public Accounts on 17th October for "an analysis of the Garden Bridge business case" (Hillier 2016). Commencing with the observation that even if one were to disregard the paucity of the material provided, its content "confirms the concerns raised at our hearing in October [2016]", Hillier then proceeds to incisively repudiate the Garden Bridge business case via its flimsy analysis. Amongst the three main concerns raised, the following features relate directly to the business case for recreation-related health benefits of the Garden Bridge and projected tourism revenue. Specifically, it was enquired further that: "[The Garden Bridge business case] stated the need for a pedestrian link between Temple Station and the Southbank" (ibid.). Hillier (2016), having raised this issue, directed criticism as to whether a configuration of the Garden Bridge's value in terms of a proposed pedestrian link would in actuality yield value for money for, as Hillier (ibid.) riposted: "This seems an extravagant solution to deal with a 'missing' walkway". Furthermore, the planned closure of the Garden Bridge "for up to 12 nights a year for private events" was deduced as counterproductive to the stated benefits of a pedestrian link; as Hillier expresses it: "Given the suggestion that the bridge would be closed for up to 12 nights a year for private events does not seem to be one that addresses the issue" (ibid.). Scepticism was also directed at the local community health benefit gains projected to be precipitated by the Bridge's installation of a pedestrian walkway connecting Temple Station and Southbank; indication of this scepticism is evident in Hillier's retort:

"Suggested journey time savings and health benefits also seem entirely tenuous" (ibid.). With specific regards to the business case claim that the Garden Bridge would increase tourism revenue, Hillier stealthily snares the virtual imaginary evident in the business case's beguiling obfuscation of quantifiable tourist revenue facts; as is evident in Hillier's shrewd and unremitting question: "You comment on the boost to tourism. What analysis is there behind this assumption?". Unsurprisingly, given the strength of the critique stealthily articulated by Meg Hillier, the 14th December 2016 letter from PAC to Tom Scholar (Permanent Secretary HM Treasury) concludes that they are dissuaded by the value for money predictions of the Garden Bridge business case and adamantly reconfirm that the Garden Bridge project was a "risk to taxpayers' money" (Hillier 2016).

MP Meg Hillier's (2016) erudite reservations concerning the predicted tourism revenue generated by the Garden Bridge encourage one to explore further TfL's Strategic Business Case for the Garden Bridge, published in May 2014, entitled: *The Garden Bridge, Summary of the Strategic Outline Business Case*. It is evident that significant emphasis was indeed placed on projected tourism revenue as a substantive justification for the Garden Bridge. For instance, the *Strategic Outline Business Case* states that while a conventional bridge might have delivered sufficient of the utility features deemed necessary, "it would fail in delivering the type of iconic development capable of attracting international attention or visitors and help unlock the full economic potential of areas surrounding the bridge on both banks of the river" (TfL 2014: 10). The expectation of an "iconic" tourist attraction presented by the Garden Bridge is amplified by its intended centrality to the auspicious Southbank riverscape vista and its prospects to connect established tourist sites within its vicinity; as evident in the following statement:

> Objective 3: To improve transport connectivity, efficiency and resilience for the South Bank area by providing a direct connection to the Underground network at Temple.
>
> This objective supports the removal of constraints to growth created by weak linkages between the key creative/cultural assets around the South Bank and commercial areas on around North Bank. Tourism potential is possibly being foregone as a result of poor access.

(TfL 2014: 7)

Nevertheless, the TfL (2014), amidst feverous expectations of spectacular deliverables, indicated some prudence in speculating Garden Bridge tourism revenue; as is evident in the following statement:

> The type of solution is constrained by the wider investment objectives relating to tourism value and the creation of green space within the centre of London. These are only possible if the standard transport is tested against some innovative approaches that address a wider spread of challenges (they have to be fixed e.g. not a ferry and above surface e.g. not a tunnel). Collectively, the investment objectives support a highly visible permanent physical connection being made between the two banks of the Thames – a bridge. (TfL 2014: 8)

Evidently straining for equivalences so as to substantiate direct revenue prospecting, the *Strategic Outline Business Case* identifies tourism survey results indicating high visitor numbers to gardens and parks thus:

> Tourism in London is a key sector and supports 226,000 jobs or around 5% of all employment in the capital and accounts for £6.6 billion 'tourism direct GVA' of £34.3 billion nationally. London is one of the most visited cities in the world with nearly 15 million international visitors annually. The average holiday visit including a stay in London in 2012 was around 5 nights, with an average spend per night of £125. The same survey results also show that 64% of all overseas visits to London include seeing a park or garden. If 5% of those overseas visitors who visit a park or garden were assumed to spend an additional hour on average in London with a Garden Bridge in place, the estimated additional annual tourism revenue generated by the Garden Bridge is £2.5 million. (TfL 2014: 16)

Marketing and advertising Garden Bridge as an international visitor attraction played a substantial part in the TfL strategic business case; as indicated in the following statements.

> Visitor exposure to new and exciting features of the London experience also helps market the capital's capability as a destination for investment. This will lead to a development of contemporary activities and uses that will generate jobs in the local economy on both sides of the river and an increase in total UK tourism revenues as London acts as a gateway. (TfL 2014: 6)

> A new Garden Bridge on the Thames has the potential to add to London's cultural offer and provide a new attractor for tourists. (ibid. 16)

Euphuistic and magniloquent projected tourism revenue benefits expose their tenuous validity when contextualised against actual costings. TfL's

(2014: 16) *Strategic Outline Business Case* provides a comprehensive costing of construction and maintenance of the Garden Bridge which does not shy away from indicating that the proposed project was an opulent endeavour. Its estimated construction cost of £120 million in 2014 was aposematic of an exorbitant expenditure, even including "an allowance of £25.6m for risk and contingency"; indeed, "when including inflation of £12.7 million and VAT of £26 [,] In total the cost rises to £159 million" (ibid.).

Marxist Ecofeminism Deconstruction of the Discourse and Rhetoric of Maintaining the Garden Bridge

In *Capital* Volume III, Karl Marx was writing in the nineteenth century, amidst the stench of an industrial capitalism woefully abnegating an ethics of care for nature; rapaciously consuming natural resources; and spewing industrial waste into rivers and habitat with equal disregard. Marx (1991) observed how, by necessity, capitalism would be forced to address its polluted industrial production but such is the rabidity of the logic of capitalist profitability it would do so in accordance with its profit maxim; thus cancelling any altruistic redress to the environment. Such paradoxical environmentalism is evident in the calculation of the maintenance cost for the Garden Bridge for its ecological features are foregrounded as the main generators of maintenance costs, as evident in the following extract:

> The cost of ongoing operation and maintenance is estimated to be £2.5 million per annum in 2014 prices. As the bridge structure is being designed so that it is very low maintenance, it will be the garden itself that will be the main source of ongoing more intensive maintenance and there will be a requirement for permanent staffing, including gardeners and supervisory staff undertaking landscape maintenance tasks most days. It could also involve the use of volunteers and incorporate education/training elements.

> The maintenance regime will cover annual planting and soil treatment requirement, maintenance of plant and equipment, provision of gardening consumables and cyclical landscaping 'renewal' and 'enhancement'. In addition to soft landscaping responsibilities, hard landscaping will require regular maintenance to keep all surfaces clean and serviceable with repairs and replacements undertaken as they become necessary. There will also be ongoing costs associated with crowd control and security.

(TfL 2014: 16)

Even the most cursory of discourse analytics applied to the TfL (2014: 16) extract makes evident paradigmatic features of a shifting discourse in the construction of the object of maintenance with regards to the Garden Bridge. Reference to the garden's "cyclical landscaping 'renewal' and 'enhancement'" reconfigures the object of maintenance; away from sustaining a lavish architectural manmade structure toward the conservation of a naturalistic garden. The transition in the narrative and discursive configuration of the Garden Bridge's maintenance is unsurprising when theorising from a Marxist ecofeminist perspective. Marxist ecofeminists such as Ariel Salleh (2009: 14) expose the reliance of capitalist production on the "meta-industrial" labour of lowly paid workers and invariably unpaid reproductive labour to provision the environment being irreparably damaged by capitalist production. In Karl Marx's *Capital* Volume III, one learns how capitalism attempts to generate business returns for its necessary environmental interventions. Marx (1991: 195) describes how "as the capitalist mode of production extends, so also does the utilization of the refuse left behind by production and consumption". Parallels can be conceived when considering the cycles of reinstatement that the Garden Bridge maintenance programme factored into its costing; parallels regarding the provision of the land from deleterious consumption borne from conserving an artificial naturalistic space, bereft of natural systems of replenishment and renewal. Some indications of the colossal cost inferred by having to artificially maintain the garden's cycles of replenishment are as follows:

> The estimated maintenance cost for the Garden Bridge is £2.5 million per year from 2018 onwards. This includes the cost of bridge maintenance as well as the running costs of the garden associated with staffing the bridge – e.g., gardeners and potentially security. The final cost is dependent on the way the bridge is managed and it is a high level estimate at this stage.
>
> The Garden Bridge Trust is the promoter of the scheme and is responsible for securing the necessary funds for both the construction and the on-going maintenance cost. Discussions have taken place with a number of parties, including one family and one charitable trust. The outcomes will depend on suitable terms being agreed and conditions of the funding.

(TfL 2014: 20)

Given the 2017 cancellation of the Garden Bridge project due to the irreconcilable issue of liability for maintenance; the outcome of the Garden Bridge Trust's "discussions" with "a number of parties" was self-evidently futile. But less obvious are the processes through which the issue of maintenance transfigured into a responsibility for the ecological conservation of the Garden Bridge. Observing the pollution of the River Thames during the height of the institution of industrial capitalism in 19th century England, Marx (1991: 195) observed: "The increase in the cost of raw materials, of course, provides the incentive to make use of waste products". In the Garden Bridge's maintenance costing can be found similar thinking; for the maintenance of the bridge to a virtualist aesthetic would have meant that the naturally occurring degeneration of vegetative materials needed to be removed from the virtualist vista of a perfectly coiffured garden. In so doing, this waste product was reformulated into a business enterprise requiring gardeners, etc. Similar conditions were prosaically foreseen by Karl Marx, as is evident in the following statement:

> The general conditions for this re-utilization are: the massive presence of this refuse, a thing which results only when labour is carried on[,] on a large scale; the improvement of machines, so that materials that were previously unusable in their given form are converted into a form suitable for new production; and finally, scientific progress – especially in chemistry, which discovers the useful properties of such waste products. (Marx, *Capital* Vol. III, 1991: 196)

Marxist ecofeminism is my preferred theoretical framework from which to challenge the positioning of the Garden Bridge maintenance as a liability in terms of ecological conservation for it is evident that the provisioning ("meta-industrial labour" Salleh 2009: 14) of the Garden Bridge involved the gardening of degenerating vegetative waste; unsightly to the virtualist aesthetics of the structure and yet entrepreneurially lucrative for the landscaping gardening commissioning, waste management and others commissioned to perfect the virtualist ecological aesthetic. Ultimately, transfiguring the issue of maintenance to one of ecology was a financially savvy attempt to deflect responsibility for the maintenance of the Garden Bridge away from soulless finance capital and towards the more publicly acceptable conservation of a naturalistic garden.

Garden Bridge Commercial Hire as Privatisation of Public Space

In September 2014, the Garden Bridge Trust published a *Draft Operation and Management Plan* for the Garden Bridge. In a section entitled "Funding these costs", the document outlines a strategy for securing funding to cover the annual running costs for the Garden Bridge. According to the funding scheme strategy proposed, the "Founding Patrons scheme" required a modest annual donation of £5,000 to award donors the status of a Founding

Patron; and this would entitle them to: (i) an "Invitation to an Annual Garden Bridge Trust Chairman's dinner" and (ii) reception of "regular updates on the progress of the project" (Garden Bridge Trust 2014: 32). It was intended that the Founding Patron Scheme would cultivate "a 'community of donors' that will provide an annual revenue stream to support the Garden Bridge" (ibid.). In an attempt to add prestige and branding kudos to this entry level programme, funding places were restricted to 200 available memberships and the Chairman of the Garden Bridge Trust was appointed as the initiative's lead. It was a grandiose estimate that the Founding Patron Scheme would generate £1,000,000 per annum (ibid.). Immediately above this scheme was proposed a Major Donor Programme, which would attract annual donations of a minimum of £5,000, targeted at funding "various aspects of the bridge activity including the work of the work of the gardeners, Garden Bridge community outreach programme(s) and the general upkeep of the bridge" (ibid.). Community outreach educational programmes are a popular feature of voluntary organisation funding streams and thus it was unsurprising that this should feature in the strategy. Furthermore, the Garden Bridge Trust had surveyed foundations experienced in charitably funding this form of community outreach scheme and these included "City Bridge Trust, Esmee Fairburn" and like-minded company trusts. The estimated annual income for this initiative: £290,000 (ibid. 33). Immediately in advance of this initiative was promoted the Corporate Membership Scheme; designed to enrol ten companies, each donating £20,000 per annum (ibid.). Appealing indirectly to Corporate Social Responsibility (CSR) branding, the modest benefits of achieving "Acknowledgement on the Garden Bridge Trust website" and "tickets to the Annual Garden Bridge Chairman's Dinner" initially appear pitiful; however, digging further into the detailing, one is informed that further benefits include "Company staff having the opportunity to volunteer on the bridge" and "The opportunity to host a 'Breakfast on the Bridge' for entertaining in one of the Gardens" (ibid.).

Emerging from the Corporate Membership Scheme is some initial indication of the complexity in the process of privatisation of public space for this process is not simply a case of enclosing from the public a space previously accessible. It was estimated that the Corporate Membership Scheme could generate £200,000 per annum (ibid.). Further evidence of the suitable modes of privatisation of public space operating through the charitable donation schemes detailed by the Garden Bridge Trust include the proposed "Annual Gala Fundraiser" whereby the Garden Bridge Trust had committed to administrating yearly a gala fundraising event directed at raising funds for the Garden Bridge. The established pool of patrons would be farmed for ticket sales alongside corporate partners and other categories of benefactors. Assuming here again the event was intended to be staged live on the Garden Bridge, this was further evidence of indirect privatisation through limiting the public's access to the bridge. It was estimated that the Annual Gala Fundraiser would generate an annual net income of £550,000. Direct modes of privatisation of the public recreational space occupied by the Garden Bridge can be identified clearly in a scheme entitled "Commercial Income – Private Hire". We are informed that: "The Garden Bridge Trust has the opportunity to hire the bridge privately, for eight events per year" (ibid.). Priority ring-fencing was scheduled to be ascribed to the finance corporation defined as "the Garden Bridge Trust's existing major corporate sponsor, Citi Bank" and also to "the Annual Chairman's Garden Bridge Event" (ibid.). The remaining private hire event days available to the Garden Bridge Trust were to be offered to companies and private individuals for a single hire evening event fee of £50,000, which was considered comparable and in accordance with the charging rates of the Shard and the Roadhouse; with both cited as running "successful hire businesses" (ibid. 33-34). The Garden Bridge Trust expressed considerable confidence at the ability of this scheme to achieve the estimated annual income of £400,000 per annum. Additional to this example of direct privatisation through restricting public access to the bridge were indirect privatisation schemes themed as temporary seasonal intermittent enterprises involving: (1) "Catering and temporary retail income" and (2) "Merchandise". In the former, direct comparison is made between New York's High Line Bridge, which allegedly "generates c £600,000 per annum from pop up catering units on the Garden itself" (ibid. 34).

Admitting that the space available was far smaller than that on the New York's High Line, it was envisaged that bijou catering units could be hosted intermittently on "the mezzanine space on the South and North Bank landing areas" (ibid.). Significantly, it was proposed that these bijou food outlets, subject to planning permission, would be available as frequently as "each weekend over the spring and summer months" (ibid.). Notwithstanding the loss of trade encountered by existing food outlets situated in vicinity to the Garden Bridge, the proposal constitutes an indirect mode of privatisation as the space that was once free for unbranded spontaneous public recreation would, during the height of the tourist season, become an enclosure for branding food outlets and bijou dining. Based on calculations of £5,000 per day for the "hire of land along Queen's Walk for pop up activities", the Trust estimated that if it were to make available for hire catering unit space "every weekend from May through to October", an estimated £500,000 net income a year could be generated (ibid.). Alongside this intermittent trade would be some limited retail trade of Garden Bridge-branded merchandise, euphemistically described as the Garden Bridge having "the opportunity to create a discreet range of merchandise as souvenirs for visitors" (ibid.). Clothing items, stationary and bags were included amongst the product offering. Acknowledging the limited space available and the need to pilot suitable products, it was decided that this venture would begin as an online sales outlet and, if successful, would be allotted space; with "some retail space available at both the north and south landing areas" enabling this venture "to grow to an annual net income of £200,000 plus per year based on figures from other South Bank retailers such as the National Theatre and the Tate" (ibid.). An estimated annual income of £50-200,000 was attributed to this merchandising initiative (ibid.).

As mentioned previously, the Garden Bridge Trust had attracted a major corporate benefactor in a tremendously successful American banking corporation. Indeed, according to the TfL (2016a: 231) compilation "of funding to date, August 2016" within the companies list of Garden Bridge funders the following features: "Citi [donation] £2 million". However, this was not the main aspect of financialisation (spread of interest-bearing capital as a financial infra-structure to the project) for the Garden Bridge Trust was dedicated to the setting-up of an endowment that would operate thus:

> Once the Capital Fundraising Campaign has been completed, (anticipated completion date December 2015), the Garden Bridge Trust will focus on raising £15 million for an Endowment Fund to deliver an annual revenue stream for operations and maintenance. At an average of 5% interest this will enable the Trust to draw down £750,000 per annum. The Endowment has been kick-started with an anonymous donation of £2 million. Estimated Income [from the endowment]: £750,000 per annum. (Garden Bridge Trust 2014: 34-35)

Written into this section of the Garden Bridge Trust (2014: 32-34) funding strategy is the proviso that realising these funding streams will be partly contingent on the trustees and the "wealth of experience from their involvement in other charitable trusts which would help ensure this level of income secured" (ibid. 35). It is my contention that securing the (above-described) income stream is determined by a privatisation of public recreational space, predicted on a model of rentier capital first identified by Karl Marx in *Capital* Volume III.

Garden Bridge Rentier Capital as the Adsensory Financialisation of Urban Decay

> Landed property thus receives its purely economic form by the stripping away of all its former political and social embellishments and admixtures, in short all those traditional accoutrements that are denounced as uselessly and absurdly superfluous by the industrial capitalists themselves, and by their theoretical spokesmen, in their passionate struggle with landed property. (Marx, *Capital* Vol. III 1991: 755)

In Part Six of *Capital* Volume III, entitled "The Transformation of Surplus Profit into Ground-Rent", Marx observes an emerging mode of capital accumulation specific to a rationalisation of agriculture on an industrial scale, materialising via "the complete impoverishment of the immediate producers", and thus contiguous with the modus operandi of previous forms of capital production (ibid. 755). The enclosure of the commons and dispossession of communality leaves only capitalist farmers, exploited by the proprietor of the land, to whom is paid "a contractually fixed sum of money (just like the interest fixed for the borrower of money capital), for the permission to employ his capital in this particular field of production" (ibid.). Marx defines as "ground-rent" money paid to a landowner in pursuit of permission to invest capital and this concept has relevance to processes of privatisation through which leasehold land destined to host the Garden Bridge would be made to yield surplus profit. Marx argues that "this sum of money is known as ground-rent irrespective of whether it is paid for agricultural land, building land, mines, fisheries, forests, etc." (ibid. 756). Suffice to say, "ground-rent is thus the form in which landed property is economically realized, valorized" (ibid.). In the subleasing of the land upon which the Garden Bridge was destined can be identified a mode of ground-rent whereby the freeholder (Lambeth Council), having leased the land to Coin Street Community Builders, did not prevent the latter leaseholder from drawing up an agreement which would have led to a subleasing tenancy. In *Capital* Volume III, Marx provides a theoretical framework applicable to adjudicating the mode of capital accumulation evident in the subleasing proffered by the Coin Street Community Builders' agreement for landed private property yields multiple dividends for the freeholder as the leaseholder sets about extracting profit via processes in which "Capital may be fixed in the earth" (Marx 1991: 756). "La terre-capital" denotes "capital incorporated into the earth" (ibid.). According to Marx (1991: 756), having gained a rental agreement, the agricultural farmer sets about cultivating the land to increase its yield; e.g., incorporation of chemical fertilisers (fixing capital in a transient manner) and/or institution of drainage fixtures (fixing capital more permanently). It is Marx's observation that:

> Interest on the capital incorporated into the earth and in the improvements that are thereby made to the soil as an instrument of production may form a portion of the rent that is paid by the farmer to the landowner, but it does not constitute ground-rent proper, which is paid for the use of the soil as such, whether this is in a state of nature or is cultivated. (Marx, *Capital* Vol. III, 1991: 756)

Consequently, the renter can potentially yield profit by improving the productive capacity of the land and in so doing "transform the earth from a mere raw material into earth-capital" (ibid. 757) regardless of whether the method of fixing capital into the soil is temporary or permanent, all of which is, in many respects, a measure of the labour of the farmer. However, all of the capital fixed into the earth by the renter is yielded by the freeholder at the end of a fixed lease term. Marx observed a particularly ostentatious mode of capital accumulation through which the freehold owner, when drawing up a new leasehold, incorporates into the value of the land the earth-capital cultivated by previous tenants of the land. As Marx expresses it:

> But as soon as the lease stipulated in the contract has expired – and this is one of the reasons why the landowner seeks to shorten the term of the lease to a minimum, as capitalist production develops – the improvements made to the land fall to the landowner as his property, as an inseparable accident of the substance of the land. When the new lease contract is concluded, the landowner adds interest on the capital incorporated into the earth to the ground-rent proper, where he leases the land again to the farmer who made the improvements or to another farmer. His rent thus swells; or, if he plans to sell the land ... its value has now risen. (Marx, *Capital* Vol. III, 1991: 757)

The expropriation is blatantly clear for the freeholder in increasing the price of the land, based on the labour of previous renters/leaseholders; and thus "he does not sell just the land, but rather the improved land, the capital incorporated into the earth, which has cost him nothing" (ibid. 757). It is my hypothetico-deductive reasoning that rentier capital operated similarly in the leasehold plans and procurement processes that enrolled Coin Street Community Builders into the Garden Bridge project.

Coin Street Community Builders' (2015) account of its leasing liability for the Garden Bridge is best described in the following extract:

> The Garden Bridge is a proposed new pedestrian crossing spanning the River Thames linking South Bank to Temple station. Designed by Thomas Heatherwick and garden designer Dan Pearson, the bridge will provide a new route from north and south and feature plants, trees, woodland and walkways. The South Bank 'landing' is on part of the Riverside Walkway by ITV London which is leased to Coin Street Community Builders. The freehold is owned by the London Borough of Lambeth.
>
> …
>
> Ensuring benefit not liability:
> The freeholder of the land is Lambeth Council. We cannot grant consent for the bridge landing unless Lambeth wish us to do so. Whatever the outcome, CSCB remains responsible for the maintenance and management of the Riverside Walkway and the area surrounding the proposed south landing of the bridge. Therefore, we have to engage in discussions and use influence to ensure there is a proper maintenance and operations plan. We will also have to increase our cleaning, management and maintenance resources to cope with the increased numbers of people the bridge will attract.
>
> Benefitting local people:
> We anticipate a collaborative relationship with the Garden Bridge Trust and the creation of a range of training and employment opportunities beneficial to our local community.
>
> (Coin Street Community Builders 2015)

As indicated in the above extract, Coin Street Community Builders were reluctant to assume responsibility for the maintenance of the Garden Bridge. Following Marx's presuppositions on value and ground-rent, it is my contention that if Coin Street Community Builders had been persuaded to assume responsibility for the maintenance of the Garden Bridge, this provisioning of the land would have yielded earth-capital and increased the value of the land to the benefit of the freeholder, a situation Marx (1991: 757) might well have described thus: "This is one of the secrets – quite apart from the movement of ground-rent as such – of the increasing enrichment of the land owners, the constant inflation of their rents and the growing money value of their estates as economic development progresses". However, and according to Marx (ibid. 772), classic economic studies of ground-rent are beset by three types of error. Firstly, regardless of the nuances of the specific forms of ground-rent, each shares a principal feature: "the appropriation of rent is the economic form in which landed property, the ownership of particular bits of the globe by certain individuals" (ibid.) for the "common character", uniting all types of rent – when assuming the latter to be "the economic realization of landed property" – is the expropriation of profit through the privatisation and "exclusive possession of particular parts of the globe" (ibid.). A second feature of ground-rent that, according to Marx, is frequently misconceived is that ground-rent fundamentally involves the expropriation, through exploitation, of surplus-value for "all ground-rent is surplus-value, the product of surplus labour" (ibid. 772-773). Finally, a frequent error evident in the analysis of ground-rent is falling short of the realisation that making profit from land property through its economic valorisation as the subject of ground-rent delivers an amount of profit that has little determinant by the actions of the landowner; rather, it is "a development of social labour that is independent of him and in which he plays no part" (ibid. 775). Marx explains this in part in terms of the added value that the farmer invests, as earth-capital, into the land so as to yield produce, above subsistence level. Thus, it is Marx's observation that one should proceed, in the analysis of ground-rent, from the following proposition: "that the worst land pays no ground-rent, or, to put it more generally, land pays ground-rent only when the individual production price of its product is below the production price that governs the market, giving rise to a surplus profit that is transformed into rent" (ibid. 882). Marx is here establishing a theoretical framework which has direct relevance to my analysis of adsensory urban ecology and the exploitation of the body as object/subject of advertising technology directed as the gentrification of post-industrial urban spaces. But prior to setting out my theory, it is necessary to detail the following feature of Marx's analysis of ground-rent: "investigate more closely the basis of the assumption that the product of the poorest land A pays no rent" (ibid. 883). This is not to assume that the landowner would lease out the land for no rent as this would be in diametric opposition to the exploitative conditions of surplus-value and capital accumulation.

Nevertheless, Marx identified anomalies in ground-rent in which "capital investment on the land can take place without payment of rent"; but for this to arise in a capitalist mode of production, this will involve "a factual – if not a legal –abolition of landed property, an abolition that can occur only under very special condition of an accidental nature" (ibid. 885). Marx identifies three examples of "where capital investment on the land can take place without the payment of rent". Firstly, if the landowner is a capitalist "or the capitalist a landowner", then it can be economically viable for the individual capitalist to cultivate their land until such time as the market price increases to justify the profitable renting of the land. As Marx states: "He can cultivate his land himself as soon as the market price has risen sufficiently to obtain the price of production from the present land A, i.e., to replace capital plus average profit" (ibid.). A rationale validating this action is that the capitalist as landowner does not have to contend with the issue of payment for the land, thus "landed property does not set any barrier to the investment of his capital" (ibid.). Consequently, the land can be taken-for-granted "as a simple natural element" and attention focused instead on "the valorization of his capital, by capitalist considerations" (ibid.). But Marx believed this to be an exception to the profit maxim of capital accumulation for, "Just as the capitalist cultivation of the land assumes a separation between functioning capital and landed property, so it generally rules out cultivation by the landed proprietor himself". As this would involve reverse engineering the model of capitalist accumulation, "i.e. that the landowner is his own farmer, up to the point that, or wherever, capital would draw no rent from cultivating the land if there were no landed property independent of it" (ibid. 885-886). Second, a plausible situation in which the landowner could viably rent the land for free is where the whole of the land is bigger than a sum of its parts; and thus the paying of no rent for part of this wider constituent of land is absorbed into the whole. As Marx describes, "A leasehold may include particular pieces of land that pay no rent at the given level of market prices, and are in fact rented free" (ibid. 886). Though, and because, the landowner is focusing on the land as a whole, this part is not considered as significantly free: "they are now viewed in this light by the landowner, since what he pays attention to is the total rental of the land leased and not the particular rent of individual component parts" (ibid.). Indeed, the sole reason the renter does not pay rent on these component parts is because they exist as an accessory to the larger mass of land from which rent is being extracted. In this situation, the landowner can enable a mixing into the portfolio of land rented substandard land that, while the renter is not required to pay rent, they, in anticipation of a capitalist drive for increased yield, might be self-motivated to invest earth-capital to enrich the land and generate some yield. In so doing, they add value to land that might have been considered unfertile and unworthy of renting. The "worse land" therefore "simply forms an inseparable filling sandwiched between the better land" (ibid.). A third example of conditions in which the landowner appears to lease land rent free is where the renter decides to sublease the land to themselves. Specifically, "a farmer may invest extra capital on his existing leasehold even though at the existing market prices the additional product obtained in this way simply yields him the price of production, the customary profit, and does not enable him to pay an additional rent" (ibid. 886). However, the landowner, not the renter, gains from this situation, as Marx explains:

> Thus for one part of the capital invested on the land he does pay ground-rent, for the other part not. But we can see from the following consideration

how little this solves the problem. If the market price (and also the fertility of the soil) enables him to obtain a surplus yield with additional capital which, like the old capital, yields him a surplus profit as well as the price of production, then he pockets this profit himself for the duration of the lease. And why? Because as long as the tenancy contract lasts, the barrier that landed property places to the investment of his capital in the land has been removed. Yet the mere fact that in order to secure this surplus profit, he must take on additional worse land and lease it separately, show irrefutably that the investment of additional capital on the old land is not sufficient to produce the increased supply needed. The one assumption rules out the other. (Marx, *Capital* Vol. III 1991: 886-887)

It needs to be appreciated that Marx's formulation, in *Capital* Volume III, of three scenarios involving the leaseholder not paying rent is far from evidence of altruism in the capitalist economy. Indeed, Marx (ibid. 884) admonishes interpretation in this respect, arguing that: "The fact that the farmer could valorize his capital at the customary profit if he paid no rent is in no way a reason for the landlord to lease out his land to the farmer for nothing, and be so philanthropic to his client as to extend him a *crédit gratuit*". Rather, in the limited situations where the farmer would be able to exploit the worst land "as long as he did not pay any rent, i.e. if he could actually treat landed property as non-existent" (ibid. 885), financial gain is ultimately harvested by the capitalist landowner. Thus it was Marx's observation that, "where capitalist investment on the land can take place without payment of rent, in a country of capitalist production, we shall find that they all involve a factual – if not a legal – abolition of landed property, an abolition that can occur only under very special conditions of an accidental nature" (ibid.). However, despite disparaging these occurrences as "accidental nature", Marx proceeded to detail the three instances of capital accumulation through the non-payment of an absolute ground-rent. I have long since been intrigued by this aspect of Marx's ground-rent thesis, endeavouring to apply it to rentier advances in advertising technologies; and specifically the development of what I have termed adsensory financialisation whereby the latter refers to the body as subject and object of advertising inscriptive technologies geared towards the financialisation of health and well-being. In a previous publication, *Adsensory Financialisation*, I formulate a theory of rentier capital that focuses on haptic biotechnology in the form of wearable biometric tracker devices used increasingly in amateur sports training. With regard now to the Garden Bridge, it is my observation that Marx's *Capital* Volume III formulation of ground-rent accumulation has relevance to some of the media installations that were proposed as security and commercial features designed to augment the Garden Bridge's tourist experience.

Mobile Phone Signal Tracking – Ethico-Synoptic Accumulation

Peter Walker (2015), in a *Guardian* article entitled "London Garden Bridge users to have mobile phone signals tracked", identified that disconcerting levels of mobile surveillance were intended to be directed at users of the Garden Bridge. Walker's (2015) article makes reference to the security and crowd control features detailed in the following document published by the Garden Bridge Trust (2014): *Garden Bridge, Draft Operation and Management Plan*. The technological innovations envisaged for the operational control of the Garden Bridge are detailed in a section entitled "Management of Bridge Operations". On reading this material, one's attention is drawn to the panoptic features of the monitoring systems envisaged. First, we are informed that monitoring of crowds will be achieved through Closed Circuit Television (CCTV) located in a "control room", which will be situated in the southern landing of the Garden Bridge (ibid. 16). Scattered elsewhere on the structure will be "local operators and security personnel" that will be connected via a "handheld radio system" and telephone in order to receive security information from their specific command centres (ibid.). The intention in installing a network of operators and CCTV is described thus: "This will ensure consolidated management of bridge operations which integrates with all other local land uses" (ibid.). It was envisaged that the need for a 24-hour staffed control room would be assessed after the first year of full operation of the Garden Bridge. However, it is evident that the labour intensive staffing envisaged for the trial period was intended to be replaced by technological surveillance, as indicated in the following extract:

> The bridge will have a comprehensive CCTV system. It will be compliant with the guidelines set out by the Information Commissioners Office (ICO) in the CCTV Code of Practice 2008. The location of the CCTV equipment will be fixed under the planning consent. It will be used to record use of the bridge but will not be observed in 'real time'. The need for a plan tilt zoom (PTZ) overlay for large events will be assessed in consultation with stakeholders and may be included in the final OMP [Operation Management Plan]. (Garden Bridge Trust 2014: 16)

Risk, Surveillance and Social Time in Garden Bridge Synoptics

Remaining with the *Garden Bridge, Draft Operation and Management Plan,* it was envisaged that access to the structure would be managed through the use of biosensors capable of crowd counting. Specifically, it is stated that: "The Garden Bridge will utilise real-time crowd counting technology in the form of ground level sensors at the access points. This will support access control decisions to ensure safe operation of the bridge, especially during 'off hours'" (ibid. 17). It is significant to review the rationale for the implementation of this level of biosensor monitor for the rhetoric leans heavily on the assumption that surveillance is a necessity not just for security but for achieving the value for money usage of the bridge and identifying consumer demand for other facilities. Thus, it is stated that "a Maximum of 2500 visitors will be permitted on the bridge as set out by fire safety regulators" (ibid.). To keep within this regulation, we are informed: "Visitor numbers will also assist the GBT [Garden Bridge Trust] in understanding how the bridge is used and assist with planning and management of bridge use and facilities" (ibid.). Enfolded into this paradigmatic language of health and safety regulation is the use of biosensors, whereby we are informed that:

> Crowd counting sensors will be installed at all bridge access points and gates. This is likely to be in the form of low level sensors. The use of a wifi crowd dynamic assessment tool is also being considered. A decision on whether to use wifi will be made only when the technology is proven. It is understood that SBEG are considering the use of this technology on the South Bank and the GBT will liaise with them about its use. (Garden Bridge Trust 2014: 17)

There exists a multitude of surveillance resonances here that encourage reference to Michel Foucault's account of disciplinary technologies while also suggesting limitations to Foucault's framework of analysis. In the writings of Michel Foucault, we are challenged to interrogate liberal humanist ethical virtues. For more than twenty years of his academic career, Foucault was concerned to trace a history of the manifold ways in Western culture "that humans develop knowledge about themselves" (1988: 18). In *Technologies of the Self*, Foucault clarifies very important conceptual tools necessary for decoding liberal humanism and rendering it intelligible as a system of knowledge with "specific 'truth games' related to specific techniques that human beings use to understand themselves" (ibid.). These techniques assume four major forms of "technologies", and each mode constitutes a vehicle of practical reason. The first is "technologies of production", which permit the transformation of natural objects into resources for the mobilisation of human interests. Foucault recognises synergies here with dialectical materialism; "for instance one sees the relation between manipulating things and domination in Karl Marx's

Capital, where every technique of production requires modification of individual conduct – not only skills but also attitudes" (ibid.). The theme of transformation is evident in "technologies of sign systems", the second mode of technology that humans use to organise social life and develop knowledge. Foucault describes this technology as modes of discourse and discursive practice "which permit us to use signs, meanings, symbols, signification" (ibid.). In Foucault's book, *Discipline and Punish*, technologies of sign systems enter into a matrix of practical reasoning that functions in a manner that exceeds a positivistic ontology of the image as representing a mirror of the world that merely needs decoding. Instead, technologies of sign systems are integrated into penal practice and in so doing operate as modes of administration, regulation and discipline.

Technologies of sign systems work in conjunction with the third specific technique that human beings have created to know themselves, i.e., "technologies of power". Foucault's focus here is premised on elucidating technologies that "determine the conduct of individuals and submit them to certain ends or domination, an objectivizing of the subject" (Foucault 1988: 18). These objectifying technologies form a recurrent theme in *Discipline and Punish*. And in Foucault's (1998, 1992, 1990) later work, technologies of power are detailed in conjunction with the fourth of Foucault's technologies, i.e., "technologies of ... self". These permit individuals to voluntarily carry out practices "on their own bodies and souls, thoughts, conduct, and way of being, so as to transform themselves in order to attain a certain state of happiness, purity, wisdom, perfection, or immortality" (Foucault 1988: 18). It is my contention that the aforementioned *Garden Bridge, Draft Operation and Management Plan* demonstrates the extent to which Foucault's four technologies of modern governance increasingly translate into sign technologies. I appreciate that this conclusion is in contrast with Foucault's conceptual and theoretical change in direction that can be deduced from his lectures in the late 1970s and early 1980s; during which time a theoretical focus on domination through the sign spectacle is displaced by a focus on "technology of self", as is evident in the following statement:

> Perhaps I've insisted too much on the technology of domination and power. I am more and more interested in the interaction between oneself and others and in the technologies of individual domination, the history of how an individual acts upon himself, in the technology of self. (Foucault 1988: 19)

It is often assumed that Michel Foucault's account of disciplinary power establishes linearity and causality as the mode by which discipline is said to

Garden Bridge, Rentier Capital as the Adsensory Financialisation of Urban Decay

structure time and space in the regulation of subjects. For example, one may interpret the surveillance system of radio and CCTV monitoring that was proposed for the Garden Bridge to be emblematic of a panoptic surveillance "based on a system of permanent registration: reports from the syndics to the intendents, from the intendants to the magistrates or mayor" (Foucault 1991: 196). Furthermore, one might initially interpret the biosensor technology proposed as epitomising a regulation of space and time in which, as Foucault (ibid. 197) has described:

> This enclosed, segmented space, observed at every point, in which the individuals are inserted in a fixed place, in which the slightest movement are supervised, in which all events are recorded, in which an uninterrupted work of writing links the centre and periphery, in which power is exercised without division, according to a continuous hierarchical figure, in which each individual is constantly located, examined and distributed among the living beings, the sick and the dead –all this constitutes a compact model of the disciplinary mechanism. (Foucault 1991: 197)

It is this language and emphasis on analytical grids, separating objectification from subjectification, and situating subjects into quantitative linear timeframes that too easily encourage prominent readers of Foucault to invariably assume that discipline operates in terms of a positivistic disciplinary space; as is evident in Dreyfus and Rabinow's (1982) *Beyond Structuralism and Hermeneutics*. Indeed, Dreyfus and Rabinow explicitly state: "In *Discipline und Punish* Foucault presents the genealogy of the modern individual as a docile and mute body by showing the inter-play of a disciplinary technology and a normative social science" (ibid. 143). Thus, from Dreyfus and Rabinow's perspective, the disciplinary effect induced by acceding to subject one's touristic experience of the Garden Bridge to a disciplinary matrix of CCTV technologies, biosensors and radio-networked security guards is similar to any other of "the technologies of discipline in which an authority effects changes on 'mute and docile bodies'" (ibid. 175). And the technologies of the self, enrolled into the self-disciplinary aspects of the Garden Bridge regime from Dreyfus and Rabinow's framework, are similar to all other disciplinary technologies – except for "one clear difference ... the modern subject is not mute; he must talk" (ibid. 175).

It might assist here to explore in further detail the type of biosensor crowd-monitoring technology that was proposed for the Garden Bridge. Recall how the *Garden Bridge, Draft Operation and Management Plan* (Garden Bridge Trust 2014) proposed biosensor technologies as a mechanism for crowd monitoring, as is evident in the following extract:

> The Garden Bridge will utilise real-time crowd counting technology in the form of ground level sensors at the access points. This will support access control decisions to ensure safe operation of the bridge, especially during 'off hours'.
>
> Monitoring and Management of Visitor Movement
> It is important that the GBT [Garden Bridge Trust] understand as accurately as possible the numbers of visitors using the bridge to ensure safe levels of operation are maintained. A maximum of 2500 visitors will be permitted on the bridge as set out by fire safety regulations. Visitor numbers will be monitored to ensure that this number is not exceeded. Monitoring will also assist the GBT in understanding how the bridge is used and assist with planning and management of bridge use and facilities.
>
> Crowd counting sensors will be installed at all bridge access points and gates. This is likely to be in the form of low level sensors. The use of a wifi crowd dynamic assessment tool is also being considered. A decision on whether to use wifi will be made only when the technology is proven. It is understood that SBEG are considering the use of this technology on the South Bank and the GBT will liaise with them about its use.
>
> (Garden Bridge Trust 2014: 17)

Exploring further the product capabilities of biosensor crowd monitoring technologies, my attention has been drawn toward the commercial provision of SensorInsight (2018). Established with over twenty years of experience "as a Systems Integrator", SensorInsight is an Industrial Internet of Things (IIoT) company (ibid.). Specifically, SensorInsight markets itself thus:

> Headquartered in Houston, Texas, SensorInsight® creates and markets an Industrial Internet of Things (IoT) platform designed to provide insight across specific domains, including energy and utilities, transportation, manufacturing, healthcare, and smarter cities. The platform works by providing deep analytics and complete access to data systems in real-time. Plus, SensorInsight takes care of the software, hardware, and upkeep so you don't have to, providing a complete IIoT Solution. (ibid.)

Key to the current SensorInsight product suite are mobile phone and video analytics biosensor crowd and pedestrian monitoring technologies, designed to detect "patterns and trends through efficient monitoring of public and private areas" (ibid.). Integral to the assemblage of techniques that constitute crowd sensing analytics are facial recognition and image profiling of objects, scenes and situations. SensorInsight proclaims that the image and facial recognition analytics can distinguish and delineate crowds in terms of age, gender, facial expression and attire; asserting that, "Working with images we can provide a description and attributes of the image in real time" (ibid.). Advances in the WiFi scanning capabilities of SensorInsight's technology have brought into being "Wifi Counting functionality", designed to collect "WiFi probe request from shoppers' smartphones". According to SensorInsight: "WiFi Counting uses a WiFi receiver to pick up unique WiFi management frames emitted from smartphones with a range of up to 100 meters" (ibid.). Speed of access, by clients, to people tracking and WiFi scanning data is a unique selling point for SensorInsight and thus much emphasis is placed on "real time" data collection and quick easily accessible data retrieval. Vertically integrated convergence technologies appear to be the key facilitator in this endeavour and indeed describes "a data collection framework designed from the ground up to connect, monitor and transform sensor data" (ibid.). Integral to the transmission of crowd analytic data from the company's server to the clients is an application programming interface (API) described thus: "SensorInsight integrated provides a complete API for accessing your data directly or pushing your data directly to your preferred platform". And the "real time" features of the people imaging applications provide the client with the option of viewing data "in a number of ways based on both static and mobile applications of the hardware" (ibid.). One might reach initially for Foucault's *Discipline and Punish* to frame, theoretically, this labyrinthine matrix of technologies as simply forming a panopticon. Indeed, the following extract derived from *Discipline and Punish* appears to be a perfect analogy for crowd monitoring technology:

> Hence the major effect of the Panopticon: to induce in the inmate a state of conscious and permanent visibility that assures the automatic functioning of power. So to arrange things that the surveillance is permanent in its effects, even if it is discontinuous in its action; that the perfection of power should tend to render its actual exercise unnecessary; that this architectural apparatus should be a machine for creating and sustaining a power relation independent of the person who exercises it; in short, that the inmates should be caught up in a power situation of which they are themselves the bearers.

(Foucault 1991: 201)

It is my contention that Dreyfus and Rabinow (1982) underestimate the value of this latter feature of Foucault's account of modern disciplinary power; they do this by subsuming this distinct human agency under the rubric that it exists as with any other linear operation of disciplinary technology. In this sense, disciplinary technologies are merely to be conceived of as interchangeable "constituent components" that can be delineated, isolated and analysed in terms of a positivist grid of delineable repertoires that "interplay" according to the ridged formulaic dynamics of linear causality (ibid. 175). Conversely, it is my contention that although biosensor technologies are similar to the disciplinary modalities which effect changes on "mute and docile bodies", one feature overrides such comparison – and that is the very fact that "the modern subject is not mute; he must talk" (Dreyfus and Rabinow 1982: 175). In short, a reading of the biosensor technologies proposed for the Garden Bridge as hyper-rationalist electronic panopticons, designed to enact a monolithic regime of control, fails to recognise the distinction between subjects being constituted through rather than by a variety of disciplinary technologies. And this requires moving beyond a linear causality model of discipline and instead focusing on the capacity of the human spirit to create meaning and inscribe affirmative beliefs into the delimitating intervals of disciplinary time. Some indication of this approach initially seems evident in Foucault's account of disciplinary time thus:

> 'seriation' of successive activities makes possible a whole investment of duration by power: the possibility of a detailed control and a regular intervention (of differentiation, correction, punishment, elimination) in each moment of time...the possibility of accumulating time and activity, of rediscovering them...Temporal dispersal is brought together to produce a profit, thus mastering a duration that would otherwise elude one's grasp.
>
> (Foucault 1991: 160)

Parallels can be made between disciplinary surveillance technologies and the seriation of biosensor monitoring events in the proposed Garden Bridge's wrap-around regulatory regime, but if one is to progress beyond arbitrarily dividing the structure and hermeneutics of the biosensor surveillance, it is evident that while power is indeed "articulated directly onto time", assuring "its control and guarantees its use" (Foucault 1991: 160), the disciplinary inscription of power into the biosensor regime is also engendering in the form of urban ecology a social time of qualitative experiential genesis. Thus, it is necessary to draw attention to the biosensor monitoring schema proposed for the Garden Bridge as potentially an illustration of how:

> The disciplinary methods reveal a linear time whose moments are integrated, one upon another, and which is orientated towards a terminal, stable point; in short, an 'evolutive' time. But it must be recalled that, at the same moment, the administrative and economic techniques of control reveal a

social time of a serial, orientated, cumulative type: the discovery of an evolution in terms of 'progress'. The disciplinary techniques reveal individual series: the discovery of an evolution in terms of 'genesis'. These two great 'discoveries' of the eighteenth century – the progress of societies and the geneses of individuals – were perhaps correlative with the new techniques of power, and more specifically, with a new way of administering time and making it useful, by segmentation, seriation, synthesis and totalization. (Foucault 1991: 160)

Foucault's exposition of disciplinary technologies as manifesting linear rationalities, calibrated into hierarchical intervals, potentially frames, effectively, a reciprocity and co-existence of the monetising calculative dianoetics of a regimented self-regulatory linear schematic disciplinary time and its opposite: a "social time" of creative meaning and agency. However, there are significant limitations in Foucault's conception of social time for in this temporal consciousness is ascribed the delimitating constructs of serialised cumulative evolutionary progress. According to Foucault, "disciplinary methods reveal a linear time whose moments are integrated, one upon another" but, similarly, "at the same moment", discipline manifests "a social time of a serial, orientated, cumulative type" (ibid.). Social time is depicted by Foucault as a time of "discovery" but this "genesis" takes only the form of an evolution through a cumulative movement towards "progress". In Dreyfus and Rabinow's (1982: 175) insistence that the subject of disciplinary technologies "must talk", there is at least an attempt to extend beyond the structure versus hermeneutic impasse in Foucault's theoretical framing of disciplinary technologies. However, neither contribution formulates effectively an antithesis to linear time's serialising evolution toward progress. It might assist the development of my argument to revisit the construction of risk, security and insurantial technologies in the Garden Bridge Trust's (2014) *Garden Bridge, Draft Operation and Management Plan*. For example, to reiterate, the document sets out risk and security in the following discursive justification for increased monitoring:

> Low watt sensor points will also be installed across the bridge at approximately 50m intervals. This will enable an understanding of dwell periods and whether visitors enter and exit at the same gate or cross the bridge. The sensors will also provide flow rates of visitors to assist in bridge management.
>
> There is also an opportunity for this to be rolled out to locations beyond the bridge footprint so assessment of the user arrival profile could also be

understood. This would enable an accurate assessment of our impact on the local community in terms of increased visitor numbers.

(Garden Bridge Trust 2014: 17)

The construction of risk, security and insurantial technologies presented in the above extract is emblematic of how biosensors have entered the terrain of advertising inscriptive technologies. Indeed, it is my contention that biosensor technologies are increasingly evident in security surveillance and, as described in the Garden Bridge Trust (2014) management plan, constitute a new terrain of advertising technology defined here as adsensory. Adsensory ethico-synoptic technology, as detailed in Odih (2016), refers to the degree to which the body is integral as both subject and object of advertising inscriptive technologies directed at the financialisation of health and social well-being. Indications of advertising aspects of the biosensors proposed for the Garden Bridge are evident in the following statements: "Monitoring will also assist the GBT in understanding how the bridge is used and assist with planning and management of bridge use and facilities"; "Low watt sensor points will also be installed across the bridge at approximately 50m intervals … The sensors will also provide flow rates of visitors to assist in bridge management" and "This would enable an accurate assessment of our impact on the local community in terms of increased visitor numbers" (Garden Bridge Trust 2014:17). In these and other similar extracts derived from Garden Bridge Trust's (ibid.) document can be discerned evidence of the transition of biosensors into advertising sensors actively seeking information about the human body so as to sell commercialised security services and extend consumer markets.

Timely Reflections; Garden Bridge Project, the Body as Rentier Capital and the Extension of Adsensory Insurantial Technology

Interviewee: ... *There are only ever two reasons why private companies might donate. One is genuine non-for-profit, so there is no real benefit to the company, the organisation except for in terms of marketing and PR and all those sorts of things. That's possibly one reason why you might get companies willing to offer funds for the Garden Bridge and really expecting nothing in return. Which is to my mind quite remarkable. The second might be that a company might want to provide funding for the Garden Bridge possibly because they have an office nearby and their staff might benefit from walking over it, [during] commute times. Or simply because they like* the aesthetic idea of the bridge. And so I don't know of anyone who's done the work, but I would have thought an interesting question would be to look at the funders who are signatories, where their offices are based. And look at their other involvement.

...

Interviewer: ... *In so doing they have managed to make financially lucrative what was only a proposition in terms of the Garden Bridge? How did it become an investable commodity when it was just an idea?*
Interviewee: *That's a good question. I am not sure it is financially lucrative for anyone involved, because clearly they are not getting a direct return on the project. So the question is: What is the indirect return?*

...

Interviewer: *If there was no direct return, I wonder what it was that was actually attracting the investment of these donors?*
Interviewee: *It's a good question. The honest answer is: I don't know. I can't speak for the investors that have put money into it. I don't really want to call them investors. Can we call them (**Interviewer:** Syndicate), yeah? Yeah, something else, to be honest, investors implies you get a return. Which I don't think they do. I think there is possibly three possible reasons. One is just marketing and PR benefit. One is, they just like the idea of the bridge; or somebody in the company does and decides that's what we want to do. The third and possibly the one you hear people talk about more, although I haven't seen any direct evidence of it, is that the Garden Bridge was also going to be closed for particular private events. Now the Garden Bridge Trust claim that for those particular events they were going to rent it out, the bridge for private functions. So that implies that for each time a private function would be held, you would be charging someone to hold it. It's unclear how you might get onto the list to hold a private event. So in making the donation, there is the implicit promise you might be able to hold an event. Or the implicit promise that you might be able to hold an event at a reduced price. But as I said, these are accusations that I have heard, but I have not seen evidence of.*

(Semi-structured Qualitative Interview: Political Researcher, Procurement Expert, London, August 2017)

Even the most cursory perusal through advertising visual cultures – used to market insurantial products – reveals that advertising creatives cultivate risks by exploiting knowledge about the phenomenology of our everyday lives. Advertising creatives are adept at assembling real scenarios drawn from the phenomenology of everyday life and crafting these into insurantial risks in terms of possible loss or protection against it. Thus, a feminist analysis of disciplinary rationalities and their application to insurantial technologies needs to focus on the discordant interplay of linear rational temporalities and their phenomenological antithesis. It is imperative that analyses of discipline engender a phenomenology of temporality (Odih 2007a) and individual self-consciousness. Returning to an analysis of the linear technological rationalities of the proposed Garden Bridge surveillance regime, its inscriptive advertising modalities are enhanced further by a focus on the regime's attempt to enter everyday life through a wrap-around surveillance of visitors to the tourist attraction. While it is evident that I am focusing on advertising as a technology of the sign, and in so doing exploring its significance as a disciplinary technology, Foucault's focus on panoptics can incline toward analysing indiscriminatingly the mechanisms through which the few extend surveillance over the lives of many. One might riposte that Foucault's formulation positions the individual as both the object and subject of surveillance; as Foucault (1991) expresses it: "Speaking of the panoptic principle ... In appearance, it is merely the solution of a technical problem; but, through it, a whole type of society emerges ... We are much less Greeks than we believe. We are neither in the amphitheatre, nor on the stage, but in the panoptic machine, invested by its effects of power, which we bring to ourselves since we are part of its mechanism" (ibid. 216-217). This statement does indeed introduce into the analysis of disciplinary technology an element of complexity. However, the empirical conditions through which Foucault might have explored further the saturation of society by technologies of the sign were less evident at the time of Foucault's writing of *Discipline and Punish* during the 1970s. It is my contention that Foucault under-estimated the significance of media to disciplinary technology and thus wholly under-appreciated the evolving trajectory of sign technologies. Nevertheless, significant inroads have been made by Foucauldian writers to augment the panoptics of disciplinary technologies so as to extend, into the contemporary realm of media, the continued relevance of Foucault's analysis of disciplinary technologies.

Of particular influence here is Thomas Mathiesen's (1997) concept of "synopticism", which is formed by the combining "of the Greek word syn", translated as meaning "at the same time", and the word "opticon", which refers to visualisation (ibid. 219). In its reference to the many watching the few, there are indeed pertinent parallels linking the operative principles of

Mathiesen's synopticism and Foucault's panopticism: (1) Similarity in their growth trajectories, "the acceleration which synopticism as well as panopticism has shown in modern times, that is, during the period 1800-2000" (ibid.); (2) panopticism and synopticism "are archaic, or 'ancient' as means or potential means of power in society" (ibid. 222). Mathiesen (ibid.) traces references in the biblical texts of the early Christian era to the use of panoptic surveillance as a technology for the taxation of populations. Synopticism is in evidence in the architectural design of amphitheatres, theatres, and coliseums of ancient societies. In contemporary times, these viewing audiences are increasingly "delocalized so that people have become isolated from each other" (ibid.); and (3) Mathiesen (ibid. 223) identifies, as further parallels between panoptics and synoptics, evidence of their development "in intimate interaction, even fusion with each other. The same institutions have often been panoptical as well as synoptical". Mathiesen identifies the Roman Catholic ritual of confession as an example of the panoptics of religious architecture, and the exterior grandeur of the Church eliciting "synoptical admiration" (ibid.). In more contemporary times, the inter-changeability of panoptics and synoptics is evident in the dashboard screens of wearable fitness technologies. Mathiesen's account of George Orwell's *1984* is an effective preliminary to this discussion: "through a screen in your living room you saw Big Brother, just as Big Brother saw you" (ibid.). Mathiesen describes how technology now enables vast populations to synoptically view advertisements "while the producers of the commodities panoptically survey everyone, controlling the consumers' ability to pay, ensuring that payment takes place, or interrupting the transaction if solvency does not obtain" (ibid. 224). Mathiesen's concept of synopticism clearly has relevance to biosensory technologies; these devices are "enabling the many to see and contemplate the few, so that the tendency for the few to see and supervise the many is contextualized by a highly significant counterpart" (ibid. 219). In so doing, one is able to discern the potential existence in the Garden Bridge management plan's regime of surveillance for the development of exploitative ethico-synoptics (Odih 2016) in which the many-watching-the-many is transformed into lucrative consumer markets for the commodification of security and the extension of adsensory technologies into the mundane everyday phenomenological time of tourism.

In the Garden Bridge Trust's (2014) *Draft Operation and Management Plan* description of biosensor crowd monitoring technology, one gains some insight into the synoptic operation and capacity of the crowd counting biosensors proposed for the Garden Bridge. Furthermore, my discussion of

220   Chapter Five

SensorInsight's suite of crowd-profiling sensor technologies provides expectation of the surveillance technologies to be rolled out elsewhere along the South Bank river space. Consider in this respect the following statement derived from the Garden Bridge Trust (2014:17): "A decision on whether to use wifi will be made only when the technology is proven. It is understood that SBEG are considering the use of this technology on the South Bank and the GBT will liaise with them about its use". If one assumes correctly that SBEG is an acronym for the South Bank Employers' Group, the magnitude of the proposed rolling out of biosensor surveillance technologies becomes worryingly apparent for the SBEG (2018) describes itself as "a unique partnership of eighteen of the major organisations in South Bank, Waterloo and Blackfriars with a long-term commitment to improving the everyday experience of the area for employees, visitors and residents alike". The scope and scale of SBEG's territory and remit provide for a vast riverscape of public recreational space, which as a consequence of the inroads made by the Garden Bridge project into biosensing crowd monitoring technology is now subject further to sign technologies intent on mobilising the body as a vehicle for the adsensory gentrification of post-industrial urban space.

Figure 5.2.: "The world smiles at us. It offers itself to us. And because *everywhere* is imagined as offering itself to us, *everywhere* is more or less the same" (John Berger, *Ways of Seeing*, 1972). Photographic Image, South Bank, Central London, August 2016.

Garden Bridge, Rentier Capital as the Adsensory Financialisation of Urban Decay

Figure 5.3.: "Colour photography is to the spectator-buyer what oil paint was to the spectator-owner. Both media use similar, highly tactile means to play upon the spectator's sense of acquiring the *real* thing which the image shows. In both cases his feeling that he can almost touch what is in the image reminds him how he might or does possess the real thing" (John Berger, *Ways of Seeing*, 1972). Photographic Image, South Bank, Central London, August 2016.

Chapter Six

Garden Bridge, Subverting the Adsensory Privatisation of Our Riverway

Figure 6.1.: "If one moment of that process is isolated, its image will seem banal and its banality, instead of serving as a bridge between two intense imaginative states, will be chilling" (John Berger, *Ways of Seeing*, 1972). Photographic Image, Southbank, London 2016.

Absolute Ground-Rent: "The worst land pays no ground-rent" (Marx 1991: 882)

One may question the futility of investigating the strategic business case, procurement and proposed maintenance management plan for a Garden Bridge project that has ceased to be a viable prospect. Empiricism as an epistemological basis for the urban ecology analysis of gentrification is unable to contend with the immaterial infrastructural exploitative relations of capital accumulation that were sediment as a result of the Garden Bridge project's existence. Conversely, in *Capital* Volume III, Marx sets out, albeit tentatively, a model of rentier capital accumulation that has application to the critical analysis of the Garden Bridge scenario, in which the structure did not materialise despite the investment of £40million of taxpayers' money. Despite not a single Garden Bridge brick being laid, it is my concluding contention that conditions for the capitalist valorisation of capital were being abundantly exploited. The following provides a precis of this chapter's key findings with regard to the application of Marx's *Capital* Volume III formulation of absolute ground-rent as a framework for the critical analysis of capital valorisation as part of the preconstruction and procurement process for the Garden Bridge.

In *Capital* Volume III, chapter 45, entitled "Absolute ground-rent", Karl Marx commences with the statement that the theory of differential ground-rent can proceed from the postulate: "Land pays ground-rent only when the individual production price of its product is below the production price that governs the market, giving rise to a surplus profit that is transformed into rent" (Marx 1991: 882). Ipso facto, Marx argues "that the worst land pays no ground-rent" (ibid.). It is crucial to appreciate that Marx's premise is not that rentier capital has an occasional altruism for, as Marx (ibid. 884) observes about the "worst land" described as "class A land": "But from the premise that capital could now be invested by the farmer on class A land under the average valorisation conditions of capital, it no way follows that this land in class A is now immediately at the farmer's disposal". Consequently, this chapter's analysis of the Garden Bridge preconstruction and procurement processes fundamentally comprehends that rentier capital gains from the payment of no rent on the worst land is, as Marx (ibid.) asserts, "no way a reason for the landlord to lease out his land to the farmer for nothing, and be so philanthropic to his client as to extend him a *crédit gratuit*". Such a misunderstanding would require conceptually abstracting from the capitalist relations of power integral to landed property and practically "abolishing landed property, whose very existence is a barrier to the investment of capital and its unrestricted valorization on the land" (ibid.). Inferentially, while my analysis suggests that rentier capital gains via the payment of no rent on the "worst land" is evident with regard to the Garden Bridge, Marx argues that in this mode of capital accumulation, the absolute existence of landed property is "a barrier that in no way collapses" (ibid. 884-885). Suffice to say, "landed property remains such a barrier even where rent in the form of differential rent disappears" (ibid. 885). Marx, nevertheless, proceeds to formulate a model of rentier capital accumulation "where rent in the form of differential rent disappears, i.e. on type A land" (ibid.); albeit ponderously caveating this model with the insistence that: "If we consider the cases where capital investment on the land can take place without payment of rent, in a country of capitalist production, we shall find that they all involve a factual – if not a legal – abolition of landed property, an abolition that can occur only under very special conditions of an accidental nature" (ibid.). On further reflection, the conception of "accidental nature" might well be supplicated by Marx's Epicurean account of the aleatory encounter; and thus suggesting situations more theoretically sophisticated than initially appears. Accepting this, it is plausible to apply to the case study of the Garden Bridge Marx's three hypothesised scenarios in which "rent in the form of differential rent disappears i.e. on type A land" (ibid.).

Marx's (ibid.) first scenario has particular resonance with the Garden Bridge procurement process for "the landowner is himself a capitalist or the capitalist a landowner". In his capacity, the landowner "can cultivate his land himself as soon as the market price has risen sufficiently to obtain the price of production from the present land" (ibid.). Marx reasons why it might be that the landowner would act in this manner; because ownership of the landed property freehold "does not set any barrier to the investment of his capital" (ibid.). Thus, as Marx contends, the freehold possessor of the landed property can "treat the land as a simple natural element" and in the absence of this concern "let his decisions be determined exclusively by considering the valorization of his capital, by capitalist considerations" (ibid.).

Although conceived as "accidental", Marx does conceive that "such cases do exist in practice, but only as exceptions" (ibid.), the contention being that "just as the capitalist cultivation of the land assumes a separation between functioning capital and landed property, so it generally rules out cultivation by the landed proprietor himself" (ibid.). Moreover, Marx argues that it would be inherently contradictory to begin from the premise of a division between capital and labour and then proceed to hypothesise a scenario in which "the landowner is his own farmer, up to the point that, or wherever, capital would draw no rent from cultivating the land if there were no landed property independent of it … This abolition of landed property is accidental. It may exist or it may not" (ibid. 885-886). It is my contention that a similar scenario was evident throughout the procurement process for the Garden Bridge. Suffice to say, Marx's (1991: 885) observation that rentier capital gains from situations where "rent in the form of differential rent disappears", for the landowner decides to "cultivate his land himself" as predicated on a scenario of "the landowner is himself a capitalist or the capitalist a landowner", correlates with the complex freehold matrix of the Garden Bridge's landownership. As a precursor to this discussion, consider the following extract:

> The Council granted planning permission, subject to conditions, for the proposed Garden Bridge, in December 2014. The Bridge is to be located between Waterloo Bridge to the west and Blackfriars Bridge to the east and will span the River Thames between Victoria Embankment and the South Bank.
> …
>
> The Council's Planning Applications Committee required that the S106 agreement cannot be signed until the GBT has a legal interest in the land.
>
> The Council is the freeholder. Therefore in 2014, the Garden Bridge Trust (GBT) approached the Council and CSCB Ltd with a view to acquiring an interest in part of the South Bank to erect a landing building, (the South Landing Building), for the proposed Garden Bridge on land adjacent to Queen's Walk. This single-storey landing building will incorporate maintenance, management and welfare facilities for GBT's operational purposes, provision of public toilets and up to 410sqm of A1, A3 and or D1 flexible floorspace with additional ancillary services and plant.
> …
>
> The long leaseholder is CSCB who have a lease, (dated 9 April 1992), with an unexpired term of approximately 75 years, but with a right for CSCB to renew on the same terms for a further period of 99 years. The passing rent is a peppercorn.
>
> The identified site and area required by GBT is within the area which is subject to the CSCB lease. A variation is required to enable the completion of the S106 legal agreement and the construction of the South Landing Building to proceed.

(Lambeth Council 2016: 2-3)

Coin Street Community Builders' (2015) *The Garden Bridge* publication describes the intention to locate the "South Bank 'landing'" of the Garden Bridge "on part of the Riverside Walkway by ITV London" which "is leased to Coin Street Community Builders". It is stated that the latter lease from the freehold owner, the London Borough of Lambeth (ibid.). Given that "landed property does not set any barrier to the investment of his capital" (Marx 1991: 885), the freeholder Lambeth Council could, as Marx (ibid.) might have expressed it, "treat the land as a simple natural element and let his decision be determined exclusively by considering the valorization of his capital, by capitalist considerations". Ipso facto, one might conceive Lambeth Council's freeholder participation in the Garden Bridge procurement process as reminiscent of Marx's (ibid.) observation "that the landowner is his own farmer, up to the point that, or wherever, capital would draw no rent from cultivating the land if there were no landed property independent of it". But what is this freeholder farming, one will no doubt ask. In respect to the case study of Garden Bridge, it is my contention that an answer to this question is: knowledge, so as to valorise the value of the land, which London Borough of Lambeth is the freehold owner. Some basis for this claim is evident in Marx's (1991: 886) account of a second scenario in which "rent in the form of differential rent disappears i.e. on type A land". In this scenario, Marx describes how a freehold landowner may lease, among a collection of land, portions of land which are not expected to yield rent payment "since what he pays attention to is the total rental of the land leased and not the particular rent of individual component parts" (ibid.). Apropos to the freehold owner of the Garden Bridge South Bank Landing, it would appear that its leasehold to Coin Street Community Builders contained a phenomenon described by Marx (ibid.) as "non-rent-bearing pieces".

Specifically, Marx (ibid.) argues that the "tracts of type-A land" are rent-free because the "worst land simply forms an inseparable filling sandwiched between the better land". Nevertheless, rentier capital gains are accumulated from this land, and this is illustrated by the subleasing scheme provisioned by Lambeth Council for the leasehold recipient Coin Street Community Builders. Some theoretical basis for this proposition is evident in Marx's formulation of a third scenario in which "rent in the form of differential rent disappears" (ibid. 885). In this scenario, the farmer appears to enter into a subleasing agreement with himself. As Marx (ibid. 886) describes: "A farmer may invest extra capital on his existing leasehold even though at the existing market prices the additional product obtained in this way simply yields him the price of production, the customary profit, and does not enable him to pay an additional rent. Thus for one part of the capital invested on the land he does pay ground-rent, for the other part not".

That this third scenario is emblematic of rentier gains through **"absolute boarder controls"** (Odih 2014, 2016) is illustrated by the following critical description of the sub-leasing arrangements proffered by Lambeth Council as a means of supporting the Garden Bridge Trust's attempt to build its permanent structure on land leased by Coin Street Community Builders. Commencing with Coin Street Community Builders rentier capital, the following extract from *Capital* volume III appears apposite: "Thus for one part of the capital invested on the land he does pay ground-rent, for the other part not" (Marx 1991: 886). More specifically, the following extract, derived from the Lambeth Council (2016) report, provides important insights into the proposed Coin Street Community Builders sub-leasing arrangement that, one might argue, has resonance with Marx's critique of ground-rent.

> The report relates to part of the Queen's Walk on the South Bank, where the Council is the freeholder … It describes a proposed variation to the existing lease with the Coin Street Community Builders Ltd, (CSCB). This has arisen as a result of a request by the Garden Bridge Trust (GBT). If supported, the negotiation and resultant variation will allow the construction and occupation of a new, permanent building ('the South Landing Building' (SLB)), which will form the landing point of the proposed Garden Bridge ('the bridge') on the South Bank. Construction of the South Landing Building is conditional upon completion of the Bridge. If the Bridge is not completed, any permanent building will have to be removed. The Council has granted planning permission for the Bridge, (Lambeth Planning ref: 14/02792/FUL), subject to 45 conditions and the completion of a S106 legal agreement to secure a number of planning obligations. The construction of the Bridge and the South Landing Building is at no cost to the Council. Agreement to the proposed draft Heads of Term is requested. The conclusion of the negotiation is to be delegated to officers in consultation with the Cabinet Member for Jobs and Growth. (Lambeth Council 2016: 1)

On 24th March 2016, Lambeth Council (2016), freeholder of the portion of the Queen's Walk situated on the South Bank, intended for the Garden Bridge south landing, published its proposed leaseholder alterations designed to enable Coin Street Community Builders Ltd to sublease land to the Garden Bridge Trust. It is my contention that the subleasing agreement exemplifies the contemporary reality and relevance of all three of Marx's (1991) conditions for the capital accumulation of rentier gains from the non-payment of rent. Firstly, given Lambeth Council's status as freeholder, it could, as Marx might describe, "farm" the land itself with incurring financial impediment. Evidence of this logic and aspect of rent-free rentier gains is provided in the following Lambeth Council (2016) statement:

> Finance summary
>
> There is no direct cost to the Council in terms of a capital contribution for the construction of the Bridge arising from this variation.
>
> The Council will not incur any financial liabilities arising from the construction/maintenance of the South Landing Building and the surrounding area in the event of GBT failing to fulfil its obligations. A guarantee has been sought from Transport for London (TFL) and the Greater London Authority to meet the obligations of the GBT for the ongoing maintenance and upkeep of the bridge and therefore the South Landing Building. This will be legally secured. The S106 Agreement secured as part of the planning permission requires GBT to make an annual payment as a contribution towards any operational and maintenance costs associated with relevant off-site impacts. In the first year after opening this will be up to a ceiling of £250,000 (index linked and subject to an open book assessment of actual costs incurred), and each year thereafter it will be a sum to be agreed with the Council based on the actual impacts derived from monitoring during the previous year. The funding must be paid to the Council as the accountable body.
>
> An undertaking by the GBT has been agreed to cover all professional costs incurred by the Council in any part of this transaction.
>
> (Lambeth Council 2016: 1-2)

That the proposed Garden Bridge Trust sublease arrangement effectively protected Lambeth Council from incurring financial liabilities is self-evident; but what is less easily deduced is evidence of what Marx (1991: 885) identifies as the freeholder treating "the land as a simple natural element" and in so doing letting "his decision be determined exclusively by considering the valorization of his capital by capitalist considerations". Lambeth Council (2016: 1-2) displays shrewd business acumen in its abnegation of finance liabilities for the subleasing of the designated land by Coin Street Community Builders to the Garden Bridge Trust. Lambeth Council (ibid.) also demonstrates dexterity here in the indirect extraction of finance capital from its leasing of freehold land. Thus, the latter illustrates a situation in which rentier capital is being expropriated through the non-payment of rent. The terms of this subleasing provide ample empirical evidence of this curious, and yet ever-so-lucrative, feature of renter capital gains, as is evident in the following extract:

> Proposal and Reasons:
>
> The terms of the existing CSCB [Coin Street Community Builders] lease do not permit any development on the land nor do they permit the grant of an under-lease or any sub-letting except in certain defined circumstances. If the Bridge is to go ahead the following sequence of events are required: Lambeth to vary the lease with CSCB; CSCB to agree a sub-lease to GBT to enable the construction of the Bridge; GBT to agree to sub lease back to CSCB so that they can occupy the new commercial premises that will be constructed as part of the South Landing Building with further sub-eases as required by CSCB with any tenants that they wish to contract with.
>
> CSCB currently benefits from an income from the sub-letting of the land in their lease to a variety of users for temporary, promotional or meanwhile activity. A recent example is the 'Virgin Holiday's treehouse'. CSCB is required to maintain the land within their lease and this source of income supports that requirement, which it is understood from CSCB can be significant. CSCB have stipulated that they should be 'no worse off' if the Bridge is constructed. The Council understands that they have required GBT to lease the commercial premises to them to ensure that they are not worse off than if the Bridge was not built. Therefore, the space lost for temporary activity when the bridge is constructed could potentially be mitigated by use of the permanent building. It should be noted that in the absence of a formal planning consent, the number of days that such activities can be carried out is limited to 28 days in any calendar year by virtue of permitted development rights granted through planning legislation.
>
> (Lambeth Council 2016: 3)

Marx (1991: 886) observed, in scenarios two and three, conditions which have resonance with aspects of the detailing of the subleasing agreement between Lambeth Council, Coin Street Community Builders and the Garden Bridge Trust. Recall that Marx (ibid.) describes a scenario in which "a leasehold may include particular pieces of land that pay no rent at the given level of market prices, and are in fact rented free, though they are not viewed in this light by the landowner, since what he pays attention to is the total rental of the land leased and not the particular rent of individual component parts".

In the Coin Street Community Builders subleasing application, we find evidence of existing "temporary" subleasing situations (e.g., Virgin

Holidays' Southbank-located treehouse) which are rent free in the sense that the freeholder (Lambeth Council) is not directly extracting rent for these "temporary" subleasing arrangements. Marx's (1991: 886) observation has resonance here in that it explains the situation of capital gains through rent-free leasing as such: "But the only reason why he pays no rent for these pieces of land is that he does pay rent for the land to which they are an accessory. In this case, the combination presupposed is precisely one in which resort does not have to be had to the worse type-A land as an independent and new field of production in order to make up the missing supply". It is my contention that here and elsewhere is evidence of rentier capital gains expropriated through the freeholder boarding the land and through absolute inscriptive sign technologies (e.g., sub leasing agreements) extracting finance capital indirectly via the proffering of the land as rent free.

One may argue that the decommissioning of the Garden Bridge project affects the relevance of these suppositions. But even the most cursory perusal through the procurement process and arrangements set in motion to reengineer time-honoured statutory leasing agreements identifies the actor network triangle of Coin Street Community Builders, Lambeth Council and Garden Bridge Trust to have set in motion a precedence for the privatisation through "**absolute boarder controls**" (Odih 2014, 2016) of public recreational post-industrial urban river space. In the following transcription is provided first-hand evidence of these processes at work and illustration of the productive mobilisation of dissent.

Garden Bridge, Subverting the Adsensory Privatisation of Our Riverway 231

Figure 6.2.: "This was the time when the ocean trade routes were being opened up for the slave trade and for the traffic which was to siphon the riches from other continents into Europe, and later supply the capital for the take-off of the Industrial Revolution" (John Berger, *Ways of Seeing*, 1972). Photographic Image, Southbank, London 2016.

Case Study, Interview Transcription – Garden Bridge, South Bank London, August 2017

Interviewer: So I am a teacher at Goldsmiths as a Sociology lecturer, which is great. And I also write for a publisher called Cambridge Scholars [Publishing]; and I write about environmental issues – which they seem to like. In addition to issues about health and biotechnology. But this project is about the environment; and particularly I am interested in water ecology. And erhm I have recently been commissioned to write another book, which is in terms of urban ecology; but it is to do with issues around the environment and the privatisation of public recreational space. Yeah ok? And I would like as a case study the Garden Bridge.
Interviewee: You picked a good one.

Interviewer: Oh yeah, I think so. And erhm, I was watching television actually and saw you being interviewed.
Interviewee: Probably yes. I wondered how you recognised me.

Interviewer: So I am very glad actually to have the opportunity to be able to interview you also.
Interviewee: Sure.

Interviewer: Thank you very much. Ok then, great. So in terms of the, could you just tell me about your organisation?
*Interviewee: It's Thames Central Open Spaces. I know it's quite a mouthful, isn't it. (**Interviewer:** "It's great, ok"). But it was formed in 2014, that September. And it came about because we were told that there was going to be a Garden Bridge built. Erhm, we were told in a public meeting in June and that wasn't acceptable to us. We just thought that it was a fait accompli, and no one had asked our permission or even if we wanted it. So I personally set up a petition. I didn't think that anything would happen of it, I just thought I'm going to Change.Org, see how many people oppose this and to my surprise hundreds did. I thought I better ask my neighbours and so I did, door to door with some of the neighbours, and almost unanimously everybody said: No, we don't want it. They felt that they could do anything. And with the help of a really brilliant organisation called Waterloo Community Development Group (WCDG). They helped me and guided me through, how to oppose a planning process, because they deal with developments in Waterloo all the time. And I felt that this was particularly inappropriate and so I asked them to help me to do something about it. And that's how the campaign started. And it, erhm, TCOS or Thames Central*

Garden Bridge, Subverting the Adsensory Privatisation of Our Riverway

Open Spaces is about, there are probably about eight people who are very keen. Whether it be people who write the blog or keep on the Twitter feed or who go door to door and do leaflet distribution I mean, that is a huge part of it. We didn't have the big machine and the cogs of the Garden Bridge Trust, who are funded by TFL, our money. And they had and they had a team, or they employed a team of professional people; media and PR people to do all their stuff. We did everything ourselves; you know the amount of man power, woman power that has gone into leafletting everybody or setting up meetings, it's all done voluntarily so I take my hat off to the entire community for taking me on board and for helping muck in. To save our public space.

Interviewer: And what was it about the threat to the public space that really did galvanise the community?
Interviewee: Well, we don't have much public, we don't have much green space; and that particular piece of land was left for the community to be used, in the lease it clearly specifies that, that piece of public space is to be used as public land.

Interviewer: Specifies in the lease?
Interviewee: It's in the lease, yes. The freeholder of the land is Lambeth Council; the leaseholders are Coin Street Community Builders. And specifically in the lease it says that this land is to be used and kept as a public right-of way for public and community use and not to be developed upon. And so Coin Street, who own the land, own the lease were trying to fudge that and obviate their lease obligations by subletting it, subleasing it through a complicated planning procedure which involved Lambeth Council allowing a variation of the lease. They permitted it, but it is a complete subversion of the very rules that are in place to protect common land for people. It is a total, it was a total subversion of the rules erhm that were clearly in place, intended to protect public land.

Interviewer: And so you said that Coin Street?
Interviewee: Coin, C O I N. This entire area, where you are sitting now in the National Theatre, wasn't much in the 1950s, 60s and by the time it got to the 70s, they said: let's develop it into corporate spaces, offices. And in the 1980s a group of people got together called Coin Street Community Builders – they called themselves – and they won the land. And the GLC, the Greater London Council, at the time, or the London Residuary Body, there were several bodies at the time that were still in existence. They conceded and with a heavily subsidised loan Coin Street Community

Builders obtained and purchased the land that the Garden Bridge is supposed to land on.

Interviewer: *So they purchased the lease?*
Interviewee: *They purchased the land; erhm, they purchased the lease, you are quite right. For £750,000, back in the 1980s. And there were certain provisos that Coin Street had to do to that land. One of which of course was to provide community housing and the other is to keep community space and it was in the lease; absolutely stipulated that piece of land in the Queen's Walk, that wonderful boulevard of trees, lit with blue lights at night must be kept as a public right-of-way and not to be developed upon. So they have failed us; Coin Street have definitely failed us, and they are still trying to develop on land for social and community use. But that's another story; that's our next battle actually, unfortunately.*

Interviewer: *Excellent, and so they subleased it to?*
Interviewee: *They subleased it to the Garden Bridge Trust. They allowed a variation on the lease to allow it to be subleased to the Garden Bridge Trust.*

Interviewer: *And this is the Community Builders?*
Interviewee: *Which is a clear obviation of the guidelines intended to protect such actions; but Lambeth Council allowed it. We took them to the Scrutiny, the Scrutiny Committee at Lambeth Council. We said this planning permission shouldn't be allowed. Erhm, unfortunately the person who chaired that Scrutiny meeting had been in talks with the development people at Lambeth Council; and who had been in touch with the Garden Bridge Trust; and we'll never know what happened behind closed doors but it is all just a bit too convenient that they all spoke to each other and low and behold, a sublease was allowed.*

Interviewer: *In terms of the Garden Bridge, were they, did they try to engage with the community?*
Interviewee: *No, the Garden Bridge Trust.*

Interviewer: *Because there is a level whereby there is the suggestion that they are actually working with the communities?*
Interviewee: *No, no, they definitely didn't. They had paved the way by speaking with Coin Street and Lambeth Council. Did you know they had spoken to Lambeth Council by the tail end of 2012? And erhm they had already had meetings with Thomas Heatherwick and TFL and then in March 2013 low and behold, the Garden Bridge has been announced. So*

they were actually in discussions with Transport for London, Thomas Heatherwick and the Garden Bridge people. By then there was no Garden Bridge Trust by then. But they had already been in discussion for a Garden Bridge in the area before the Garden Bridge even became a thing. It is just so corrupt, I can't tell you. So they had already agreed nominally to this project and then they thought: Well, let's put it out there and have some consultation. And it was during 2013 that consultation, and I use that in the loosest possible term; two months of consultation on the TFL website; very little widespread press about the Garden Bridge at all. And so when they came to us in 2014 and said: Oh, we've done some consultation and the results are very positive. And they said that 87% of Londoners were in favour of the project. When I asked specifically about the statistics, it turned out that, that 87% came from comments from the visitor book that totalled about 258 signatures. Unbelievably corrupt, but they will use those figures and fudge them to their advantage. I think that figure still may remain on their website to this day.

Interviewer: In terms of the land, why is the land so valuable? Has value been added to the land?
Interviewee: The land is incredibly valuable because of its location; its wonderful riverside location. It would be prime real estate for any developer. You would be mad not to want to, if you were a developer, not to make the best of and exploit the best views of London. So much so that right where we are, there are protected views of London, that you can't develop upon it because it will ruin the views, the sight lines of Saint Paul's Cathedral. However, once again, the Garden Bridge Trust were going to obviate that in their planning application the English Heritage clearly stated: Yes, you will actually ruin viewing point, 16 point "a" I think it is, of the views of Saint Paul's. So three clear violations of, have you heard of London View Management Framework (LVFM)? That was set up directly to protect the views of Saint Paul's and treasured views of London. Sadly, the person who oversees all of that is the Mayor of London and of course at the time that was Boris Johnson. So he and English Heritage said the views on the Garden Bridge would outweigh the damage done to the loss of views, to the loss of protected views that already exist. And this was a clear joke because new views from the Garden Bridge had not been created. So we weren't able to see even visualisations of what the views might be and yet it still passed planning permission. It still got planning permission. Despite the fact that we had not seen images of what those new views might be; so that's another travesty. Going over it all again just makes my blood boil, it really does. Boris Johnson had deemed, and with British Heritage, which is

a shocking, shocking revelation, they had both agreed that the new views from this private bridge would outweigh the benefits, would outweigh the damage done to existing views. But also in Westminster planning committee; Westminster themselves had said: Had this been a private project, there is no way we would have allowed planning permission. But because there is some TFL funding and some public engagement via the Mayor of London Boris Johnson, we will allow it. They had clearly stipulated had it been a private project: ah, ah no way. **(Interviewer:** *"And who would have said?").* Westminster Planning, Lambeth are somewhat desperate and so I would say: They are desperate for a feather in their cap. They want something to show off their borough. It is not that they don't have enough: National Theatre and the London Eye. They wanted something else: a feather in their cap. And we firmly believe they wanted this to pass at all cost. It might have had something to do with the fact that the Garden Bridge Trust used money from TFL, thousands of money, to fast track the application. So they had a job to do, Lambeth. But Westminster were more canny and they have, they are more powerful in that they have more conservation concerns and they don't want a tacky tourist attraction on their side of the river. So they were more canny and they had more stipulations, one of which was a guarantee; Robert Davis was the leader of the planning committee and he stipulated: The Garden Bridge, yes, all right, you can build, but you must have a guarantee or a surety from somebody who can guarantee your maintenance costs of £3.5 million. Lambeth didn't ask for such a guarantee. As I say, they would have let the bridge happen and had it gone belly-up, then we would have picked up the bill. So we took them to court over that and we won the guarantee for Lambeth. It is crazy that the local community had to do that in order to safeguard are own concerns. We realised that Lambeth was so reckless we had to take them to a High Court and the High Court judge said: Yes, you have got a case. And so we settled by saying: You must give us a guarantee. And it was on the basis, on the lack of that guarantee, that the Garden Bridge failed. Otherwise it could have gone ahead.

Interviewer: Yeah, in terms of the actual bridge and what was being promised about the bridge. So were you concerned about the actual bridge? (Interviewee: *"Yes, it's huge absolutely huge").* **So we talked about procurement; just in terms of the Bridge.**
Interviewee: Well, procurement is a whole new, gosh, that's an entire degree subject, that is. But they bypassed procurement; they fast tracked everything. There were clear signs that Thomas Heatherwick had gone to San Francesco with Boris Johnson in 2012; you probably know about that?

He didn't go with Johanna Lumley, but Boris took his chief of staff Ed Lister and Isabel Dedring. They were the head honchos at TFL at the time. They went to Apple and tried to get money (Interviewer: "Oh yeah, Apple"). Low and behold, Thomas Heatherwick happened to be in Apple in San Francisco at the same time. And so he joined them. They were clearly trying to get funding before Garden Bridge even became a project and passed by TFL. This is just corruption (Interviewer: "Concerning"). Very concerning. Yeah, that's procurement, but as for the Bridge itself, several architects, including Alistair Lenczner, who was the architect for a project called the Millau Viaduct, which is a beautiful bridge in France. Ian Ritchie is a well-esteemed architect. So many people we know have opposed it on the grounds of aesthetics, design. It's a huge clunky thing, I mean, even if you were to stand under Waterloo Bridge, that's nowhere near the size the Garden Bridge would have been, which is only there [gesturing in the direction of Waterloo Bridge]. It would have been thirty metres wide at its widest point and that's bigger than a football pitch. The narrowest point would have been six metres wide, which is ridiculous; that is a bottleneck beyond belief: from thirty to six metres, crazy. And the actual entrance to the Bridge itself would have only been four metres wide. So ridiculous proportions; a massive span in an area that is already covered by several bridges. In this two-mile span of the Thames, you have got twelve bridges. Ten that can be crossed on foot. It's just ridiculous.

Interviewer: And there were claims that it was going to be ecologically environmentally friendly. Did you challenge?
Interviewee: Yeah, it's called greenwash. It would have been 15,000 tonnes of concrete being poured into the Thames, which has a delicate eco-system as it is. We have only just managed to get the Thames up to scratch so that flora and fauna can survive within the Thames. You know, we actually have fish now swimming within the Thames; we've cleaned up the Thames.

Interviewer: I know; it was biologically dead in the 50s.
Interviewee: To dump 15,000 tonnes of concrete, which would have also, would have affected the shoreline. Which a lot of birds, as you know, just come to perch when they are not flying; or want to sit a while and sup from the Thames. All of that would have been destroyed. The river bed itself would have been sunk and any of the, for example, a huge amount of archaeological finds that you can still find on the Thames Bank, like clay pipes or whatever; because the Thames was London's receptacle for everything back in medieval times. So all of that history is just being gradually eroded away by over-development by man. But, yeah,

ecologically it would have been a disaster. And also it would have been totally private and the actual green space that was allowed on the Bridge, you do know that it is 2,500 square metres of green on a 6,500 square-metre bridge? So a third of it might have been green. But that equals, the 2,500 square metres that they proposed for the green space, equals what we have here [gesturing to the Southbank wharf] with all these trees and the grass and whatever. So you are taking one and you are putting one on top of the river; but you are privatising it. It was a complete smokescreen; but their trees would not have been, nowhere near as big as our wonderful London Plane [tree] here. There were 270 trees, and I use that in the loose term because if you take 270 trees, you could not put them on 500 square metres of space. They would have been lollipop trees or shrubs. I have trees in my back garden that are classed as trees but they are practically bonsai. The Garden Bridge Trust's loose interpretation of replacing thirty-eight trees with 270 was once again just a smoke -screen: greenwash. And we call it greenwash because it was sponsored by companies who needed to make their reputation greener. In particular Glencore, who wanted to cover the Bridge in their copper nickel alloy. It would have changed in time from a gold to a rust colour. But this copper nickel was mined from places in the Congo and Zambia, which have an appalling human rights record; pollution records are terrible, they pollute rivers in the Congo. Glencore have such a bad reputation for tax dodging. It is probably one of the most ecologically unsound, vile mining conglomerates; if you mention Glencore to most people, there will be close associations with a lot of controversy. So to make themselves greener, they align themselves with the Garden Bridge Trust. They said that they would donate £10million so long as they would use that ten million on their copper nickel. So these kind of things are called greenwash. And Sky, for example, you can imagine all the big bad things that Sky are associated with; but they donated £5million to name a garden after them. So they would have had a Sky Garden. There was a lot of greenwashing going on; purporting to be green but hiding an awful lot of associations you don't really want to have out in the public. It's like the National Theatre, you know, they might get a green sponsor to make themselves look good but actually the National Theatre is a charity, that's probably a bad idea. But say, for example, Shell or BP Oil, they need to pick a fluffy project in order to make their reputation greener. And that's exactly what the Garden Bridge Trust did, they aligned themselves with people with the promise of making their reputation greener.

Interviewer: And so the companies that were attracted to the syndicate, they were involved, you think, because the wanted to greenwash their brands?
Interviewee: The Garden Bridge Trust needed funding and so they did approach people to donate. I'm not sure about, say for example, Harrods? Or Ernst and Young, I suspect they, you know, aligning themselves with an allegedly green project can't be a bad idea. But if you look deeper, you'll clearly see that it is not, it is furthest from a green project. It is quite the opposite. But Royal Mail is now a private entity and they donated a huge amount. Bizarrely there was something called the Monument Trust, they are to do with Sainsbury's; and they gave, I believe they are winding up the Monument Trust, the Sainsbury's Foundation and they had money in the bank. Like most people who have budgets, you have to offload that money so they decided to give £20million to the Garden Bridge Trust. Because I believe they are winding up their operations, the Monument Trust. And it was almost a case of we have to give it to someone, let's give it to the Garden Bridge Trust. So that was their single biggest donation and we are shocked that the Monument Trust, which is supposed to be aligned to really good things: whether it is homelessness; cancer, erhm Heart Foundation, would give £20million, that was one of the biggest shockers for us. There is so much that you can go on with £20million, you can fill a school with £20million. And yet they chose to give to the Garden Bridge Trust. It was only a pledge, so we don't think the money's gone. Hopefully it can be reallocated elsewhere. But that really shocked us: Good people giving good money to bad people.

Interviewer: Was that an indication of how well connected they were in terms of trying to gain financing?
Interviewee: I can't speak to why they did it. But it does go to how well-connected people in the Garden Bridge Trust were. All of the trustees are multi-millionaires; and not one of them is liable so far for the £50million that we're potentially liable for the cancellation of their bridge. At the moment it stands at about £46 to £47million. We need a full itemised breakdown of all that spend is. Sadiq Khan doesn't support that; but we need to see it, it is public money.

Interviewer: So in terms of, we are only half way through the interview, ok? So in terms of your engagement; apparently Sadiq Khan was initially quite on board? It is interesting why the sudden change, and then the 14th August the various messages that were sent out by the Mayor of London and then the Garden Bridge. And they were quite terse.

Interviewee: Sadiq during his mayoral campaign said it was a ridiculous idea. We don't know whether it was a political thing because clearly Boris was championing it and Sadiq was clearly the favourite to become mayor. So that was one of his mayoral pledges: that if he became mayor, he would take the money pledge for the Garden Bridge and use it for pedestrianising Oxford Street. So when he got in, he suddenly realised actually, well we strongly suspect, that the Evening Standard, for example, is a very, very powerful machine in London and you can't win elections without something like the Evening Standard. [Alexander] Lebedev owns the Evening Standard, closely aligned with Joanna Lumley and [Thomas] Heatherwick, they are personal friends. And so there came about a U-turn. He also realised that he had to remain allies with developers and TFL, who are closely bonded with this Garden Bridge project. And so he did a U-turn. The leader of Lambeth Council initially said: Actually, I am looking at the figures here and it doesn't look right to me. I am not going to allow you the permission to land on Lambeth. And then TFL, Thomas Heatherwick, Joanna Lumley had a further meeting with Lambeth and they did a U-turn, they said: Actually we are going to use £30million from TFL: We have asked the mayor to commit the £30million from TFL and to transform £20million of it into a loan. So even though the Garden Bridge have got £60million from the Department for Transport and they have got £60million from TFL, £20million of that we are going to convert into a loan. And that is down to me [**** name redacted] from Lambeth Council, I did that; and I have also talked Sadiq Khan into agreeing with me. So from initially saying: Ok, we want the Bridge, to [saying]: No, actually we don't know that we have looked at the figures. And then they have flipped again and said: Right, we do want the Bridge; but the £20million from TFL will be treated as a loan. But once again if you look at the loan agreement, you'll see it was practically interest free; with no penalty clauses if they didn't pay. So it was a sham of a loan but it made them look good. So Sadiq turning again, we wondered if it was as (**Interviewer:** "Did you personally actually, in terms of your organisation, actually engage with this U-turn? Did you actually experience, witness?"). Oh yes, we were there, we were actually sitting with Nick Bowes, who is Sadiq's director of policy before he became mayor. We were actually in a coffee shop with Nick Bowes discussing the foibles of the Garden Bridge when news came in that Sadiq had done a U-turn. that he was now backing it because of this sham loan arranged by Lambeth Council. And he sat there, shell-shocked, and I don't think even he knew what to say to us. We wondered if he had known all along but he seemed surprised at this U-turn as well. But now that U-turn had happened, they had to go with it, they had to say: It could be good for London so long as more public money goes into it, and that's the line Sadiq has taken ever since. It could be good for London as long as no more taxpayers' money that he's responsible for could go into it. So I actually think, personally, that it was the long game that he was thinking of. And he played it very well because on the surface of it he seemed to be saying: I am for the Garden Bridge, we want to show London is open; it's a great thing for London but we don't want any taxpayers to fork out any more than has been committed already. And that was a nigh on impossible task for the Garden Bridge Trust to get round because Sadiq was clearly the only person who could give a viable trustee for the Bridge. No one else other than a public body could possibly commit £3.5million every year as a guarantee. Unless some very foolish millionaire, billionaire, was prepared to put £100million into an endowment trust in order to bail out the Bridge forever. It was a monumental task for the Garden Bridge Trust to overcome and they clearly didn't do it.

Interviewer: *So you said the long game. So the long game that Sadiq was playing?*
Interviewee: *Well, Sadiq started by saying no then yes, and then stuck with that yes, with the proviso that no more taxpayers' money would go into it. But every meeting, and I have attended several, I have attended several Mayor's Question Time, they have a People's Question Time where the Mayor attends; we attended the O$_2$, a group of our TCOS, supporters, yelled out to him: What about the money? And he said no more taxpayers' money that I am responsible for. I think that it could be a good thing for London. We kind of heckled but it made the headlines, it was on LBC. He was clearly on the back foot, he never answered my question straight: Are you going to commit £3.5million or £3.1million for the guarantee, and he just would not; I have got video clips of him answering in a very round-about-way. He completely circumvented anything that came near to an answer that anyone wanted to hear. He just wouldn't answer a straight question about whether he would commit £3.5million. He just spelt out the mantra time and time again. I will not commit further public money other than that I am responsible for blah, blah, blah. You ask him a straight question, he wouldn't do that. I was really frustrated; I thought he's not meeting with us! We have met with everybody, we have met with Zac Goldsmith, we met with Caroline Pidgeon, everybody who was running for mayor. Everybody but Sadiq Khan would meet with us. But it turns out, having read Lord Mervyn Davies' letter, he's the chairman of the Garden Bridge Trust, it turns out that he wouldn't even meet them; Sadiq wouldn't even meet them. So that, we are pleasantly surprised about that, so he was kinda avoiding*

controversy by not meeting either side. By not being accused of having met one side and not the other. So we are pleasantly surprised by that. We still welcome the opportunity to talk to him now about it because we don't think that it is the right way of engaging: You need to talk to both sides, you can't just draw your own conclusion from people who were very closely associated, for example, with the procurement fiasco. He's been guided by TFL and they are so culpable in messing this up. They have so many questions to answer, including people who are now hugely instrumental in getting the Garden Bridge off the ground. Who are now working for Arup, for example, who are the Garden Bridge contractors and engineers. There is clearly some sort of nepotism and some cross fertilisation going on where chums are scratching each other's backs and helping each other out. I would be very interested to find where the head honchoes of the Garden Bridge now end up. I wouldn't be at all surprised if it is something closely connected with Arup. In fact, did you know that the Garden Bridge Trust team are largely made up of the people who did the Olympic delivery team? **(Interviewer:** *"Arup?"). ARUP, A.R.U.P. ARUP are huge engineering construction contractors, they provide information on design development, feasibility. As well as employing the construction people as well. They are huge! Absolutely huge! They are giants enough to take on board whoever is going to suffer from the fall out of the Garden Bridge Trust collapsing, I would think. They earned £8million from it so far.*

Interviewer: I am also interested in the way in which the experience, the tourist experience; and the way in which that was being sold in terms of technology. I wonder if you have any background to that in terms of how they were trying to sell the experience to the community? That this would be an enhanced experience of a bridge.
Interviewee: They used the green-credentials very heavily by saying that it would be a quiet oasis and an idyllic place for you to relax. But that was just ridiculous given that they factored into their plans a Disney-style queuing system. They also mentioned that the maximum capacity for the bridge will be 2,500 people. And they acknowledged in the planning application that for the first three years the Garden Bridge would be chock-a-block; it would be one of the most visited popular tourist attractions in the country, if not Europe. That's what they were always comparing themselves to: Disneyland Paris. So how that can be an idyllic peaceful place with 2,500 people and Disney-style queuing? What a joke! What an absolute joke.

Interviewer: *Was there the suggestion of factoring, the possibility of making this a pay-to-use space? Was the infrastructure present in that suggestion?*
Interviewee: They had plans for an Oyster card-style reader at either end; but that would have also been something challengeable in the High Court. Because their very raison d'être was to be a free public; sorry a publicly accessibly space. It was never going to be a public space. There are clear, it is clearly written in the planning application that this will be a private space managed by the Garden Bridge Trust. (***Interviewer:*** "Oh, ok"). So whenever they kept going on: it will be for the public; that was an absolute lie. It was a complete misleading of the public. It was privately owned public space. (***Interviewer:*** "Perfect"). That's not the same as public space; [in] public space you can protest, you can sit and do want you want; you can fall asleep there if you wanted to. You could not have done that on the Garden Bridge. So yeah.

Interviewer: *So there was a suggestion, ok, so there was an obvious privatisation. I was just wondering whether there were any connections? You know, you said that Sky was interested; a media connection they aimed to introduce in terms of the way in which people experienced the Bridge?*
Interviewee: They had, in their initial business plans, for example, they had written down that they could use it for world record attempts. The one thing that the Garden Bridge didn't do, even though they kept saying: it will be open every single day of the year, except for maybe twelve half-days (or whatever); we are going to have corporate events where we need to fund raise. Well, that was all bull as well because, I don't about you but if you organise a public event, you are going to need more than half a day to set that up. They had talked about doing things like theatrical performances; corporate parties; gala, the Garden Bridge gala. There were going to be two Garden Bridge galas. These things do not take half a day to set up. You are going to close off massive parts of this area, the Queen's Walk. This is called the Queen's Walk, by the way [gesturing to the pedestrian wharf alongside the National Theatre, London]. They were going to close off huge parts of that just to set up the toilets, the catering; you name it. There is no way that, that would have been just two-and-a- half days. But they always constantly, consistently fail to mention that, in addition to the twelve closure days there would be public holidays as well; like New Year's Eve, things for the Thames Festival. Or any other memorial occasion; a flotilla that might come down the Thames. So those were in addition to the twelve closed days. But they compared themselves to other places, like the Royal Parks or the

National Theatre or something like that; but if you look at those institutions, they can offer so much more in terms of membership, if you like. You could have had membership of the Garden Bridge but there are very limited opportunities for you to do anything as a member of the Garden Bridge compared to the National Theatre, where you can come and see a play. And hire a space; the Garden Bridge was incredibly limited in what you could actually do. You can't hire out a part of the Garden unless you severely hamper your whole raison d'être, which is a public space. It had so many flaws in their plans for their, raison d'être, that it fell apart. Anyone with any intelligence could see it wasn't going to work. Sorry, that was rather harsh.

Interviewer: No, that was excellent. And so as we come towards the end now. So, I'm interested in that change. There seems to be a U-turn now that starts to become more defined, yeah? And we have the situation on Monday with the Garden Bridge [Trust] announcement and Sadiq Khan's announcement. In terms of your experiences and that of your organisation's experience, what insights were you able to gain in terms of why the announcements happened, when they happened and the content of the announcements?

Interviewee: *I can't say exactly why they happened. I can only give you my guess that clearly announcements for anything this major are clearly timed. Press releases always are. And it just so happens that many of the Garden Bridge announcements have been made during the Easter holiday, Christmas time; things that are buried. For example, when there was permission for works to be done to Temple tube station last year, that was massive; that's a public building. A private company wanted to reinforce Temple tube station for their bridge. That was all buried in December by Christmas time. We were given two weeks to respond to this proposal to build on Temple tube; and it was buried amongst Christmas, New Year's Eve. I said it is really unfair. You haven't given people opportunities to properly analyse your documents; we're all going to be on holiday, away whatever; drunk; this is really poor timing. They always do that on purpose. Boris Johnson for example, released his information about the guarantee a day or so before he left office. Just crept; all these things are cleverly and carefully timed. So whenever the Margaret Hodges review came out, I just think that she didn't have an infinite time to do this review, so it has to come out at some stage. And that wasn't at a particularly awkward time. But I do think that the Garden Bridge Trust announcement for winding up has come at the height of the summer holidays; everyone is away; Parliament is in recess. They want to go away with as little fanfare as possible. But we are* not going to let it get away because there are still more questions to be answered, massive corruption to be investigated.

Interviewer: And so when you say that Sadiq Khan announced, the announcement on Monday?
Interviewee: Oh no, he announced the withdrawal of his support for the Garden Bridge on the basis of Margaret Hodges' review some time ago. That was around April.
Interviewer: Yes, the letter, the letter sent to Margaret Hodge.
Interviewee: I don't think there was anything monumental happening around that time. Brexit had already happened; and I don't think there was anything being hidden there ... I said Brexit happened, sorry, it was the General Election I was thinking of.

Interviewer: And so on Monday he announces; his mayoral announcement ... He says he cannot give any more taxpayers' money.
Interviewee: If the Garden Bridge Trust had chosen to wind up there and then, then he clearly, his office would have had to make a comment, a comment pretty damn quick afterwards. We do, if we read about something, we try and get something in on that day ...

Interviewer: And then Sadiq he says, he actually says, that it is an indefinite amount that seems to be promised and that it wasn't value for money. So the indefinite amount seems to be the arrangement of £3.5million a year.
Interviewee: Well, it became, it started off as £2million, then it became £3.5million at its highest then it went down to £3.1million. Sorry, you were saying?

Interviewer: So there is, in the Garden Bridge response, they do suggest that it is the maintenance. The issue is that the Mayor has no longer agreed to underwrite the maintenance?
Interviewee: Yes; but actually their wording goes beyond that. Not only is it the maintenance. This project cannot continue without the Mayor's full approval. And if the Mayor is clearly not; that is a fudge again. The Mayor did commit his support; so long as he didn't give any more money to it. So the Garden Bridge Trust are very much twisting that to have a swipe at Sadiq Khan, which is wholly unjustified given they have so many faults and reasons why they themselves couldn't make it work. To be very childish and swipe that blame at Sadiq Khan when he has actually said: I do support this, so long as Londoners don't have to fork out anymore; we've given them

enough; you need to find your own way. I think that's wholly fair; but they were very ungracious in attacking Sadiq Khan for protecting Londoners' interests. Very disingenuous indeed.

Interviewer: I agree by far and I thought that it did seem disingenuous, by far. And so, and so just finally, do you feel that the situation has been resolved now? Resolved and succeeded?
Interviewee: *Yes, absolutely, it is a complete victory for the people of Waterloo who started this campaign and fought really hard. I mean, we are talking day and night. There have been nights when a group of us have been transcribing a meeting or whatever; and we have been emailing each other at five in the morning, saying: Have you got this far: have you got this chapter? I can't tell you the countless nights that we have actually gone through with a fine tooth comb every document that's been going in order to get our facts straight and to present it to people who can make a difference. Whether it is members of the GLA or our MP Kate Hoey, who raised a question in the Commons; you know, it got as far as the House of Commons, a debate. And the media interest as well, we have to be able to give clear and informed facts to them as well otherwise we just don't look good. And so an awful lot of effort has gone into this. It is not quite the end, although the overall result is what we wanted; which is a stoppage of the Bridge. Unfortunately, more questions have arisen out of the dishonesty of those who made it happen in the first place. Questions are going to arise: What else are they going to push forward again without transparency and openness? We can't let this kind of, it is criminal behaviour. We can't condone that; so that kind of thing needs to be investigated now ...*

Interviewer: I am very in support of your campaign by far. I think that what you have done is very brave.
Interviewee: *I take my hat off for everybody who supported us around here. Before them I think the last big campaign was in the 1980s for Coin Street themselves and the community to rally round to win this land. I can't think of another huge campaign. To stop something as gigantic as this. It had support from the very top, from the Prime Minister David Cameron and George Osbourne, who supported it. It is just like, wooh, we are so the underdogs here. It just really fired the imagination of everybody too. It is really telling that all the people who wanted the project are very, quite well to do. You know artists, creatives and whatever. The feedback is quite: what are you talking about? But it was cross party. The opposition was very cross party. We had GLA people, Andrew Boff, for example, was very against it and said: It's a ridiculous waste of money. Even UKIP hated it [laughter].*

It was totally cross party; the Greens very supportive. Caroline Pigeon from the Liberal Democrats, one of the first people to really grasp hold of this. Its iniquitous ways; she really got behind this; and highlighted it from the start.

Interviewer: And so you worked with these organisations? Did you ally with these organisations? So you worked as a network?
Interviewee: *We networked with them, yes; clearly, we had to talk to them to get things done. There were key decision makers, people like Tom Copley, the Labour representative at the GLA. Florence Eshalomi as well as, it was Val Shawcross, who is now the deputy commissioner for transport at TFL. They were Lambeth and Southwark representatives at the time who we clearly had to go to. Surprisingly Zac Goldsmith, we just pointed out to him, this is not a green project. You used to be working for the ecologists; you are Mr Green, ok, you are a Tory now; but you were; can you not see all of this? He was a real disappointment; he turned to align himself with the Tories. We had to talk to; we tried to talk to Occupy because we had people who were prepared to chain themselves against the trees; stop them from being cut down. We aligned ourselves with so many people. There were certain people we didn't align ourselves with. Other projects that didn't quite tally with ours; erhm, different agendas. Even people like the TaxPayers' Alliance, who are very; seen as Tories, Tory supporters. It is clearly a waste of taxpayers' money. So it is clearly in their interests to align with us if you like but we never actually had a definite association with them. Some people saw us as trouble makers; some people saw us as a bit too contentious. Although we never said anything vitriolic or anything. Generally, people don't want to stand next to people shouting with banners. We did do some shouting with banners, you know. But that's always the campaign. You always get people who don't want to have that link, I suppose, with anything slightly controversial.*

Interviewer: And finally your identification with the space, with the river, it seems to be a very sort of embodied relation to it. Did you see the Garden Bridge as invading that particular way of relating?
Interviewee: *Completely.*

Interviewer: In terms of your identity, what was it that you identified with in terms of the river and space?
Interviewee: *I suppose the people around here, as I say, don't have gardens or open space. It is terribly built up round here; and the one thing that we come to is the river for our respite; and just to breathe. That wonderful open*

space was in between two bottlenecks. You walk along the path from the National Theatre to this wonderful open space and then you enter another bottleneck going through the OXO Tower towards the Millennium Bridge. So just the preservation of what little we have; and also what little green we have; we have trees that have stood here for fifty years; that are over twenty-five metres high. They would do much better than any lollypop tree that needs a bit if nurturing in the dark. That would have taken another fifty years to get to any decent height. I don't think it is difficult to see why we wanted to keep this space for us. It is currently a public right-of-way, we don't want to start privatising public space. That's exactly what the Garden Bridge was hoping to do ... Disgrace, it's a disgrace [laughter].

Interviewer: Thank you so much.
Interviewee: *You are very welcome.*

Interviewer: You are so knowledgeable and clear; and erhm you have given me insights: the subleasing is very important; and I hadn't realised the extent to which that had happened.
Interviewee: *By hook or by crook, they were going to sublease that, no matter what. Did you know that the director of Coin Street Community Builders, his name is Iain Tuckett, he wasn't even one of the Community, he actually worked for the GLA. He came on board to be their champion, to spearhead the Community into winning the land. He had been approached by Joanna Lumley, did you know, in 2002? Joanna Lumley wrote about it in her book; ironically called: No Room for Secrets. And she had approached not only Thomas Heatherwick and Iain Tuckett from Coin Street; she also approached ARUP back in 2002, early 2000s. She already had it in her head: Diana, Princess Diana has died, I want this Bridge; will you help me? And they went: yeah, ok. Then they waited until Boris came to power; they waited until somebody that could help them; but for them to even know already this is what Ms Lumley wants was shocking.*

Interviewer: Yes, it is by far; and so congratulations.
Interviewee: *Thank you very much.*

(Semi-Structured Qualitative Interview: Member of Thames Central Open Spaces, South Bank, London, August 2017)

Garden Bridge, Subverting the Adsensory Privatisation of Our Riverway 249

Figure 6.3.: "Publicity is, in essence, nostalgic. It has to sell the past to the future. It cannot itself supply the standards of its own claims. And so all its references to quality are bound to be retrospective and traditional. It would lack both confidence and credibility if it used a strictly contemporary language" (John Berger, *Ways of Seeing*, 1972). Photographic Image, Southbank, London 2016.

Figure 6.4.: "Publicity is addressed to those who constitute the market, to the spectator-buyer who is also the consumer-producer from whom profits are made twice over — as worker and then as buyer. The only places relatively free of publicity are the quarters of the very rich; their money is theirs to keep" (John Berger, *Ways of Seeing*, 1972). Photographic Image, Southbank, London 2016.

CHAPTER SEVEN

GARDEN BRIDGE, CULTURE INDUSTRY MEDIATIONS: FRAMING TELEVISUAL ECOFEMINIST CARE ETHICS

Figure 7.1.: "Publicity images also belong to the moment in the sense that they must be continually renewed and made up-to-date. Yet they never speak of the present. Often they refer to the past and always they speak of the future" (*Ways of Seeing*, 1972). Photographic Image, Environmental Activist, Central London, August 2016.

Garden Bridge, Psychosocial Mediations: Framing Celebrity Ecofeminist Care Ethics

Dame Margaret Hodge (MH): I'm looking at value for money and whether proper procedures were followed.

Joanna Lumley (JL): I wanted Bee to write down anything that I can't answer on the dot. Can I do something really, really cheeky, which is to just do the very, very beginning of the bridge, not the good or bad idea but just how it started?

MH: Yes, I would like to hear that because I've heard lots of things.

JL: I think that's important otherwise you won't know and it's important that you have all the information.

MH: Yes.

JL: After the Princess of Wales died, there was a competition for a memorial, what was it going to be, and everybody thought of everything under the sun. Because I'd always loved bridges and have drawn them all through my life and everything, I'd always thought of a bridge as something pretty special and pretty spectacular. So I thought, 'A bridge'.

Originally I thought of it as a built bridge, a London bridge, with architects each taking a slice each and making shops and restaurants and things. Fabulous. That was out of the window, bang. Health and safety wouldn't have it. Then I thought of this idea of a garden bridge where you walk on to it but can't see across because it's just trees and stuff painted, wandering paths, but it's useful. I thought that the memorial must be something useful for London and spectacular for the Princess. I thought it must be essentially useful for Londoners but memorable. So we put it into the competition and we came second.

MH: You put it into the competition? Were you doing it with Thomas?

JL: No, no, this is far before. This is far before. And I only brought this so just that you have sight of – This was – for instance, this is 1999, 'Lumley calls for river tribute to Princess'.

…

I had to raise money for it and I wanted to use the name Diana because it was going to be called the Diana Bridge. The Diana Memorial Trust said I may not use her name in raising the money for this bridge. So that was a bit of a bummer because I could have raised the money in two dinners in America and the lottery. I went to Camelot and said, 'Could you have one lottery because I don't think that would be bad idea and we'll get the thing done?'

Anyway, so eventually it went in, no drawings, but the idea went in. It came second to the round water feature, which won.

…

So I kept it, kept it, kept it. At the very end of it I'd met, through Terence Conran, Thomas Heatherwick who said, 'This sounds fantastic'. I said, 'It is fantastic' and Terence Conran said, 'If ever you want this bridge built, this is the boy who should design it'. It goes back into the cupboard; nothing happens. Every year I get a Christmas card from Thomas, the ones he used to make himself, which were just works of art, which I've kept all of those, 'Dear Joanna, Love Thomas' because we'd met.

Then suddenly in 2012 I get a call here from Thomas Heatherwick which says, 'Shall we talk about your bridge? There's an idea that maybe there is a footbridge being planned in London. Can we talk about it?' So he'd got wind of it. Somebody had said, either Transport for London, because Thomas had done all those buses, 'What can this brilliant boy do next?' the Leonardo da Vinci, as Conran called him, of our day, and so presumably that's how it happened. Anyway, the only reason Thomas would have come to me was connected with the bridge. So we thought this would be fantastic. We talked about it; nothing happened. Not nothing happened but time went by, time went by.

The next thing I see here is the fourth plinth. I do stuff for London. I love it. So, whichever mayor asks me to do stuff I do it. I unveiled the fourth statue plinth. None of this matters to you but I'm a Londoner and I live in Lambeth and I do stuff for London all the time.

This is the Boris myth. I sat for Boris's mother, who is a painter, who painted me for *The Breaking of Bumbo* in 1971. At that time there were children creeping about on the floor so I said I must have met Boris when he was a child. This has turned into he was my childhood friend. I was a grownup actress being painted by his mother, so this is an awful myth. I don't know Boris. I've met him now.

…

MH: So you'd met them before you met … you wrote to Boris, didn't you?

(Hodge, 2016: 1-4; "This transcription has been disclosed by the GLA [Greater London Authority] in response to a request under the Environmental Information Regulations (EIR)" Garden Bridge Review Meeting Transcript, Event: Dame Margaret Hodge and Joanna Lumley, 1st December 2016)

In October 2016 Sadiq Khan, as mayor of London, appointed Dame Margaret Hodge MP to direct an independent review of the pre-constructed Garden Bridge. The remit of the independent review was strictly confined to ascertaining "whether value for money has been achieved from taxpayers' contributions" and to "investigate the work of TFL, the GLA and other relevant authorities on the Garden Bridge, going back to when it was first proposed" (London Assembly 2018). Dame Margaret Hodge's final report, entitled, *The Garden Bridge*, published in April 2017, was profoundly comprehensive in its critical elucidation of the inherent contradictions and predicaments engulfing the project's continued viability. On the vexing question of value for money, Hodge castigated the politicisation of the Garden Bridge and its mobilisation as an egotistic accolade by populist mayoral propaganda. Hodge (2017: 1) convincingly argues that "a weak business case" accentuated confusion that blighted the project from its inception for it appears that this anaemic business case was formulated after contracts had been procured and financial outlays invested. Incompetency in business planning rapidly untethered from private sector investment risk into public sector financial liability, as detailed in the following extract:

> The original ambition to fund the Garden Bridge solely through private finance has been abandoned. Furthermore, the goalposts have moved several times and each time the risks to the taxpayer have intensified. Looking to the future, the costs of construction have escalated and are likely to increase further. What started life as a project costing an estimated £60 million is likely to end up costing over £200 million. At the same time, the Garden Bridge Trust has lost two major donors and has only secured £69 million in private funding pledges, leaving a gap of at least £70 million that needs to be raised for the capital investment. No new pledges have been obtained since August 2016. (Hodge 2017: 1)

So concerned was Hodge (2017) about the chaotic spiralling of the Garden Bridge's capital costs that the mayor of London was advised, with urgency, to desist from signing further "guarantees until it is confirmed that the private capital money to build the bridge has been secured by the Garden Bridge Trust" (ibid.1). Highly sceptical of the capacity of the Garden Bridge Trust to independently raise the private monies to meet spiralling capital costs, Hodge (ibid.) warned against public money being used to float the sinking project. Awareness of the growing public disquiet about the project seems to have provided some empirical support in Hodge's calculation of the Garden Bridge Trust as having hit the buffers of private capital investment. It was becoming increasingly apparent that "if the Garden Bridge is not treasured by the public in the same way that it is by its creators, then the business model, based on raising private finance, is far less likely to succeed" (ibid. 1-2). Indeed, declining public and private capital enthusiasm for the Garden Bridge appeared to converge around a disillusionment with regards to its capacity to fulfil an increasingly mythical providence as an ecologically focused garden bridge. Consequently, declining public belief in the urban ecology of the Garden Bridge coupled with ambiguity over its maintenance presented the independent review with a fait accompli; the report concluded against the Garden Bridge project as value for money. As detailed in the following extract:

> The project has already used £37.4 million of public money and the agreement to underwrite cancelation costs by the Government could bring the bill to the taxpayer up to £46.4 million. I believe it is better for the taxpayer to accept the loss than to risk the additional demands if the project proceeds. In the present climate, with continuing pressures on public spending, it is difficult to justify further public investment in the Garden bridge. (Hodge 2017: 2)

An area of particular critical focus in the Hodge (ibid.) report was the "conduct and procedure of Transport for London and the Greater London Authority", especially with regards to evidence of a clique loosely aligned with an urban ecological architectural aesthetic and commitment to the notion of a garden bridge. Principal agents within this clique include Heatherwick Studio, seemingly guided by the celebrity ecofeminist philosophical vision of actress and activist Joanna Lumley. While it is not my intention to cast any aspersions on the integrity of these actor-networked agents, it is noteworthy that the Hodge report states that:

> The procurement subject to this review comprised one contract that was awarded to Heatherwick Studio for design and consulting services and one contract that was awarded to Arup for engineering and project management services. These were not open, fair or competitive procurements and my review revealed systematic failures and ineffective control systems at many levels. (ibid. 2)

In December 2016, Dame Margaret Hodge interviewed the actress and peace activist Joanna Lumley as part of the value for money review of London's Garden Bridge project. The transcription extract presented above provides an illustration of a tradition of ecological activism made manifest, in the gender dynamics of the culture, by its mediated celebrity care-centred ethic. And this chapter has as its focus, the expropriation of this ethic into a sign technology mobilised in the pursuit of a financialisation of river conservation. In the endeavour to substantiate theoretically this observation, one is required to develop further the feminist concept of care ethics.

Celebrity Ecofeminism and the Ethics of Care; Case Study of Joanna Lumley's Ecofeminist Garden Bridge

"Incorporating ecological costs, in short, will have the same social and economic consequences as the oil crisis" (Gorz 1983: 6). *Ecology as Politics* provides for an incisive counter position to the efficaciousness of capitalist pollution control as part of capitalism's commodification of ecological interventions into rectifying environmental degradation. Advancing from orthodox Marxism's dystopian vision of irreconcilable disparities inevitably misaligning the objectives of a capitalist environmentalism, André Gorz presents a techno-promethean vision in which technology can potentially be mobilised in the advocacy of environmentalism. According to Gorz (ibid.), when faced with environmental disaster, capitalist manufacturing capital, "far from succumbing to this crisis", deftly applies market capitalist logic to the environmental interventions of its competitors; and in so doing, transforms environmentalism into a market capitalist venture. While it is evident that Karl Marx's *Capital* Volume III preceded this paradigm of ecological critical theory, André Gorz (1983) is particularly distinguished in advancing a critical framework for analysing the intervention of capitalist technology into environmental politics. According to Gorz (ibid. 6), the state operates to assuage capitalism's endeavour to capitalise environmental degradation for it is evident that in times of environmental crisis, the capabilities of the state to collate information so as to regulate forms of industrial practice provide the basis for market capitalism to compete in a race to the bottom of profit maximum environmental provision. As Gorz (ibid. 6-7) describes:

> The state will reinforce its power over society: its technocrats will calculate 'optimal' norms of pollution control and of production, issue regulations, and extend the domain of 'programmed' activity and thus the scope of the repressive apparatus. Popular resentment will be diverted with compensatory myths and directed towards readily available scapegoats (racial or ethnic minorities, migrant workers, young people, other countries). (ibid.)

Gorz's observation regarding the scapegoating of folk devils and minority groups as part of ecological capitalism's co-operation with state apparatus is particularly interesting when examined in relation to technology. Although adamant that "the ecological perspective is incompatible with the rationality of capitalism", Gorz (ibid. 18) proceeds to make innovative inroads into "prevailing technologies" as apparatus for ecology politics. Specifically, Gorz (ibid.) theorises technology as one of the "material prerequisites of the economy system"; consequently, the prevailing informationalised instrumentally rationalising mode of technology is axiomatic with the current capitalist system in that it operates to "reflect and determine the relations of the producers to their products, of the workers to their work, of the individual to the group and the society, of people to the environment" (ibid.). Moreover, capitalism preferences those technologies that advance its profit maximum; and in this sense, "technology is the matrix in which the distribution of power, the social relations of production, and the hierarchical division of labor are embedded" (ibid. 18-19). Given that Gorz (ibid. 19) proposes that "capitalist relations of production and exchange are already inscribed in the technologies which capitalism bequeaths to us", a Marxist technological intervention into ecological politics appears to be premised on inherent incompatibilities. Nevertheless, Gorz's techno-promethean vision assails this impasse in its advocacy that "the struggle for different technologies is essential to the struggle for a different society" (ibid.). "Alternative technologies" is an integral feature of the ecological transformations that Gorz's (1983: 19) *Ecology as Politics* seeks to facilitate and thus, "The theoretical and practical definition of alternative technologies, and the struggle of communities and individuals to win, collectively and individually, control over their own destinies must be the permanent focus of political action" (ibid. 19-20). It is from this techno-promethean perspective that this chapter explores the ethics of care central to the hyper-mediated celebrity ecofeminism that pervaded much of the Garden Bridge's ecological politics.

Celebrity Ecofeminism as "a Different Voice"?

We went along and the Mayor had asked us to look at a site between Battersea and Pimlico. So we went down there, dutifully, and looked at it and there was not one single human being there. I said if we were going to put a bridge there it would be just a complete waste of time. Nobody needed from Pimlico to go to Nine Elms or vice versa. There were no shops in Pimlico. There was no reason for a crossing there. A cycle path perhaps but not a pedestrian bridge.

I said to Thomas, 'Come and see my old idea, Aldwych, to complete the Aldwych', because I changed it from Horse Guards to the Aldwych. I took him there. We walked, we too photographs, we took photographs down Arundel Street looking straight across. We went across then to the other side, to the patch of Coin Street-owned grass in front of ITV Studios, which I know well because it's where the fans stick their autograph books through the thing. There was not a human being on it on this bright sunny Sunday, people walking up and down. We looked at it, we looked across the river, and we said this would be a brilliant place because people who want to get from the South Bank culture hub across through Aldwych to the culture hub up there, people who want to come from Waterloo station and walk to their offices in Holborn, ... it doesn't matter where you say, this crossing will be used by people. Then I had this balance of it going transport, footbridge, transport, which can be train or cars, footbridge. So that's how it goes now, there footbridges are crossed by London things. So Thomas agreed that this would be a sensational place, added to which it's going to be pretty daring. This was years before the High Line.

(Hodge, 2016: 1-4; "This transcription has been disclosed by the GLA [Greater London Authority] in response to a request under the Environmental Information Regulations (EIR)" (ibid.). Garden Bridge Review Meeting Transcript, Event: Dame Margaret Hodge and Joanna Lumley, 1st December 2016)

Carol Gilligan's (1982) *In a Different Voice* is emblematic of the radical critical intervention into the hegemony of Freudian psychoanalysis analysis presented by second-wave feminism. Prior to this feminist breakthrough, analysis of ethics was modelled according to the psychosocial development of the male psyche. Freud had attributed to the psychosocial development of the male psyche the propensity for individuation achieved through the disassociation and detachment from embodied relations of care associated with the maternal primary carer. Gilligan (ibid. 8), recognising this model, identifies individuation to be an integral feature of the development of male identity: "For boys and men, separation and individuation are critically tied to gender identity since separation from the mother is essential for the development of masculinity". Conversely, female identity is not accomplished through dissociative individuation from the mother as primary carer for female identity is cultivated through emulation of the mothering role. Gilligan (ibid.) observes that a consequence of male dissociative individuation from the mother role is a fear of intimacy; as such, emotional engagement is reminiscent of the nurturing primary care giver role that male identity strives to distance itself from. Specifically, Gilligan says, "Since masculinity is defined through separation while femininity is defined through attachment, male gender identity is threatened by intimacy while female gender identity is threatened by separation" (ibid.). Consequently, males struggle with embodied situations requiring intimacy and emotional engagement whereas females experience difficulties in achieving detached, objective separation and individuation (ibid.). Freudian psychoanalysis translates the femaleness of embodiment and its struggles to transition through to an individuation as "developmental liabilities" (ibid. 9). Suffice to say, "Women's failure to separate then becomes by definition a failure to develop" (ibid.); and this has direct implications for a Freudian psychoanalytical model of moral development.

Given that the psychosocial development of the female is axiomatic with motherhood, Freud's (1994) analysis presupposed limits to the capacity for individuation in the female psyche, thus formulating a muted ineffectual notion of female ethical judgement. Gilligan's (1982) *In a Different Voice* is primarily a riposte to the Freudian assumption that "women's failure to separate then becomes by definition a failure to develop" (ibid. 9). Freud asserted that the ethical judgement of the female is compromised and degenerated by centrality to the sense of self, of a continuity between the female subject and her primary mothering care giver. As Gilligan (ibid. 18) describes: "The criticism that Freud makes of women's sense of justice, seeing it as compromised in its refusal of blind impartiality", a feature which Gillian identifies as appearing also "in the work of Piaget but also in that of Kohlberg" (ibid.). In an attempt to valorise the Othering of female embodiment and its entangled ethics, Kohlberg, according to Gilligan, constructs the conception of "goodness", which is assumed to be functional as an ethic when restricted to the domestic sphere (ibid.). Of particular concern, and with regards to the latter, is that embodied, care-centred traits associated with "the 'goodness' of women, their care for and sensitivity to the needs of others are those that mark them as deficient in moral development" (ibid.). Axiomatic to this phallocentric male-orientated frame of moral development is linear taxonomy predicated on male experience, which makes manifest "the importance of individuation in their development" (ibid.). Conversely, according to Gilligan, where inquiry into ethics and gendered subjectivity commences with the analysis of women, modelling the developmental structure directly in relation to their lives, a configuration of moral development at variance with the Freudian psychosocial developmental process becomes eminently apparent. In the *different voice* of female moral maturation, "the moral problem arises from conflicting responsibilities rather than from competing rights and requires for its resolution, a mode of thinking that is contextual and narrative rather than formal and abstract" (ibid. 19). Embodiment and relational circumspection configure female moral development, according to Gilligan; and this contrasts with the detached instrumental rationality of male moral development. Relationality and embodiment are prominent conceptual features of Gilligan's ascription of a *different voice* to female moral maturity whereby relationality involves selfless consideration of others and the situation of one's self in the nurturing of their well-being. As Gilligan (ibid.) expresses it, "This conception of morality as concerned with the activity of care centers moral development around the understanding of responsibility and relationships, just as the conception of morality as fairness ties moral development to the understanding of rights and rules" (ibid.). Embodied and embedded in the complexities of other people's lives, the moral development of females entangles in ways that mitigate against delineating an apex and trajectory of efficient culmination. Efficacious delineable resolution to moral dilemma, while characteristic of the Freudian male archetype, is anachronistic to the emotional entanglement of female moral development.

As Gilligan (ibid. 21-22) describes, whereas the linear nomenclature depicting stages of development, evident in Freudian psychosocial moral frameworks, designates "arriving at an objectively fair or just resolution to moral dilemmas upon which all rational persons could agree, the responsibility conception focuses instead on the limitations of any particular resolution and describes the conflicts that remain". It is Gilligan's observation that the centrality of contextual relativism to female morality makes anathema the pursuit of disentangled objectively and categorically delineable resolutions to moral dilemma. Indeed, Gilligan presupposes apprehension to be a logical female reaction to circumstances in which the imposition of categorical resolution is the only option available. As Gilligan expresses it, "Thus it becomes clear why a morality of rights and non-interference may appear frightening to women in its potential justification of indifference and unconcern" (ibid. 22). Considering the equivalent male response, it becomes apparent that contextual relativism is anathema to a rationalising, instrumental efficiency that seeks to achieve a delineable solution to a moral dilemma. Thus, "At the same time, it becomes clear why, from a male perspective, a morality of responsibility appears inconclusive and diffuse, given its insistent contextual relativism" (ibid.).

Remaining within the orthodoxy while unshackling from its phallocentric bias, Gilligan argues that female moral development maps onto the unflinching care-centred maternal embodiment of female psychosocial development but at one and the same time, the entangled embodied moral resolutions so evidently female "also provide an alternative conception of maturity by which these differences can be assessed and their implications traced" (ibid.). More specifically,

> The psychology of women that has consistently been described as distinctive in its greater orientation toward relationships and interdependence implies a

more contextual mode of judgement and a different moral understanding. Given the differences in women's conception of self and morality, women bring to the life cycle a different point of view and order human experience in terms of different priorities. (ibid.)

Viewed through the lens of Gilligan's model of *a different voice*, Joanna Lumley's inchoate sensibility to bridge (albeit arbitrarily) the disparate concrete viaducts of public spaces, via the construction of a garden bridge, is emblematic of an "ethic of care" whose *different voice* tends toward perceiving actors as networks of alliances rather than competing factions. This is not to abnegate responsibility for alliances made but rather to suggest that when framed within an "ethic of care", the *different voice* of female moral judgement seeks resolution to moral dilemma by "activating" networks and "strengthening rather than severing connections" (ibid. 30-31). Suffice to say, it is my contention here that from Gilligan's model of *a different voice*, one could plausibly frame Joanna Lumley's ecology politics as manifesting an "ethic of care" whereby Gilligan argues that "the logic underlying an ethic of care is a psychological logic of relationships, which contrasts with the formal logic of fairness that informs the justice approach" (ibid. 73). The "ethic of care" is, however, riddled with irreconcilable contradictions, as Gilligan identifies: "the language of rights ... recognizes clearly the importance of self-determination and respect", and in this sense, "the concept of rights remains in tension with an ethic of care" (ibid. 136). In her whimsical delight in constructing a garden to arbitrarily bridge public recreational river spaces, Joanna Lumley's care ethics might well be described as ethical relativism destined to encounter interminably its abject impracticalities. And herein resides indication of the debilitating actualities of applying Gilligan's "ethic of care" to exploitative situations and/or contexts which abnegate responsibility and negate its value. Gilligan provides some indication of this problematic as follows:

> This confusion is captured in Kohlberg's definition of the third stage of moral development which joins the need for approval with the wish to care for and help others. When thus caught between the passivity of dependence and the activity of care, the woman becomes suspended in a paralysis of initiative with respect to both action and thought. (ibid. 82)

Gilligan's tendency to conflate woman with the "ethic of care" makes it difficult to agree with the principal assertion expressed in this extract. An alternative approach is to comprehend care ethics in terms of gendered time (Odih 2007, Odih 2014). One can then more easily comprehend how the discursively constructed female identity, in seeking to achieve affirmation through recognition of its selfless relational giving of time to service the care needs of others, becomes caught up and entangled in an endless spiral of caring. Applying this conceptual development of gendered time to Gilligan's (1982) presupposition, it becomes more understandable thus: where there occurs a joining of "the need for approval with the wish to care for and help others", the female in its ambition to accomplish self-worth becomes caught in an endless spiral of care (ibid. 82). And this is compounded by contradictions in the female imperative of an "absolute injunction against hurting others" (ibid. 165). For Gilligan (ibid. 171), an antidote to this situation is to unshackle the "ethic of care" from a need for approval for "when the distinction between helping and pleasing frees the activity of taking care from the wish for approval by others, the ethic of responsibility can become a self-chosen anchor of personal integrity and strength" (ibid.). While wholly sympathetic with this endeavour, the idea and conceptual tools to achieve this situation of self-reliant care ethics are tenuously available in Gilligan's theoretical framework of *a different voice*. The psychosocial development of the female is predicated on a forbiddance towards detachment, any foray into which is relentlessly punished, as is implicitly indicated in Gilligan's recounting of the Greek myth of Demeter and Persephone.

Gilligan's feminist challenge to the Freudian phallocentric conception of morality extends into the realms of Greek mythology and the corresponding oscillations of light and dark that define Demeter and Persephone. Indeed, parallels can be drawn between the symbolic mediations of Joanna Lumley's characterisation in the Garden Bridge project's initial stages and that of Carol Gilligan's (1982) feminist interpretation of the Eleusinian myth of Demeter and Persephone. Of significance is Joanna Lumley's consistent reference to the death of Princess Diana as an impetus to the engenderment of the garden bridge idea whereby Princess Diana symbolically represents Persephone, extracted from the sovereign Demeter's maternal security and propelled into the ravages of Hades. Although Gilligan's feminist psychoanalysis of the Greek myth is rooted in a Eurocentric tradition (e.g., preference for Demeter and displacement of Isis as mother nature c.f. Odih 2014), the critical analysis has relevance when applied to a deconstruction of the symbolically mediated portrayal, in the Garden Bridge review interviews by Dame Margaret Hodge, of Joanna Lumley's ecological activism. According to Gilligan (1982: 22), Freud's immense impact on psychology extends into life-cycle theories depicting mother and daughter relations. Citing the life-cycle analysis of McClelland (1975), Gilligan comments on an account of "the feminine attitude toward power" evident in McClelland's (1975) interpretation of the Greek myth of Demeter and Persephone. As Gilligan (1982: 22) states:

> The myth of Demeter and Persephone, which McClelland (1975) cites as exemplifying the feminine attitude toward power, was associated with the Eleusinian Mysteries celebrated in ancient Greece for over two thousand years. As told in the Homeric Hymn to Demeter, the story of Persephone indicates the strengths of interdependence, building up resources and giving, that McClelland found in his research on power motivation to characterize the mature feminine style.

Gilligan, however, makes evident an unresolved contradiction in McClelland's interpretation of the myth of Demeter and Persephone; for its exemplification of the Greek myth as a religious cult "organized by and for women, especially at the onset before men by means of the cult of Dionysos began to take them over" (McClelland 1975, cited in Gilligan 1982: 22) insufficiently addresses the ancient Greek myth's intention to formulate an integral interdependence of male and female value systems. Thus Gilligan (1982: 22) quotes critically McClelland's notion of the myth "[as] a special presentation of feminine psychology" (McClelland 1975, cited in Gilligan 1982: 22). Keen to accent an integral interplay of value systems evident in the Greek myth, Gilligan recounts the narrative thus:

> Persephone, the daughter of Demeter, while playing in a meadow with her girlfriends, sees a beautiful narcissus which she runs to pick. As she does so, the earth opens and she is snatched away by Hades, who takes her to his underworld kingdom. Demeter, goddess of the earth, so mourns the loss of her daughter that she refuses to allow anything to grow. The crops that sustain life on earth shrivel up, killing men and animals alike, until Zeus takes pity on man's suffering and persuades his brother to return Persephone to her mother. But before she leaves, Persephone eats some pomegranate seeds, which ensures that she will spend part of every year with Hades in the underworld. (Gilligan 1982: 22-23)

Gilligan's feminist interpretation of the Eleusinian mystery of Demeter and Persephone evidences a history of Greek mythology that valorised the interdependence of embodiment and reasoned ethics for "the elusive mystery of women's development lies in its recognition of the continuing importance of attachment in the human life-cycle" (ibid. 23). The feminist vision perpetuated is that of a female psyche geared towards embodiment, overcoming a tradition of Freudian analysis that has derided its care ethic; seeking now its supplicant so as to ameliorate the excesses of reason in the human life-cycle. Thus Gilligan (ibid.) describes how a "woman's place in man's life cycle is to protect this recognition while the developmental litany intones the celebration of separation, autonomy, individuation, and natural rights". Conversely, Gilligan's feminist interpretation cites the mystery of Demeter and Persephone as testament to the integral reality and necessity of attachment. Excessive individuation and detachment are personified "by reminding us that narcissism leads to death, that fertility of the earth is in some mysterious way tied to the continuation of the mother-daughter relationship, and that the life-cycle itself arises from an alternation between the world of women and that of men" (ibid.). Parallels can be drawn between the symbolic mediation of Joanna Lumley's garden bridge ecological activism and Carol Gilligan's interpretation of the Eleusinian mystery of Demeter and Persephone for both characterisations depict a care ethic that ameliorates the excess individuation of male judgement: Joanna Lumley's introduction of a fertile garden bridge into the sterile concrete architectural proposals for the Princess Diana memorial; and Carol Gilligan's alternating world view of Persephone's plight for part of the year in Hades. Gilligan concludes the feminist analysis of the Eleusinian mystery with a statement rallying "life-cycle theorists [to] divide their attention and begin to live with women as they have lived with men" for only then "will their vision encompass the experience of both sexes and their theories become correspondingly more fertile" (ibid.). Similar conceptions of parallel worldviews are evident in Joanna Lumley's account of the embryonic generation of a garden bridge traversing opposite river banks. For example, in her interview with Dame Margaret Hodge, Joanna Lumley describes traversing opposite spaces when exploring a suitable place for a garden bridge; as she expresses it:

> So I went and walked up and down, taking photographs of the Thames from both sides and studying maps and things like this and relocated it in my mind and wrote back to all my supporters, who were a fantastic list of people. Anyway, so I walked up and down and saw the place where I thought it would be better to serve people using it, because bridges must be for people to walk across. If people aren't walking there they're not going to cross it.

> (Hodge, 2016: 3; "This transcription has been disclosed by the GLA [Greater London Authority] in response to a request under the Environmental Information Regulations (EIR)" (ibid.). Garden Bridge Review Meeting Transcript, Event: Dame Margaret Hodge and Joanna Lumley, 1st December 2016)

As with Carol Gilligan's assertion that the Eleusinian mystery of Demeter and Persephone should be interpreted in terms of parallel worlds intersected, so it is that Joanna Lumley's account of exploring opposing spaces to traverse with a garden bridge evokes the metaphor of intersecting parallel worlds. Furthermore, Joanna Lumley's care ethic as espoused in the Garden Bridge review interview (ibid.) is highly reminiscent of a care ethic articulated by Gilligan (1982) although generic to celebrity ecofeminism second-wave feminism. This female care ethic is introduced by Gilligan as follows:

> The psychology of women that has consistently been described as distinctive in its greater orientation toward relationships and interdependence implies a more contextual mode of judgement and a different moral understanding. Given the differences in women's conceptions of self and morality, women bring to the life cycle a different point of view and order human experience in terms of different priorities. (ibid. 22)

Gilligan reconceives Freud's psychosocial drama of attachment so as to valorise a female conception of self and morality. In contrast to the model of detached judgement ascribed to the individuated male psyche, Gilligan formulates a feminist turn in perspective "toward increasingly differentiated comprehensive and reflective forms of thought" associated with "women's responses to both actual and hypothetical dilemmas" (ibid. 73). Axiomatic to these divergences in male and female moral domains is Gilligan's proposition that the maternal attachment derived as part of the psychosocial development of the female child precipitates the cultivation of embodied and contextual response to moral dilemma. As Gilligan (ibid.) expresses it: "Women's construction of the moral problem as a problem of care and responsibility in relationships rather than as one of rights and rules ties the development of their moral thinking to changes in their understanding of responsibility and relationships, just as the conception of morality as justice ties development to the logic of equality and reciprocity". This construct of justice relates to Gilligan's assertion that the pragmatisms and detachment evident in the psychosocial development of the male child manifests an individuation that aligns with an ethic based on the efficacious pursuit of justice. As Gilligan expresses it: "Thus the logic underlying an ethic of care is a psychological logic of relationships, which contrasts with the formal logic of fairness that informs the justice approach" (ibid.). Gilligan's *In a Different Voice* provides plentiful empirical illustrations of moral judgements emblematic of distinctly gendered care ethics. In a discussion of an interviewee named Amy, some tentative parallels can be traced with a model of Joanna Lumley's celebrity ecofeminism. Gilligan's description of Amy's moral judgements and "restorative activity of care" (ibid. 30-31) has similarities with Lumley's celebrity ecofeminist endeavour to activate an environmentalist network through communication and the cultivation of social capital. This apparent relationality in finding an ecological resolution to the Garden Bridge project might be described as emblematic of what Gilligan (ibid. 73) describes as "women's construction of the moral problem as a problem of care and responsibility in relationships"; Gilligan contrasts this with an ethics that has as its focus quantitative, rational individuated justice. Here and elsewhere, Gilligan's care ethics assumes a seemingly crude binary formulation such that "the logic underlying an ethic of care is a psychological logic of relationships, which contrasts with the formal logic of fairness that informs the justice approach" (ibid.). By extension, the ethic of care is resourced with "comprehension of the dynamics of social interaction", of which one assumes the ethic of justice is bereft (ibid. 74). Accumulated through embodied social relations with self and others, the relational dimension of the ethic of care orientates "around a central insight, that self and other are interdependent" (ibid.).

Inferred in Gilligan's focus on cumulative knowledge is a suggestion of development in the maturity of feminine care and this has significance to a case study analysis of Joanna Lumley's Garden Bridge celebrity ecofeminism and its saccharine media care ethic. It is my observation, gained from a close reading of the Dame Margaret Hodge (2016) transcription, that Joanna Lumley's care ethics is awkwardly stuck in what Gilligan (1982:74) derides as an initial immature stage of the psycho-social development of the ethic of care. Prior to examining Gilligan's conception of stages in the development of the ethic of care, consider the following transcription extract of Joanna Lumley discussing the fate of the heritage trees that were to be felled as a part of the Garden Bridge development:

> Coin Street wanted this very, very much bigger building on the South Bank, which means we cut down far more trees, but now there are notices tied all around the trees saying we are murdering the trees and yet Coin Street have insisted on the size of this building, which we've got to pay them money for and they want the thing. We understand this deal but the fact that we're taking the flak for a much bigger building, cutting down far more trees. I can understand Coin Street hating the idea of more people on their patch but we live in London. All of us have got our skylines desecrated, our roads shot to pieces. This is called living in London, so I'm anxious that they aren't the only voices heard.
>
> I'm anxious that Londoners, walkers particularly, people who can't afford a bicycle or a car, might not even be able to afford a bus fare, can walk across the bridge. A lot has been done for cyclists and nothing really has [been] done for pedestrians, except enormous patches for tourists. This is for Londoners. This is for Londoners and it's so strange, Dame Margaret, that

something that I dreamed of almost calling the people's bridge, because it would be funded by the very rich for people who have nothing, for perpetuity, for people, has suddenly been turned round into the toffs bridge, and you go, 'Where did this happen?'.

So it's so odd and … anyway, it doesn't matter. Whine, whine, whine. I've been told not to whine to you and I'm not going to but you suddenly feel the injustice and you go, 'This is the people's bridge for the people, a thing of utter beauty'.

(Hodge, 2016: 19; "This transcription has been disclosed by the GLA [Greater London Authority] in response to a request under the Environmental Information Regulations (EIR)" (ibid.). Garden Bridge Review Meeting Transcript, Event: Dame Margaret Hodge and Joanna Lumley, 1st December 2016)

Gilligan (1982) identifies a trio of moral perspectives which "denote a sequence in the development of the ethic of care" (ibid. 74). Methodologically, Gilligan's analysis emphasises language as an expression of inter-subjective meaning and drills down to the use of morally coded words to discern principled judgement. In applying these research techniques, Gilligan elucidates from the empirical research an initial stage of female ethical development in which caring for others is centre-staged but evocation of care endeavours to assuage anxiety by the woman for social acceptance. As Gilligan (ibid.) observes, "the initial focus on caring for the self in order to ensure survival". Psycho-social development of the female subject transitions dialectically from this initial stage as it comes to be interpreted as selfish. The latter critical self-introjection "signals a new understanding of the connection between self and others which is articulated by the concept of responsibility" (ibid.). Gilligan introduces here a conception of "maternal morality" so as to formulate a first transition in which caring for self-survival is displaced by focused commitment to a maternal responsibility in which "good is equated with caring for others" (ibid.). Inevitably, the focus on others as legitimate "recipients of the woman's care" to "the exclusion of herself" creates problems in managing relationships as her life becomes overloaded by the care demands of others. According to Gilligan (ibid.), a second transition is precipitated "in an effort to sort out the confusion between self-sacrifice and care inherent in the conventions of feminine goodness". The third phase of psycho-social development of the ethic of care attempts to reconcile the initial stage's self-centred self-sacrifice with the second stage's excesses of responsibility; this requires renegotiating relations between self and other. In this latter stage of development in the ethic of care:

> Care becomes the self-chosen principle of a judgement that remains psychological in its concern with relationships and response but becomes universal in its condemnation of exploitation and hurt. Thus a progressively more adequate understanding of the psychology of human relationships – an increasing differentiation of self and other and a growing comprehension of the dynamics of social interaction – informs the development of an ethic of care. (Gilligan 1982: 74)

It is evident that in maturity the ethic of care exceeds the immediacy of emotional demands as it becomes "universal" in its embodied commitment to a deontological philosophical stance that eschews any justification for violence; its zero tolerance and adamant refusal to accept that any one person (child or adult) should be sacrificed to the utilitarian principles of a greater good for the greater number speaks to the immediacy of care and a broader, more universal human rights endeavour.

Paul Adams' (2015) "In Defence Of Care: Gilligan's Relevance For Primary Education" advances "an approach that sees care, not in opposition to justice, but rather as a partner to its cold, rational orientation". In support of this proposition, Adams (ibid. 292) argues that "Gilligan eschewed the idea that justice and care are separate; rather she saw them as intertwined: care as conceived through the prism of justice and care as a perspective on moral action". Indeed, Adams (ibid.) goes as far as to suggest that Gilligan "came to view the justice perspective as incomplete without the addition of the care perspective", arguing further that Gilligan proposed "the idea that relational and autonomous selves ... different modes of being but are two aspects of human existence: self can only be experienced in relationship with others and relationship can only be experienced through the differentiation of self from other" (ibid.). While in some agreement with this latter part of Adams' (2015:292) reading of Gilligan, one needs to adopt circumspection as to whether Gilligan is assuming a notion of "completion" with regards to the interdependence of the ethic of care and the ethic of justice. In this respect, consider the following extract derived from *In a Different Voice*:

> Women's construction of the moral problem as a problem of care and responsibility in relationships rather than as one of rights and rules ties the development of their moral thinking to changes in their understanding of responsibility and relationships, just as the conception of morality as justice ties development to the logic of equality and reciprocity. Thus the logic underlying an ethic of care is a psychological logic of relationships, which contrasts with the formal logic of fairness that informs the justice approach. (Gilligan 1982: 73)

Adams (2015) correctly observes a maturing in Gilligan's theoretical framework whereby Gilligan's logical conclusions involve a recognition of human development as necessitating autonomous and relational dimensions. As Adams (ibid. 292) expresses it: "For Gilligan, maturity is evidenced through the convergence of justice and care resulting in a dialogue". However, there appear to be limitations in Adams' (ibid. 293) comprehension of this "dialogue", judging from the following illustration of the concept that Adams provides: "In a challenge to Piaget, Gilligan identifies that male egocentrism is not inherent but that it develops as a result of boy's socialisation through the roles adopted by mothers. Thus she challenges the definition of 'human' as separate, autonomous and egocentric ... replacing it instead with a dualistic theory of moral development" (ibid.).

While it is evident that Gilligan (1982) does challenge the validity of absolute individuation, it is my understanding that the interconnected duality of Gilligan's care ethics does not derive from the fore fronting of the mothering role. Rather it is evident that the issue of absolute is relevant to Gilligan's assertion that at the absolute ends of the spectrum of the ethic of care and ethics of justice are realisations of reciprocity and a co-dependency of an ethic of care on an ethic of justice (and visa-versa). For taken to its utmost logical conclusion, even the most objective of judgements needs care if it is to be considered humane, as Gilligan (1982: 100) alludes in the following extract: "In the development of a postconventional ethical understanding, women come to see the violence inherent in equality, while men come to see the limitations of a conception of justice blinded to the difference in human life".

While it is the case that a gender binary distinction of care ethics pervades *In a Different Voice*, towards its conclusion there is indeed evidence of complexity, which is developed further in Gilligan's more recent writing. Particularly in the book's final paragraphs, Gilligan describes again situations in which the voices of male programmatic, individuated moral justice reverberate notions of ethics; such that the nuanced, embodied relationality of an ethic of care is marginalised and subjugated. But in the suppression of the latter resides a paradox, Gilligan concludes, for "in the difference voice of women lies the truth of an ethic of care, the tie between relationship and responsibility, and the origins of aggression in the failure of connection" (ibid. 173). Inability to appreciate this *different voice*, according to Gilligan, arises from an inflexible singularity in the framing of human experience and in its exegesis. Introducing into this pervasive rigidly programmatic schema a different ethics of care engenders "a more complex rendition of human experience which sees the truth of separation and attachment in the lives of women and men" (ibid. 174). Recognition of a different truth encourages appreciation of how "the truth of separation and attachment" is conveyed "by different modes of language and thought" (ibid.). In this comprehension of a *different voice* and appreciation of "how the tension between responsibilities and rights sustains the dialectic of human development", Gilligan begins to conclude "the integrity of two disparate modes of experience that are in the end connected" (ibid.). Evidence of this integration is presented in terms of the ethic of justice as premised on achieving equality for all; and the ethic of care as premised on a deontological ethos committed to achieving nonviolent resolution. Connecting both ethical premises is their endeavour to prevent injustice through an ethics of care. As Gilligan (ibid.) expresses it, "both perspectives converge in the realization that just as inequality adversely affects both parties in an unequal relationship, so too violence is destructive for everyone involved". Consequently, one might refer more specifically to an ethics of justice that is in actuality about care, and so is its nominal counterpart, the ethic of care. However, Gilligan is reluctant to abandon the male/female binary through which the formulation of the ethic of care emerges. Thus *In a Different Voice* concludes with reference to the phallocentric bias of Freud and Piaget's psycho-social model of individuated maturity and how "a recognition of the differences in women's experience and understanding expands our vision of maturity and points to the contextual nature of developmental truths" (ibid.).

In recent years, and partly in response to a barrage of criticism and accusations of essentialism, Gilligan's (2011/2016) *Joining the Resistance* revisits the central propositions of *In a Different Voice*. With admirably steadfast valour, Gilligan (2011/2016) reasserts the existence of a hegemonic masculine morality that establishes its power "by enforcing women's silence in the name of goodness" (ibid. 17). In this discourse of the good woman is ascribed selfless listening and unbounded kindness but as Gilligan consistently contends, "this ethic of feminine goodness was holding in place so-called normal, everyday conversations in which men spoke as if the omission of women was irrelevant or inconsequential and women overlooked or excused the omission of themselves" (ibid.). *Joining the Resistance* makes clearer that the "ethic of care resists these divisions" (ibid.) for Gilligan's concept of "care is a relational ethic, grounded in a premise of interdependence" (ibid. 23). When exploring the embattled concept of care within mainstream discourse of political justice, Gilligan observes the value of a relational ethic of care for "a feminist ethic of care is a *different voice* within a patriarchal culture because it joins reason with emotion, mind with body, self with relationships, men with women, resisting the divisions that maintain the patriarchal order" (ibid. 22). When reading through Joanna Lumley's interview with Dame Margaret Hodge as part of the Garden Bridge value for money review, one is drawn to a discernible portrayal of selflessness in the paradigmatic sequencing of the speech. Gilligan's (2011/2016: 20) account of morality and the female subject has resonance, most especially in the following reflection:

> Listening to women, I was struck over and over again by the power of the opposition between selfishness and selflessness to shape women's moral judgements and guide the choices they made. I would hear women call whatever they wanted to do (whether to have the baby or have an abortion) 'selfish' while describing what others wanted them to do as good. (ibid. 21)

Focusing on the theme of political justice, Gilligan (ibid. 20) proposes a "thick" conception of democracy; one that is in reception to different voices alongside and in relation to the objective, reasoned detached pragmatics of justice that pervade Western democratic institutions. Axiomatic to Gilligan's feminist care ethic is the intention to challenge the marginalising, within a "patriarchal framework", of care as an ostensible "feminine ethic" (ibid. 22). The "different voice" of care aligned with the female is contextually abridging the dualities that pervade a patriarchal order of justice; this is because it affiliates "reason with emotion, mind with body, self with relationships" (ibid.). Similar attempts to abridge patriarchal dualities are discernible in Joanna Lumley's speech; for example, in the following description, disputing an excessive individualism in preference for a care ethic based on the affirmation of others: "So I went and walked up and down, taking photographs of the Thames from both sides and studying maps and things like this and relocated it in my mind and wrote back to all my supporters, who were a fantastic list of people" (Hodge 2016: 3). Apparently immersed in care for others, the ecological activist motivation to enter a garden bridge into the competition to design a memorial for the late Princess Diana might plausibly be designated within a "thick" conception of democracy for, as Gilligan (2011/2016:22) contends, "A thin interpretation of democracy homogenizes differences in the name of equality, whereas thick democracy rests on the premise that different voices are integral to the vitality of a democratic society". In response to Dame Margaret Hodge's inference, when questioning Joanna Lumley, that the Garden Bridge project decision makers were more oligarchic than democratic, Lumley depicts an ethic of care as the basis for her positioning within the Garden Bridge project's powerful political network. For example, when accounting for her connections with Boris Johnson MP, Joanna Lumley states:

> JL: This is the Boris myth. I sat for Boris's mother, who is a painter, who painted me for *The Breaking of Bumbo* in 1971. At that time there were children creeping about on the floor so I said I must have met Boris when he was a child. This has turned into he was my childhood friend. I was a grownup actress being painted by his mother, so this is an awful myth. I don't know Boris. I've met him now.
>
> …
>
> MH: Yes, I think it is about then. What I've got is you wrote to Boris after the election and then you went to see and you had a meeting with Isabel and Ed. That's what I think.
>
> JL: No, I wrote to Boris after. Because I'd done something for him and I nearly broke my back trying to do a photograph with him on the South Bank for recycled furniture. It was one of the Mayor's charities and he sent me a bunch of flowers. I wrote back and thanked him for the bunch of flowers, which I noticed went into the papers as if he sent me flowers. Anyway, it doesn't matter. It makes me enraged because people are implying that we're some old mates. Anyway, we went to see Ed and Isabel and they said, 'Come back and let's talk to the Mayor about it later on'. Then Thomas and I wrote to the Mayor and said, 'Please consider this idea if it's to be a bridge'.
>
> We went along and the Mayor had asked us to look at a site between Battersea and Pimlico. So we went down there, dutifully, and looked at it and there was not one single human being there. I said if we were going to put a bridge there it would be just a complete waste of time. Nobody needed from Pimlico to go to Nine Elms or vice versa. There were no shops in Pimlico. There was no reason for crossing there. A cycle path perhaps but not a pedestrian bridge.
>
> (Hodge, 2016: 3; "This transcription has been disclosed by the GLA [Greater London Authority] in response to a request under the Environmental Information Regulations (EIR)" (ibid.). Garden Bridge Review Meeting Transcript, Event: Dame Margaret Hodge and Joanna Lumley, 1st December 2016)

Joanna Lumley's dialogue is replete with symbols of a maternal care ethic; indeed, the essentialising conflation of care ethic with female-centred motherhood presents limits to the ecofeminist parallels I am attempting to formulate regarding Gilligan's (1982) conception of an ethic of care. *Joining the Resistance* attempts to respond to a generation of critique directed at Gilligan's feminist intervention into Freudian psychoanalysis as part of a valorisation of a feminine ethic of care. Cognizant of the indictment of essentialism, *Joining the Resistance* advances Gilligan's original supposition of parallel and intersecting feminine (ethic of care) and masculine (ethic of justice) ethics of care. It recognises that "the gains in the 1960s and '70s toward realizing the promise of a truly democratic society included direct challenges to patriarchal constructions of masculinity and femininity on the part of the anti-war movement, the women's movement, and the gay liberation movement" (Gilligan 2011/2016: 22-23). Recognising the epistemological problematics of essentialism, Gilligan (ibid. 23) concedes that "to be a man did not necessarily mean becoming a soldier or preparing oneself for war; to be a woman did not necessitate becoming a mother or preparing oneself to bear and raise children". In this reformulation of the ethic of care, the concept of care exceeds the boundaries of male vs female duality as it embraces the notion of care and humanity for "care and caring are not women's issues, they are human concerns" (ibid.). *Joining the Resistance* is thus an intervention into a patriarchal order of justice which prioritises detached objectivity. In contrast to the disembodied logic of justice, the ostensibly feminine ethic of care cultivates care as "a relational ethic, grounded in a premise of interdependence" (ibid.). Consequently, in *Joining the Resistance* "the different voice, then is identified not by gender but by theme" (ibid. 24). From this more advanced feminist perspective, one might interpret the ethic of care evident in Joanna Lumley's speech as thematic and motivated by an ecological activism, distinguished as Gilligan (ibid.) might describe: "Its difference arises from joining reason with emotion, self with relationships. Undoing patriarchal splits and hierarchies, it articulates democratic norms and values: the importance of everyone having a voice, being listened to carefully, and heard with respect". Unquestionable genuineness cascades over the conception of a thematic application of the ethic of care but Gilligan's *Joining the Resistance* struggles to thoroughly explicate the issue of essentialism, as is evident in the following statement: "The association of a care voice with women was an empirical observation, admitting exceptions and by no means limited to women, but for reasons I will go into, women are more apt to resist separating themselves from relationships" (ibid.). The limitations of essentialism that blight Gilligan's feminist ethic of care extend into its application to ecology activism, as observed and replicated in the *Radical Ecology* of Carolyn Merchant (2005).

Carolyn Merchant's (2005) *Radical Ecology*, at initial inclination, apparently ameliorates many of the conceptual limitations evident in Carol Gilligan's (1982) ethic of care. Unlike the latter's apolitical juxtaposition of gender and care, axiomatic with Merchant's (2005) radical ecology is "a sense of crisis in the industrialized world" (ibid. 4). Contiguous with critical configurations of ecofeminism, Merchant (2005) espouses interconnectivity in the "domination of nature" and the subjugation "of human beings along lines of race, class and gender" (ibid.). Radical ecology confronts an industrial capitalist logic seemingly oblivious to its flagrant neglect of nature. "It seeks a new ethic of the nurture of nature and the nurture of people", advocating an inculcation into cultural political practice of a new albeit ambiguous conception of relationality (ibid.). Less ambiguous is the concession that radical ecology interpolates with social ecology for it shares a concern to scrutinise economic production and political and social institutions in conjunction with their impact on nature. Capitalist production is consumed by deleterious contradictions, which "creates accumulating ecological stresses on air, water, soil, and biota (including human beings) and on society's ability to maintain and reproduce itself over time" (ibid. 9). Contradictions of primary concern relate to "the assaults of production on ecology"; Merchant incorporates into this the production of warfare alongside the polluting biodegradation resulting from industrial waste (ibid.). In global capitalism, local incidents of biodegradation rapidly circulate through global circuits of production, and as Merchant (ibid.) observes: "These assaults of production on global ecology are circulated by means of the biogeochemical cycles and thermodynamic energy exchanges through soils, plants, animals and bacteria". Accepting this, it is a truism that the latter's effects will be differentially experienced by "First, Second, and Third Worlds and by people of different races, classes and sexes" (ibid.). Less self-evident is Merchant's observation that a perilous contradiction in capitalist production "arises from the assaults of production on biological and social reproduction" (ibid.). Biochemical reengineering coupled with a massification of mono-agricultural production assault "the biological (intergenerational) reproduction of both human and nonhuman species" (ibid.). Social reproduction is likewise affected as societies struggle to sustain reciprocity in care ethics and relations of trust while withstanding encroaching urban decay and environmental devastation. The compound affect, according to Merchant (ibid. 9), "of these deepening contradictions generated by the dynamics between production and ecology and by those between reproduction and production" is an accelerating "global ecological crisis". Retrenching from grandiose meta-exclamation, Merchant recognises that the depth and extent of ecological crisis need to be configured in conjunction with the industrial history and economic development of a country "as well as its linkages to global political economies" (ibid.). Thus, radical ecology advocates with "guarded optimism" direct cultural political intervention at the axis of immense magnitude of ecological stress to invert environmental degradation. Ethically, radical ecology evokes a belief that "the goals of production need to be subordinated to the reproduction of life through the fulfilment of human needs and the preservation of local ecologies" (ibid.). Axiomatic to Carolyn Merchant's ecofeminist care ethic is the concept of "an ethic of partnership between humans and nonhuman nature" (ibid.). "Partnership" is mobilised, conceptually, by Merchant (ibid. 196) so as to ameliorate the essentialist presuppositions of a conventional ecofeminism that attempts to "constrain traditional ethics based on rights, rules, and utilities, with considerations based on care, love, and trust". Of particular concern is the tendency for conventional ecofeminist care ethics to conflate nurturing with an essential female nature. Merchant's (ibid.) conception of "partnerships" purports to avoid essentialism in so far as it allegedly traverses gendered dichotomies; as Merchant expresses it:

> My own approach to resolving these contradictions is through a partnership ethic that treats humans (including male partners and female partners) as equals in personal, household, and political relations and humans as equal partners with (rather than controlled by or dominant over) nonhuman nature. (ibid. 196)

Barely avoiding a heterosexual normative consensus, Merchant's (ibid.) ecofeminism configures "partnerships" according to a utopian ideal of domestic division of labour, as is evident in the following extracts derived from *Radical Ecology*:

> Just as human partners, regardless of sex, race, or class, must give each other space, time, and care, allowing each other to grow and develop individually within supportive non-dominating relationships, so humans must give nonhuman nature space, time, and care, allowing it to reproduce, evolve, and respond to human actions. (ibid. 196)
>
> ...
>
> Constructing nature as a partner allows for the possibility of a personal or intimate (but not necessarily spiritual) relationship with nature and for feelings of compassion for nonhumans as well as for people who are sexually, racially, or culturally different from ourselves. It avoids gendering nature as a nurturing mother or a goddess and avoids the ecocentric dilemma that humans are only one of many equal parts of an ecological web and therefore morally equal to a bacterium or a mosquito. (ibid. 197)

Purporting to confront all aspects of social political life that exploit nature, radical ecology nevertheless retains conventional ecofeminism's opacity of self-interrogation for it also falls short of interrogating its positionality in formidable nexuses of power. Merchant (ibid. 8) blithely exclaims that radical ecology "supports social movements for removing the causes of environmental deterioration and raising the quality of life for people of every race, class, and sex". Omitted in this integrity is recognition of the intersectionalities of race, gender and class in determining one's positionality in powerful nexuses of power and privilege. Acknowledging positionality is crucial because it compels us to apprehend, as ecofeminists, our situational privilege in environs of structured inequalities of power in conjunction with the partialities and propensities borne from our embeddedness in structures of power. Axiomatic with reflexivity of positionality is an unavoidable confrontation with accountability for our research methodology, status as subjects in the subject-object research dyad, and moral obligation to take care in the representations, exegesis and elucidation produced (Madison 2011: 8). Positionality disputes claims toward the validity of a universal standpoint evident in conventional ecofeminism; it also challenges Merchant's (2005) conception of "partnerships". With specific regard to the latter, in its insistence on making transparent the value-laden taxonomies of structure and partial leanings of subjectivity, positionality stimulates an attentive scepticism of the possibilities of developing "partnerships" devoid of superimposition by subjects on their Others. While avidly concerned to investigate the unjust assaults on nature dispatched by powerful multinationals, Merchant's (2005) taciturnity on positionality is conspicuously mute. Parallels here with Joanna Lumley's mediated ecofeminism are less than factitious for both *radical* feminist positions obfuscate a questioning of their positionality; and in so doing, shield the vulnerability of their judgement to accusations of inadvertently being self-centred supplicants to structured relations of power. It suffices to say that, in emphasising the necessity of disclosing positionality, "we are inviting an ethics of accountability" (Madison 2011:9) by compelling the chance that we may be proven wanting in our own ethics of care. Commitment to a cognizance of positionality is perilously oblivious throughout the, admittedly redacted, Johanna Lumley presentation to Dame Margaret Hodge (1st December 2016); and this is acutely evident in the following transcription extract:

> MH [Margaret Hodge]: So the original tender was a concept tender and by that time you were also an associate with Heatherwick, I gather.

JL [Joanna Lumley]: Yes. Because I realised people didn't understand what a garden bridge or a green bridge or a living bridge would be; in the olden days, I had made – in 1999, from Lez Brotherston, who is a great stage designer, his assistant, Stefan, made me. I said, 'Model it on Lambeth Bridge. It doesn't matter. Make a bridge, clad it in Lalique-y glass stuff (which is what I always thought would be divine, a glass bridge) stick some trees on it so that when you sit down at one end and look like that you can't see across it'. I then carried that about. I've got it in the attic at home. I carried this metre-long thing around to every meeting I went to and put it on the table. I made it. Nobody asked me to make it. I made it so that people could understand what a garden bridge was.

That's probably why people have to make something for a tender because otherwise people literally don't know. Iain Tuckett said, 'You mean with grass growing along the side of it?' You go, 'No, with trees going across', but people who haven't got that can't imagine that, so I just wanted to say that.

I wasn't an associate but that's a word. What Thomas wanted to do is he knew that he was going to be putting it forward and he knew that this was my idea. He thought that if he didn't acknowledge me somehow I wouldn't be part of it. I wanted very much to be part of it if it was going to be a success, which is why I'm a trustee. You probably think I'm a flaky trustee. I know that you criticised some of our trustees and I can see that I'm easily the lightest weight but the truth is it was my idea and I've done quite a lot of work on it.

MH [Margaret Hodge]: I don't t think I've suggested that at all.

JL [Joanna Lumley]: Trying to find out from people, taxi drivers, people in bus queues and things, I've stopped doing it now but in the old days I'd say, 'What do you think, what do you think?' Everybody was mad about it. So I became connected with it. It was my idea, it's my baby, and you say, 'Did you want your baby?' and you go, 'Yes'. Why else would I fight for something as lovely as this? I'm not doing it because I think there is a prize in it; I'm doing it because there is money in it. I set up the whole first thing, which vanished away, and this time I know it's only £100,000 but that's what I've put into it. You don't receive even a bus fare in our position, so it's not really for money.

MH [Margaret Hodge]: Just for the record, you never got money from Heatherwick?

JL [Joanna Lumley]: Never. Never, never, never. That was a word; 'associate' meant because we dreamt up the idea.

BE [Bee Emmott]: And that has been confirmed in writing back in the day because as a charity we wanted to understand what that relationship was.

JL [Joanna Lumley]: I don't get money from anybody.

BE [Bee Emmott]: So we've got a document between Heatherwick and Joanna that says this is just a term used for recognition of your idea, so Heatherwick had provided it.

(Dame Margaret Hodge 2016: 11-12; "This transcription has been disclosed by the GLA [Greater London Authority] in response to a request under the Environmental Information Regulations (EIR)" (ibid.). Garden Bridge Review Meeting Transcript, Event: Dame Margaret Hodge and Joanna Lumley, 1st December 2016)

It is not my intention to question or besmirch these testimonies but rather the critical analysis is directed at making manifest the formulation of ecofeminism that is (in)advertently mobilised so as to accomplish the integrity of the testimony. Indeed, the above transcription extract exposes a profound vulnerability in a conventional liberal ecofeminist ethics of care, which is oblivious to its positionality in structured relations of power and privilege. While unwaveringly insistent that Joanna Lumley's "associate" status was non-transactional, "never" involving money payments, it is difficult to dismiss an incipient sense of exploitative gendered relations of power at work. In the exquisite Marxist ecofeminism of Ariel Salleh (2009), one gains appreciation of complex capitalist machinations in which ecological environmental physical exertion provides for the "meta-industrial labour" necessary for capitalist production. Salleh's (2009) path-breaking concept of "meta-industrial" labour is advanced further when applied to the question of epistemology and the production of knowledge. Indeed, when Salleh's (2009) concept of "meta-industrial labour" is considered in relation to inscriptive sign-technologies (Odih 2010), one apprehends revelatory insights into capitalism's expropriation of urban ecological practices involving the encoding of knowledge into space. It is my contention that the liberal ecofeminism portrayed by Joanna Lumley in the Garden Bridge testimony presented to Dame Margaret Hodge reveals and makes manifest: (a) the mediation of ecofeminism as a cultural production and façade; and (b) liberal ecofeminism's a-political care ethic is particularly vulnerable to capitalism's rapacious exploitation of the knowledge-based labour necessary in the privatisation of public recreational spaces. The latter involves an advance on Salleh's (2009) concept of "meta-industrial labour" so as to consider uniquely inscriptive sign-technologies (Odih 2010). Salleh's (2009) account of "Ecological debt: Embodied debt" in *Eco-Sufficiency and Global Justice* identifies capitalist production to be reliant on the expropriation of unpaid reproductive labour and measly remunerated labour of workers that "undertake regenerative or meta-industrial labour" (ibid. 7). Unmediated, natural and embodied meta-industrial labour is visceral in its conditionality on the materiality of the human body. Salleh incisively elucidates:

> Unlike factory work, or academic work, the labour of these socially diverse groupings oversees biological flows and sustains matter/energy exchanges in nature. It is certainly no exaggeration to say that the entire machinery of global capital rests on the material transactions of this reproductive labour force. (ibid. 7)

Salleh (ibid.) convincingly argues that global capitalism systematically exploits meta-industrial labour while simultaneously abnegating responsibility for its sufficient remuneration. Indeed, "Embodied debt is accrued by the global North when it denies forms of value generated by this gendered and racialised labour" (ibid.). Significantly, Salleh (ibid.) convincingly contends that the agents of meta-industrial labour are involved in the practice of "an alternative economics and an alternative epistemology". The economics of meta-industrial labour necessitate a new epistemological formulation, contends Salleh (ibid.); a formulation of knowledge predicated at the molecular level of capitalism's metabolic rift with nature. Axiomatic with Salleh's advance on the notion of "an epistemology of the South" is the cultivation of an epistemology based on "the counter-entropic logic of regeneration" contrasted against "a knowledge-based-bio-economy" in which "the addictive processes of molecular biology" are accorded competitive primacy (ibid.). Conversely, an epistemology centralising "meta-industrial provisioning" can facilitate the modelling "of eco-sufficiency" attained through "local autonomy and resource sovereignty – and by these means, global justice" (ibid. 8). Supporting and valuing in principle, Salleh's cultivation of an epistemology is relevant to eco-sufficiency and sustainable development in the global South, the concept of meta-industrial labour as application to knowledge-based coding of urban ecological and the privatisation of urban recreational riverscapes.

Marxist Ecofeminism

Central to my theoretical framework is the feminist principle that the ecological understanding of water sustainability interrogates the market form of environmental degradation. It is equally important to expand the notion of economy so as to encompass "the multiple contributions of women's reproductive labour to the maintenance of capital" (Salleh 2010: 208). Ecofeminist ideals are not new to the lexicon of feminist struggles to preserve communities and enable equality of opportunity for all women. Global capitalism's increasingly rapacious extension into the natural environment has raised the imperative of an ecofeminist challenge to "corporate globalization" as it relentlessly "expands and contracts, leaving no stone unturned, no body unused" (Salleh 2014: ix).

I appreciate the Marxist feminist belief that neoliberal capitalist expropriations of the natural world necessitate robust and resourceful challenge; "resourcing of women and of nature are structurally interconnected in the capitalist patriarchal system" (ibid. xi). "The stranglehold of global neoliberalism" (ibid.) has indeed tightened and Marxist ecofeminism constitutes a formidable part of the feminist challenge. While in agreement with Marxist ecofeminists, it is necessary to explore further the complexities of dialectical materialism, advance beyond economic deterministic ecology politics, critically engage with the governmentality of symbolic mediation, and engage reflexively with the intersectionalities of class, race and feminist environmental activism.

Marxist feminists recognise that nature "enfolds human being" (Mellor, 1997: 184-85); rather than presupposing an idea of transcendence from nature, Mary Mellor (ibid. 185) convincingly proclaims the imperative of assuming humans as "immanent beings". The condition of immanence is located outside of an Archimedean timeline and thus it is recognised that: "The dynamics of the natural world exist in their own right with or without conscious human intervention...humanity cannot have a 'grand narrative' to explain its own position...Ecologically, humanity exists in a condition of radical uncertainty" (ibid.). These and other Marxist ecofeminist principles partly inform the theoretical ideas that have framed my empirical research of river restoration. The following discussion presents critical ethnographic fieldwork I conducted in 2013-2014 while exploring river conservation along the London foreshore of the River Thames (Odih 2014). My ecofeminist theoretical framework inductively emerged from this critical ethnographic research; as is evident in its empirically led confluence of Marxist ecofeminism and Foucauldian post-structuralism.

In *The Subject and Power*, Michel Foucault (1982) explores "the question of the subject". Foucault committed decades of scholarship to composing a history of the contrasting techniques "by which, in our culture, human beings are made subjects" (ibid. 208). Central to Foucault's theoretical framework is his attempt to elicit processes of "objectification" and "subjectification". With regards to the former, Foucault (ibid.) asserts that his entire oeuvre has been concerned with the exploration of three modes of rendering human subjects into calculable objects amenable to surveillance and programmes of administration. Forms of investigation that attempt to ascribe scientific status to their operation constitute the first of Foucault's three modes of objectification. Foucault presents "the objectivising of the speaking subject" in structural linguistics: "grammaire générale, philology and linguistics" (ibid.) as examples of processes through which human beings are transformed into objective phenomena. Also significant are the objective rationalities of finance, economics and "the analysis of wealth". Foucault highlights the scientific prerogative of the natural sciences as powerful enclaves in which the existence of the human, as a living being, is subject to processes of nomenclature, aggregation and allocation. These processes through which scientific discourse is mobilized as part of a classificatory analysis of the subject were apparent in Odih (2014) analysis of the European Union's Water Framework Directive. The latter dictate necessitates that local governance agencies work with river conservation charities and environmental specialists as part of a determining of river conservation and community prerequisites. Such programmes resonate with "the objectivizing of the speaking subject" for they attempt to render knowable the opinions of environmental citizens and subject these ideals to governmental techniques of scientific enquiry. Classification is a feature of the second of Foucault's investigations into objectivizing technologies. Foucault identifies modern governance as pervaded by "dividing practices" through which subjects are distinguished from themselves and each other. "Dividing practices" are discernible in the technologies of the advertising sign, used to inscribe meaning into space, place and social practices.

The issue of visibility is illustrative of the operation of sign technologies. Foucault (1982: 208) describes how "dividing practices" have the effect of rendering the subject "either divided inside himself or divided from others". Visibility is an inscriptive sign technology that objectivises subjects. At the same time, visibility provides an axis through which "a human being turns him – or herself into a subject" (ibid.). The interviewee refers to visibility as indexed to processes of self-learning and consciousness raising. Visibility is a technology of the sign; a mechanism through which individuals come to learn to recognise themselves as both subject and object of the sign. This suggests that the focus of post-structural analysis is not power per se but rather the dynamic interplay between the subject and power. In my interviews with the river restoration volunteers, it was evident that individuals are integrally involved in the sign mediation of ecological activism. Foucault (ibid. 209) states that "the human subject is placed in relations of production and of signification".

Thus, the complexities of the subject of ecology and power are discernible when the analysis is concerned not so much to individuate a possessor of power or identify power as residing within an institution. Foucault (1982: 212) defines power as a "technique":

> This form of power applies itself to immediate everyday life which categorizes the individual, marks him by his own individuality, attaches him to his own identity, imposes a law of truth on him which he must recognize and which others have to recognize in him. It is a form of power which makes individuals subjects. (ibid.)

Nothing surely clarifies so well the subject of symbolic mediation than a focus on power as existing "when it is put into action, even if, of course, it is integrated into a disparate field of possibilities brought to bear upon permanent structures" (ibid. 219). Focusing in this way on power can open up the symbolic mediations through which ecological activism can be communicated. Relations of definition and meaning are certainly informed by power, but an integral feature of the circulation of signs is the subject. The power of symbolic mediations is relational; and thus the mobilization of the feminine ideal in visual cultures of ecological activism needs to be comprehended in terms of an intercourse of power. As Foucault states:

> In effect, what defines a relationship of power is that it is a mode of action which does not act directly and immediately on others. Instead it acts upon their actions: an action upon an action, on existing actions or on those which may arise in the present or the future. (ibid. 220)

The symbolic mediation of ecological activism is clearly allied to the exercise of power as action on the existing on-going symbolic mediations of subjects. Signs engage subjects that are themselves engaged in the production of signification. Consequently, the relationality of signs opens up the possibility of resistance. As Foucault (1982: 221) expresses it: "Power is exercised only over free subjects, and only insofar as they are free". Sign constellations mediate free actions and thus individuals are presented with a "field of possibilities in which several ways of behaving, several reactions and diverse comportments may be realized" (ibid.). Freedom is axiomatic to the power of symbolic mediations: "In this game, freedom may well appear as the condition for the exercise of power" (ibid.). The decisive problem is not that of acquiescence to symbolic mediations but rather the provocation of resistance to the "hail" (Althusser 1971) of the sign. As Foucault (1982: 221-222) expresses it: "At the very heart of the power relationship, and constantly provoking it, are the recalcitrance of the will and the intransigence of freedom". Signs are mediated by the intransigence of the spirit, and relationships of antagonism best describe the sign mediations of ecological activism. In this sense: "It would be better to speak of an 'agonism' – of a relationship which is at the same time reciprocal incitation and struggle" (ibid. 222).

Foucault (1982: 222) describes "the exercise of power as a way in which certain actions may structure the field of other possible actions". It has been a consistent theme of this chapter that river restoration is symbolically mediated by the spectre of the feminine ideal. Gender identities are embedded in the social milieu; they are actively composed by conscious human beings and thus "not reconstituted 'above' society as a supplementary structure whose radical effacement one could perhaps dream of" (ibid.). Central to my theoretical formulation of a poststructural ethics of care is an appreciation of gender identities as discursive, i.e., constituted in and through language, social practice, institutions, economy, politics and regimes of governance. The integration of the symbolic into the discursivity of gender identity far exceeds a notion of discourse as communication. Indeed:

> It is necessary to distinguish power relations from relationships of communication which transmit information by means of a language, a system of signs, or any other symbolic medium. No doubt communicating is always a certain way of acting upon another person or persons. But the production and circulation of elements of meaning can have as their objective or as their consequence certain results in the realm of power; the latter are not simply an aspect of the former. (Foucault 1982: 217)

To this end, symbolic mediations should not be merely conflated with power as part of the construction of gendered identity; but this does not mean that power relationships and sign relationships exist in different domains. As Foucault expresses it:

> Power relations, relationships of communication, objective capacities should not therefore be confused. This is not to say that there is a question of three separate domains. Nor that there is on one hand the field of things, of perfected technique, work, and the transformation of the real; on the other that of signs, communication, reciprocity, and the production of meaning; finally that of the domination of the means of constraint, of inequality and the action of men upon other men. It is a question of three types of

relationships which in fact always overlap one another, support one another reciprocally, and use each other mutually as means to an end. (ibid. 217-218)

Foucault (1988: 18) identifies inter-relationships between sign technologies (signs, meanings, signification), technologies of production (transformation of material things), technologies of power (objectivising categorisation), and technologies of the self (self-regulating abilities of subjects to impact discourse on the cultivation of body and soul). Formulating an account of gender and ecological activism therefore requires examining "the application of objective capacities" in terms of the "relationships of communication" that circulate in and through the discursive constructs of gender identity. Symbolic mediations are inextricably bound to the objectivizing capacity of technologies of power ("whether they consist of obligatory tasks" or processes of visibility) (Foucault 1982: 218). Symbolic mediations are meaningful communications for they "imply finalized activities (even if only the correct putting into operation of elements of meaning) and, by virtue of the modifying the field of information between partners, produce effects of power" (ibid. 218). Consequently,

> [Symbolic mediations] can scarcely be dissociated from activities brought to their final term, be they those which permit the exercise of this power (such as training techniques, processes of domination, the means by which obedience is obtained) or those which in order to develop their potential call upon relations of power (the division of labor and the hierarchy of tasks). (ibid. 218)

In this analysis of the subject of gender and ecological activism, it is appreciated that the "transformation of the real" (technologies of production); "signs, communication, reciprocity, and the production of meaning" (technologies of the sign); and "domination of the means of constraint" (technologies of power) are interrelated features of symbolic mediations (ibid.). Nevertheless, their application is never uniform and invariant because "in a given society there is no general type of equilibrium between finalised activities, systems of communication, and power relations" (ibid.). Rather,

> The activity which ensures ... the acquisition of aptitudes or types of behaviour is developed there by means of a whole ensemble of regulated communication (lessons, questions and answers, orders, exhortations, coded signs of obedience, differentiation marks of the 'value' of each person and of the levels of knowledge) and by the means of a whole series of power processes (enclosure, surveillance, reward and punishment, the pyramidal hierarchy). (ibid. 218-219)

Part of Foucault's thinking here derives from his advocacy for a definition of "government" that extends beyond the formal institutions and structures of politics and the state. Rather, "government" refers to a shifting assemblage of formal and informal agencies, practices and institutions that variously and differentially align the self-regulating ability of subjects with the design, objectives and scope of a regime of governance. As Foucault expresses it:

> The exercise of power consists in guiding the possibility of conduct and putting in order the possible outcome. Basically power is less a confrontation between two adversaries or the linking of one to the other than a question of government. This word must be allowed the very broad meaning which it had in the sixteenth century. 'Government' did not refer only to political structures or to the management of states; rather it designated the way in which the conduct of individuals or of groups might be directed: the government of children, of souls, of communities, of families, of the sick. (ibid. 221)

Symbolic mediations are inextricably linked to the exercise of power in government, i.e., they are involved in the designation of "the way in which the conduct of individuals or of groups might be directed" (ibid.). A consistent feature of my research into the feminine ideal, as part of a symbolic mediation of river restoration, involved focusing on governance both in terms of conventional political structures and "also modes of action, more or less considered and calculated, which were destined to act upon the possibilities of action of other people" (ibid.). Thus, for example, I have empirically researched the impact of the European Union's Water Framework Directive on river conservation charities. My interviews with three river conservation charities produced primary data which has been triangulated with data derived from my interviews along the foreshore of the River Thames. Both sets of data have trace elements of government in the sense of "political structures or ...the managements of states" (ibid.); but the data also illustrates "the exercise of power as a mode of action upon the actions of others" (ibid.). Emerging from this triangulation of data is the suggestion that the coordination of technologies of production, signs, and power constitutes a shifting and irregular field of practice. Symbolic mediations of ecological activism tend not to easily slot into the formal apparatuses of political institutions and environmental organisations. Rather, and as Foucault observes:

> [T]here are diverse forms, diverse places, diverse circumstances or occasions in which these interrelationships establish themselves according to a specific model. But there are also 'blocks' in which the adjustment of

abilities, the resources of communication, and power relations constitute regulated and concerted systems. (ibid. 218)

The symbolic mediation of ecological activism is constituted through a complex milieu of moderated communications (environmental citizenship programmes, advertising signs and scheduled events) and, less formally, "by the means of a whole series of power processes (enclosure, surveillance ...)" (ibid. 219). Further to the operation of assemblages of actions upon actions, it is evident that these symbolic mediations of ecological activism, in terms of the feminine ideal, were not prescriptive or directly imposed upon the subject. Rather, symbolic mediations of ecological activism exemplify the manifold ways in which the exercise of power opens up a field of possibilities in the cultivation of gender identities.

Timely Reflections, Culture Industry Mediations on Marxist Ecofeminism

One may query the relevance of applying Marxist ecofeminist critical engagement to an application process for a garden bridge, which will, now, never be built. It is my contention that the Garden Bridge, in its application and now its legacy, is part of a wider process of privatised financialisation of the River Thames and its immediate surroundings. Indeed, recent venture capitalist manoeuvring with regards to finance capital investment in Thames Water substantially supports concerns about a financialisation of the river, its surrounding spaces and its conservation. Consider in this regards the following material:

Monday 22/06/2015, 18:15

Dear Christian Wolmar,

Thank you for receiving my communication. I am writing to you with regards to your declared interest in the forthcoming 2016 London Mayoral election. I am a senior lecturer at Goldsmiths University of London and specialist in European Union water directives and their implications for community cohesion and nationalist identity. It is my opinion that your mayoral campaign requires further focus and engagement with London's current water strategy. Moreover, your campaign requires further focus on the crucial inter-connections linking European Union water directives, voluntary sector river conservation and a rise of ethnic nationalism in European Union urban cities. I have conducted extensive research on this issue, and I would like to introduce you to my current specialist research which focuses on the European Union Water Framework Directive and river conservation of the River Thames. My recently published book entitled 'Watersheds in Marxist Ecofeminism', provides unique political and economic insights which are valuable to your mayoral campaign. My book provides a detailed empirically informed critique of London's current water strategy, which as you know is entitled 'Securing London's Water Future'.

As we accelerate towards a European Union referendum, can your campaign afford to remain insufficiently informed about the centrality of London's water strategy decentralising English ethnic identities and the uncompromising legislative force of a centralising European Union Water Framework Directive? My book will be a valuable resource to your campaign; my book is entitled 'Watersheds in Marxist Ecofeminism'. It's time for your campaign to think of the future of London's River Thames; it's time to develop a water strategy for London that builds integrated urban communities; it's time to place the river that connect us at the center of current debates regarding the European Union.

...

Best wishes,
Pamela Odih
https://www.gold.ac.uk/sociology/staff/odih/

In June 2015, I wrote to the then Labour Party mayoral candidate Christian Wolmar to express concerns about the incumbent Mayor of London's Water Strategy, situating this within the context of the centralising tendencies of the European Union's Water Framework Directive. While I did not receive a response from Christian Wolmar directly, the following appeared soon after in the *Evening Standard*'s Londoner's Diary feature:

Thursday 23 July 2015, 15:20

A feminist watershed for Wolmar

At this stage of their campaigns, what should contenders for the London mayor be thinking about? Housing? Heathrow? No, the key issue at stake here is how 'neoliberal environmental governance of river conservation, coupled with the organizational modernization imposed and sustained by the European Union's water directives, engenders Other Spaces of feminist ecological alignment'. Obviously. Such is the opinion of one Pamela Odih, senior lecturer at Goldsmiths and 'specialist in European Union water directives and their implications for community cohesion and nationalist identity'. Labour candidate and transport expert Christian Wolmar, pictured, yesterday got an email from Odih, insisting that her recent book, *Watersheds in Marxist Ecofeminism*, would be a 'valuable resource to your campaign'. 'As we accelerate towards a European Union referendum,' Odih writes, 'can your campaign afford to remain insufficiently informed about the centrality of London's water strategy to decentralising English ethnic identities and the uncompromising legislative force of a centralising European Union Water Framework directive?' So could Wolmar for Watersheds prove the ultimate vote-winner? ...

(Londoner's Diary 2015)

Platitudes to one side, I was reservedly intrigued to feature in the iconic Evening Standard Londoner's Diary, given its iconic longevity across a century literary reverie. *Watersheds in Marxist Ecofeminism* raises highly contentious issues that proved prophetic and insightful given the scapegoating of immigrants, heartrendingly accepted as collateral damage for a soulless toxic 2016 referendum's Brexit campaign, and the accelerated pace by which finance capital is financialising Thames Water. Indeed, I shall conclude this chapter's Marxist ecofeminist scrutiny of the Garden Bridge project with a discussion in more graphic detail of ethnic identity, nationalism and the adsensory financialisation of the urban decay that is the deteriorating service delivery of Thames Water.

> Holding Thames Water to account ... The previous ultimate controller, Macquarie, has sold out to Canadian Borealis and Middle-Eastern Wren House, whom we welcome to the sector. Responsible investors can benefit from helping us drive performance up and prices down ... It's a privilege for a company to hold a monopoly franchise, in perpetuity. Ofwat will always take action where necessary to protect customers and step in when necessary. We challenge companies to do the very best for the communities they serve and to provide clarity and transparency so that customers have the information they need and the service they expect. (Johnson Cox, Chair, Water Services Regulation Authority; Ofwat 2017: 1-2)

On 14th March 2017, Macquarie announced that its European Infrastructure Fund, in conjunction with several other Macquarie-managed funds, had acceded to the sale of an incorporated 26.3 per cent stake in Kemble Water Holdings Limited, the ultimate parent company of Thames Water Utilities (Macquarie 2017). On 14th August 2017, the Garden Bridge Trust announced the termination of its project to build and manage a garden bridge across the River Thames in central London (Garden Bridge Trust 2017). Presupposing these encounters as aleatory materialist dialectics (Odih 2014) involves contemplating one's proximal place in time and space. Stuart Hall's (1987: 44) *Minimal Selves* offers "a few adjectival thoughts" pertinent to one's sense of identity amidst the foreclosure of place by absolute transpositions of time. Meditative and thoughtful, Hall (ibid.)

discloses the intimate realisation that his "own sense of identity" has always been inextricably dependent "on the fact of being a *migrant*, on the *difference* from the rest of you". Hall's realisation yields fascination in the context of decentring English ethnic nationalism; borne from which Hall (ibid.) quips the irony: "to find myself centred at last". Postmodernity is targeted in *Minimal Selves* as a troublesome conceptual framework, propitious for critical intervention for "now that, in the postmodern age, you all feel so dispersed, I become centered" (ibid.). Dispersal and fragmentation exist in Hall's experience but this is attributed to configurations of modernity, as Hall (ibid.) expresses it: "What I've thought of as dispersed and fragmented comes, paradoxically, to be *the* representative modern experience!" Hall providences postmodern, decentring of English ethnic identity with the poignant salutation: "This is 'coming home' with a vengeance! … welcome to migranthood" (ibid.). Extending and engaging with the theme of "welcome to migranthood", this chapter's conclusion replaces Hall's account of decentring identity in postmodernity with a focus on absolute disjunctures of time and space in the adsensory financialisation of urban ecological decay.

Figure 7.2.: "The world smiles at us. It offers itself to us. And because *everywhere* is imagined as offering itself to us, *everywhere* is more or less the same" (John Berger, *Ways of Seeing*, 1972). Photographic Image, Environmental Activist, Central London, August 2016.

Garden Bridge, Culture Industry Mediations: Framing Televisual Ecofeminist Care Ethics

Figure 7.3.: "Let us first be sure about what we are not saying. We are not saying that there is nothing left to experience before original works of art except a sense of awe because they have survived" (John Berger, *Ways of Seeing*, 1972). Photographic Image, Southbank, London, 2016.

Figure 7.4.: "Capitalism survives by forcing the majority, whom it exploits, to define their own interests as narrowly as possible. This was once achieved by extensive deprivation. Today in the developed countries it is being achieved by imposing a false standard of what is and what is not desirable" (John Berger, *Ways of Seeing*, 1972). Photographic Image, Southbank, London, 2016.

Garden Bridge, Culture Industry Mediations: Framing Televisual Ecofeminist Care Ethics 293

Figure 7.5.: "A people or a class which is cut off from its own past is far less free to choose and to act as a people or class than one that has been able to situate itself in history" (John Berger, *Ways of Seeing*, 1972). Photographic Image, Southbank, London, 2016.

Chapter Eight

Garden Bridge, Forecasting Troubled Waters: English Ethnic Nationalism In European Union Brexit Times

Figure 8.1.: "Publicity images also belong to the moment in the sense that they must be continually renewed and made up-to-date. Yet they never speak of the present. Often they refer to the past and always they speak of the future" (*Ways of Seeing*, 1972). Photographic Image, Environmental Activist, Central London, August 2016.

English Ethnic Nationalism Brexit Time's River Tales

> Not something I would naturally rush to hear, but Macquarie; The Tale of the River Bank is the must-listen of my week. I didn't think anyone made unflashy, meticulous documentaries like this any more. Financial journalist Michael Robinson began his report in a lovely part of the world, on the banks of the Thames in Little Marlow. He listened to locals telling him about a time, a few years ago, when the river was not so pretty. When brown foam rolled over the river ripples and tampons, sanitary towels, condoms and 'large lumps of matter' clustered around houseboats. Why was this happening?

(Sawyer 2017)

As an avid listener to Radio 4 and keen advocate of BBC speech radio, the Observer radio columnist Miranda Sawyer is a dedicated Sunday ritual read. In September 2017, Sawyer (2017) published a fascinating review of a radio programme entitled "Macquarie: The Tale of the River Bank". Sawyer's (ibid.) review was deftly written and thought provoking in its inference that jingoistic rhetoric, around an increasing foreign national share ownership in Thames Water, is obscuring the privatisation of Thames Water through the banking sector. Sawyer's review article is ingenuously brief and worthy of further development, with respect to a more detailed survey of Environment Agency reports. Nevertheless, it has provided for a further development of my existing interest in financialisation and the River Thames water ecology (Odih 2014). Of particular relevance and thought provoking inspiration for further investigation is the following aspect of Sawyer's (2017) review:

> The voices in the programme – financial experts, watchdogs, journalists – were all reasonable. And they all said the same thing. Macquarie's structures were not transparent, money was moving through offshore subsidiaries and the UK watchdog, Ofwat, just waved everything through. 'Bankers are always a few steps ahead,' said one expert, pointing out that by the time a parliamentary inquiry has been conducted, the bankers have made their money and moved on to the next deal. All rather depressing, but well worth your time.

Intellectually intrigued by Miranda Sawyer's (2017) incisive introjection, I indeed, listened to the Radio 4 broadcast documentary by Michael Robinson (2017) entitled: *Macquarie: The Tale of the River Bank*. Further exploration and review has facilitated the formulation of a similar conclusion to that of Robinson (2017) and Sawyer (2017), that is: complexity resides behind the jingoistic rhetoric of increasing foreign national share ownership of Thames Water.

Thames Water Utilities Ltd (Thames Water) was, on 22nd March 2017, assigned an unprecedented £20,361,140.06 in aggregate of penalty fines, imposed for a succession of cataclysmic pollution incidents on London's River Thames (Environment Agency 2017). The prosecution collated six prescinded pollution cases, stemming from 2012 to2014, involving Thames Water sewage treatment works in Aylesbury (polluted the River Thames), Didcot (polluted a River Thames tributary, the Moor Ditch), Henley (sewage treatment works polluted the Thames), Little Marlow (polluted the Thames) and Arborfield (polluted a tributary of the River Loddon, Barkham Brook) and Littlemore (sewage station polluted the Thames); presenting these at one hearing in the Aylesbury Crown Court. The court ascertained that Thames Water Utilities Ltd recurrently debouched illegal discharges of untreated sewage directly into the River Thames and its tributaries, resulting "in major environmental damage including visible sewage along 14 kilometres of the river, and the death of birds, fish and invertebrates" (ibid.). The profusion of pollution incidents disgorging from Thames Water's sewage water sites in Oxfordshire, Buckinghamshire and Berkshire precipitated ominous desolation and anguish among those directly afflicted. Customary heritage events such as River Thames sailing regattas were interrupted. Investigative scrutiny undertaken by Environment Agency officers provided Aylesbury Crown Court with a litany of incidents involving "repeated discharges of untreated or poorly treated raw sewage" continually discharged "for weeks" and "amounting to millions of litres per day" entering into the Thames' rivers having been diverted from their capacitated destination, the Thames Water treatment processing works (ibid.).

Astonishingly, it was revealed that: "In many instances less than half of the incoming sewage was sent for treatment" (ibid.). Many of those directly affected were Thames Water consumers, actively paying water bills for water treatment services that were casuistically neglected. The presiding judge, his Honour Judge Sheridan, is stated to have condemned Thames Water's operation as "disgraceful conduct", stating further that the episodes were "a very dark period in the history of Thames Water [demonstrating] … Scant regard for the law, with dreadful results for people who live in the area" (ibid.). Keen to impede the transference of the penalty fine onto its consumer-base, Honour Judge Sheridan required the fine's denouement to be attributable directly to the company Thames Water Utilities Ltd (ibid.).

Additionally, in 2017, the water regulators Ofwat (2017a), following Thames Water's release of its Annual Report and Accounts 2016-17, administered a penalty fine of £8.55 million "as a consequence of missing its commitment on leakage". Furthermore, the fine is the maximum penalty that can be automatically triggered "under the performance commitment regime for missing this specific target" (ibid.). Also keen to prevent transference of the penalty onto the customers, Ofwat (ibid.) stated: "The penalty is borne by the company alone and cannot be passed on to customers". The Financial Times' (2017) 4th May 2017 lead article entitled "Thames Water: The murky structure of a utility company" tenaciously quibbles with the extent to which the fines will be borne solely by Thames Water for, according to the Financial Times (2017), English urban river restoration charities will enter into market-based competitive tendering for finances to subsidise programmes to restore the River Thames water ecology, as evident in the following extract:

> The Environment Agency declined to put an exact amount on the cost of bringing the pollution case against Thames Water. But it said the cost has 'run into hundreds of thousands of pounds'. It added: 'Once sewage pollution is mixed into the river it is almost impossible to remove'. (ibid.)
>
> Although Thames Water has put together a £1.5m fund to restore both rivers, charities have to bid for the money, which is all under the company's control. The £20m raised from the fine will go straight to the Treasury and equates to about two weeks of operating profits at the company. (ibld.)

Timely Reminders: Troubled Waters, Financialisation Masquerading as Disenchanted English Nationalism

Similar processes positioning English nationalism at the centre of centrifugal financialising forces were reared, fabricated and fostered in Spring 2017 amidst a maelstrom of repudiation concerning the Macquarie Group's sale of all of its remaining 26.3 percent stake in Thames Water (Financial Times 2017a). Maelstrom is a deserved description of the swirling mix of financial indignation at Thames Water's derisory consumer service, tinged with a ripple of disenchanted English nationalist ethnicity. Consider for a moment the following provocative newspaper headlines issued during and in the immediate aftermath of the announcement of the sale of the Macquarie Group's stake in Thames Water:

Aussies revamp Green Bank after £2.3 billion UK sell-off.
(Evening Standard – 18 August 2017)

Britain is still a world-beater at one thing: Ripping off its own citizens.
(Guardian – 3 August 2017a)

Thames Water's foreign owners rinsing millions in dividends despite firm not paying corporation tax and being hit by fines.
(This is Money – 14 June 2017)

Ontario Municipal teams with Kuwait Investment Authority for Stake in Thames Water.
(Pensions and Investments – 15 March 2017)

Canadian and Kuwaiti investors buy 26% stake in Thames Water.
(The Independent – 14 March 2017)

Australian investment bank Macquarie sells last of its stake in Thames Water to Canadian and Kuwaiti Funds.
(City A.M. – 14 March 2017)

Canadian, Kuwaiti investors take stake in UK's Thames Water.
(Reuters – 14 March 2017)

These newspaper media headlines featured an insidious provocation, malignly positioning foreign companies as a threat to the English ethnically inscribed nationalism of the accouchement of Thames Water, i.e., the River Thames. Precariously enfolded into this context is the increasingly arbitrary English ethnic identity upon which the misadventures of the "Vote Leave" campaign mattered, together with its populism. But even the most cursory of perusals beyond the ethnically charged Thames Water sale headlines reveals the machinations of a centralising financialisation labyrinthine, with financial capital flows that extend irrespective of territory, nationality and ethnicity. Thames Water PLC, emerging from the 1989 Water Act's facilitation of the transition into the private sector of water companies, had long since been integral to the privatisation of the water utility in London and the Thames Valley (Thames Water 2017). Accelerating the international capitalist features of Thames Water's privatisation, in 2001, Thames Water announced that it had been "acquired by multi-utility RWE", detailing this acquisition as "Thames water became RWE's Water Division, taking control of its water and wastewater operations worldwide, and RWE's existing operations in Germany and Eastern Europe" (ibid.). By 2006, the infrastructure for the financialisation of Thames Water had been secured in its acquisition, on 1 December 2006, by "Kemble Water Limited, a consortium of institutional investors managed by the Macquarie Capital Funds (Europe) Limited" (ibid.). On 14 March 2017, Macquarie Group announced that its Macquarie European Infrastructure Fund 2 (MEIF2), in conjunction with two other Macquarie- managed funds, had acceded to sell an aggregate 26.3 per cent stake in Kemble Water Holdings Limited, the consummate holding company of Thames Water Utilities Limited (Macquarie 2017). Macquarie describes further the detailing of the sale thus:

> MEIF2 is managed by the Macquarie Infrastructure and Real Assets (MIRA) division of Macquarie.
>
> The Sale Interest is being acquired by Borealis Infrastructure, the infrastructure investment manager of OMERS, and Wren House Infrastructure Management Limited, the infrastructure investing arm of the Kuwait Investment Authority. MEIF2, which holds the majority of the Sale Interest, is divesting its stake as the fund is approaching maturity. The Sale Interest is the final divestment by Macquarie of its stakes in the business.

(Macquarie 2017)

One might presuppose that the featuring of a Canadian pensions fund and Kuwait sovereign wealth fund provides some confirmation of the nationalist anxieties relayed in the afore-stated newspaper headlines. However, a brief perusal into the ownership structure of Thames Water reveals similarities of interest-bearing capital financial investment, for financialisation and not the immigrant Other, is transparently evident in the predominance of finance capital institutional investors in Thames Water.

Figure 8.2.: "Capitalism survives by forcing the majority, whom it exploits, to define their own interests as narrowly as possible. This was once achieved by extensive deprivation. Today in the developed countries it is being achieved by imposing a false standard of what is and what is not desirable" (John Berger, *Ways of Seeing*, 1972). Photographic Image, Southbank, London, 2016.

CONCLUSION

ADSENSORY FAÇADE GENTRIFICATION: "HISTORY ALWAYS CONSTITUTES THE RELATION BETWEEN A PRESENT AND ITS PAST" (BERGER)

Figure C.1.: *Love Assisst(f)*: "One may remember or forget these messages but briefly one takes them in, and for a moment they stimulate the imagination by way of either memory or expectation" (John Berger, *Ways of Seeing*, 1972). Photographic Image, Grenfell Tower National Memorial Service, St Paul's Cathedral, December 2017.

Commemoration into Memory

Interviewee: It's supposed to be a democracy ... I think [it's] quite a big mistake.
Interviewer: Sorry, what's a big mistake? I'm just filming something.
Interviewee: Oops.
Interviewer: Oh no, no [reassuring]. What's a big mistake?
Interviewee: You have to speak to my agent [said jovially].
Interviewer: Oh OK, I'm just a university teacher and I just wanted to find out ... But what did you say the big mistake was?
Interviewee: Not to invite the Council ... I think that decision not to invite the Council... I think should have been thought out a lot more clearly. Because the Council made a massive error; a huge mistake in dealing with the Grenfell victims. A huge mistake, I think they, they have to make amends for that. I do think that they should; they should be here. They should be here, to make account of themselves. To make a proper account of themselves, they should be here. And I didn't think it was right to exclude them. But then again, the saying is that the community felt they should be excluded; but it's the community's wishes. But I think that the Council should be here to make an account of themselves. You've got the whole nation, the whole public; everyone is here and they should be here.
Interviewer: Am I allowed to quote you, sir?
Interviewee: Yes, of course.
Interviewer: Thank you very much, sir.

(Thematically Structured Qualitative Interview; Video Transcription: Journalist photographer, with companion in journalist enclosure at Saint Paul's Cathedral Grenfell Tower memorial, London, 14th December 2017)

Thursday, the 14th of December, 2017 designated a poignant episode of remembrance for the victims of the Grenfell Tower. St Paul's Cathedral hosted a prodigious "service of remembrance, hope and unity" entitled the Grenfell Tower National Memorial Service (St Paul's Cathedral 2017). Mingling among the conglomeration of journalists and international press media, one could sense the febrile expectation of the nonchalant arrival of unbidden guests, for conspicuous in their absence were members of the Royal Borough of Kensington and Chelsea council, who had unceremoniously self-excluded, having heeded the chorus of rejection resounding from the Grenfell Tower community leaders, relatives and friends of the victims. Indeed, the community's animated refusal to provide the council a public stage from which to ameliorate culpability and publicly portray lamentation constituted a defining moment, establishing the albeit fragile working consensus on how to remember and commemorate into collective memory the victims of the Grenfell Tower tragedy. An indication of this quandary is expressed in my interview with the journalist photographer:

Interviewee: *To give an account of themselves, to say: Listen this is what we did, we are sorry. To say it in front of God, in front of the nation: We are sorry. So I think that the idea to exclude them from this meeting could not be the best possible idea. And we know the council very well.*
Interviewer: How do you know the council?
Interviewee: *Notting Hill Gate is nothing new to us. Everybody remembers Notting Hill Gate from the days of the riots and stuff. So Notting Hill Gate is not a new territory. One thing is that, this tragic incident, that Grenfell happened, which brought the whole area into the public view again, and that's something awful; and it has to be addressed. Every party being involved, that's how it has to be addressed. It can't be addressed in splinter group sort of things; it has to be addressed with everyone actively getting involved and doing something about this real tragedy. It is a tragedy [pause ... looks sorrowfully into my eyes]. Sad. Very, very sad; very sad, sad ... [Interviewee turns and slowly walks away].*

(Thematically Structured Qualitative Interview; Video Transcription: Journalist photographer, with companion in journalist enclosure at Saint Paul's Cathedral Grenfell Tower memorial, London, 14th December 2017)

Following Daniel Bell's (1999) theory of the codification of knowledge as an axial feature of the structuring of post-industrial society, this book's first case study focuses on the regeneration of the Grenfell Tower – once situated in North Kensington, London. Much attention has been drawn to the polyethylene-insulated cladding tiles installed on the Grenfell Tower building as part of a wider project of energy efficiency and aesthetic gentrification. During the early hours of June 14th, 2017, Grenfell Tower was tragically engulfed by fire and this heart-breaking incident precipitated a justifiably angry chorus of condemnation directed initially at North Kensington's administration then spiralled to include an exploitative political economy of urban regeneration. Political economy makes apparent policies and practices that, in their rapacious scurrying for exploitative profit, are divested of any consciousness of apprehending the obvious negligence of covering decades-old buildings in glittering, flammable, highly combustible cladding materials. Neoliberal re-engineered social housing façades provide the focus of this book's second case study. The concept of adsensory features, in terms of an aesthetically driven coding of urban regeneration knowledge, into which an urban ecological coding of the human body has become integral.

This book's second case study focuses on the gentrification problematics presented by the proposed and partially enacted Garden Bridge. "It's my duty to ensure taxpayers' money is spent responsibly" (Khan 2017) is the first line of the terse *Statement from the Mayor on the Closure of the Garden Bridge Trust,* issued Monday, 14th August 2017. Precipitately citing Dame Margaret Hodge's independent cost evaluation of the Garden Bridge (2017), London mayor Sadiq Khan's statement provides a scathing indictment of Boris Johnson's irresponsibly commissioned Garden Bridge project. Khan's incendiary statement of closure accentuates an astonishing revelation elucidated by *The Garden Bridge* report – the project had an irreconcilable "funding gap of over £70 million, potentially unlimited costs to London taxpayers to fund the bridge in the future, systemic failing in the procurement process" compounded by "decisions not being driven by value for money" (Khan 2017). Clearly exasperated by the lavish, improvident extravagance of the Garden Bridge project, Khan's (ibid.) statement heroically exclaims "I could not permit a single penny more of London taxpayers' money being spent on it". In response, the Garden Bridge Trust issued a contrite resignation establishing that the charity's intention to build what amounted to an artificial green park space across the River Thames had ceased to be a viable proposition and that they were "winding up the project" (Garden Bridge Trust 2017). Barely able to camouflage its disaccord, the Garden Bridge Trust nonchalantly personalises the root incongruity thus: "On 28 April, Sadiq Khan wrote to Lord Mervyn Davies, Chairman of the Garden Bridge Trust, stating that he was not prepared to sign the guarantee for the annual maintenance costs of the Bridge, a condition of planning consent, despite previous assurances given about his support for the project". The aphoristic displacement of the unviability of the project is also endured by the syndicate of financiers: "Unfortunately, the benefactor concerned and the Trustees have all concluded that they cannot proceed with what was always designed to be a public project in the heart of the capital without the support of the Mayor of London" (ibid.). In full retreat from any hint of assigning blame, the statement concludes: "The Garden Bridge project will now be formally closed. This includes terminating contracts, and concluding donor funding agreements. The Trust itself will then be wound up in accordance with the Companies Acts" (ibid.). Transport for London (2019), recently published: "a detailed breakdown of the [Garden Bridge] Trust's final expenditure on the project, which shows a total of almost £53.5m was spent on the project". The central objective of this second case study featuring the Garden Bridge project is to further ascertain the significance of adsensory financialisation to the privatisation of the urban ecology of riverside recreational spaces. Specifically, in this book's Garden Bridge case study, I reconfigure Karl Marx's conception of rentier capitalism as part of a techno-Prometheus ecofeminist critical analysis of the privatisation of public recreational urban river space.

Adsensory Financialisation, the human body as both object and subject of inscriptive advertising technologies, is integral to a Western capitalist insurantial financialisation of health and wellbeing. Developing further the theme of adsensory technologies of the sign, in conjunction with Daniel Bell's theory of the codification of knowledge as an axial feature of the structuring of post-industrial society, this book, *Adsensory Urban Ecology* (Volume One) case studies gentrification in heterotopic (Foucault) post-industrial urban spaces: London's Grenfell Tower, perilous façadism refurbishment and London's Garden Bridge project, speculative capital regeneration. In so doing, these case studies illustrate, empirically, the extent to which advertising adsensory technologies have become integral to the gentrification of post-industrial urban spaces. For example, aspects of the case studies engage critically with the empirical observation that, in the post-industrial urban ecology of inner-city regeneration, adsensory technologies extend avariciously into the infrastructure of neoliberal managerialist audit-cultured "best value" gentrification. More specifically, adsensory refers to the significance of a sensory codification of the body to the market-based urban ecological codification of knowledge relevance in the managerialist gentrification of post-industrial urban spaces. With regard to the research question that has guided my critical ethnography, it is thus: What form of capital accumulation is emerging from the integration of adsensory technology into the gentrification of post-industrial urban spaces? The empirical ethnographic case studies identify disruptive encounters between adsensory gentrification and embodied urban ecology. In so doing, this book has examined empirically a new form of capital accumulation in inner-city gentrification, predicated on the (de)generative integrity of adsensory financialisation.

Epilogue

Timely Reflections

Figure E.i.: "One may remember or forget these messages but briefly one takes them in, and for a moment they stimulate the imagination by way of either memory or expectation" (John Berger, *Ways of Seeing*, 1972). Photographic Image, St Paul's Cathedral, Grenfell Tower Memorial Service, London, December 2017.

> **Interviewee:** Labour Party Councillor, Royal Borough of Kensington and Chelsea Council.
> **Interview Date:** September 2017.
> **Interview Technique and Location:** Management science, semi-structured qualitative interview; Labour RBKC council offices.
> **Interview Thematic Features:** Grenfell Tower refurbishment; intellectual reflections on Grenfell Tower regeneration, procurement strategic management; and experiential dialogic engagement with the organisational culture of RBKC council.
> **Empirical Findings:** KTMO contract culture management; RBKC council managerialism; Grenfell Tower refurbishment in the context of market-based managerialism; RBKC council organisational culture; political decision-making, conflict management, leadership and negotiated consensus; and changed management in transition.

Verbatim Full Transcription

Is the cladding a red herring?

Interviewer: Firstly, thank you very much, it is very kind of you to invite me here. And in our correspondence I sent you some of the questions I was going to ask.
Interviewee: Yes, you sent them.

Interviewer: It's very nice offices; it's quite nice round here.
Interviewee: Yes, it is the cheapest street in the constituency. This is the best we could manage ...

Interviewer: Yes, so I have some questions. Firstly, if you could just, tell me about your role on the Council.
Interviewee: I am the leader of the Labour group. I have been a councillor for twenty three years. I have always specialised in education and young people; I have done a bit of planning. I have never got myself involved in the housing matters, so my detailed knowledge as to what happens or is happening or the circumstances of Grenfell is not great. Other than the fact, that I am the ward councillor, for Grenfell Tower and I was involved in the complaints that the residents made about how badly they have been treated, in as part of the process. Erhm, and the Council very smugly, well in essence said: These people are lucky that we are spending 10 million pounds on them, so they ought to be grateful. And they certainly never looked carefully

into the way it was happening or what was happening. And I was outraged when I did visit the tower during the work. Because the point was that, they had done, they started the, they did the project with the residents still in situ. And they gave the residents undertakings that their privacy would be respected; that there's two lifts and only one lift would ever be used by the building workers and none of that was adhered to when I visited at 9 O'clock in the morning I found that the, that the workmen were using both lifts. Therefore, making all the residents late for work; children late for work; the place was left dirty; the workmen walked in and out of flats willy nilly, showed very little respect for the residents. So I was outraged about their treatment. I never raised any questions about the safety of the works; because as I say I wasn't a housing councillor. And I assumed that the council, would have proper experts to guide the contracts and to ensure compliance. I should have course realised that as they, the building contractors weren't complying with their undertakings about their respect for the residents. We should have looked more carefully as to whether they were complying with other aspects of the contract. I would also say that: the residents were represented by **** [redacted name] who I have, had dealings with he had previously objected to the rebuilding of the school; the rebuilding of the sports centre; the redesign of the, sort of the park area around; and erhm he has a very scatter gun approach to everything and quite honestly he made so many mistakes about many things, erhm, that I suspect the authorities took very little notice of him. Erhm, which turned out to be a huge mistake. Erhm, I think that's as much as I want to say on that [pause]. Erhm, by the way that's my background and how I got involved in the, in what turned out to be a disaster. Mr **** [redacted name] very late in the day, did query the safety of the building regulations, but that was sort of, he had raised a hundred points, two of which referred to the safety. So, all those concerns were sort of lost in the overall state. Of course everybody now beats themselves up, because on this he happened to be right. But it also has to be said, that nobody queried, as far as I'm aware, nobody queried the safety of the cladding, until after it had happened.

Interviewer: And in terms of the Grenfell Tower Action groups: did they not query the safety of the cladding?
Interviewee: *I am not sure that they did. Erhm, certainly if they did I wasn't aware of that aspect. Now I don't think they did. They raised other things. Not so much the material, but the lack of sprinklers, or whatever; all of which was valid. But the cladding, I don't think cladding was raised.*

Interviewer: *And erhm, [glancing through my prepared interview theme/topic guide] … Oh yes, in terms of the management culture, I am particularly interested in and I was just wondering if you could tell me something further about.*
Interviewee: *Oh yes, I am very happy to. The Tenant Management Organisation, is supposed to be a tenant run organisation that ran the housing stock. What it turned into was an organisation that had very hostile relations with the tenants. We've always said, in the end, they were managing the tenants, rather than managing the properties; and you will see not only the hostility, to the TMO (Tenant Management Organisation) from those directly affected by the Grenfell Tower; but all the way across Kensington, among the nine thousand social housing units the tenants are completely antagonistic to the TMO because the TMO has treated the tenants badly; has treated them without respect; has a very poor record in terms of its maintenance arrangements so erhm.*

Interviewer: Is there a history to this?
Interviewee: *Yes it was, I mean, Kensington and Chelsea started it originally; it was one of the first TMO organisations; it was one of the largest and they run their Council's entire housing stock, which of itself presents problems because it does mean that the big estates get more attention and have more representation than people who live on small estates; because simply in a democratic process if you live on the Lancaster West and you run as a Lancaster West tenant you can get more people to turn out to vote for you than you can for someone who lives in a small box, somewhere else. So the whole structure (**Interviewer** [interruption]: "Could you tell me about the structure of the TMO?"). I'm not quite sure of the numbers, you can look them up. But I think there are five tenant reps, and then there are so called independent representatives and there are a minority of councillor representatives proportionate to erhm: so we have got one Labour member, one Labour member and I think there are two Tory councillor members. But it is, it is supposedly independent, was set up as independent; but it is a monopsony situation. Because the TMO their only customer is Kensington and Chelsea Council; and erhm Kensington and Chelsea and the other way round Kensington and Chelsea Council previously has dealt only with the TMO. So it's a monopoly provider and a monopoly customer. The other interesting thing that's different from most of the other tenant management organisations is that the TMO do not own the housing stock. The property still belongs to the Council. So they are a management company; most TMOs, I think what happens is that the housing stock is made over to, is owned by the organisation. So Kensington and*

Chelsea and one of the problems they have got now is that they have no assets. They have a turn over, 11 million pounds a year and they are facing insurance claims and all kinds of other claims, legal costs which are going to be in the tens of millions and they can't flog off the property to pay for any of this because it doesn't belong to them, it belongs to the Council. So in brief it was an arrangement whereby, when central government wanted local government to get rid of its housing stock Kensington and Chelsea, aware of the value of its properties didn't want to lose control of it so the setting up of the TMO was a way to get round the government requirement; but they still in effect control it, and control it now – maybe we can come on later to discuss what the current situation is – but at the moment the TMO unbelievably are claiming that they still can recover from this. That they will face; that there will be a new ballot in the autumn, of the Council's tenants as to whether they should keep the contract and unbelievably the TMO still claim that they think they can win this ballot. Now the way they have won the ballot on previous occasions has been to terrify the tenants and say: well we at least keep the rents down. If the properties are made over to a housing association or to a commercial property management company, they would jack-up your rents so that's how they have sort of kept control of it until now; but that's not going to be good enough this time round.

Interviewer: So the TMO didn't actually own the housing stock it is owned by the Kensington and Chelsea Council?
Interviewee: *No. It's still; ultimately we [Kensington and Chelsea Council] are the freeholders. So that, so then that; so that then raises questions, which I hope the judge will sort out; because I don't start to understand it: Is who is liable? You can have a tenant's management organisation who could possibly run repairs; who could collect rents; who could organise tenant's meetings and wot not. But they're not capable of organising massive capital projects that they were asked to undertake. And again hindsight is a wonderful thing; but the TMO should never have been left to run the, run the, restoration contract for Grenfell Tower. And at the end they didn't because it was still the cabinet member for; because the Borough had to come up with the capital to pay for the modernisation and it was the Cabinet minister for housing [Cllr] Rock Feilding-Mellen who was the one, who sort of said: Right you have got 10 million quid, if it costs more than that, you have to cut back. And he was the one, who sort of set the original specification, which was drawn up by the contractors, was too expensive and they had to cut it. So that's the circumstances in which they went for cheaper products. Oh and the other thing that needs to be said is, as I say*

*part of the problem was that the tenants were left in situ whilst the building works were being done. Now there's two reasons for that: the 125, 126 units of accommodation if they had decanted the residents somewhere else, the council would not have been able to find 126 residential accommodations, so it wasn't available for them. One of the reasons why the tenants accepted this was they feared that once they were moved out of the {**Interviewer**: "they would be ..."} they would never be allowed to come back. Because that has happened in the past, as well, oh move out temporally and we'll move you back in again. So they were prepared to put up with it. They had no idea that the project was going to be as problematic as it turned out to be.*

Interviewer: Hmm by far ... So the culture of the actual Council you think was?

Interviewee: *As I say, I have been a councillor for a very long time; and when I've, and I have checked this with people who have been around for as long as me, just to make sure that I am not seeing this through rose tinted spectacles. But other people who have been around, said that the culture of the Council at one stage was very old fashioned patrician, erhm patrician approach of: We are a wealthy local authority with a number of poorer people and we will do the best we can for them; because we can, because we are a very wealthy local authority. Kensington and Chelsea decided to become Thatcherite just at the point when everybody else decided that erhm. And so they then sort of started to want to redevelop the area, and to pay for the, {**Interviewer**. "So when was this?" "When did they decide this?"}. Oh I would say about twelve years ago: there was a change in the leadership of the Council; there was certainly a change [in culture] and Rock Feilding-Mellen holds a lot of responsibility for this, cos his background, is, is whilst he's posh he reckons he's a very good, he reckons he's a property developer. He's been a very successful property developer, but he certainly sought to use the portfolio of the Council and his idea was that we would redevelop the large estates, making them more "socially balanced" by which he meant he would move in private owners. Yeah and there is an argument, I mean we all in theory believe in mixed tenancies. But he wasn't offering to move Council Tenants into private estates, he was offering to move, to sell, to sell off, or to build new properties within the Council, within existing estates and to sell them off. It was moving rich people into share the space that was available on the estate, rather than, as I say there was no suggestion that poorer people would, they would provide properties for poorer people in the wealthy areas of the Borough. So they started to sort of, and Grenfell Tower was supposed to be one of the, no, no I am getting ahead of myself* now. There are other estates, where they had been built properly according to Parker, Parker ... what's the standard? Anyway the old GLC which specified the size of rooms and Parker – oh I'll think about it and go and look it up later. And so they had, they had sort of gardens; they'd had open public spaces [referring to the Kensington and Chelsea social housing that were built during the era of the Greater London Council (GLC) and incorporated Lord Justice Parker's housing design proposals]. So our estates, our existing estates built at that time do have open public spaces around them, they saw this as an opportunity to squeeze in, to build into the estates more properties. Now, given that we are the most built up local authority in the country there's an argument in favour of that; erhm but the key being that they wanted to sell them off rather than use them for social housing. His theory was: we'll sell off a certain amount and erhm make some money and well use that to pay for the upgrading of what was left. But actually they were flogging stuff off as much as quickly as possible. So when they are accused of "social cleansing" there's a lot to be said for that. I forget, we are going around slightly in circles, but that's why the tenants were reluctant to leave Grenfell Tower and put up with all this shit of the way they were treated [referring to the inconvenience of the refurbishment and KCTMO actions]. Because, the thought was, at least at the end of the day: I will still be occupying, my flat which will have been updated. And contrary to sort of popular belief the flats inside, were very good; were to a high; were built to a high standard. You see in some of the national press reports that these, that it was a slum property or whatever. A slum property full of immigrants is what the tabloid newspaper would like you to believe. That's not true it was property built to a very high standard and the majority of tenants had been there for a very long time. In fact I have got figures that the average length of tenancy of that block was twelve and a half, was getting onto thirteen years. And I know myself some people who have been there for more than thirty years. So it was a stable balanced, balanced community. Now of those 126, 17 had been sold off. So you are dealing with lease holders in those circumstances. Once the flats were owned by someone from outside they had the right to rent them out to whomsoever they wanted. And I think a number of those are the flats, the ones it's proving difficult to find out who was living there. Cos they were renting stuff out and not declaring it. So, anyway, it's getting a long way, away from your question.

Interviewer: In terms of the refurbishment renovation and: was it part of a bigger project?
Interviewee: It was originally going to be, what they talked about originally was the total redevelopment of the Lancaster West estate. But then they

*found out two things: One that there was massive opposition from the tenants. Secondly, they then worked out that even the wealthiest local authority in the country couldn't afford to do that; couldn't afford to do it. So it was gradually scaled down. And the way in which the Grenfell Tower was chosen is, it was sort of recognised that the tenants had, had to put up with a lot of disturbance around them, because the borough had squeezed in a new secondary school at the base of the Tower and had built a new sports centre at the base of the Tower. So basically, they had already put up with six years of building work and at one stage it was decided that, as a way of rewarding people; rewarding? – oh anyway [interviewee considerately deliberating expression] ... compensating people, they would at the same time, update the flats. So at least tenants could say: Yes, I am living in the middle of a building site, but at least my flats going to be done up. The way it worked out, again, because of their incompetence in the end and their cheese pairing; because at one stage it was proposed that the contractors who had done the school and sports centre would also do the tower at the same time. There's two arguments; there's alternative arguments for that: The Council argued that the contractors, having got the first two contracts, were then, then got greedy and asked too much money for the project. Now the original contractors said well given the spec of what you have; what you've asked for this is the legitimate rate for erhm, the Council said that's too much and that's when they started squeezing from it. Because they made a mess of that they fell out with the original contractors, the project kept getting pushed back. So basically, the poor tenants having put up for six years with the school and the sports centre. Was, as that was being finished that was when they started the renovation of the, of the Tower. So in the end they had to put up with building works for eight years {**Interviewer:** "Wow"}. Again, because of the incompetence and squeezing by Kensington and Chelsea. And they got a cheaper contractor, one of the contractors, some of the subcontractors then when bankrupt so that caused further delays. And of course Rydon got the contract in the end because, they were the cheapest; found that they couldn't do it so the Council had to give them extra money anyway. So it's, irrespective of the tragedy of the fire, in terms of the efficiency of the contract it was very badly done.*

Interviewer: That's interesting, yeah. So you think that there were inefficiencies in terms of the contract?
Interviewee: *Oh yeah.*

Interviewer: Do you think these inefficiencies were a reflection of the Kensington and Chelsea Tenant Management Organisation actually responding to sort of political issues?
Interviewee: Yes, yes, yes. There are, and this will come out in the enquiry, that as they were negotiating the revisions of the contracts and things, they thought they had got an arrangement; but there is an infamous email, which is in the public records, sort of saying: this is still too much, we have to cut another million or two off to keep the Cabinet member happy. So he had looked at the revised contract and said: no this is still too much. {*Interviewer:* "Mellen, Rock Feilding-Mellen"} Yes, [returning to account of Rock Feilding-Mellen's intervention] you've got till Monday morning to knock another million off it. So that was the culture in which those decisions were made.

Interviewer: And is this culture responding to external pressures in terms of the political environment or is something happening to the culture itself; to the organisation itself? Whereby, itis almost independently starting to act in this sort of, Tory, Thatcherite, Neoliberal we often say, did it suddenly become [Neoliberal]?
Interviewee: Yes, I am a Labour councillor, so I would say that my disposition is this way anyway... in the same way, I would argue, in the same way the building societies all decided they were going to become banks and the people were brought up in the culture of a building society; then decided they were going to be bankers; paid themselves massive salaries and bankrupted all of the building societies. None of the building societies are there anymore; they are all screwed up, they have all been taken over by banks. So that whole culture of cooperation and valuing public service it was just completely got rid of on the grounds that capitalism was more efficient. We have now seen that capitalism wasn't more efficient. And I think the same: the people running the TMO, whilst their market might have started out with an interest in public housing then decided they were going to be property developers and they were just very bad at it.

Interviewer: And why do you think; why would they decide upon property development? It's almost like it mutates, like you said, this culture of valuing public service suddenly mutated into a culture in which they wanted to become property developers.
Interviewee: Several reasons, one is vanity, that was the sort of the, the ethos of the world: that business knows best, we have to run things in a professional capitalist manner. And also then there is the political pressure

they came under the Council to do that. And as I started off by saying, the Council had this patrician culture and attitude. They too decided, rather than being a council Kensington and Chelsea we'll be bastards like the bastards are or like Wandsworth and again as a Council I saw that, because I saw the change in the leadership of the Council.

Interviewer: So, oh yes. How might they have been rewarded for becoming, like you said: more business knows best?
Interviewee: I can only really talk about the Council. The leader of the Council was given a Knighthood, the Chief Executive, and was well on the way to getting his peerage. The Chief Executive of the Council also got a Knighthood and he went off to run Barnardo's? No Shelter for a couple of years ... because he too was on his way to having a peerage. So they were going to make money out of it. And got gongs and things.

Interviewer: When you say they were going to make money out of it?
Interviewee: Well, I think certainly in **** [redacted name] case, he certainly wanted company directorships and things like that. It would be interested to look at **** [redacted name].

Interviewer: But there wasn't any direct commission that was encouraging this culture of property?
Interviewee: I wouldn't know. I would be the last person in the entire Borough that they would tell, I am the leader of the opposition.

Interviewer: Was there a sort of pride in the status?
Interviewee: Oh yes, Kensington and Chelsea Council applied for went to, applied for status; it got a triple "A" credit rating. And they were terribly, terribly proud of that. We are the first local authority in Western Europe to be given a triple "A" credit rating. To which I [said], absolutely great: So now we can borrow lots of money very cheaply; of course they didn't want to do that. And then that, again all this is part of the culture of building up reserves. Notoriously we had 250 million pounds in reserves. Even Eric pickles said was too much.

Interviewer: What I am understanding here is that there seem to be merit rewards in terms of Peerages, possibly in terms of becoming directors as well and then there were various credit ratings. So there were various external bodies that were somehow fuelling or encouraging this culture towards property development.
Intervlewee: Yes!

Interviewer: And in what ways was this culture of property development being challenged, successfully?
Interviewee: It wasn't challenged successfully because it was going ahead. It certainly was challenged by the Labour Group; I could show you my. Remind me at the end I could send you my budget speech from last April, I might even be able to find my budget speech for the year before. That will give you an example of what the culture was like and what we feared before the fire.

Interviewer: Yes, I think I have made real progress here in terms of understanding a culture of property development and you're saying that this was being encouraged by various reward systems etc., And they're sort of personal; individuals were able to gain from this {Interviewee: "Yes"} indirectly?
Interviewee: Yes. And again, we are unusual in the fact that property land here is worth more than anywhere else. This model of development you couldn't possibly do it in Rotherham because nobody wants to live in Rotherham. And it's all this attitude of, and this happens in other global cities: let's move all the poor people out the middle of the cities because the rich people want to live in the middle. And in Kensington and Chelsea's case it's not just rich English people, it's actually the international global elite that wish to live in Kensington and Chelsea. As a long serving councillor I really like seeing the old rich of Chelsea resenting very much the internationally rich, who are massively more wealthy than English wealthy people. They loathe each other; they loathe the idea of an American banker can come in and decide that they are going to have a triple basement. As I have said, I sat on the planning committee and so you will get Sir Henry whatever turning up saying: my wife and I have lived here for thirty five years and now this new comer comes in and they wish to build a triple basement and this can't be allowed. It is almost comic because as I say, old fashioned wealthy Chelsea people have always got their own way in the past. To suddenly find that they can't actually stop the rich American bankers from building basements is almost comic. Anyway, that's getting a long way from what your research is.

Interviewer: Well not really; staying with the culture of property development, I was looking through the strategy, some strategy documents in relation to Kensington and Chelsea [KCTMO] and a particular phrase kept coming up, which was Value for Money. And I just wondered to what extent was that being translated; how was that being interpreted in the

property culture? Was Value for Money becoming something defined in terms of the property culture?
Interviewee: *In an attempt to be fair this is in the context of central government taking money away from local government. We too have lost 13, 14% of the money we previously got from central government. Then again Kensington and Chelsea refused to increase our council tax; we increase our council tax once every seven years. And then notoriously, for the last, twice in the year of a council election, we give a refund {**Interviewer:** "Hundred Pounds"} Yes! But that's only to people who pay the council tax and of course poorer people don't pay the council tax so they don't get the refund. So you live in a 25 million pound house in Chelsea and it was just bizarre and three months before the council election you get back 100 pounds of your own money. I mean a hundred pounds is neither here nor there, it was a very naïve attitude that people would change their vote for the sake of a 100 pound bribe, but the fact that they did it twice is an indication that they thought it was productive. They could say, we are such a well-run authority that we can even give you back some of your own money. So again that was indicative of what the culture was at the time.*

Interviewer: And the issue about Value for Money, you said that central government was actually putting on the pressure.
Interviewee: *On all local authorities and again some of the other things that have happened in other local authorities, and again the Rotherham's, the Liverpool's and the Lambeth's and whatnot: they did lose all their money; they are poor. Kensington and Chelsea was rich. We chose; we didn't need, we didn't really need the money because we got this 250, 300 million – whichever way you counted it – extra money. So the cuts that we made were all ideological rather than because they were actually needed. And the way they, and again I will send you my speech. The way they built up these reserves was systematically underspending their spending budgets and then at the end of the year, any under spend was automatically transferred into the capital reserves. So, that's how you did it. So you then made cuts in revenue expenditure when you didn't need to. {**Interviewer:** "Yeah I understand"}. I am trying to think of Value for Money. I mean.*

Interviewer: So you said there was a systematic underspending of [Interviewee: "Revenue budgets"]. Yes, perfect.
Interviewee: *And it was Council policy that any underspend, wouldn't be spent on alternative projects it would be automatically transferred into the reserves. Now they argued that they needed these reserves. They needed these reserves for two things: One because they wanted to spend them on*

the big capital projects like the rebuilding of Holland park school and they moaned that they had lost so much money from central government that they had to find money were they can. But every year they kept [building reserves], it was always: We need to build up these reserves for a rainy day. Which never came. In the twenty odd years I have been on the Council we never had, we never had financial problems; or any risk of financial problems. Year after year, the reserves went up [short seconds of reflective pause], and the circumstance we're in now: central government is saying they won't give us; they won't give the Council any financial support or backing until all the reserves are spent. We have to demonstrate that the reserves are; that the piggy bank is empty.

Interviewer: This is really interesting, by far. So this systematic under spending might have actually been part of the pressure therefore in terms of selecting cheaper or trying to haggle cheaper contractual arrangements (Interviewee: "Yes") etc., in terms of procurement.
Interviewee: And as I say, I'll give you might speech so that I can prove that wasn't a retrospective analysis of what was happening. We said, all this before the fire took place.

Interviewer: Ok, and so some final questions specifically about the refurbishment contract. Are there any insights that you can provide? Rydon actually gains the maintenance contract from what I understand?
Interviewee: Yes, erhm. No, I mean, I started off by saying in the beginning: I was never on the TMO, I was never shown the contracts. I never taken an interest in housing; one of the reasons why I didn't take an interest in housing is that right from the beginning I knew it was a very depressing story. And I didn't want to bang my head against a brick wall. I have spent my entire time, as I say doing education and there was a time the Borough was very proud of its education and was prepared to spend money. And developed a very good education department which I was proud to take part in. They then spent the last six years dismantling cos central government has decided that local government has no role in education. So that has been, from my point of view, a rear guard action to fighting all the way. I've lost; all our secondary schools are now academies; we have no influence on the way in which the secondary schools, and increasingly we have no influence in the way in which the primary schools are run.

Interviewer: And so; and so moving forward now as we close. I watched the webcast of Cllr Elizabeth Campbell's inauguration. Did you speak then? (Interviewee: "yes"). You did, yes it was you and so did the MP for

Kensington *{Interviewee: "Emma Dent Coad"}. Yes, yes, and I wonder are there any reflections there? Her reception [Cllr Elizabeth Campbell]. There were real issues in terms of how she was being received. You gave a very eloquent speech about your concerns. At the same time, I thought you were quite generous when you actually said that you thought she was a nice person [Cllr Elizabeth Campbell].*
Interviewee: *I didn't say she was a nice person. No what I said, what I said was, that she showed courage. Which she has done, well I am happy to say this for sort of academic ... I can put that in the context of, as the disaster was happening. I phoned the then leader of the Council and said: Where the fuck are you? I'm here surrounded by total chaos and the residents are saying: Where is the Council? And he said: "I have been advised not to be seen in North Kensington". And I said: "Well that's just the wrong; just the wrong advice. You need to be here". I said: "I'm being shouted at and spat at, because I'm the only representative of the Council that people can see. Get here!". And he said: "I've been advised that I shouldn't". And I said: "You've got the wrong advice". And I pushed it in the end and he said: "Oh well the police have told me that" -after few days- "The police have told me I'm toxic and that I will only make the situation worse". And I said: "That's because you haven't been seen for the last week. If you had shown any leadership, at all, the situation could have been". He kept saying: "I've been advised". Which I'm shouting at him: "The advice you got is wrong". So, and I don't know if you saw the, there was the notorious cabinet meeting, which was supposed to be held in public and then in private. At that meeting, I turned up to that meeting, genuinely thinking we are going to have a debate. And we as the representatives for North Kensington could feed in ideas. I didn't think; I knew they didn't know what was happening. So I turned up to that meeting to say: this is what you need to do this is what my residents tell you to do. He then, read out a speech. And then said: right the press here, we can't continue with this meeting. That's the point I stood up and I said: "this is utterly outrageous, you are now making an apology you should have made ten days ago; you have now had your speech again; and you are not allowing anybody else to speak; you need to resign!". And I think, I just happened to be in the right place at the right time and I was the one who could articulate the conclusion that the rest of the country had come to. As apparently had the prime minister. The prime minister had also told him that he needed to resign. {**Interviewer:** "This is not Paget-Brown?"}. This is [Nicholas] Paget-Brown. Paget-Brown was totally overwhelmed by the entire situation, had no idea how to handle it; showed no leadership. So anyway, the point of that being, when he then got [pause] I'm telling you this for academic reasons .. When the now leader of the*

Council, phoned me up and said I am running to be leader of the Conservative Group, I sort of laughed up my sleeve. Cos I thought: there's not a cat in hell's chance that you will get it; because you have no background in housing; you're are not the ... Councillor, she's not. She's not ... She said, well what should I do? I said: "There are a number of things I will tell you, you need to do". I said: "You need to apologise; and keep apologising in an unequivocal manner". And secondly: "You need to be seen in North Kensington". And thirdly: "You need to dissolve the Tenant Management Organisation, because it is so toxic". *{Interviewer: "Wow"}.* And the point in which I said she's shown courage is because she's done those things. When she became leader the first thing she did: was to apologise publicly in front of the media and came to North Kensington and has apologised, and apologised and apologised. Without making any excuses.

Interviewer: I remember she was interviewed by Michelle Husain on Radio 4 and Michelle Hussain asked her if she had ever been to any of the tower blocks.
Interviewee: Yeah. So she's apologised; she's been seen; she's repeatedly come to North Kensington and had done what the previous leader should have done, which is to stand there: to be shouted at and screamed at and spat at and in the end once people have got it out of their system, the run out of; if you take it for long enough they eventually stop and ask you: what you're going to do and she has managed to do that. No as I say she's not very ... But then again our Council has been run by bright Oxbridge educated men for a very long time and look at the mess it's got us in! I would argue that leadership doesn't necessarily have to be academically bright. You have to show empathy; which I think she has done; you have to show courage; which she has done. But, what you're going to say: She's still not qualified! Because she is a rich privileged woman. She represents the richest ward in Chelsea. Way down on the river, you couldn't get further, physically you couldn't get further away from North Kensington and still be in the borough. Her sons go to Eton. She's absolutely classic rich woman. And this was shown to the entire nation: Have you ever been in a Tower block? [Mimicking the caricature of an aristocratic female voice]: "Oh I have never been in a tower block. There aren't any tower blocks in my ward; I represent royal hospital". Which shows a number of things: One it shows you that she's politically very naïve *{Interviewer: "Or honest"}.* Or honest, yes. I'm sitting their shouting at the television: Lie you silly woman! Lie!

Interviewer: *[Laughter] No she'd be found out.*
Interviewee: *[Laughter] We'll I'm not sure she would have done. [Laughter]. Yes so, yes OK we'll agree to all of that.*

Interviewer: *It was shocking; it was interesting.*
Interviewee: *But it does show, that she's actually not qualified for the [job]. She knows nothing about housing what's so ever. She knows nothing about North Kensington. And her redeeming qualities are that she showed empathy and she showed courage. So to go back to your question, that was why I did pay tribute to her when she became leader. I honestly balanced it: you have shown courage but that's still not. I said, I said: courage is required, but not of itself, is not sufficient.*

Interviewer: *But it was very generous, because it was quite hostile, from what we could see, hostile environment. I thought that was very generous of you by far. So you think that she will effectively be able to respond to the aftermath?*
Interviewee: *No never, I think.*
Interviewer: *You said that she dissolved the TMO, I remember there was an article, I remember there was the suggestion that Theresa May had actually come to Grenfell and that she had met with the survivors and then she gave a statement that the TMO would be dissolved. So where is the impetus here is it coming from Theresa May?*

…

Interviewee: *I still think, that no matter what they do they are never going to get their credibility back. Because she is associated with the old regime [Cllr Elizabeth Campbell]. She was a Cabinet member under the old regime; she did undertake cuts which were unnecessary. Including in her own children's brief, but that's a separate story. And Theresa May has made this infinitely worse. In everything that she's done.*

Interviewer: *In what ways?*
Interviewee: *Well again I can give you another example: as the crisis was happening Theresa May issued this statement, about "we are going to rehouse everybody within the borough"; "We are going to find everybody accommodation within three weeks"; "And we are going to house them permanently within a year". So I phoned up the then leader of the Council Nick Paget-Brown and said: "How the fuck are you going to do this"? And he said: "I don't know, she didn't ask me!". She made that statement*

*without any consultation with the Council what's so ever. She just said it was going to happen. Because nationally it was politically required. And then you see they have carried on with those type of statements. So she said that people will be rehoused within the borough; they will get the same or better flats that they had previously; that they will carry on paying the same rents as they paid in Grenfell and they would have the right to buy. All of which, means that any property that the borough is going to buy to then compensate the tenants is going to cost four times as much as it would do if you were buying it on the open market. Cos they've gone to the housing associations and the housing associations have said: yes, you can have properties with us; but with housing associations you don't have the right to buy. So then the borough is then stuck; it can't use those properties; because the housing associations either won't let them have the properties or the housing associations themselves will want compensation for the flats that they are going to lose forever. So that's Theresa May continuing to make problems; to make unsolvable; to make insolvable problems for Kensington and Chelsea without giving them the money to do so. So we have gone, and this is something I have really only realised in the last couple of weeks; we've gone from being the wealthiest local authority in Europe to being completely bankrupt. We'll, I'm perhaps exaggerating. But we can't do it with the resources we've got. The only way it can be done is if we get money from central government. It is central government that has made those pledges. So again I am sounding more sympathetic to them than I actually should do [gasp of exasperation]. If central government has made those pledges, then central government should bloody well provide the money as well. Because the borough itself can't. We will not have the money to be able to {**Interviewer:** "The reserves aren't sufficient?"}. No. Cos you are talking hundreds of millions of pounds if you are going to do it. {**Interviewer:** "And the reserves are about 300 million"}. Depending on which way you, calculate it. But again, government requires there is a formula, that is to be a minimum level of reserves that the authority has. And one of reasons why I am concerned is that there is a project to rebuild a school and to build a new centre for special educational needs which is fifty million pound project. Which is almost finished. The design has been done; the contractors have been found; it's all been agreed but they haven't signed the contact because now they realise that the fifty million pounds that was put aside for this new educational facility is going to be required for compensation, for Grenfell. You can't argue, we have to find it. But it does mean; we threw a hundred million pounds at the rebuilding of Holland park school. Cos we had plenty of money. And we financed the rebuilding of Holland Park school by selling off some properties. We were property* *speculating then. This school is not going to happen. Because as I say, we've gone from being the wealthiest local authority in Europe to, we don't; I very much fear we will not have the means to carry on. Certainly can't provide the level of services we are providing until now. Because the, what's the analogy? The yawning demands and requirements of the, of those 126 families. And the rebuilding of the Lancaster West estate. Because it's not just Grenfell Tower it's those properties that were damaged in the area. So the Council's in a mess and I just don't see that they can win back any type of public support between now and the Council elections which are due in nine months, eight, nine months' time. And again the Government has sent in these four, we asked for commissioners;* **{Interviewer:** *"Yes this is interesting, the task force"*}. *The task force, isn't to provide services; or to take care of the needs of the Grenfell survivors. The task force is sent in, by central government, to keep an eye on what the hell is happening in Kensington and Chelsea. And they will at some point, they'll either say yes, they can probably scrape by and we might let them survive. Or far more likely in the end they are going to say, they are not credible. You need to dissolve the Council and reconstitute the Council.* **{Interviewer:** *"It is a Conservative council have they tried to control?"*}. *Yes, that is why they haven't sent in commissioners; had it been a Labour Council we would have been thrown out on our ear immediately, like they did with Rotherham or like they did with Tower Hamlets. The only reason they didn't send in commissioners is because it would be criticised, so: we have sent in this task force. As I say, I'm absolutely astonished, I thought the task force was going to undertake the rebuilding of the Council. No it's not! It is to keep an eye on; it is to report back on what is happening. In actual fact our new chief executive, is the one who, is actually digging us out of the hole ... We are up for re-election in the beginning of May [2018], such is the unpopularity of the Council, there is a distinct possibility that I will end up being the leader of the largest group on the Council, which is something I wanted for the last twenty odd years. But the point in which I would become leader of the Council is the point at which we have no money at all. So I will be left to sort out the Grenfell problem whilst the Council is bankrupt.* **{Interviewer:** *"It wasn't due to your management issues etc., etc.,"*}. *No, but I'll still get blamed, wont' I.* **{Interviewer:** *"It's a very likely situation"*}. *Yes: when I cut back on the window boxes down on the Kings Road; and I cut the grant to Holland Park opera; and I stopped the twice a week street cleaning; twice a week bin emptying. I think all of that is going to happen; I think it's going to have to happen, but I don't want to be the leader of the Council when that happens.*

Interviewer: The situation is looking very positive, if it's appropriate for me to suggest that it would be a Labour Council. If it were a case that Labour did become the dominant representation within the Council how would you, as we close now, how would you resolve the issues? What would you do? If it is the case that you do become the majority Council representation.
Interviewee: Hmm we are getting, beyond your academic briefing.

Interviewer: Ok, ok.
Interviewee: I would shift the priorities. I would be spending; it would be a labour priority so I would be spending it on housing; I would be spending it on social services; I would be spending it on children; and I would genuinely look as to who has the most needs.

Interviewer: Because some of things that I noticed, finally in terms of the planning permission document there was a focus very much on aesthetics; a statement kept on coming through that, for example the exterior refurbishment had to be befitting of the estate and the work they had done. Would a Labour Council have been concerned [Interviewee: "With aesthetics?"]. With the branding, possibly the cladding, the use of aluminium panels with the polyethylene core? Would you have done that?
Interviewee: I would have genuinely taken advice from people who really are experts.

Interviewer: Would you have been as seduced as they seemed to have been about how the building will look?
Interviewee: I mean I would want to make anything look ugly, but my priority; my priority would have been for it to be really what it said it was all about which was to cut down on the heating expenses of people. Because there was a centralised heating system and the logic was that people would then; they all have different needs; and that they would control the thermostat and that they would pay their own bills. Now to help people do that you then apply better standards of insulation. So yes I would have demanded standards of insulation. I would also have wanted to; the first thing I would do, if I were to become leader of the Council, is I would require that the obligation to provide a percentage of social housing, in all developments, was actually adhered to. In Kensington and Chelsea this has never happened. So if you are going to be building in Kensington and Chelsea and you are building five flats, one of those flats where ever it is; even if it is in sodden Knightsbridge is going to be for social housing.

Interviewer: And so to my understanding, what was happening is that a lot of the property builders would actually initially promise to uphold the percentage of social housing and then they would [Interviewee: "Come back and say we can't afford it"]. And then they would give some sort of compensation? Is that [correct]?
Interviewee: *Oh yes, there's several things happening with that. {Interviewer: "I did some reading, obviously before"}. Yeah, the, I can't remember what the percentage is. But it was supposed to be that for any development of more than five, thirty to fifty percent, I think Ken Livingston wanted fifty percent and I think that Sadiq Khan has now gone back to saying fifty percent has to be social housing. They would do a number of things. First of all they would promise anything, and then once the building started to happen they would say: Oh it's no longer viable we can't carry on with this building unless you let us off our social obligations. And again because we are amateurs about these things, we had no idea about how much money the developers were making. Then repeatedly: "Oh I'm terribly sorry that you can't afford it. We'll having promised to give us 40 and we'll let you off with five". And that's not just in Kensington and Chelsea, that's happened all the way across central London, I think one Wandsworth is one that has been caught up recently.*

Interviewer: And was there a compensation then given by the property developers to the Council?
Interviewee: *Yes, that's the other thing; two other things to be said about it: One they then said, because I was in planning and so I do know a little bit more about this. From Section 106 money: let us make squillions and we might build you a new zebra crossing or we will give you money for [xyz]. Of course the Borough or the people drawing up these contracts had no idea how much the developers were actually making. And so we will proudly say: Oh we have got 200 thousand pounds to spend on the Borough's education department little knowing that the developers in Knightsbridge are making 200 million, it's just small change. So the Section 106 money was just farcical we would have argued that actually the type of things we were taking Section 106 money to do were things that should have been paid for out of the Council tax anyway. So we've been very bad compared to other Councils at ... the developers to get the Section 106 money that we should have done. And the other thing that we've allowed to happen; so we didn't ask enough money from them in the first place; we let them then renege on the developments once you got into the contract; the third thing they would do and this has been going on for much longer is: Oh rather than providing for one social housing unit in Knightsbridge if you let us, if*

you let us develop the social housing units in Merton or Milton Keynes or whatever, we can then give eight social housing units up there. So the exported; So we never required the developers to; and initially we said.

Interviewer: Building in Milton Keynes was that a set promise?
Interviewee: Oh there was a time that the leader of the local Council was actually, made a deal with the leader of Hereford, not Hereford, Hertfordshire Council. That had this brilliant idea, this policy that Kensington and Chelsea was going to build in corporation with the developers *{Interviewer: "Is it satellites?"}*. Estate housing in Hertfordshire. This was a private arrangement between [redacted name] the then leader of our Council and whoever the Tory county council leader in Hereford, in Hertfordshire was. They thought it was a great wheeze until the Tory group in Hertfordshire realised that we were exporting our poorer people: So these poor people would come along and they would have children and they would want to put their children into Hertfordshire schools. They would want to have to make; they will want to have GPs and they will want to continue receiving benefits. The backbench Hertfordshire county council have said: "You're Nuts". There is no way we are going to take your problems. So that bit the dust and I think that the leader of Hertfordshire county council was removed by his own group for being absolutely stupid. And to make more; one of the reasons why there hasn't been better agreement in London about, across London about where we build new properties is precisely because of that. So Redbridge ... they're not keen to take the poorer people from Kensington and Chelsea, even for temporary housing reasons; for once they are there for two years they then become the responsibility of Redbridge, then Redbridge has to find the schools; Kensington and Chelsea washes its hands of them; it really is the exportation of its poor people. That was; that was an undeclared policy. I don't think I can ever find ... I can't find a public statement from Rock Feilding-Mellen; we certainly have accused him of that. And one of my councillors was severely reprieved, reproved for he made a speech and said that this was: Ethnic cleansing. Because, disproportionately the poorer people in the Borough, are not white Anglo-Saxons. Yes, the objective was social cleansing, but it is also, it is also ethnic cleansing as well. And a big fuss made of the Council. I mean you can see it; one of the great things about Kensington and Chelsea is that we are; we are multi ethnic and we have had our problems in the past. And at the moment it isn't a problem; that's a wide generalisation there are still; it is less of problem than it is in other areas because people embrace the multi-ethnic nature of the Borough.

But disproportionately, the people, the poor people that have been moved out are not white.

Interviewer: *And so finally, if it were a case that labour had a majority in the Council, how would you have responded to the building regulation issues that are arising?*
Interviewee: *You see the other issues I wanted; I keep going from one thing to another; but because we ran down the number of council officers we used to have experts in house, who knew about these things {**Interviewer:** "Oh this is interesting"}. And who had served in the Borough throughout their careers, for twenty, thirty years, they would know the area; they would have expertise in fire regulation or whatever. But as part of the running down of local authorities generally, suddenly it is decided that a local authority doesn't need to have fire experts of its own: You out source that; you go to other independently set up fire – I mean this is one of the things that has appalled me - I knew nothing about it. The important thing is, is to get a fire certificate. The fact that your fire certificate is provided by your, provided by your tame contractor round the back, who is more or less a John Ball. Erhm, what was important was the certificate not the quality of the certificate, of the advice. But the certificate meant that it wasn't the responsibility of the local authority; it wasn't the responsibility of the TMO. But this expert took it upon themselves to say that fire regulations or building regulations had been; had been complied with. I'm sure that the investigation will show that most of this was bogus.*

Interviewer: *So I can imagine here that a Labour response would not have been to reduce the expertise, the pool of expertise. So that's interesting.*
Interviewee: *It goes back to the whole idea that the private sector knows best and that the fat complacent ideal unimaginative public sector don't know their arse from their elbow. But in fact it turned out not to be the case; because I swear that when I first became a councillor, the then director of housing, who was an e-military man, who always used to click his heals and call me sir even though he was twenty years older than me, erhm, he knew every ounce of the Council's buildings stock. He knew most of the tenants. Erhm, yeah they took a pride in the service they provided his name was Martin Kingslet. And all that level, these issues: Oh we are over staffed, this is not necessary, we shouldn't be providing services or expertise, or permanent staff of our own. This should all be outsourced. Because if it is outsourced, it will be done cheaper and it will be done more efficiently. And the result is Grenfell. It's extremely distressing. [pause – commemorative]. {**Interviewer:** "I'm sorry"}. I, I wandered away from your last question.*

Interviewer: *No that's perfect. This gives, it's an incredible response, because my question was: how might labour respond? And it wasn't a yes or no. You responded in terms of your understanding about the management and the infrastructure and the outsourcing of expertise. It's an incredible answer and really academically, I mean I can just imagine when students read this they will understand culture and organisations; not in a negative: I'm Labour so I'm going to be critical. But in the way that you have answered it, it is to do with the structure and the management issues and this notion that the expertise, so they are becoming less and less valued in this more neoliberal culture. Which at an academic level, this actually does help a student to actually be able to understand?*

Interviewee: *Let me say one more thing in relation to that: As the Council took on this: Let's be capitalist about it attitude, those who were part of the old culture decided that this is not what I came into local government for so a number of them took early retirement. So that is one of the reasons why you lost expertise. And once it started to happen and they were understaffed on things the younger members of staff who were ambitious and who were being over worked and who were not getting, where not able to provide the services they wanted to, they all buggered off as well. So the old ones took retirement; the young clever ones; the ones who could see the writing on the wall and the ones who came into local government to provide services; they also left. So you were left with, those who were not terribly ambitious, or those who were far enough along in their career would know that they couldn't get a new job somewhere else, so we were left with the dross. The talent left or retired so the calibre of the officers that we had; it became a self-fulfilling function really. We had been efficient, we eventually became less efficient, because we lost the expertise and we lost clever people. Course the whole thing has now gone completely the other way, what's going to happen in May is that loads of councillors will retire or just give up and it's going to be difficult to find young Tory Councillors. Because it used to be: Oh if you put it on your political CV, that I've been a councillor in Kensington and Chelsea for four years ... well done. But now they are going to have to lie aren't they. They are not going to admit that they were a member, a Conservative member of the worst Council in Europe. But the other thing, that's happening of course is that we are losing what talented young Council officer we've got in the interest of their own careers, they're buggering off as well. They don't want to have it on their CV that they worked for this terrible Council that through its own negligence it's killed its tenants. I have seen that, the officers that I do, the ones that I know and I value, they are precisely the ones that have gone. And the new chief* executive has an enormous job on his hands to try and keep the talent, get rid of the rubbish; have a culture change; because they have got to try and change it back again now. He's going to have difficulty in recruiting it.

Interviewer: Just staying with the theme: what would a Labour Council have done? There was an eco-funding that Rydon worked with the KCTMO to actually gain. Do you know anything more about that?
Interviewee: No, I do know that I thought it was a good thing and I was going to be really supportive of it, I don't know what happened.

Interviewer: Do you have any literature about that?
Interviewee: No and the other thing is, talking to you I realised of course come the Enquiry I am going to have to give, you know I am going to have to give evidence. But I have never kept the paperwork. So in that respect I don't have the paperwork. Why don't you, send me an email about that, cos I have got colleagues who are better at keeping files than I am. If I can find it I will send it to you.

Interviewer: That's perfect.
Interviewee: Be as specific as you can and I will look for it.

Interviewer: It's just that one, cos I came across, Rydon mention it in one of their last brochures about the completion of the works. They talk about the ECO-funding grant that they are really proud of in the statement, but there's no paperwork, and I have tried [to locate it].
Interviewee: I'll find it, you send it to me and I will find it. And I will send you my speech. When you go home, send me an email reminding me that I owed you my speech, I can then attach my speech and send it to you. And once you go home if you have other questions I will be very happy ...

Interviewer: And do you think that the focus on the exterior and the cladding, do you think it is a red herring?
Interviewee: I do.

Interviewer: Oh my god! Really? There has been so much focused around this cladding; and the Communities Secretary and all the tests that have been done on all the buildings and the councils that have been insisting on taking off the [cladding].
Interviewee: That is public hysteria.

Interviewer: *Do you think so?*
Interviewee: *I need to qualify that. Undoubtedly, the reason why the block burned in the way it did, I mean you've seen the pictures, it's absolutely horrendous. And you could see, right from the very beginning. On the first morning, I went back to the then, the now discredited and sacked Town Clark and I said to him: The outside of the building is burning, that's what's done it. And he said: "Oh it's far too soon to speculate. You might find it's done". I said: All you need to do is look at it, you could see that the cladding was burning. But the whole strategy of, the whole policy of staying in your flats and the fire brigade will come and rescue you was that each unit was like sort of like erhm; what you have for bees, cells. Each cell was supposed to be water, was supposed to be fire proof. But they did a number of things, I think in doing it cheaply; they drilled through the concrete; and also the cladding went from one flat up to another. So on the outside, it led the fire from one flat to another. So it was [the refurbishment] breaking this cellular security. {**Interviewer:** "The containment"}. Yes, and I don't see; we know that, that was done in Kensington and Chelsea in the case of Grenfell Tower. I don't think it's been done widely, I'm certainly sure it has not been done widely. So this idea: Let's rip off the cladding of every building. Is not right, cos in most cases the fire walls have not been breached. But and again we will see this I am sure, this is what the judge is going to find, that: the fire doors were not, the fire door didn't have closures on them; the fire doors were done cheaply; they put gas pipes up the middle of the fire escape. It's, it's, I'm sure that no matter, even the inadequate building regulations that we have got were broken in the case of Grenfell; and in the case of the other flats, I think in other areas there might not be live[ing] up to the new standards. Or the standards which we were asked following the fire in Southwark the one that Harriet Harman got so angry about because there was a similar fire in Southwark, in which six people {**Interviewer:** "Yeah Lakanal House"}. Yes, yes, yes!*

Interviewer: *The coroner [for the Lakanal House fire] suggested that they should introduce sprinklers; and she wrote to Eric Pickles; and his response to the councils. Have you got the response? It's disappeared; it's been redacted.*
Interviewee: *I don't have it, but I know it is there and it will be produced by other people [councillors that received the letter will publish/submit it]. I mean the leader, to go back to our case again; the leader of the Council, when he was asked about why we hadn't put sprinklers on the system, he said because the building works had gone on for so long, that the tenants were sick to death of building contractors and they didn't want it. Which,*

that offended me more than anything else. Cos I was the one that had said to him: how dare you put my tenants through six years of absolute hell and at the time, this is when he came back with they ought to be grateful, that we spent ten million pounds on them, that's what Rock Feilding-Mellen said. After the fire, he then suddenly discovered; he remembers that the tenants didn't want the building work to go on and he said that the tenants had said that they didn't want sprinklers. There is no evidence, that anybody said they didn't want sprinklers. So whilst, going back to hindsight is a wonderful thing: I don't think anybody queried the cladding; they definitely did query the lack of sprinklers.

Interviewer: *That's a really important insight that you have provided there. Thank you so much for your time and the detailed responses, especially about the way in which expertise became less and less valued. For me that was revelatory it really was. At an academic level it provides; I think students reading this as a book to understand issues around culture and management cultures would actually sort of understand how infrastructures go wrong; but go wrong around these issues, rather than say that: they were bad. So much of the hysteria has been [Interviewee: "They were wicked people"]. That's why I am so impressed when you actually said: Elizabeth Campbell was courageous; because the sentiment, the panic, the moral outrage has been so despondent in relation to the Council. Anyway, I just want to say that your responses have actually veered away from that, they have actually been based on experienced, based on an incredible wealth of knowledge and providing an informed understanding. Not one that's denigrating the Council, but one that is actually saying: these were the structural problems. It's unfortunate that you weren't able to intervene more effectively to try to stop what you obviously were seeing as being really problematic.*

Interviewee: Well I mean, they reduced the number of Council meetings; they shortened Council meetings; they stopped taking, issuing verbatim minutes; they did everything they possibly could to discourage public interest or participation in local government. And you'll be aware that there are in effect, no longer local newspapers, in Britain and what's happening. Only thing that every got reported really, you would occasionally get stuff on planning matters, but that was, as I say, possibly somebody very annoyed and it is outrageous that their building; so planning stuff gets reported, but nothing else ever gets reported and the Council's freebee newspaper has never been distributed in North Kensington anyway.

Interviewer: *Wow, thank you so much.*

Figure E.ii.: "By refusing to enter a conspiracy, one remains innocent of that conspiracy. But to remain innocent may also be to remain ignorant" (John Berger, *Ways of Seeing*, 1972). Photographic Image, St Paul's Cathedral, Grenfell Tower Memorial Service, London, December 2017.

Figure E.iii.: "If the new language of images were used differently, it would, through its use, confer a new kind of power" (John Berger, *Ways of Seeing*, 1972). Photographic Image, St Paul's Cathedral, Grenfell Tower Memorial Service, London, December 2017.

Figure E.iv.: "If the new language of images were used differently, it would, through its use, confer a new kind of power. Within it we could begin to define our experiences more precisely in areas where words are inadequate" (John Berger, *Ways of Seeing*, 1972). Photographic Image, St Paul's Cathedral, Grenfell Tower Memorial Service, London, December 2017.

Figure E.v.: "Capitalism survives by forcing the majority, whom it exploits, to define their own interests as narrowly as possible. This was once achieved by extensive deprivation. Today in the developed countries it is being achieved by imposing a false standard of what is and what is not desirable" (John Berger, *Ways of Seeing*, 1972). Photographic Image, St Paul's Cathedral, Grenfell Tower Memorial Service, London, December 2017.

Epilogue

Timely Reflections

Photographic Diary 15th June 2017

Figure Evi.: "Colour photography is to the spectator-buyer what oil paint was to the spectator-owner. Both media use similar, highly tactile means to play upon the spectator's sense of acquiring the *real* thing which the image shows. In both cases his feeling that he can almost touch what is in the image reminds him how he might or does possess the real thing" (John Berger, *Ways of Seeing*, 1972). Photographic Image, Vicinity of Grenfell Tower, North Kensington, London, 15th June 2017.

Figure Evii.: "Publicity is addressed to those who constitute the market, to the spectator-buyer who is also the consumer-producer from whom profits are made twice over — as worker and then as buyer. The only places relatively free of publicity are the quarters of the very rich; their money is theirs to keep" (John Berger, *Ways of Seeing*, 1972). Photographic Image, Vicinity of Grenfell Tower, North Kensington, London, 15th June 2017.

Figure Evii.: "Publicity is addressed to those who constitute the market, to the spectator-buyer who is also the consumer-producer from whom profits are made twice over — as worker and then as buyer. The only places relatively free of publicity are the quarters of the very rich; their money is theirs to keep" (John Berger, *Ways of Seeing*, 1972). Photographic Image, Vicinity of Grenfell Tower, North Kensington, London, 15th June 2017.

Figure E.viii.: "Publicity speaks in the future tense and yet the achievement of this future is endlessly deferred. How then does publicity remain credible - or credible enough to exert the influence it does? It remains credible because the truthfulness of publicity is judged, not by the real fulfilment of its promises, but by the relevance of its fantasies to those of the spectator- buyer. Its essential application is not to reality but to day-dreams" (John Berger, *Ways of Seeing*, 1972). Photographic Image, Vicinity of Grenfell Tower, North Kensington, London, 15th June 2017.

Figure E.viii.: "Publicity speaks in the future tense and yet the achievement of this future is endlessly deferred. How then does publicity remain credible - or credible enough to exert the influence it does? It remains credible because the truthfulness of publicity is judged, not by the real fulfilment of its promises, but by the relevance of its fantasies to those of the spectator- buyer. Its essential application is not to reality but to day-dreams" (John Berger, *Ways of Seeing*, 1972). Photographic Image, Vicinity of Grenfell Tower, North Kensington, London, 15th June 2017.

Figure E.viii.: "Publicity speaks in the future tense and yet the achievement of this future is endlessly deferred. How then does publicity remain credible - or credible enough to exert the influence it does? It remains credible because the truthfulness of publicity is judged, not by the real fulfilment of its promises, but by the relevance of its fantasies to those of the spectator- buyer. Its essential application is not to reality but to day-dreams" (John Berger, *Ways of Seeing*, 1972). Photographic Image, Vicinity of Grenfell Tower, North Kensington, London, 15th June 2017.

Figure E.ix.: "The entire world becomes a setting for the fulfilment of publicity's promise of the good life. The world smiles at us. It offers itself to us. And because *everywhere* is imagined as offering itself to us, *everywhere* is more or less the same" (John Berger, *Ways of Seeing*, 1972). Photographic Image, Vicinity of Grenfell Tower; Lancaster West Estate, North Kensington, London, 15th June 2017.

Figure E.ix.: "The entire world becomes a setting for the fulfilment of publicity's promise of the good life. The world smiles at us. It offers itself to us. And because *everywhere* is imagined as offering itself to us, *everywhere* is more or less the same" (John Berger, *Ways of Seeing*, 1972). Photographic Image, Vicinity of Grenfell Tower; Lancaster West Estate, North Kensington, London, 15th June 2017.

Figure E.ix.: "The entire world becomes a setting for the fulfilment of publicity's promise of the good life. The world smiles at us. It offers itself to us. And because *everywhere* is imagined as offering itself to us, *everywhere* is more or less the same" (John Berger, *Ways of Seeing*, 1972). Photographic Image, Vicinity of Grenfell Tower; Lancaster West Estate, North Kensington, London, 15th June 2017.

Figure E.ix.: "The entire world becomes a setting for the fulfilment of publicity's promise of the good life. The world smiles at us. It offers itself to us. And because *everywhere* is imagined as offering itself to us, *everywhere* is more or less the same" (John Berger, *Ways of Seeing*, 1972), Photographic Image, Vicinity of Grenfell Tower; Lancaster West Estate, North Kensington, London, 15th June 2017.

Figure E.ix.: "The entire world becomes a setting for the fulfilment of publicity's promise of the good life. The world smiles at us. It offers itself to us. And because *everywhere* is imagined as offering itself to us, *everywhere* is more or less the same" (John Berger, *Ways of Seeing*, 1972). Photographic Image, Vicinity of Grenfell Tower; Lancaster West Estate, North Kensington, London, 15th June 2017.

Figure E.x.: "Capitalism survives by forcing the majority, whom it exploits, to define their own interests as narrowly as possible. This was once achieved by extensive deprivation. Today in the developed countries it is being achieved by imposing a false standard of what is and what is not desirable" (John Berger, *Ways of Seeing*, 1972). Photographic Image, Vicinity of Grenfell Tower; Lancaster West Estate, North Kensington, London, 15th June 2017.

Figure E.x.: "Capitalism survives by forcing the majority, whom it exploits, to define their own interests as narrowly as possible. This was once achieved by extensive deprivation. Today in the developed countries it is being achieved by imposing a false standard of what is and what is not desirable" (John Berger, *Ways of Seeing*, 1972). Photographic Image, Vicinity of Grenfell Tower; Lancaster West Estate, North Kensington, London, 15th June 2017.

Figure E.xi.: "We never look at just one thing; we are always looking at the relation between things and ourselves. Our vision is continually active, continually moving, continually holding things in a circle around itself, constituting what is present to us as we are" (John Berger, *Ways of Seeing*, 1972). Photographic Image, Vicinity of Grenfell Tower; Lancaster West Estate, North Kensington, London, 15th June 2017.

Figure Exii.: "A people or a class which is cut off from its own past is far less free to choose and to act as a people or class than one that has been able to situate itself in history" (John Berger, *Ways of Seeing*, 1972). Photographic Image, Vicinity of Grenfell Tower; Lancaster West Estate, North Kensington, London, 15th June 2017.

Figure Exiii.: "The inherent contradiction in perspective was that it structured all images of reality to address a single spectator who, unlike God, could only be in one place at a time" (John Berger, *Ways of Seeing*, 1972). Photographic Image, North Kensington, London, 15th June 2017.

Figure Exiv.: "Alternatively the anxiety on which publicity plays is the fear that having nothing you will be nothing" (John Berger, *Ways of Seeing*, 1972). Photographic Image, Vicinity of Grenfell Tower; Lancaster West Estate, North Kensington, London, 15th June 2017.

Figure Exv.: "Publicity helps to mask and compensate for all that is undemocratic within society. And it also masks what is happening in the rest of the world" (John Berger, *Ways of Seeing*, 1972). Photographic Image, Vicinity of Grenfell Tower; Lancaster West Estate, North Kensington, London, 15th June 2017.

Figure Exvi.: *Love Assisst(f)*: "One may remember or forget these messages but briefly one takes them in, and for a moment they stimulate the imagination by way of either memory or expectation" (John Berger, *Ways of Seeing*, 1972). Photographic Image, Vicinity of Grenfell Tower; Lancaster West Estate, North Kensington, London, 15th June 2017.

Epilogue

Timely Reflections

Photographic Diary 16th June 2017

Figure Exvii.: "Colour photography is to the spectator-buyer what oil paint was to the spectator-owner. Both media use similar, highly tactile means to play upon the spectator's sense of acquiring the *real* thing which the image shows. In both cases his feeling that he can almost touch what is in the image reminds him how he might or does possess the real thing" (John Berger, *Ways of Seeing*, 1972). Photographic Image, Vicinity of Grenfell Tower, North Kensington, London, 16th June 2017.

Figure Exviii.: "Publicity is addressed to those who constitute the market, to the spectator-buyer who is also the consumer-producer from whom profits are made twice over — as worker and then as buyer. The only places relatively free of publicity are the quarters of the very rich; their money is theirs to keep" (John Berger, *Ways of Seeing*, 1972). Photographic Image, Vicinity of Grenfell Tower, North Kensington, London, 16th June 2017.

Figure E.xix.: "Publicity speaks in the future tense and yet the achievement of this future is endlessly deferred. How then does publicity remain credible - or credible enough to exert the influence it does? It remains credible because the truthfulness of publicity is judged, not by the real fulfilment of its promises, but by the relevance of its fantasies to those of the spectator- buyer. Its essential application is not to reality but to day-dreams" (John Berger, *Ways of Seeing*, 1972). Photographic Image, Vicinity of Grenfell Tower, North Kensington, London, 16th June 2017.

Figure E.xx.: "The entire world becomes a setting for the fulfilment of publicity's promise of the good life. The world smiles at us. It offers itself to us. And because *everywhere* is imagined as offering itself to us, *everywhere* is more or less the same" (John Berger, *Ways of Seeing*, 1972). Photographic Image, Vicinity of Grenfell Tower; Lancaster West Estate, North Kensington, London, 16th June 2017.

Figure E.xxi.: "Capitalism survives by forcing the majority, whom it exploits, to define their own interests as narrowly as possible. This was once achieved by extensive deprivation. Today in the developed countries it is being achieved by imposing a false standard of what is and what is not desirable" (John Berger, *Ways of Seeing*, 1972). Photographic Image, Vicinity of Grenfell Tower; Lancaster West Estate, North Kensington, London, 16th June 2017.

Figure E.xxii.: "We never look at just one thing; we are always looking at the relation between things and ourselves. Our vision is continually active, continually moving, continually holding things in a circle around itself, constituting what is present to us as we are" (John Berger, *Ways of Seeing*, 1972). Photographic Image, Vicinity of Grenfell Tower; Lancaster West Estate, North Kensington, London, 16th June 2017.

Figure Exxiii.: "A people or a class which is cut off from its own past is far less free to choose and to act as a people or class than one that has been able to situate itself in history" (John Berger, *Ways of Seeing*, 1972). Photographic Image, Vicinity of Grenfell Tower; Lancaster West Estate, North Kensington, London, 16th June 2017.

Figure Exxiv.: "The inherent contradiction in perspective was that it structured all images of reality to address a single spectator who, unlike God, could only be in one place at a time" (John Berger, *Ways of Seeing*, 1972). Photographic Image, Vicinity of Grenfell Tower; Lancaster West Estate, North Kensington, London, 16th June 2017.

Figure Exxv.: "Alternatively the anxiety on which publicity plays is the fear that having nothing you will be nothing" (John Berger, *Ways of Seeing*, 1972). Photographic Image, Vicinity of Grenfell Tower; Lancaster West Estate North Kensington, London, 16th June 2017.

Figure Exxvi.: "Publicity helps to mask and compensate for all that is undemocratic within society. And it also masks what is happening in the rest of the world" (John Berger, *Ways of Seeing*, 1972). Photographic Image, Vicinity of Grenfell Tower; Lancaster West Estate, North Kensington, London, 16th June 2017.

Figure Exxvii.: *Love Assisst(f)*: "One may remember or forget these messages but briefly one takes them in, and for a moment they stimulate the imagination by way of either memory or expectation" (John Berger, *Ways of Seeing*, 1972). Photographic Image, Vicinity of Grenfell Tower; Lancaster West Estate, North Kensington, London, 16th June 2017.

Epilogue

Timely Reflections

Photographic Diary 18th June 2017

Figure Exxviii.: "This has the effect of closing the distance in time between the painting of the picture and one's own act of looking at it. In this special sense all paintings are contemporary. Hence the immediacy of their testimony. Their historical moment is literally there before our eyes" (John Berger, *Ways of Seeing*, 1972). Photographic Image, Vicinity of Grenfell Tower; Lancaster West Estate, North Kensington, London, 18th June 2017.

Figure Exxix.: "To great Omnipotence a debt can owe? Or owing, can repay it? Would'st thou dare Barter upon equality!" (Ann Yearsley, *On Jephthah's Vow, Taken in a Literal Sense*, 1787). Photographic Image, Vicinity of Grenfell Tower; Lancaster West Estate, North Kensington, London, 18th June 2017.

Figure Exxx.: "But there is the evidence of the paintings themselves: the evidence of a group of men and a group of women as seen by another man, the painter. Study this evidence and judge for yourself" (John Berger, *Ways of Seeing*, 1972). Photographic Image, Vicinity of Grenfell Tower; Lancaster West Estate, North Kensington, London, 18th June 2017.

Figure Exxxi.: "These relations between conqueror and colonized tended to be self-perpetuating" (John Berger, *Ways of Seeing*, 1972). Photographic Image, Vicinity of Grenfell Tower; Lancaster West Estate, North Kensington, London, 18th June 2017.

Epilogue

Timely Reflections

Photographic Diary 20th June 2017

Figure Exxxii.: "The artificiality is deep within its own terms of seeing, because the subject has to be seen simultaneously from close-to and from afar" (John Berger, *Ways of Seeing*, 1972). Photographic Image, Vicinity of Grenfell Tower; Lancaster West Estate, North Kensington, London, 20th June 2017.

Figure Exxxiii.: *Love Assisst(f)*: "One may remember or forget these messages but briefly one takes them in, and for a moment they stimulate the imagination by way of either memory or expectation" (John Berger, *Ways of Seeing*, 1972). Photographic Image, Vicinity of Grenfell Tower; Lancaster West Estate, North Kensington, London, 20th June 2017.

Figure Exxxiv.: "No other kind of relic or text from the past can offer such a direct testimony about the world" (John Berger, *Ways of Seeing*, 1972). Photographic Image, Vicinity of Grenfell Tower; Lancaster West Estate, North Kensington, London, 20th June 2017.

Figure Exxxv.: "The compositional unity of a painting contributes fundamentally to the power of its image. It is reasonable to consider a painting's composition. But here the composition is written about as though it were in itself the emotional charge of the painting" (John Berger, *Ways of Seeing*, 1972). Photographic Image, Vicinity of Grenfell Tower; Lancaster West Estate, North Kensington, London, 20th June 2017.

Figure Exxxvi.: "On each board all the images belong to the same language and all are more or less equal within it, because they have been chosen in a highly personal way to match and express the experience of the room's inhabitant" (John Berger, *Ways of Seeing*, 1972). Photographic Image, Vicinity of Grenfell Tower; Lancaster West Estate, North Kensington, London, 20th June 2017.

Figure E.xxxvii.: "A people or a class which is cut off from its own past is far less free to choose and to act as a people or class than one that has been able to situate itself in history" (John Berger, *Ways of Seeing*, 1972). Photographic Image, Vicinity of Grenfell Tower; Lancaster West Estate, North Kensington, London, 20th June 2017.

Figure Exxxviii.: "A people or a class which is cut off from its own past is far less free to choose and to act as a people or class than one that has been able to situate itself in history. This is why – and this is the only reason why – the entire art of the past has now become a political issue" (John Berger, *Ways of Seeing*, 1972). Photographic Image, Vicinity of Grenfell Tower; Lancaster West Estate, North Kensington, London, 20th June 2017.

Figure Exxxix.: "This value is affirmed and gauged by the price it fetches on the market" (John Berger, *Ways of Seeing*, 1972). Photographic Image, Vicinity of Grenfell Tower; Lancaster West Estate, North Kensington, London, 20th June 2017.

Figure Ex1.: "Yet the spiritual value of an object, as distinct from a message or an example, can only be explained in terms of magic or religion" (John Berger, *Ways of Seeing*, 1972). Photographic Image, Vicinity of Grenfell Tower; Lancaster West Estate, North Kensington, London, 20th June 2017.

Figure Exli.: "It is the final empty claim for the continuing values of an oligarchic, undemocratic culture" (John Berger, *Ways of Seeing*, 1972). Photographic Image, Vicinity of Grenfell Tower, North Kensington, London, 20th June 2017.

Figure Exlii.: "By refusing to enter a conspiracy, one remains innocent of that conspiracy. But to remain innocent may also be to remain ignorant" (John Berger, *Ways of Seeing*, 1972). Photographic Image, Vicinity of Grenfell Tower, North Kensington, London, 20th June 2017.

Figure Exliii.: "If the new language of images were used differently, it would, through its use, confer a new kind of power" (John Berger, *Ways of Seeing*, 1972). Photographic Image, Vicinity of Grenfell Tower, North Kensington, London, 20th June 2017.

Figure Exliv: "If the new language of images were used differently, it would, through its use, confer a new kind of power. Within it we could begin to define our experiences more precisely in areas where words are inadequate" (John Berger, *Ways of Seeing*, 1972). Photographic Image, Vicinity of Grenfell Tower, North Kensington, London, 20th June 2017.

Figure Exlv.: "Serving as a bridge between two intense imaginative states" (John Berger *Ways of Seeing*, 1972). Photographic Image, Vicinity of Grenfell Tower, North Kensington, London, 20th June 2017.

Figure Exlvi.: "A people or a class which is cut off from its own past is far less free to choose and to act as a people or class than one that has been able to situate itself in history. This is why - and this is the only reason why - the entire art of the past has now become a political issue" (John Berger, *Ways of Seeing*, 1972). Photographic Image, Vicinity of Grenfell Tower, North Kensington, London, 20th June 2017.

Figure Exlvii.: "A people or a class which is cut off from its own past is far less free to choose and to act as a people or class than one that has been able to situate itself in history" (John Berger, *Ways of Seeing*, 1972). Photographic Image, Vicinity of Grenfell Tower; Lancaster West Estate, North Kensington, London, 20th June 2017.

Figure Exlviii.: "If one moment of that process is isolated, its image will seem banal and its banality, instead of serving as a bridge between two intense imaginative states, will be chilling" (John Berger, *Ways of Seeing*, 1972). Photographic Image, Vicinity of Grenfell Tower; Lancaster West Estate, North Kensington, London, 20th June 2017.

Figure Exlix.: "This was the time when the ocean trade routes were being opened up for the slave trade and for the traffic which was to siphon the riches from other continents into Europe, and later supply the capital for the take-off of the Industrial Revolution" (John Berger, *Ways of Seeing*, 1972). Photographic Image, Vicinity of Grenfell Tower; Lancaster West Estate, North Kensington, London, 20th June 2017.

Figure EL.: "Publicity is, in essence, nostalgic. It has to sell the past to the future. It cannot itself supply the standards of its own claims. And so all its references to quality are bound to be retrospective and traditional. It would lack both confidence and credibility if it used a strictly contemporary language" (John Berger, *Ways of Seeing*, 1972). Photographic Image, Vicinity of Grenfell Tower; Lancaster West Estate, North Kensington, London, 20th June 2017.

Figure ELi.: "Publicity is addressed to those who constitute the market, to the spectator-buyer who is also the consumer-producer from whom profits are made twice over — as worker and then as buyer. The only places relatively free of publicity are the quarters of the very rich; their money is theirs to keep" (John Berger, *Ways of Seeing*, 1972). Photographic Image, Vicinity of Grenfell Tower; Lancaster West Estate, North Kensington, London, 20th June 2017.

Figure ELii.: "Capitalism survives by forcing the majority, whom it exploits, to define their own interests as narrowly as possible. This was once achieved by extensive deprivation. Today in the developed countries it is being achieved by imposing a false standard of what is and what is not desirable" (John Berger, *Ways of Seeing*, 1972). Photographic Image, St Paul's Cathedral, Grenfell Tower Memorial Service, London, December 2017.

REFERENCES

Abergel, F., Aoyama, H., Chakrabarti, B., Chakrabarti, A., and Ghosh, A., (2015); *Econophysics and Data Driven Modelling of Market Dynamics*, London: Springer.

Abramson, K., Keefe, B., and Chou, W., (2015); Communicating About Cancer Through Facebook: A Qualitative Analysis of a Breast Cancer Awareness Page, *Journal of Health Communication,* Vol. 20, pp., 237-243.

acast (2018); *Reasons to be Cheerful with Ed Miliband and Geoff Lloyd. Reversing the Cycle of Gang Violence: Lessons from Scotland.* Available at: https://www.acast.com/reasonstobecheerful/reversingthecycleofviolence-lessonsfromscotland

Adam, B., (1995); *Timewatch, The Social Analysis of Time*, Cambridge: Polity Press.

Adams, P., (2015); In Defence of Care: Gilligan's Relevance for Primary Education, *Pedagogy, Culture & Society,* Vol. 23, No. 2, pp., 281-300.

Adorno, T., (1941); On Popular Music, *Studies in Philosophy and Social Science,* Vol. 9, pp., 17-48.

Adorno, T., and Horkheimer, M., (1944/2010); *Dialectic of Enlightenment,* London: Verso.

Adorno, T., and Eisler, H., (1947/2007); *Composing for the Films*, London: Continuum.

Ahn, S., (2015); Incorporating Immersive Virtual Environments in Health Promotion Campaigns: A Construal Level Theory Approach, *Health Communication*, Vol. 30, pp., 545-556.

Althusser, L., (1971); Ideology and Ideological State Apparatuses, in *Lenin and Philosophy and Other Essays* by Althusser, L., trans., Brewster, B., New York: Monthly Review Press.

—. (1971/2001); Ideology and Ideological State Apparatuses, in *Lenin and Philosophy and Other Essays* by Althusser, L., trans., Brewster, B., New York: Monthly Review Press.

—. (2006); *Philosophy of the Encounter, Later Writings, 1978-1987*, London: Verso.

Amazon.co.uk (2018); *Busking Equipment* [keyword search]. Available at: https://www.amazon.co.uk/s/?ie=UTF8&keywords=busking+equipment&index=aps&tag

Amazon.co.uk (2018a); *Home Music Production* [keyword search]. Available at: https://www.amazon.co.uk/Focusrite-Scarlett-Audio-Interface-Tools/dp/B01E6T56CM/ref=sr

Amazon.co.uk (2018b); *Loop Station Performer* [keyword search]. Available at: https://www.amazon.co.uk/Boss-RC-505-Loop-Station/dp

Android (2015); *Android Wear. Wear What You Want*. Available at: http://www.android.com/wear/

Antenna (2012); *Connecting the World to Culture*, Antenna International. Available at: https://tsdrapi.uspto.gov/ts/cd/casedocs/bundle.pdf?sn=85748430&type=SPE&fromdate=2012-10-08&todate=2012-10-08

Antenna (2018); *Innovative Content Grows Revenue at the National Gallery About Us*. Antenna International. Available at: https://antennainternational.com/case-studies/national-gallery-innovative-content-grows-revenue/

Antenna (2018a; *Projects we have Partnered with National Gallery, London on: Innovative Content Grows Revenue at the National Gallery*, Antenna International. Available at: https://antennainternational.com/client/national-gallery-london/

Antonucci, T.C., and Jackson, J.S., (1990); The Role of Reciprocity in Social Support. In B.R. Sarason, I.G. Sarason, and G.R. Pierce (Eds.), *Social Support: An Interactionist View* (pp. 173-198), New York: Wiley.

Arconic (2017); *Building Construction: Reynobond*, Reynolux. Available at: https://www.arconic.com/aap/europe/en/info_page/market_building_construction.asp.

Aristotle, (1977); *Aristotle's De Anima Books II, III,* Oxford, University Press: Oxford at the Clarendon Press.

Ashcroft, B., (2001); *Post-Colonial Transformation*, London: Routledge.

—. (2001a); *On Post-Colonial Futures*, London: Continuum.

—. (1995); Interpolation and Post-colonial Agency, Factions and Frictions, Special Issue of *New Literatures Review*, ed. Sharrad, P., et al., 28/29, pp., 176-189.

—. (1989); Griffiths, G., Tiffin, H., *The Empire Writes Back: Theory and Practice in Post-Colonial Literatures*, London: Routledge.

Attorney General (2018); *Legal Advice to Cabinet on the Withdrawal Agreement and the Protocol on Ireland/Northern Ireland,* 13th November 2018, Attorney General, Attorney General's Office. Department for Exiting the European Union, Published 5th December 2018. Available at:
https://assets.publishing.service.gov.uk/government/uploads/system/uploads/attachment_data/file/761852/05_December-_EU_Exit_Attorney_General_s_legal_advice_to_Cabinet_on_the_Withdrawal_Agreement_and_the_Protocol_on_Ireland-Northern_Ireland.pdf

Attorney General (2019); *Protocol on Ireland/Northern Ireland – Exchange of Letters, Attorney General,* Attorney General's Office London, Published 14th January 2019. Available at:
https://www.consilium.europa.eu/en/press/press-releases/2019/01/14/joint-letter-of-president-tusk-and-president-juncker-to-theresa-may-prime-minister-of-the-united-kingdom/pdf

Austin, L. J., (1964); *Sense and Sensibilia,* Oxford: Oxford University Press.

Back, L., (1996/2005); *New Ethnicities and Urban Culture; Racisms and Multiculture in Young Lives,* London: Routledge.

Baker, A., (2016); *The Life of Sir Isaac Pitman, (Inventor of Phonography),* Charleston, South Carolina: BiblioLife, LLC.

Baronian, L., (2013); *Marx and Living Labour,* Oxfordshire: Routledge.

Bateman, V., (2015); *Welfare Reform: Why Subsidising Other People's Kids Must Have Limits,* CapX, London Office 57 Tufton Street, London SW1P 3QL. Available at:
https://capx.co/welfare-reform-why-susbsidising-other-peoples-kids-must-have-limits/

Bath Heritage Watchdog (2010); *The 3RD Public Events,* Bath Heritage Watchdog. Available at:
http://www.bathheritagewatchdog.org/bpress.htm

Bath Heritage Watchdog (2011); *Bath Press News, Bath Heritage Watchdog.* Available at:
https://www.bbc.co.uk/news/av/10318089/bbc-news-channel

Bath Heritage Watchdog (2018); *Home [Page],* Bath Heritage Watchdog. Available at: http://www.bathheritagewatchdog.org/index.html

Bath and North East Somerset Council Planning Services (2008); *Locally Important Buildings. Supplementary Planning Document, Consultation Draft – April 2008,* Bath and North East Somerset Council. Available at:

www.bathnes.gov.uk/sites/default/files/...and.../LocallyImportantBuildingsSPD.pdf

Baudrillard, J., (1968/2005); *The System of Objects*, trans., Benedict, J., London: Verso.

—. (1983); *Simulations*, trans., Foss, P., Patton, P., and Beitchman, P., New York: Semiotext(e), Inc.

—. (1994); *Simulacra and Simulation*. Ann Arbor: The University of Michigan Press.

—. (2001); *Impossible Exchange*, trans., Turner, C., London: Verso.

—. (2003); *The Consumer Society. Myths and Structures,* trans., Turner, C., London: Sage.

—. (2003a); *Passwords*, (second edition), London: Verso.

—. (2005/2007); *The Intelligence of Evil or the Lucidity Pact*, Oxford: Berg.

—. (2013); *The Intelligence of Evil or the Lucidity Pact*, London: Bloomsbury.

BBC (2017); *Grenfell Tower Fire: New Council Leader Heckled by Public*, Video Extract, British Broadcasting Company News. Available at: http://www.bbc.co.uk/news/uk-40663512

BBC Newsnight (2017); @BBCNewsnight , *The Traumatic Account Of How Two Families Escaped The Grenfell Tower Blaze From The 21st Floor #newsnight*. Available at: https://twitter.com/BBCNewsnight/status/913160662473482241

BBC Breaking News, @BBCBreaking (2019); *UK PM Theresa May Loses MPs' #BrexitVote on Her Deal by 432 votes to 202 – the Biggest Government Defeat Since 1924*. BBC Breaking News, @BBCBreaking. Tuesday 15th January 2019, posted 19:30hrs. Available at: https://twitter.com/BBCBreaking/status/1085260422935207937

BEIS (2017); *The Clean Growth Strategy. Leading the Way to a Low Carbon Future*. Department for Business, Energy & Industrial Strategy, Low Carbon Technologies and Industrial Strategy, 12 October 2017, HM Government. Available at: https://www.gov.uk/government/publications/clean-growth-strategy

Bell, D., (1999); *The Coming of Post-Industrial Society. A Venture in Social Forecasting,* New York: Basic Books/ Perseus Books Group.

Berger, J., (1972); *Ways of Seeing*, London: British Broadcasting Corporation and Penguin Books.

Berger, J., (1972a); *Ways of Seeing*, CPI Bath, Bath: British Broadcasting Corporation and Penguin Books.

Berger, J., (1972/1977); *Ways of Seeing*, London: British Broadcasting Corporation and Penguin Books.

Berger, P., and Luckmann, T., (1966); *The Social Construction of Reality*, Garden City, N.Y.: Doubleday.

Bertho, M., Crawford, B., Fogarty, E., (2008); The Impact of Globalization on the United State, *Culture and Society*, Volume 1, Westport, Conn.: Praeger.

Blumer, H., (1969); *Symbolic Interactionism, Perspective and Method*, Englewood Cliffs, New Jersey: Prentice-Hall, Inc.

Booker, C., (2017); *The Grenfell Tower Fire Would Not Have Happened Without the EU and Global Warming*, London, 08 July 2017, Telegraph.co.uk. Available at: https://0-search.proquest.com.catalogue.libraries.london.ac.uk/docview/1917085838/citation/566DC70B71E4AAAPQ/1?accountid=14565

Boorstin, D., (1961/1982); *The Image. A Guide to Pseudo-Events in America*, New York: Atheneum.

Bourdieu, P., (1984/2010); *Distinction*, London and New York: Routledge.

Bourdieu, P., (1990/2017); *The Logic of Practice*, trans., Nice, R., Cambridge: Polity Press.

Bourdieu, P., (2005/2018); *The Social Structures of the Economy*, Cambridge: Polity Press.

BRAC (2017); *Membership, Building Regulations Advisory Committee*. Available at: https://www.gov.uk/government/organisations/building-regulations-advisory-committee

BREEAM (2012); *Grenfell Tower Regeneration Project, BREEAM Pre-Assessment (REV B), Planning Application*, October 2012., Syntegra Consulting Intelligent and Green Building Solutions. Available at: https://www.rbkc.gov.uk/idoxWAM/doc/Other-959896.pdf?extension=.pdf&id=959896&location=VOLUME2&contentType=application/pdf&pageCount=1

Brennan, P., and Fink, S., (1997); Health Promotion, Social Support and Computer Networks, in (eds.) Street, R., Gold, W., and Manning, T., *Health Promotion and Interactive Technology. Theoretical Applications and Future Directions*, London: Lawrence Erlbaum Associates, Publishers.

Busk in London (2018); *Busk in London*. Available at: http://buskinlondon.com

@BuskinLondon (2018); *Busk in London*. Available at: https://twitter.com/BuskInLondon

Cadwalladr, C., (2015); *Is the Dotcom Bubble About to Burst (again)?* Available at: wwwtheguardian.com/technology/2015/oct/04/is-dotcom bubble- about-to-burst-again.

Callon, M., (1986); Some Elements of a Sociology of Translation: Domestication of the Scallops and the Fisherman of St Brieuc Bay, in (ed.) Law, J., *Power, Action and Belief. A New Sociology of Knowledge?* London, Boston and Henley: Routledge & Kegan Paul.

—. (1986a); The Sociology of an Actor-Network: The Case of the Electric Vehicle, in (eds.) Callon, M., Law, J., and Rip, A., *Mapping the Dynamics of Science and Technology. Sociology of Science in the Real World*, Hampshire: The MacMillan Press LTC.

Canon (2018); *Canon EOS 5D Mark II*, Canon. Available at: http://gdlp01.c-wss.com/gds/0/0300004270/02/eos5dmkii-im5-c-en.pdf

CapX (2019); *CapX Brings You the best Writing on Politics, Economics, Technology and Ideas*, CapX, London Office 57 Tufton Street, London SW1P 3QL. Available at: https://capx.co/about/

Cardiff, J., (1999); *Artangel Audio Walk, The Missing Voice: Case Study B [1999]*, Guides Visitors On a Physical and Psychological Journey Through the Streets of Spitalfields, Whitechapel Gallery. Available at: http://www.whitechapelgallery.org/exhibitions/social-sculpture/

Casey, A., (2018); *Letter Correspondence to Odih, P., from: Adele Casey, Facilities Manager,* Greater London Authority [GLA] 26th July 2018.

Castells, M., (2000); *The Rise of the Network Society*, Oxford: Blackwell.

—. (1996); The Net and the Self., Working Notes for a Critical Theory of the Informational Society., *Critique of Anthropology*, Vol., 16, Issue, 1, pp., 9-38.

—. (1996/2010); *The Rise of the Network Society*, Oxford: Wiley-Blackwell.

—. (1997/2002); *The Power of Identity*, Oxford: Blackwells Publishers.

—. (1996/2010a); *The Power of Identity*, Oxford: Blackwells Publishers.

—. (2000a); Urban Sustainability in the Information Age., *City: Analysis of Urban Trends, Culture, Theory, Policy Action*, Vol. 4, Issue, 1, pp., 118-122.

—. (2004); Informationalism, Networks, and the Network Society: a Theoretical Blueprint, in (ed) Castells, M., *The Network Society. A Cross-cultural Perspective*, Cheltenham, Glos: Edward Elgar Publishing.

—. (2005); The Message is the Medium, *Global Media and Communication*, Volume, 1, Issue 2, pp., 135-147.

—. (2004); *The Network Society. A Cross-Cultural Perspective*, Cheltenham: Northampton.

—. (2010); *The Rise of the Network Society*, Sussex: Wiley-Blackwell.

—. (2012); *Aftermath: The Cultures of the Economic Crisis*, Oxford: Oxford

University Press.

Celotext (2017); *Update - Friday 23rd June. Grenfell Tower: Celotex Is To Stop The Supply Of RS5000 For Use In Rainscreen Cladding Systems In Buildings Over 18m Tall*, Celotex Saint-Gobain. Available at: https://www.celotex.co.uk/

Celotex (2017a); *History, Timeline*, Celotex Saint-Gobain Available at: https://www.celotex.co.uk/about/history

Celotex (2017b); *Celotex RS5000: Promotional Document*. Celotex Saint-Gobain. Available at: https://www.celotex.co.uk/products/.../5c73880a-6017-4854-88fe-923fff569a4f

Celotex (2017c); *Celotex RS5000*. Celotex Saint-Gobain. Available at: https://www.celotex.co.uk/products/.../5c73880a-6017-4854-88fe-923fff569a4f

Channel 4 News (2018); *UK Drill Music Gang Banned from Making Violent Music*, Channel 4 News, June 15, 2018. Available at: https://www.youtube.com/watch?v=KXX0b4hka4g

CheerfulPodcast (2018); *50 Reversing the Cycle of Gang Violence: Lessons from Scotland*; Reasons to be Cheerful with Miliband and Geoff Lloyd, Acast. Available at: https://www.acast.com/reasonstobecheerful/reversingthecycleofviolence-lessonsfromscotland

CityA.M. (2017); *Australian investment bank Macquarie sells last of its stake in Thames Water to Canadian and Kuwaiti Funds*, CityA.M. Available at: http://www.cityam.com/260875/australian-investment-bank-macquarie-sells-last-its-stake

City of Westminster (2016); P*lanning Applications Committee: Creation of 6 no. Pitches on the North Terrace of Trafalgar Square*, City of Westminster, 20th September 2016. Available at: http://committees.westminster.gov.uk/documents/s19502/ITEM%2006%20-%20TRAFALGAR%20SQUARE%20LONDON.pdf

City of Westminster (2016a); *Planning Applications Sub-Committee (2), Tuesday 20th September, 2016 6:30pm*, City of Westminster. Available at: http://committees.westminster.gov.uk/ieListDocuments.aspx?CId=168&MId=4078&Ver=4

Clark, M., Scholze-Stubenrecht, W., Sykes, J., and Thyen, O., (1999); *Oxford-Duden German Dictionary*, Oxford: Oxford University Press.

Clark, B., Bellamy, J., and York, R., (2007); The Critique of Intelligent Design: Epicurus, Marx, Darwin, and Freud and the Materialist Defense of Science, *Theory and Society*, Vo., 36, No. 6 (Dec), pp., 515-546.

Coad, E, D., (2017); *Maiden Speech, (ed.) Corbyn, J., Today @EmmaDentCoad, the new Kensington MP, Gave a Powerful Maiden Speech About Poverty in her Constituency & the Tragedy of Grenfell Tower*, @jeremycorbyn. Available at: https://twitter.com/jeremycorbyn/status/877979528282243073

Cohen, S., (1972/2002); *Folk Devils and Moral Panics; The Creation of the Mods and Rockers*, London and New York: Routledge.

Coin Street Community Builders (2015); *The Garden Bridge, Coin Street Community Builders*. Available at: https://coinstreet.org/the-garden-bridge/

Collins (1995); *Collins Concise Dictionary. Third Edition*, Glasgow: HarperCollins Publishers.

Commons Select Committee PAC (2016); *PAC [Public Accounts Committee] Submits Evidence to Mayor's Review of Garden Bridge Project*, Commons Select Committee, Public Accounts Committee, 28 October 2016. Available at: https://www.parliament.uk/business/committees/committees-a-z/commons-select/public-accounts-committee/news-parliament-2015/garden-bridge-mayor-evidence-16-17/

Construction Manager (2017); *News: Grenfell: Corporate Manslaughter Raised by Police*, Construction Manager. Available at: http://www.constructionmanagermagazine.com/news/grenfell-corporate-manslaughter-considered-police/

Corbin, J., and Strauss, A., (2008); *Basics of Qualitative Research, Techniques and Procedures for Developing Grounded Theory*, 3e, London: Sage.

Corbyn, J., (2017); *Grenfell Tower; Response to PM Theresa May's 22nd June 2017 Statement*. Available at: https://hansard.parliament.uk/Commons/2017-06-22/debates/E4B84F46-4699-4725-BBE4-AA724C3A0191/GrenfellTower?highlight=79%20people%20dead#contribution-BA735503-B381-4B69-8727-9225127D18F7

Couch, D., Han, G., Robinson, P., and Komesaroff, P., (2015); Public Health Surveillance and the Media: a Dyad of Panoptic and Synoptic Social Control, *Health Psychology and Behaviour Medicine*, Vol. 3, No. 1, pp., 128-141.

Council Meeting Webcast (2017); *Royal Borough of Kensington and Chelsea, Council Meeting Webcast (19th July 2017)*, Royal Borough of Kensington and Chelsea. Available at: https://www.rbkc.gov.uk/council-and-democracy/council-meeting-webcast-19-july-2017

Available also at: https://www.youtube.com/watch?v=I8mpvkPLpoI&feature=youtu.be

CoventryLive (2018); *Watch: Disturbing Coventry 'Drill Music' Videos Glamorise Knife and Gun Crime*, CoventryLive, 15:29, 5 September 2018. Available at: https://www.coventrytelegraph.net/news/coventry-news/drill-music-rap-guns-knives-15114481

Creative Europe Desk UK (2019); *Creative Europe Brexit Update*, Creative Europe Desk UK, 20 June 2019. Available at: http://www.creativeeuropeuk.eu/news/update-creative-europe-and-outcome-eu-referendum

Davies, K., (1990); *Women, Time and the Weaving of the Strands of Everyday Life*, Aldershot, Hants: Avebury.

Davis, G., and Bonsall, P., (2006); *A History of Bath: Image and Reality*, Lancaster: Carnegie Publishing.

DBEIS (2017); *Energy Company Obligation – Flexible Eligibility*, Department for Business, Energy and Industrial Strategy. Available at: https://assets.publishing.service.gov.uk/government/uploads/system/uploads/attachment_data/file/608042/ECO_Help_to_Heat_flexible_eligibility_guidance_for_LAs.pdf

DCLG (2013); *Former Bath Press, Lower Bristol Road Bath (ref: 2191952, 18 December 2013)*, Department for Communities and Local Government. Available at: https://www.gov.uk/government/publications/recovered-appeal-former-bath-press-lower-bristol-road-bath-ref-2191952-18-december-2013

DCLG (2017); *Independent Report, Fire Test Report: DCLG BS 8414 Test no.1*. Part of Grenfell Tower, 28th July 2017, Department for Communities and Local Government. Available at: https://www.gov.uk/government/publications/fire-test-report-dclg-bs-8414-test-no1

DCLG (2017a); *Independent Review of Building Regulations and Fire Safety: Publication of Terms of Reference*. Part of Grenfell Tower, 30th August 2017, Department for Communities and Local Government. Available at: https://www.gov.uk/government/news/independent-review-of-building-regulations-and-fire-safety-publication-of-terms-of-reference

DCLG (2017b); *Independent Review of Building Regulations and Fire Safety: Terms of Reference*. Part of Grenfell Tower, 30th August 2017, Department for Communities and Local Government. Available at: https://www.gov.uk/government/publications/independent-review-of-building-regulations-and-fire-safety-terms-of-reference

DCLG (2017c); *New Taskforce to Support Recovery from Grenfell Fire Disaster*. Part of Grenfell Tower, 26th July 2017, Department for Communities and Local Government. Available at: https://www.gov.uk/government/news/new-taskforce-to-support-recovery-from-grenfell-fire-disaster

DDCMS, (2011); *Technology Project puts Worldwide Art at your Fingertips*, Department for Digital, Culture, Media and Sport. Available at: https://www.gov.uk/government/news/technology-project-puts-worldwide-art-at-your-fingertips

DDCMS (2018); *Culture is Digital*, Department for Digital, Culture, Media and Sport. Available at: https://www.gov.uk/government/publications/culture-is-digital/culture-is-digital

Debord, G., (1967/2006); *The Society of the Spectacle*, Zone Books: New York.

DEEU (2018); *The Future Relationship Between the United Kingdom and the European Union*, Department for Exiting the European Union (DEEU). Available at: https://assets.publishing.service.gov.uk/government/uploads/system/uploads/attachment_data/file/725288/The_future_relationship_between_the_United_Kingdom_and_the_European_Union.pdf

Denzin, N., (1989); *The Research Act: a Theoretical Introduction to Sociological Methods*, London: Prentice Hall.

Denzin, N., (2009); *The Research Act*, New Jersey: Transaction Publishers.

Department for Communities and Local Government (2013); *Section 106 Affordable Housing Requirements; Review and Appeal*, Department for Communities and Local Government. Available at: https://assets.publishing.service.gov.uk/government/uploads/system/uploads/attachment_data/file/192641/Section_106_affordable_housing_requirements_-_Review_and_appeal.pdf

Department for Exiting the European Union (2018); *Exiting the EU: Publication of Legal Advice*, Publication of the Attorney General's Legal Advice to Cabinet on the Withdrawal Agreement and the Protocol on Ireland/Northern Ireland, Published December 5th 2019. Available at: https://www.gov.uk/government/publications/exiting-the-eu-publication-of-legal-advice

Derrida, J., (1984); *Signéponge = Signsponge*, translated by Rand., R., New York: Columbia University Press.

Diacritics (1986); Des Espace Autres And Published by the French Journal Architecture-Mouvement-Continuité in October, 1984, was the basis of a Lecture Given by Michel Foucault in March 1967, *Diacritics* Vol. 16, No. 1 (Spring, 1986), pp. 22-27.

Dicks, B., (2003); *Culture on Display, The Production of Contemporary Visitability*, Berkshire: Open University Press.

Dimbleby, J., (1998); *The Prince of Wales*, London: Warner Books.

Dreyfus, H., and Rabinow, P., (1982); *Beyond Structuralism and Hermeneutics*. London: Harvester and Wheatsheaf.

@EL4JC (2017); *2013: Boris Johnson Tells Labour Opponent to 'Get Stuffed' when Questioned on Fire Service Cuts*. Available at: https://twitter.com/EL4JC/status/874986965766205441

Environment Agency (2017); *Thames Water Ordered to Pay Record £20 million for River Pollution*. Available at: https://www.gov.uk/government/news/thames-water-ordered-to-pay-record-20-million-for-river-pollution

Epicurus, (1993); *The Essential Epicurus. Letters, Principal Doctrines, Vatican Sayings, and Fragments*, trans., and intro., O'Connor, E., New York: Prometheus Books.

Ermarth, E., (1995); Ph(r)ase Time: Chaos Theory and Postmodern Reports on Knowledge, *Time and Society*, Vol., 4, No., 1, pp., 91-110.

Escobar, M., (2014); The Power of (dis)placement: Pigeons and Urban Regeneration in Trafalgar Square, *Cultural Geographies*, Vol. 21, Issue 3, pp., 363-387.

Esperdy, G., (2005); The Odd-Job Alleyway of Building: Modernization, Marketing and Architectural Practice in the 1930s, *Journal of Architectural Education*, Vol., 58:4, pp., 25-40.

European Broadcasting Union (2014); R 128 *Loudness Normalisation and Permitted Maximum Level of Audio Signals; Status: EBU Recommendation*, Geneva June 2014. Available at: https://tech.ebu.ch/docs/r/r128-2014.pdf

European Commission (2018); *Regulation 2015/751 on Interchange Fees*. European Commission. Available at: http://ec.europa.eu/competition/sectors/financial_services/sepa_en.html

European Council (2019); *Joint Letter of President Tusk and President Juncker to Theresa May, Prime Minister of the United Kingdom, Press Lease, European Council*, Council of the European Union. Available at: https://www.consilium.europa.eu/en/press/press-releases/2019/01/14/joint-letter-of-president-tusk-and-president-juncker-to-theresa-may-prime-minister-of-the-united-kingdom/pdf

European Parliament (2018a); *Free Movement of Workers*, European Parliament. Available at: http://www.europarl.europa.eu/ftu/pdf/en/FTU_2.1.5.pdf

Evening Standard [ES] (2018); *Spare Us Buskers On Elizabeth Line,* Evening Standard, The Reader, Evening Standard. Available at: https://www.standard.co.uk/comment/letters/the-reader-the-uk-is-bullying-its-overseas-territories-and-trust-is-being-lost-a3834196.html

Ewald, F. (1991); Insurance and Risk, in J. Burchell, C. Gordon and P. Miller, *The Foucault Effect: Studies in Governmentality*. Hemel Hempstead: Harvester.

Fairclough, N., (2001); The Discourse of New Labour: Critical Discourse Analysis, in (eds.) Wetherell, M., Taylor, S., and Yates, S., *Discourse as Data; A Guide for Analysis*, London: Sage.

Fenves, P., (1986); Marx's Doctoral Thesis on Two Greek Atomists and the Post-Kantian Interpretations, *Journal of the History of Ideas*, Vol. 47, No., 3 (Jul. – Sep., 1986) pp., 433-452.

Ferlie, E., Ashburner, L., Fitzgerald, L, and Pettigrew, A., (1997); *The New Public Management in Action*, Oxford: Oxford University Press.

Financial Times (2017); *Thames Water: The Murky Structure of a Utility Company*, Financial Times. Available at: https://www.ft.com/content/5413ebf8-24f1-11e7-8691-d5f7e0cd0a16

Financial Times (2017a); *Macquarie Sells its 26% Stake in Thames Water*, Financial Times. Available at: https://www.ft.com/content/9c34ac2b-48de-3031-a6de-395c9ab64b59

Fitton, L., Hussain, A., and Leaning, B., (2015); *Twitter for Dummies*, New Jersey: John Wiley & Sons, Inc.

Foster and Partners (2003); *Transformation of Trafalgar Square,* Press Release 02 July 2003, Foster + Partners. Available at: https://www.fosterandpartners.com/news/archive/2003/07/transformation-of-trafalgar-square/

Foucault, M., (1979/2010); *The Birth of Biopolitics. Lectures at the College De France 1978-1979.*, Basingstoke/New York: Picador, Palgrave Macmillan.

Foucault, M., (1982); The Subject and Power, in (eds.) Dreyfus, H. and Rabinow, P. *Michel Foucault. Beyond Structuralism and Hermeneutics*, London: Harvester Wheatsheaf.

—. (1986); Of Other Spaces, *Diacritics*, trans., Miskowiec, J., Vol. 16, No. 1, (Spring, 1986), pp., 22-27.

—. (1988); Technologies of the Self, in Martin, L., (eds.) Gutman, H. and Hutton, P., *Technologies of the Self; A Seminar with Michel Foucault*, London: Tavistock Publication.

—. (1990); *The Care of the Self; The History of Sexuality Vol. 3*. London: Penguin Books.

—. (1991); *Discipline and Punish; The Birth of the Prison.* trans., Sheridan, A., London: Penguin Books.
—. (1992); *The Use of Pleasure, The History of Sexuality Volume 2*, London: Penguin.
—. (1997); *The Order of Things*, London: Routledge.
—. (1998); *The Will to Knowledge, The History of Sexuality Volume 1*, Hurley, R., trans., London: Penguin
—. (2001); *Fearless Speech*, Los Angeles: Semiotext(e).
Freres, G., (1875); *Nouveau Dictionnaire Classique de la Française.* Available at: https://books.google.co.uk/books?id=BYgPAAAAYAAJ&printsec=frontcover&source=gbs_ge_summary_r&cad=0#v=onepage&q&f=false
Freud, S., (1994); *The Interpretation of Dreams*, trans., Brill, A., New York: Random House.
Fu, C., Komar, V., Rose, R., Shoaub, U., and Yap, L., (2016); *Coming in from the Cold: A Case Study of Community Engagement in Tackling Fuel Poverty*. Available at: http://www.lse.ac.uk/intranet/students/LSE-LIFE/Resources/undergraduateStudents/forms/LSE-GROUPS-2016-research-papers/CHENXU-FU-688601-assignsubmission-file-Group-6-Paper.pdf
Fuchs, C., (2014); *Digital Labour and Karl Marx*, London: Routledge.
—. (2015); *Culture and Economy in the Age of Social Media*, Oxon: Routledge.
Fumagalli, A., and Mezzadra, S., (2010); Crisis *in the Global Economy: Financial Markets, Social Struggles, and New Political Scenarios*, Cambridge Mass: Semiotext(e), The MIT Press.
Gabriel, Y., and Lang, T., (1995); *The Unmanageable Consumer,* London: Sage.
—. (2006); *The Unmanageable Consumer*, London: Sage.
—. (2015); *The Unmanageable Consumer*, London: Sage.
Garden Bridge Trust (2014); *Garden Bridge, Draft Operation and Management Plan*, September 2014, Garden Bridge Trust. Available at: https://www.london.gov.uk/sites/default/files/ffs_garden_bridge_emails_redacted.pdf
Garden Bridge Trust (2017); *Garden Bridge Trust Announces the Closure of the Project*, 14th August 2017 Press Release. Available at: https://www.gardenbridge.london/news/article/garden-bridge-trust-announces-the-closure-of-the-project
@geraldi23591291(2017); *Pam xXx New Book: Adsensory Financialisation.* Available at: https://twitter.com/geraldi23591291
Gilligan, C., (1982); *In A Different Voice. Psychological Theory and*

Women's Development, Cambridge, Massachusetts, and London: Harvard University Press.

Gilligan, C., (1993); *In A Different Voice. Psychological Theory and Women's Development*, London: Harvard University Press.

Gilligan, C., (2000); *In A Different Voice. Psychological Theory and Women's Development*, London: Harvard University Press.

Gilligan, C., (2015); Moral Orientation and Moral Development. In *Justice and Care: Essential Readings in Feminist Ethics,* (ed.) Held, V., pp., 31-46. Oxford: Westview Press.

Gillian, C., (2011/2016); *Joining the Resistance*, Cambridge: Polity Press.

Godfrey, R., Jack, G., and Jones, C., (2004); Sucking, Bleeding, Breaking: On the Dialectics of Vampirism, Capital, and Time, *Culture and Organisation*, March, Vol. 10, Issue 1., pp., 25-36.

Goetz, S., and Taliaferro, C., (2011); *A Brief History of the Soul*, Sussex: John Wiley & Sons Ltd.

Gordon, C., (1980); *Power/Knowledge: Selected Interviews and Other Writings, 1972-1977*, New York: Pantheon Books.

Gorry, A., Harris, L., Silva, J., and Eaglin, J., (1995); Health Care as Teamwork: The Internet Collaboratory, in (ed.) Harris, L., *Health and the New Media. Technologies Transforming Personal and Public Health*, New Jersey: Lawrence Erlbaum Associates.

Gorz, A., (1983); *Ecology as Politics*, London: Pluto Press.

Government Equalities Office, (2015); *Explanatory Memorandum on the Report From the European Commission to the European Parliament, The Council and the European Economic and Social Committee*, Submitted by Government Equalities Office, Department for Culture Media and Sport on 3rd June 2015. Available at: http://europeanmemoranda.cabinetoffice.gov.uk/files/2015/06/150603_Report_on_the_application_of_Council_Directive_2004_113_EC__equal_treatment_between_men_and_women_-_FINAL.pdf

Gov.UK (2017); Appendix 8: Energy Company Obligation. Gov.uk. Available at: https://www.gov.uk/government/publications/2010-to-2015-government-policy-household-energy/2010-to-2015-government-policy-household-energy#appendix-8-energy-company-obligation-eco

Gov.UK (2017a); *Climate Change Act 2008,* 2008 Chapter 27. Legislation.gov.uk. Available at: https://www.legislation.gov.uk/ukpga/2008/27/introduction

Gov.UK (2018); *Energy Companies Obligation: Brokerage*, Department for Business, Energy and Industrial Strategy and Ofgem. Gov.UK. Available at: https://www.gov.uk/guidance/energy-companies-obligation-brokerage

Gov.UK (2018a); *Settled and Pre-Settled Status for EU Citizens and their Families*, Gov.UK. Available at: https://www.gov.uk/settled-status-eu-citizens-families/what-settled-and-presettled-status-means

Greater London Authority (2012); *Greater London Authority, Trafalgar Square Byelaws 2012*, Greater London Authority. Available at: https://www.london.gov.uk/sites/default/files/trafalgar_square_byelaws.pdf

Greater London Authority (2018); *Request for Information Regarding the Trafalgar Square Pedestrian Piazza*, Adele Casey, Facilities Manager – Hard Services, Greater London Authority, London: Greater London Authority.

Greater London Authority (2018a); *World Squares for All Planning Conditions and Proposals for North Terrace*, Compendium of Greater London Authority Reports About Trafalgar Square North Terrace. Bespoke Compilation Prepared on Request and by the Information and Governance Department. London: Greater London Authority.

Greener, I., (2009); *Public Management a Critical Text*, Basingstoke, Hampshire: Palgrave Macmillan.

Grenfell Action Group (2015); *Grenfell Residents Resist TMO Intransigence*, Posted on March 11 2015, Grenfell Action Group. Available at: https://grenfellactiongroup.wordpress.com/2015/03/11/grenfell-residents-resist-tmo-intransigence/

Grenfell Action Group (2016); *Grenfell Tower Residents Address RBKC Scrutiny Committee*, Grenfell Action Group. Available at: https://grenfellactiongroup.wordpress.com/speech/

Grenfell Action Group (2016a); *KCTMO – Playing with Fire!* Grenfell Action Group. Available at: https://grenfellactiongroup.wordpress.com/2016/11/20/kctmo-playing-with-fire/

Grenfell Action Group (2017); *In the Matter of the Royal Borough of Kensington and Chelsea Tenant Management Organisation Limited. And in the Matter of an Annual General Meeting Scheduled for 17 October 2017*, Grenfell Action Group. Available at: https://grenfellactiongroup.files.wordpress.com/2017/10/urgent-advice-on-tmo-agm.pdf

Grenfell Action Group (2017a); *ICO [Information Commissioner's Office] Complicit in KCTMO Grenfell Cover Up*, Grenfell Action Group. Available at: https://grenfellactiongroup.wordpress.com/2017/10/31/ico-complicit-in-kctmo-grenfell-cover-up/

Grimme, K., (2017); *Impressionism*, Taschen: Köln.
Grossman, M., (1972); On the Concept of Health Capital and the Demand for Health, *Journal of Political Economy*, Vol. 80, No.2, pp., 223-255.
Gsöllpointner, K., Schnell, R., Schuler, R., (2016); *Digital Synaesthesia: A Model for the Aesthetics of Digital Art*, Berlin: Walter de Gruyter GmbH & Co KG.
Guardian (2015); *Wearable Fitness Gadget Maker Fitbit Valued at More Than £2.5bn*. Available at: www.theguardian.com/business/2015/jun/18/wearable-fitness-gadgetmaker-fitbit-valued-at-more-than-25bn.
Guardian (2017); *Grenfell Tower: Fire-proof Cladding Specified by Architects Used Only on Ground Floor*, Guardian. Available at: https://www.theguardian.com/uk-news/2017/jul/06/grenfell-fire-proof-cladding-specified-by-architects-only-used-on-ground-floor
Guardian (2017a); *Britain Is Still A World-Beater At One Thing: Ripping Off Its Own Citizens*, Guardian. Available at: https://www.theguardian.com/commentisfree/2017/aug/03/britain-world-beater-ripping-off-citizens-rail-fares-water-energy-bills
Guardian (2018); *Yanny or Laurel: Why Do Some People Hear A Different Word?* Guardian. Available at: https://www.theguardian.com/technology/2018/may/16/yanny-or-laurel-sound-illusion-sets-off-ear-splitting-arguments
Hall, S., (1987); Minimal Selves, in (eds.), Bhabha, H., and Appignanesi, L., *Identity: The Real Me: Post-Modernism and the Question of Identity*, London: ICA (Institute of Contemporary Arts).
Hall, S., (2018); *Professor Stuart Hall and Isaac Julien*, Series 2, Unforgettable, BBC Radio 4.
Available at: https://www.bbc.co.uk/programmes/b0bclvxv
Hamlyn, D., (1977); Introduction, to *Aristotle's De Anima Books II, III*, Oxford, University Press: Oxford at the Clarendon Press.
—. (2002); *De Anima: Books II and III* (with Passages from Book I), Trans. Hamlyn, D., Clarendon Press: Oxford.
HM Treasury (2015); *Spending Review and Autumn Statement 2015, HM Treasury*. Available at: https://www.gov.uk/government/uploads/system/uploads/attachment_data/file/479749/52229_Blue_Book_PU1865_Web_Accessible.pdf
Hansard (1990); *Heliport (Cannon Street Station),* House of Commons Debate 24 May, 1990, Vol., 173 cc483-90. Available at: https://api.parliament.uk/historic-hansard/commons/1990/may/24/heliport-cannon-street-station

Hansard (1995); *Local Government*, Hansard, House of Commons, Commons Chamber, 30 June 1995, Volume 262. Available at: https://hansard.parliament.uk/Commons/1995-06-30/debates/01dbc686-7ffa-4803-bac4-60c6a3d11947/LocalGovernment?highlight=golliwog#contribution-139c7eba-c4aa-4968-af5d-a929105185db

Hansard (1999); *Trafalgar Square*, Hansard; HL deb 25 October 1999, Vol. 606 cc127-34. Available at: https://api.parliament.uk/historic-hansard/lords/1999/oct/25/trafalgar-square

Hansard (2017); Grenfell Tower, 22 June 2017, *House of Commons Hansard*, Vol. 626. Available at: https://hansard.parliament.uk/Commons/2017-06-22/debates/E4B84F46-4699-4725-BBE4-AA724C3A0191/GrenfellTower

@HansardSociety (2018); *Hansard Society*. Available at: https://twitter.com/hansardsociety?lang=en

Hansard Society (2011); *A Place for People, Proposals for Enhancing Visitor Engagement with Parliament's Environs*, Hansard Society. Available at: https://www.hansardsociety.org.uk/publications/a-place-for-people-proposals-for-enhancing-visitor-engagement-with-parliaments-environs

Harvey, D., (2005); *The Condition of Postmodernity. An Enquiry into the Origins of Cultural Change*, Oxford: Blackwell.

Hawking, S., (1995); *A Brief History of Time. From the Big Bang to Black Holes*, London: Bantam Books.

Hebdige, D., (1979/1988); *Subculture the Meaning of Style*, Oxon: Routledge.

Heraclitus (2003); *Heraclitus, Fragments*, London: Penguin.

Heyes, C., (2006); Foucault Goes to Weight Watchers, *Hypatia*, Vol. 21, No., 2, pp., 126—149.

Hillier, M., (2016); *Letter to Tom Scholar Permanent Secretary, HM Treasury From Meg Hillier MP (Chair of the Committee of Public Accounts), 14th December 2016*, Committee of Public Accounts. Available at: https://www.parliament.uk/documents/commons-committees/public-accounts/Correspondence/2015-20-Parliament/161214-Chair-to-Perm-Sec-HM-Treasury-re-Garden-Bridge.pdf

Hine, C., (2000); *Virtual Ethnography*, London: Sage.

Hodge, M., (2016); *Garden Bridge Review Meeting Transcript, Event: MH/ Joanna Lumley, 1st December 2016*. Present Dame Margaret Hodge MP, Joanna Lumley, Bee Emmott, Claire Hamilton. Published by GLA in response to an information request within the auspices of the Environmental Information Regulation (EIR). Available at:

https://www.london.gov.uk/sites/default/files/gb_transcript_-_joanna_lumley.pdf

Hodge, M., (2017); *The Garden Bridge*. Available at: https://www.london.gov.uk/sites/default/files/md2108_appendix_garden_bridge_review.pdf

Hodge, H., (2017a); *Independent Review of the Garden Bridge*, April 2017, London Assembly. Available at: https://www.london.gov.uk/independent-review-garden-bridge-project

Home Office (2018); *EU citizens and their families will need to apply to the EU Settlement Scheme to continue living in the UK after 31 December 2020*, @ukhomeoffice, 27 December 2018. Available at: https://twitter.com/ukhomeoffice/status/1078206349148708865

@ukhomeoffice (2018); *The Home Office is the Lead UK Government Department for Immigration and Passports*. Available at: https://twitter.com/ukhomeoffice

Hough, M., (2004); *Cities and Natural Process, a Basis for Sustainability*, Second Edition, London: Routledge.

Hough, D., (2017); *ECO, the Energy Company Obligation, Briefing Paper, Number CBP 06814, 29 March 2017*, House of Commons Library. Available at: researchbriefings.files.parliament.uk/documents/SN06814/SN06814.pdf

House of Commons (2017): *Fuel Poverty: Written Question – 64520*, Parliamentary Business, Publications and Records. Available at: http://www.parliament.uk/written-questions-answers-statements/written-question/commons/2017-02-20/64520

House of Lords (2014); *Revised Transcript of Evidence Taken Before The Select Committee on Economic Affairs Inquiry into High-Frequency Trading, Evidence Session No.1, Heard in Public, Questions 1-12, Tuesday 22 July 2014, 2:30pm, Witness: Brad Katsuyama*, House of Lords. Available at: https://www.parliament.uk/documents/lords-committees/economic-affairs/High-Frequency-Trading-and-Going-Concern/cEAC20140722Ev1.pdf

Huisman, F., (2015); *Health and Citizenship: Political Cultures of Health in Modern Europe*, Oxon: Routledge.

Independent (2017); *Canadian and Kuwaiti investors buy 26% stake in Thames Water*, Independent. Available at: https://www.independent.co.uk/news/business/news/canadian-and-kuwaiti-investors-buy-26-stake-in-thames-water-macquarie-a7630041.html

International Institute of Social Research (1934); *A Short Description of Its History and Aims*, International Institute of Social Research, American Branch: New York.

Intelligent Environments (2016); *World's First Internet of Things Bank Helps You Take Control of Your Finances and Kerb Overspending.* Intelligent Environments Digital Financial Solutions. Available at: http://www.intelligentenvironments.com/info-centre/press releases/world-s-first-internet-of-things-bank-helps-you-take-controlof-your-finances-and-kerb-overspending.

Inwood, B., and Gerson, L.P., (1994); *The Epicurus Reader. Selected Writings and Testimonia*, Cambridge: Hackett Publishing Company Inc.

Isin, E., and Wood, P., (1999); *Citizenship and Identity*, London: Sage.

iZettle (2018); *About Us*, iZettle. Available at: https://www.izettle.com/gb/about-us

iZettle (2018a); Tap, Insert or Swipe. Available at: https://www.izettle.com/gb/card-readers

iZettle (2018b); *About iZettle Cash Advance; My Advance Offer; Repayment.* Available at: https://www.izettle.com/gb/help/articles/2107029-izettle-cash-advance

@JackHardy9 (2017); *Here is the Letter Grenfell Tower Residents Received Telling Them About the Developing Investigation Concerning RBKC and KCTMO.* Available at: https://twitter.com/JackHardy9/status/890629625667362817

Jameson, F., (1995); *The Geopolitical Aesthetic. Cinema and Space in the World System*, Bloomington, Indiana/London: Indiana University Press/British Film Institute.

Johnson, B., (2018); *Denmark has got it wrong. Yes, the burka is oppressive and ridiculous – but that's still no reason to ban it*, The Telegraph News. Available at: https://www.telegraph.co.uk/news/2018/08/05/denmark-has-got-wrong-yes-burka-oppressive-ridiculous-still/

Johnson, B., and Halegoua, G., (2015); Can Social Media Save a Neighbourhood Organization? *Planning, Practice and Research*, Vol. 30, No. 3, pp. 248-269.

Johnson, S., and Todd, H., (1837); *A Dictionary Of The English Language In Which The Words Are Deduced From Their Originals*. London: Longman, Rees, Orme and Company.

Katz, D., (1989); *The World of Touch*, trans., Krueger, L., Lawrence Erlbaum Associates: Hillsdale, New Jersey.

KCCM (2014); *The Royal Borough of Kensington and Chelsea Cabinet Meeting – 19 June 2014. Report By The Director Of Housing Grenfell*

Tower Major Works And Hidden Homes Project, The Royal Borough of Kensington and Chelsea. Available at: https://www.rbkc.gov.uk/committees/Document.ashx?czJKcaeAi5tUF L1DTL2UE4zNRBcoShgo=

KCHPSC (2013); *Housing and Property Scrutiny Committee, 16th July 2013: An Update on Grenfell Tower Improvement Works and the Recent Power Surges*, The Royal Borough of Kensington and Chelsea Housing and Property Scrutiny Committee. Available at: https://grenfellactiongroup.files.wordpress.com/2017/06/a5-grenfell-tower-update.pdf

KCHPSC (2016); *Housing and Property Scrutiny Committee 11th May 2016; Grenfell Tower Report by the Director of Housing*, The Royal Borough of Kensington and Chelsea Housing and Property Scrutiny Committee. Available at: https://www.rbkc.gov.uk/committees/Document.ashx?czJKcaeAi5tUF L1DTL2UE4zNRBcoShgo=

KCTMO (2012); The Royal Borough of Kensington and Chelsea Tenant Management Organisation. Notes from Grenfell Tower Evening Meeting, 29th May 2012 at 19:00pm, in (ed.) Studio E., *Grenfell Tower Regeneration Project, Engagement Statement; Planning Application October 2012*, Kensington and Chelsea TMO. Available at: https://www.rbkc.gov.uk/idoxWAM/doc/Other960662.pdf?extension=.pdf&id=960662&location=VOLUME2&contentType=application/pdf&pageCount=1

KCTMO (2012a); The Royal Borough of Kensington and Chelsea Tenant Management Organisation. Notes from Meeting with Head of Grenfell Tower Nursery, 12th July 2012 at Lancaster West Estate Office, *Grenfell Tower Regeneration Project, Engagement Statement; Planning Application October 2012*, Kensington and Chelsea TMO. Available at: https://www.rbkc.gov.uk/idoxWAM/doc/Other960662.pdf?extension=.pdf&id=960662&location=VOLUME2&contentType=application/pdf&pageCount=1

KCTMO (2012b); The Royal Borough of Kensington and Chelsea Tenant Management Organisation. Appendix C Minutes/Notes from Pre-Planning Meeting 19th July 2012, *Grenfell Tower Regeneration Project, Engagement Statement; Planning Application October 2012*, Kensington and Chelsea TMO. Available at: https://www.rbkc.gov.uk/idoxWAM/doc/Other960662.pdf?extension=.pdf&id=960662&location=VOLUME2&contentType=application/pdf&pageCount=1

KCTMO (2012c); The Royal Borough of Kensington and Chelsea Tenant Management Organisation. Appendix C Minutes/Notes from Pre-Planning Meeting 19th July 2012, *Grenfell Tower Regeneration Project, Engagement Statement; Planning Application October 2012*, Kensington and Chelsea TMO. Available at: https://www.rbkc.gov.uk/idoxWAM/doc/Other-960662.pdf?extension=.pdf&id=960662&location=VOLUME2&contentType=application/pdf&pageCount=1

KCTMO (2013); *Grenfell Tower Regeneration: Feedback from the Last Residents' Meeting on 15 August 2013 was Circulated to all Households in a Meeting Report*. Kensington and Chelsea Tenant Management Organisation. Available at: http://www.kctmo.org.uk/files/102250_september_2013_grenfell_tower_newsletter.pdf

KCTMO (2013a); *Grenfell Tower Regeneration Newsletter, November 2013*, Kensington and Chelsea Tenant Management Organisation. Available at: http://www.kctmo.org.uk/files/102319_november_2013_grenfell_tower_newsletter.pdf

KCTMO (2014); *Grenfell Tower Regeneration Newsletter, April 2014, It's All Systems Go!* Kensington and Chelsea TMO. Available at: https://www.rbkc.gov.uk/pdf/Grenfell%20tower%20regeneration%20April%202014.pdf

KCTMO (2014a); *Grenfell Tower Regeneration Newsletter, October 2014: What's Been Happening?* Kensington and Chelsea Tenant Management Organisation. Available at: http://www.kctmo.org.uk/files/boardmeetings/092940_kctmo_rydon_grenfell_tower_newsletter_october_vff.pdf

KCTMO (2015); *Grenfell Tower Regeneration Newsletter, January 2015*. Kensington and Chelsea Tenant Management Organisation. Available at: http://www.kctmo.org.uk/files/boardmeetings/154724_vfff_grenfell_tower_regeneration_newsletter_january_2015.pdf

KCTMO (2015a); *Grenfell Tower Regeneration Newsletter, February 2015*. Available at: http://www.kctmo.org.uk/files/155737_kctmo_rydon_grenfell_tower_newsletter_february_vff.pdf

KCTMO (2017a); *Value for Money Strategy 2014-2017. Quality Working Together Integrity Innovation Commitment,* Kensington and Chelsea Tenant Management Organisation. Available at:

http://www.kctmo.org.uk/files/091723_value_for_money_strategy_20 14-17.pdf

Kensington and Chelsea (2014); *Town and Country Planning Act 1990, Town and County Planning (Development Management Procedure) Order 2010. Permission for Development (Conditional), Grenfell Tower*, Ref:/PP/12/04097, The Royal Borough of Kensington and Chelsea. Available at: https://www.rbkc.gov.uk/idoxWAM/doc/Decision1180274.pdf?extension=.pdf&id=1180274&location=Volume2&contentType=application/pdf&pageCount=1

Kensington and Chelsea Council (2017); *Council Leader Pledges Hundreds of New Social Housing Units and a Reformed Council "Changed Forever" by the Grenfell Fire*. The Royal Borough of Kensington and Chelsea. Available at: https://www.rbkc.gov.uk/press-release/council-leader-pledges-hundreds-new-social-housing-units-and-reformed-council-"changed

Khan, S., (2017); *Statement from the Mayor on the Closure of the Garden Bridge Trust*, Mayor of London, London Assembly. Available at: https://www.london.gov.uk/city-hall-blog/statement-mayor-closure-garden-bridge-trust

King James Bible (1991); *Holy Bible King James Version*, Edinburgh: Collins.

King, M, L., (2014); *The Autobiography of Martin Luther King, JR.*, (ed.) Carson, C., London: Abacus.

Kline, S., Dyer-Witheford, N., De-Reuter, G., (2003); *Digital Play: The Interaction of Technology Culture and Marketing*, Montreal: McGill-Queen's University Press.

Knights, D., and Odih, P., (1993); *Gender, Time and Financial Services Consumption*, Paper Presented at the Rethinking Marketing Conference, Warwick: University of Warwick.

Knights, D., and Odih, P., (1995); "It's About Time": The Significance of Gendered Time for Financial Services Consumption, *Time & Society*, June, 4, pp., 205-231.

Knights, D., and Odih, P., (1999); It's a Matter of Time: The Significance of the Women's Market in Consumption, in (eds.) Brownlie, D., Saren, M., Wensley, R., and Whittington, R., *Rethinking Marketing. Towards Critical Marketing Accountings*, London: Sage.

Kohn, M., (2004/2010); *Brave New Neighbourhoods*, Madison Ave: Routledge.

Kvale, S., and Brinkmann, S., (2009); *Interview, Learning the Craft of Qualitative Research Interviewing*, Second Edition, London: Sage.

Lambeth Council (2016); *Proposed Changes to the Lease hold by the Coin Street Community Builders Relating to Land on the South Bank.* Lambeth Council. Publication date: 16/03/2016. Available at: https://moderngov.lambeth.gov.uk/documents/s80244/Proposed%20ch anges%20to%20the%20lease%20held%20by%20the%20Coin%20Stre et%20Community%20Builders%20relating%20to%20land%20on%20t he%20Sou.pdf

Lambeth Planning, (2014); *Lambeth Planning Applications Committee, Case Number: 14/02792/FUL. Application: The Garden Bridge Trust, Address: London.* Available at: https://moderngov.lambeth.gov.uk/documents/s69725/06_garden%20b ridge%20PAC%20report.pdf

Latour, B., (2007); *Reassembling the Social. An Introduction to Actor-Network-Theory*, Oxford: Oxford University Press.

Lieberman, S., (2013-2014); *English Learner's Guide to Homophones and Heteronyms,* North Carolina: Lulu.

Lisvane, Lord, (2016); *European Communities Act 1972.* Interview on Week in Westminster, Radio 4, 9th July 2016. Interviewer Waugh, P., Available at: http://www.bbc.co.uk/programmes/b07jqm79

London Assembly (2012); *Gigs: Big Busk 2012*, London Assembly. Available at: https://www.london.gov.uk/what-we-do/arts-and-culture/ vision-and-strategy/gigs-big-busk-2012

London Assembly (2012a); *Hunt on for Musicians to Join London's Biggest Gigs Competition*, London Assembly. Available at: https://www.london.gov.uk/press-releases-4754

London Assembly (2012b); *Mayor of London Presents ... A Summer Like No Other!* London Assembly. Available at: https://www.london.gov.uk/press-releases-4743

London Assembly (2013): *London's Hottest New Music Talent to be Crowned Gigs Champion 2013*, London Assembly. Available at: https://www.london.gov.uk/press-releases-5779

London Assembly (2013a); *Mayor and Singer Misha B Launch Gigs 2013 Competition*, London Assembly. Available at: https://www.london.gov.uk/press-releases-5013

London Assembly (2014); *Young Musicians Hit Streets in Bid to be Crowned Busker of the Year*, Mayor of London, London Assembly. Available at: https://www.london.gov.uk/press-releases-6228

London Assembly (2014a); *Five Month Search Almost Over as 18 Acts Compete for Top Honours*, London Assembly. Available at: https://www.london.gov.uk/press-releases-6272

London Assembly (2014b); *Don't Let London Become a No Go Area for Buskers, Warns Mayor*, London Assembly. Available at: https://www.london.gov.uk/press-releases-6132

London Assembly (2015); *National Busking Day*, London Assembly. Available at: https://www.london.gov.uk/events/2015-07-18/national-busking-day

London Assembly (2015a); *National Busking Day*, Mayor of London, London Assembly. Available at: https://www.london.gov.uk/events/2015-07-18/national-busking-day

London Assembly (2015b); *MD1501 Busk in London*, Mayor of London, London Assembly. Available at: https://www.london.gov.uk/decisions/md1501-busk-london

London Assembly (2016*)*; *International Busking Day and Busk in London Festival*, London Assembly. Available at: https://www.london.gov.uk/events/2016-07-23/international-busking-day-and-busk-london-festival

London Assembly (2016a); *DD2045 London Music Board and Music Tourism*, London Assembly. Available at: https://www.london.gov.uk/decisions/dd2045-london-music-board-and-music-tourism-campaign

London Assembly (2016b); *MD1603 Creative Industries Investment and Culture Strategy Support*, London Assembly. Available at: https://www.london.gov.uk/decisions/md1603-creative-industries-investment-and-culture-strategy-support

London Assembly (2017); *Gigs- London's Biggest Busking Competition*, London Assembly. Available at: https://www.london.gov.uk/what-we-do/arts-and-culture/current-culture-projects/gigs-londons-biggest-busking-competition

London Assembly (2017a); *Busking Talent on the Road in Next Phase of Mayor's Gigs Competition*, Mayor of London, London Assembly. Available at: https://www.london.gov.uk/press-releases/mayoral/buskers-performing-on-london-buses-this-weekend

London Assembly (2017b); *MD2127 Night Time Economy and Music*, London Assembly. Available at: https://www.london.gov.uk/decisions/md2127-night-time-economy-and-music

London Assembly (2018); *Independent Review of the Garden Bridge Project*, London Assembly. Available at: https://www.london.gov.uk/independent-review-garden-bridge-project

London Assembly (2018a); *London Leads Global Busking Celebration with Festivals at Wembley Park*, London Assembly. Available at:

https://www.london.gov.uk/press-releases/mayoral/london-leads-busking-celebration-at-wembley-park

London Assembly (2018b); *Gigs – London's Biggest Busking Competition*, London Assembly. Available at: https://www.london.gov.uk/what-we-do/arts-and-culture/current-culture-projects/gigs-londons-biggest-busking-competition

London Assembly (2018c); *London's Streets Are Paved With Talent*, London Assembly. Available at: https://www.london.gov.uk/what-we-do/arts-and-culture/current-culture-projects/londons-streets-are-paved-talent

London Assembly (2018d); *News from Navin Shah: Wembley Park to Lead Celebrations for International Busking Day*, London Assembly. Available at: https://www.london.gov.uk/press-releases/assembly/navin-shah/wembley-park-to-host-international-busking-day

London Assembly (2018e); *DD2248 Busk in London and London Music Fund*, London Assembly. Available at: https://www.london.gov.uk/decisions/dd2248-busk-london-london-music-fund

London Assembly (2018f); *Mayor Announces Plans for St Patrick's Day Festival Across Entire City*, Mayor of London, London Assembly. Available at: https://www.london.gov.uk/press-releases/mayoral/biggest-st-patricks-festival-to-be-held-in-london

London Assembly (2019); *Mayor Announces London is Open for St Patrick's Day Celebrations*, Mayor of London, London Assembly. Available at: https://www.london.gov.uk/press-releases/mayoral/london-is-open-for-st-patricks-day-celebrations

Londoner's Diary, (2015); *A Feminist Watershed for Wolmar, Evening Standard*, Evening Standard Londoner's Diary, Thursday 23 July 2015. Available at: https://www.standard.co.uk/news/londoners-diary/londoners-diary-mark-carney-foists-keynes-into-george-osborne-s-life-10410613.html

Lourenço, M., (2005); *Between Two Worlds. The Distinct Nature and Contemporary Significance of University Museums and Collections in Europe*. Available at: http://webpages.fc.ul.pt/~mclourenco/

Lucretius, T., (2007); *The Nature of Things*. London: Penguin Books.

Lund, P., (2011); *Massively Networked. How the Convergence of Social Media and Technology is Changing Your Life*, San Francisco: PLI Media.

Lupton, D., (2014); *Self-Tracking Cultures: Towards A Sociology Of Personal Informatics*, Proceedings of the 26th Australian Computer-Human Interaction Conference: Designing Futures, the Future of Design. Available at: http://www.canberra.edu.au/researchrepository/items/89265416-5c81-4d4c-bed3-948c2d9a0734/1/

Mace, R., (1976/2005); *Trafalgar Square Emblem of Empire*, London: Lawrence and Wishart.

Macquarie (2017); *Macquarie Reaches Agreement to Sell Its Final Stake In Thames Water To Institutional Infrastructure Investors*. Available at: https://www.macquarie.com/uk/about/newsroom/2017/agreement-to-sell-final-stake-in-thames-water-to-institutional-infrastructure-investors/

Madison, D.S., (2011); *Critical Ethnography: Method, Ethics, and Performance*, Second Edition, London: Sage.

MailOnline (2018): *Stab Gang Who Posted Violent 'Drill' Music Videos on YouTube Six Days Before [redacted] ... Are Jailed for Life*, Duell, M., for Mailonline, Daily Mail, 5 September 2018. Available at: http://www.dailymail.co.uk/news/article-6133495/Stab-gangs-violent-drill-music-videos-online-begin-life-sentences.html

Marcuse, H., (1941/2002); Some Social Implications of Modern Technology, in Arato, A. and Gebhardt, E. (Eds) *The Essential Frankfurt School Reader,* New York: Continuum.

—. (1956/1998); *Eros and Civilization. A Philosophical Inquiry into Freud*, London: Routledge.

—. (1964); *One Dimensional Man. Studies in the Ideology of Advanced Industrial Society*, London: Routledge & Kegan Paul Ltd.

—. (1964/1986); *One-Dimensional Man. Studies in the Ideology of Advanced Industrial Society,* London: ARK Paperbacks/Routledge & Kegan Paul plc.

—. (1970); *Der eindimensionale Mensch,* Sammlung Luchterhand: Luchterhand Verlag.

Marshall, P., Krance, K., and Meloche, T., (2015); *Ultimate Guide to Facebook Advertising,* Irvine California: Entrepreneur Press.

Marshall (2018); *World Square, London. Marshall Transforming Britain's Landscape.* Available at: http://www.stonefed.org.uk/uploads/companydirectory/id192/pdf/world.pdf

Marx, K., (1835/1997); Reflections of a Youth on Choosing an Occupation, in (ed.) Easton, L., and Guddat, K., *Writings of the Young Marx on Philosophy and Society*, Cambridge: Hackett Publishing Company.

—. (1841/2006); Difference Between the Democritean and Epicurean Philosophy of Nature, in (ed.) Schafer, P., *The First Writings of Karl Marx*, Brooklyn, New York: Ig Publishing.

—. (1844/ 2007); *Economic and Philosophic Manuscripts of 1844*, New York: Dover.

—. (1857/1973); *Grundrisse; Foundations of the Critique of Political Economy* (Rough Draft), Translated with a Forward by Nicolaus, M., Middlesex: Penguin Books.

—. (1867/1887/2003); *Capital, Vol. 1: A Critical Analysis of Capitalist Production*, trans., Moore, S., and Aveling, E., Edited by Engels, F., London: Lawrence & Wishart.

—. (1885/1978); *Capital: A Critique Of Political Economy*, Vol., II; introduced by Ernest Mandel; translated by Fernbach, D., Harmondsworth: Penguin Books in association with New Left Review.

—. (1894/1981); *Capital, A Critique of Political Economy Volume Three*, Intro., Mandel, E., and trans., Fernbach, D., Middlesex: Penguin.

—. (1991); *Capital, A Critique of Political Economy Volume Three*, Intro. Mandel, E., and trans., Fernbach, D., London: Penguin.

—. (1991a); *Capital, A Critique of Political Economy Volume Three*, Intro., Mandel, E., and trans., Fernbach, D., Middlesex: Penguin.

Marx, K., and Engels, F., (1848/1970); *The Communist Manifesto*, Middlesex: Penguin Books.

Mason, R., and Sherwood, H., (2017); *Grenfell Tower Fire: May Accepts Tory-led Council Did Not Help Quickly Enough, Guardian, Wednesday 23rd August 2017*. Available at: https://www.theguardian.com/uk-news/2017/aug/23/grenfell-tower-fire-may-accepts-tory-led-council-did-not-help-quickly-enough

Mathiesen, T., (1997); The Viewer Society, Michel Foucault's 'Panopticon' Revisited, *Theoretical Criminology*, Vol. 1(2), pp., 215-234.

Mayor of London (2016); *A City for all Londoners*. Greater London Authority. Available at: https://www.london.gov.uk/sites/default/files/city_for_all_londoners_nov_2016.pdf

Mayor of London, London Assembly (2018); *Book Trafalgar Square*, Mayor of London, London Assembly. Available at: https://www.london.gov.uk/about-us/venue-hire/book-trafalgar-square

@MayorofLondon (2018); *Capital's Talented Street Performers Contactless Cards*. Available at: https://twitter.com/MayorofLondon/status/1000672963706966016

McCann, G., (2007); New Introduction, in Adorno, T., and Eisler, H., (1947/2007); *Composing for the Films*, London: Continuum.

McClelland, D., (1975); *Power: The Inner Experience*, New York: Irvington.

McFall, L., (2015); Is Digital Disruption the End of Health Insurance? Some Thoughts on the Devising of Risk. *Economic Sociology the European Electronic Newsletter*, Volume 17, Number 1, pp., 32- 44.

McLoughlin, P., (2016); *Garden Bridge Letter From The Secretary Of State For Transport,* Department for Transport. Available at: https://assets.publishing.service.gov.uk/government/uploads/system/uploads/attachment_data/file/558981/garden-bridge-letter-from-the-secretary-of-state-for-transport-to-the-dft-permanent-secretary.pdf

McLuhan, M., (1964); *Understanding Media; The Extensions of Man*, New York: McGraw-Hill Book Company: Routledge.

—. (1964/2004); *Understanding Media; The Extensions of Man*, London: Routledge.

Mellor, M., (1997); *Feminism and Ecology*, Oxford: Polity Press.

Merchant, C., (2005); *Radical Ecology. The Search for a Livable World*, Second Edition, New York and London: Routledge.

Metropolitan Police (2018); *Gang Sentenced in Shepherds Bush GBH and Violent Disorder*, Metropolitan Police News, Sep 14, 2018 14:27 BST. Available at: http://news.met.police.uk/news/gang-sentenced-in-shepherds-bush-gbh-and-violent-disorder-322172

Miller, V., (2005); *Consuming Religion: Christian Faith and Practice in a Consumer Religion*, London: Continuum.

Minogue, J., and Jones, M.G., (2006); Haptics in Education: Exploring an Untapped Sensory Modality, *Review of Educational Research*, Vol. 76, No., 3, pp., 317-348.

Mirror (2018); *[Redacted] Gang who Posted Violent 'Drill' music on YouTube before [redacted] ... are Jailed*, Mirror, 15:56, 5 September 2018. Available at: https://www.mirror.co.uk/news/uk-news/machete-gang-who-posted-violent-13197467

Mishler, E., (1991); *Research Interviewing, Context and Narrative*, Cambridge, MA: Harvard University Press.

Moore-Bick, M., (2017); *Chairman's Opening Statement, Grenfell Tower Inquiry*. Available at: https://www.grenfelltowerinquiry.org.uk/wp-content/uploads/2017/09/OPENING-STATEMENT-14-September-2017.pdf

Murray, P., and Stevens, M, A., (1996); *Living Bridges. The Inhabited Bridge, Past, Present and Future*, London: Royal Academy of Arts.

National Audit Office (2016); *Green Deal Energy Company Obligation, Report by the Comptroller and Auditor General, Department of Energy and Climate Change.* Available at: https://www.nao.org.uk/wp-content/uploads/2016/04/Green-Deal-and-Energy-Company-Obligation.pdf

National Gallery (2007); *The National Gallery and HP Bring Works of Art to the Streets of London,* Issued June 2007. Available at: https://www.nationalgallery.org.uk/about-us/press-and-media/press-releases/the-grand-tour

National Gallery (2007a); *The Grand Tour.* Available at: http://www.thegrandtour.org.uk

National Gallery (2014); *The Review of the Year April 2013 – March 2014 National Gallery,* London: National Gallery. Available at: https://www.nationalgallery.org.uk/media/16294/annual-review_2013-2014.pdf

National Gallery (2017); *The National Gallery Annual Report and accounts for the Year End 31 March 2017,* Presented to Parliament Pursuant to Section 9(8) of the Museums and Galleries Act 1992, Ordered by the House of Commons to be Printed 13 July 2017. Available at: https://assets.publishing.service.gov.uk/government/uploads/system/uploads/attachment_data/file/629007/59954_HC_144_Text_A4.pdf

National Institute for Health and Care Excellence (NICE) (2014); *Weight Management: Lifestyle Services for Overweight or Obese Adults. Public Health Guideline,* Published 28th May 2014. National Institute for Health and Care Excellence. Available at: https://www.nice.org.uk/guidance/ph53/resources/weightmanagement-lifestyle-services-for-overweight-or-obese-adults-1996416726469.

NEA (2017); *NEA Respond to the Mayor of London's "A City for All Londoners" Consultation.* National Energy Action. Available at: http://www.nea.org.uk/resources/publications-and-resources/nea-respond-mayor-londons-city-londoners-consultation/

Neate, R., (2016); Fitbit Stock Sinks After Company Warns Shareholders Over Profits, *The Guardian,* Tuesday 23rd February 2016. Available at: https://www.theguardian.com/business/2016/feb/22/fitbit-shares-fallafter-hours-profits?CMP=share_btn_link

Negri, A., (2003); *Time for Revolution.* London: Bloomsbury Academic, Imprint Bloomsbury Publishing PLC.

Netlytic (2015); *Netlytic Tutorials: Importing Data, Netlytic:Twitter* by Netlytic. Available at: https://www.youtube.com/watch?v=U4mLzxfAjTE&index=2&list=PL-jLxGsSNm3cVmV9SXoiAwfGaDIxDVpe-

—. (2015a); *Netlytic Network Analysis Part 1,* Published Nov 10, 2015. Available at: https://www.youtube.com/watch?v=uxT1EIyq4Gs

. (2015b); *Netlytic: Facebook.* Available at:

https://www.youtube.com/watch?v=JptSa3nX950
—. (2016); *Netlytic Making Sense of Online Conversations*. Available at: https://netlytic.org/home/
Nicholson, M., and Hoye, R., (2008); *Sport and Social Capital*, Oxford: Elsevier.
Nouveau Dictionnaire Classique de la Française (1875); *Nouveau Dictionnaire Classique De La Langue Française: Précédé D'un Tableau Complet De La Conjugaison Des Verbes Réguliers Et Irréguliers Etc.*
Available at: https://books.google.co.uk/books?id=BYgPAAAAYAAJ&dq=Nouveau+Dictionnaire+Classique+de+la+Française+(1875)&source=gbs_navlinks_s
Nowak, R., and Whelan, A., (2016); *Networked Music Cultures: Contemporary Approaches, Emerging Issues*, London: Palgrave Macmillan.
@OccupyCoscienza (2017); altor @OccupyCoscienza, Replying to @Telegraph @geraldi23591291. Available at: https://twitter.com/OccupyCoscienza/status/910192799802327041
Odih, P., (2007a); *Gender and Work in Capitalist Economies*, Maidenhead: Open University Press.
—. (2007b); *Advertising in Modern and Postmodern Times*, London: Sage.
—. (2010); *Advertising and Cultural Politics in Global Times*, Farnham: Ashgate.
—. (2013); *Visual Media and Culture of 'Occupy'*, Newcastle Upon Tyne: Cambridge Scholars Publishing.
—. (2014); *Watersheds in Marxist Ecofeminism*, Newcastle Upon Tyne: Cambridge Scholars Publishing.
—. (2016); *Adsensory Financialisation*, Newcastle Upon Tyne: Cambridge Scholars Publishing
—. (2016a); *Advertising and Cultural Politics in Global Times*, Oxon: Routledge.
Ofgem (2017); *Energy Suppliers*. Ofgem. Available at: https://www.ofgem.gov.uk/environmental-programmes/eco/energy-suppliers
Ofgem (2017a); *Energy Company Obligation 2017 – 18 (ECO2t) Guidance*: Delivery; 12th April 2017; Information Type: Guidance; Policy Areas: Environmental Programmes ECO., Ofgem. Available at: https://www.ofgem.gov.uk/publications-and-updates/energy-company-obligation-2017-18-eco2t-guidance-delivery

Ofgem (2018); *What is ECO?* Energy Company Obligation, Ofgem. Available at: https://www.ofgem.gov.uk/environmental-programmes/eco/about-eco-scheme

Ofwat (2017); *Holding Thames Water to Account – Utility Week Column by Johnson Cox, Chair of Ofwat.* Available at: https://www.ofwat.gov.uk/wp-content/uploads/2017/06/Holding-Thames-Water-to-account-Utility-Week-column-by-Jonson-Cox.pdf

Ofwat (2017a); *Ofwat Statement on Thames water Leakage Commitments.* Available at: https://www.ofwat.gov.uk/ofwat-statement-thames-water-leakage-commitments/

O'Neill, S., (2017); Grenfell Cladding Boss is a Government Adviser, *The Times*, Saturday July 1 2017, pp., 6.

Parliamentary Papers (1998); *Pedestrianisation of Parliament Square*, Early Day Motion 911; Parliamentary Papers; Session: 1997-1998; Date Tables: 05.03.1998. Available at: https://www.parliament.uk/edm/1997-98/911

Payment Systems Regulator (2018); *Contactless Mobile Payments, A PSR Report.* Available at: https://www.psr.org.uk/sites/default/files/media/PDF/Contactless_mobile_payments_July_2018.pdf

Pensions and Investments (2017); *Ontario Municipal Teams with Kuwait Investment Authority for Stake in Thames Water, Pensions and Investments.* Available at: https://www.pionline.com/article/20170315/ONLINE/170319933/ontario-municipal-teams-with-kuwait-investment-authority-for-stake-in-thames-water

People's Assembly Against Austerity (2019); *Open Letter from the People's Assembly Against Austerity*, People's Assembly Against Austerity. Available at: http://www.thepeoplesassembly.org.uk

6, Perri (1997); The New Politics of Welfare Contracting, in Perri 6 and Kendall, J., (eds.); *The Contract Culture in Public Services; Studies from Britain, Europe and the USA*, Arena Ashgate Publishing Limited: Aldershot Hants.

6, Perri and Kendall, J., (1997); *The Contract Culture in Public Services; Studies from Britain, Europe and the USA*, Arena Ashgate Publishing Limited: Aldershot Hants.

Pitman, I., (1837); *Stenographic Sound-Hand,* London: Samuel Bagster. Available at:

https://books.google.co.uk/books/reader?id=DkcEAAAAQAAJ&printsec=frontcover&output=reader&pg=GBS.PP7

Pitman, I., (1852); *Phonographic and Pronouncing Vocabulary of the English Language*, Second Edition, London: Fred. Pitman, Phonetic Depot, 20, Paternoster Row.

Pitman, I., (1853); *The Reporter's Companion: An Adaptation of Phonography, to Verbatim Reporting*, London: Fred. Pitman, Phonetic Depot, 20, Paternoster Row; Bath: Isaac Pitman, Phonetic Institution, 1, Albion Place.

Pitman, I., (1855); *A Manual of Phonography, or Writing by Sound: Method of Writing by Signs that Represent Spoken Sounds; Adapted to the English Language as a Complete System of Phonetic Shorthand*, London: Fred. Pitman, Phonetic Depot; Bath: Isaac Pitman, Phonetic Institution, Parsonage Lane.

Pitman, I., (1877); *The Phonographic Phrase Book*, London: F. Pitman, Phonetic Depot, Paternoster Row; Bath: Isaac Pitman, Phonetic Institute.

Planning Advisory Service, (2018); *S106 Obligations Overview*, Planning Advisory Service, Local Government Association. Available at: https://www.local.gov.uk/pas/pas-topics/infrastructure/s106-obligations-overview

Prime Minister's Office (2017); *Statement on Grenfell Tower: 14 June 2017*, Prime Minister's Office, 10 Downing Street. Available at: https://www.gov.uk/government/news/statement-on-grenfell-tower-14-june-2017

Public Accounts Committee [PAC] (2016); *Public Accounts Committee Submission to the Garden Bridge Project Review*, Public Accounts Committee, October 2016. Available at: https://www.parliament.uk/documents/commons-committees/public-accounts/written-evidence/2015-20-Parliament/pac-submission-garden-bridge-project-review-281016.pdf

Radio 4 Unforgettable (2018); *Professor Stuart Hall and Isaac Julien*, Radio 4 Unforgettable, Assistant Producer: Philippa Geering, Producer: Adam Fowler. Unforgettable: An Overtone production for BBC Radio 4. Available at: https://www.bbc.co.uk/programmes/b0bclvxv

RBKC (2012); *Report by Councillor Nicholas Paget-Brown, Cabinet Member for Transport, Environment and Leisure Current Issues, Public Realm Scrutiny Committee – 12 March 2012*, The Royal Borough of Kensington and Chelsea. Available at: https://www.rbkc.gov.uk/COMMITTEES/Document.ashx?czJKcaeAi5tUFL1DTL2UE4zNRBcoS

RBKC (2012a); *Energy Efficiency, Fuel Poverty and Environmental Health. Information and Advice for Private Sector Landlords*, Royal Borough of Kensington and Chelsea. Available at: https://www.rbkc.gov.uk/pdf/Energy%20efficiency%20landlords%20pack.pdf

RBKC (2012b); *Grenfell Tower Regeneration Project, Planning Application, October 2012, Design and Access Statement*. Available at: https://www.rbkc.gov.uk/idoxWAM/doc/Other-959901.pdf?extension=.pdf&id=959901&location=VOLUME2&contentType=application/pdf&pageCount=1

RBKC (2012c); *Grenfell Tower Regeneration Project, Planning Application, October 2012, Sustainability and Energy Statement*. Royal Borough of Kensington and Chelsea. Available at: https://www.rbkc.gov.uk/idoxWAM/doc/Other-952368.pdf?extension=.pdf&id=952368&location=VOLUME2&contentType=application/pdf&pageCount=1

RBKC (2012d); *Grenfell Tower Regeneration Project, Planning Application, August 2012, Sustainability and Energy Statement*, Royal Borough of Kensington and Chelsea, Kensington and Chelsea TMO. Available at: https://www.rbkc.gov.uk/idoxWAM/doc/Other-919218.pdf?extension=.pdf&id=919218&location=VOLUME2&contentType=application/pdf&pageCount=27

RBKC (2014); *Town and Country Planning Act 1990. Town and Country Planning (Development Management Procedure) Order 2010, Decision -1180274, Date: 10/01/2014*, The Royal Borough of Kensington and Chelsea. Available at: https://www.rbkc.gov.uk/idoxWAM/doc/Report-1180275.pdf?extension=.pdf&id=1180275&location=Volume2&contentType=application%2Fpdf&pageCount=1

RBKC (2014a); *Grenfell Tower Refurbishment Contract Agreed*, 09 April 2014, The Royal Borough of Kensington and Chelsea. Available at: https://www.rbkc.gov.uk/pressrelease/pressreleasePage.aspx?id=4714

RBKC (2016); *North Kensington Tower Block Transformed by £10m Refurbishment, 13 May 2016*, The Royal Borough of Kensington and Chelsea. Available at: https://www.rbkc.gov.uk/pressrelease/pressreleasePage.aspx?id=6994

RBKC (2017); *Notice of Meeting, The Royal Borough of Kensington and Chelsea, Council, Public Agenda,* Royal Borough of Kensington and Chelsea. Available at: https://www.rbkc.gov.uk/committees/Document.ashx

RBKC (2017a); *Royal Borough of Kensington and Chelsea, Council Meeting – 19 July 2017, Petition in Respect of the Cabinet, Grenfell Tower and Regeneration*, Royal Borough of Kensington and Chelsea. Available at: https://www.rbkc.gov.uk/committees/Document.ashx

RBKC (2017b); *Royal Borough of Kensington and Chelsea, Notice of Meeting, Council Public Agenda – 27 September 2017 at 6.30pm*, Royal Borough of Kensington and Chelsea. Available at: https://www.rbkc.gov.uk/sites/default/files/atoms/files/Council%20Meeting%20Public%20Agenda%20%28Wednesday%2027%20September%202017%29_1.pdf

RBKC (2017c); *Council Meeting Webcasts: Council Meeting: Wednesday 27 September 2017*, Royal Borough of Kensington and Chelsea. Available at: https://www.rbkc.gov.uk/council-and-democracy/council-meeting-webcasts

RBKC (2017d); *KCTMO and Council Working Together to Secure Orderly Transition*, Royal Borough of Kensington and Chelsea. Available at: https://www.rbkc.gov.uk/newsroom/all-council-statements/kctmo-and-council-working-together-secure-orderly-transition

RBKC (2018); *Declaration of results of poll; Election of a Member of Parliament for Kensington on Thursday 8 June 2017*, UK Parliamentary General Election 2017 The Result, The Royal Borough of Kensington and Chelsea. Available at: https://www.rbkc.gov.uk/council-and-democracy/local-democracy-and-elections/uk-parliamentary-general-election-2017-result

Reuters (2017); *Canadian, Kuwaiti Investors Take Stake In UK's Thames Water,* Reuters. Available at: https://www.reuters.com/article/us-britain-m-a-thames/canadian-kuwaiti-investors-take-stake-in-uks-thames-water-idUSKBN16L0W3

Richmond, P., Mimkes, J., and Hutzler. S., (2013); *Econophysics and Physical Economics*, Oxford: Oxford University Press.

Rist, M., (1972); *Epicurus. An Introduction*, London: Cambridge at the University Press.

Robinson, M., (2017); *Macquarie: The Tale of the River Bank*, BBC Radio 4. Available at: https://www.bbc.co.uk/programmes/b0931hl5

@RoseEGillott (2018); *@jennydavidmusic Hi guys! I'm messaging from James Whale's show on talkRadio. James loves your music and we'd love to get you on the show. What's the best way to contact you? Rosie*, Twitter. Available at: https://twitter.com/RoseEGillott/status/1019211299883028480

Royal Borough of Kensington and Chelsea (2015); *Planning and Borough Development, Strategic Developments Service Standard: 28/04/2015,* The Royal Borough of Kensington and Chelsea. Available at: https://www.rbkc.gov.uk/idoxWAM/doc/Decision-1454972.pdf?extension=.pdf&id=1454972&location=VOLUME2&contentType=application/pdf&pageCount=1

Rydon, (2016/2017); *Rydon Lands Grenfell Tower Refurbishment.* July 2016, Rydon. Available at: http://www.rydon.co.uk/news/rydon-lands-grenfell-tower-refurbishment-

Rydon Construction (2017); *Rydon, Local Authority Partnerships.* Available at: http://www.rydon.co.uk/?q=Grenfell+Tower

Rydon Construction (2017a); *Rydon, Refurbishment Case Studies, Grenfell Tower.* Rydon Maintenance. Available at: http://archive.li/PKkH3

Rydon (2017b); *Sustainable Development Environment.* Rydon. Available at: http://www.rydon.co.uk/sustainable-development/environment

Salleh, A., (1991); Eco-Socialism/Eco-Feminism, *Capitalism, Nature, Socialism,* Vol. 2(1):129–37.

—. (1995); Nature, Woman, Labour, Capital: Living the Deepest Contradiction, *Capitalism, Nature, Socialism,* Vol. 6, No., 1, pp., 21–39.

—. (2001); Sustaining Marx or Sustaining Nature?. An Ecofeminist Response to Foster and Burkett, *Organization and Environment,* 14(4): 443–50.

—. (2003); Ecofeminism as Sociology, Feminism and Ecology, *Capitalism, Nature, Socialism,* 14(1): 61–74.

—. (2005); Moving to an Embodied Materialism, *Capitalism, Nature, Socialism,* 16(2): 9–14.

—. (2006); Embodying the Deepest Contradiction: A Rejoinder to Alan Rudy, *Capitalism Nature Socialism,* Vol. 17, Number 14, pp., 115- 124.

—. (2009); Ecological Debt: Embodied Debt, in Salleh, A., (ed.) *Eco-sufficiency and Global Justice, Women Write Political Ecology,* London and North Melbourne Vic: Pluto Press and Spinifex Press.

—. (2010); From Metabolic Rift to 'Metabolic Value': Reflections on Environmental Sociology and the Alternative Globalization Movement, *Organization and Environment,* 23(2): 205–19.

—. (2014); Forward, in (eds) Mies, M., and Vandana S., *Ecofeminism,* London: Zed Books.

Salleh, A., and O'Connor, M., (1991); Eco-socialism/Eco-feminism, *Capitalism Nature Socialism,* Vol., 2, Issue 1, pp., 129-137

Sanders, J., (2007); *Shakespeare and Music. Afterlives and Borrowings,* Cambridge: Polity Press.

Savoiu, G., (2013); *Econophysics. Background and Applications in Economics, Finance, and Sociophysics*, Elsevier: London.

Sawyer, M., (2017); *The Week in Radio: Macquarie: The Tale of the River Bank; Hey, It's OK ...; The Red*, The Observer, Sunday, 10th September 2017. Available at: https://www.theguardian.com/tv-and-radio/2017/sep/10/macquarie-tale-river-bank-hey-its-ok-glamour-red-marcus-brigstocke-review

SBEG (2018); *25 Years of Success Improving London's South Bank*. Available at: http://sbeg.co.uk

Scheerhorn, D., (1997); Creating Illness-Related Communities in Cyberspace, in (eds.) Harris, L., *Health and the New Media Technologies Transforming Personal and Public Health*, New Jersey: Lawrence Erlbaum Associates.

Schumacher, T., (2010); Façadism Returns, or the Advent of the "Duckorated Shed", *Journal of Architectural Education*, Vol. 63:2, pp., 128-137.

SensorInsight (2018); *People and Crowd Monitoring. Cell Phone and Video Analytics*. Available at: http://sensorinsight.io/people-and-crowd-monitoring/

Sheridan, A., (1994); *Michel Foucault the Will to Truth*, London: Routledge.

Siisiäninen, L., (2013); *Foucault and the Politics of Hearing*, London: Routledge.

Simon, R.I, and Dippo, D., (1986); On Critical Ethnographic Work, *Anthropology and Education Quarterly*, Vol. 17, issue, 4., pp., 195- 202.

Simons, J., (2005); *Public Realm in London: An Overview*, Sister City Program Public Art Summit White Papers, February 17-18, The Sister City Program of the City of New York. Available at: http://www.nyc.gov/html/ia/gp/downloads/pdf/art_london.pdf

Simun, M., (2009); My Music, My World: Using the MP3 Player to Shape Experience in London, *New Media and Society*, Vol. 11, Issue 6, pp., 921-941.

Sky News (2017); *"You've let the Dead Down, Now You Want to Come for the Living?" Grenfell Tower Victims Call for Council Leader to Stand Down*, Sky News – 19th July 2017, @SkyNews. Available at: https://twitter.com/SkyNews/status/887754202260193280

Sky News (2018); *Grenfell Insulation Passed Fire Safety Tests After Being Covered in Boarding*, Sky News, Thursday 14 June 2018, 09.57 UK. Available at: https://news.sky.com/story/grenfell-cladding-passed-fire-safety-tests-after-being-covered-in-boarding-11403887

St Paul's Cathedral (2017); *St Paul's to Host Grenfell Tower Memorial Service Six Months On. St Paul's Cathedral.* Available at: https://www.stpauls.co.uk/search-results/Grenfell

Strauss, A., and Corbin, J., (1990); *Basics of Qualitative Research; Grounded Theory Procedures and Techniques*, London: Sage.

@stevethesmiths (2017); Let's Hope They Get the Justice they deserve. #JusticeForGrenfell. Available at: https://twitter.com/stevethesmiths/status/914444425341882368

Swiss Re (2015); *Sigma. Life Insurance in the Digital Age: Fundamental Transformation Ahead.* Swiss Re Ltd, Economic Research & Consulting. Available at: www.biztositasiszemle.hu/files/201512/sigma6_2015_en.pdf

Symonds, T., and De Simone, D., (2017); *Grenfell Tower: Cladding 'Changed to Cheaper Version'*, BBC News. Available at: http://www.bbc.co.uk/news/uk-40453054

@TanyaGKasim (2018); Oct 1 [2018] Replying to @geraldi23591291 @dimbleby_jd "Wasn't he Prince Charles' biographer?". Available at: https://twitter.com/TanyaGKasim/status/1046736000461021184

Tesco, (2010); *The Bath Press. Statement of Community Involvement. Mixed-use Redevelopment. Submitted on Behalf of St James's Investments Limited and Tesco UK Stores Limited*, London: Terence O'Rourke Ltd.

@Telegraph (2017); *The public inquiry into the Grenfell Tower fire has descended into chaos on day one after its chairman snubbed a lawyer representing victims,* @Telegraph. Available at: https://twitter.com/Telegraph/status/908303074707439619

@THEJamesWhale (2108); *Love this Music*. Available at: https://twitter.com/THEJamesWhale/status/1018859579537612801

TfL (2014); *The Garden Bridge, Summary of the Strategic Outline Business Case*, May 2014, Transport for London [TfL]. Available at: https://www.london.gov.uk/sites/default/files/gla_migrate_files_destination/MD1355%20Appendix%20B%20-%20Summary%20of%20Garden%20Bridge%20Business%20Case_0.pdf

TfL (2016); *Commercial in Confidence, Draft Operations and Maintenance Business Plan, March 2016, version 11, 30.03.15*, Transport for London (TfL). Available at: http://content.tfl.gov.uk/garden-bridge-business-plan-march-2016.pdf

TfL (2016a); *Mike Brown MVO Responses to Dame Margaret Hodge MP Review*, Transport for London. Available at: http://content.tfl.gov.uk/mike-brown-margaret-hodge-correspondence-

and-info-30092016-part1.pdf

TFL (2019); *Transport for London Publishes Detailed Final Cost of the Undelivered Garden Bridge Project*, Transport for London. Available at: https://tfl.gov.uk/info-for/media/press-releases/2019/february/transport-for-london-publishes-detailed-final-cost-of-the-undelivered-garden-bridge-project

Thames Water (2017); *Our History*, Thames Water. Available at: https://corporate.thameswater.co.uk/about-us/our-business/our-history

This is Money (2017); *Thames Water's foreign owners rinsing millions in dividends despite firm not paying corporation tax and being hit by fines*, This is Money. Available at: https://www.thisismoney.co.uk/money/markets/article-4604506/Thames-Water-s-foreign-owners-rinsing-dividends.html

Thomas, J., (1993); *Doing Critical Ethnography*, Volume 26 of Qualitative Research Methods, London: Sage.

Thomson, B., (2000); *Impressionism, Origins, Practice, Reception*, London: Thames & Hudson World of Art.

Tonks, A., Lyons, A., and Goodwin, I., (2015); Researching Online Visual Displays on Social Networking Sites: Methodologies and Meanings, *Qualitative Research in Psychology*, Vol. 12, pp., 326-339.

Trafalgar Square Byelaws (2012); *Greater London Authority, Trafalgar Square Byelaws 2012*. Greater London Authority Act 1999, Section 385(1), (2) and (4) Local Government Act 1972, Section 236B. Available at: https://www.london.gov.uk/sites/default/files/trafalgar_square_byelaws.pdf

Transport for London (2019); *Transport for London Publishes Detailed Final Cost of the Undelivered Garden Bridge Project*, Transport for London. Available at: https://tfl.gov.uk/info-for/media/press-releases/2019/february/transport-for-london-publishes-detailed-final-cost-of-the-undelivered-garden-bridge-project

Triple D, (2018); *Professional 3D Rendering, High Quality CGIs*, Triple D Illustrations. Available at: https://www.studiotripled.com/?campaign=1486634306&content=284451541089&keyword=%2Barchitecture%20%2Bvirtual&gclid=CjwKCAjwtIXbBRBhEiwAWV-5nhiNPLtndfl_8GrNwvzbSehhUcd9bL-o3GuGktbk7FRXiyyBFGHp7hoC6I4QAvD_BwE

Tricoglus, G., (2001); Living the Theoretical Principles of "Critical Ethnography" in Educational Research, *Educational Action Research*,

Vol., 9, Issue, 1, pp., 135-148.
Twain, M., and Warner, C., (1874/2005); *The Gilded Age, a Tale of To-Day*, Harvard College Library.
Twitter (2018a); *How to like a Tweet or Moment*, Twitter. Available at: https://help.twitter.com/en/using-twitter/liking-tweets-and-moments
Twitter (2018b); *Retweet FAQs; What is a Retweet?* Twitter. Available at: https://help.twitter.com/en/using-twitter/retweet-faqs
Twitter (2018c); *How To View Video Analytics In Media Studio*, Twitter. Available at: https://help.twitter.com/en/using-twitter/media-studio-analytics
Vahl, A., Haydon, J., and Zimmerman, J., (2014); *Facebook Marketing All-in-One For Dummies*, New Jersey: John Wiley & Sons.
Van Dijck, J., (2013); *The Culture of Connectivity: A Critical History of Social Media*, New York: Oxford University Press.
Van Hoyweghen, I., (2007); *Risks in the Making. Travels in Life Insurance and Genetics*. Amsterdam: Amsterdam University Press.
Van Maanen, J., (1988); *Tales of the Field, on Writing Ethnography*, Chicago and London: The University of Chicago Press.
Venturi, R., Scott Brown, D., and Izenour, S., (1977); *Learning from Las Vegas: The Forgotten Symbolism of Architectural Form*, Cambridge, Massachusetts and London: MIT Press.
Vercellone, C., (2010); The Crisis of the Law of Value and the Becoming-Rent of Profit, in (eds.) Fumagalli, A., and Mezzadra, S., *Crisis in the global economy: Financial Markets, Social Struggles, and New Political Scenarios*, Cambridge Mass: Semiotext(e), The MIT Press.
Urry, J., (1990); *Tourist Gaze: Leisure and Travel in Contemporary Societies*, London: Sage.
—. (2008); Speeding Up and Slowing Down, in (ed) H., Rosa, and Scheuerman, W., *High-Speed Society*, Pennsylvania: The Pennsylvania State University Press.
—. (2009); Speeding Up and Slowing Down, in (eds) Rosa, H., and Scheverman, W., *High-speed Social Acceleration, Power and Modernity*, Pennsylvania: The Pennsylvania State University Press.
—. (2010); Consuming the Planet to Excess, *Theory Culture and Society*, Vol., 27, Issue 2-3, pp., 191-212.
Wacquant, L., (1993); From Ruling Class to Field of Power: An Interview with Pierre Bourdieu on La Noblesse d'Etat, *Theory, Culture and Society*, Vol., 10, No., 3., pp., 19-44.
Walker, P., (2015); *London Garden Bridge Users to Have Mobile Phone Signals Tracked*, Guardian, Friday 6th November 2015:18:30 GMT. Available at: https://www.theguardian.com/uk-news/2015/nov/06/

garden-bridge-mobile-phone-signals-tracking-london

Walsh, K., (1995); *Public services and Market Mechanisms. Competition, Contracting and the New Public Management*, Basingstoke, Hampshire: Macmillan.

Webster (2005); *Webster II New College Dictionary*, Boston: Houghton Mifflin Company.

Wentworth De Witt, N., (1976); *Epicurus and His Philosophy*. Westport: Greenwood.

West, P., and Carrier, J., (2004); Ecotourism and Authenticity. Getting Away from It All? *Current Anthropology,* Volume 45, Number 4, August-October pp., 483-498.

Which (2017); *Home Grants Energy Company Obligation (ECO)*. Available at: http://www.which.co.uk/reviews/home-grants/article/home-grants/energy-company-obligation-eco

White, N., and Delichatsios, M., (2015); *Fire Hazards of Exterior Wall Assemblies Containing Combustible Components*, London: Springer.

Yearsley, A., (1787); *Poems on Various Subjects*, British Library, Historical Print Editions.

—. (1796); *The Rural Lyre; a Volume of Poems*, British Library, Historical Print Editions.

—. (1795); *The Royal Captives: a Fragment of Secret History*, Vol. 1 and 2, Philadelphia: Robert Campbell. Reproduced by, Gale ECCO Print Editions.

Yin, R., (2009); *Case Study Research, Design and Methods*, London: Sage.

INDEX

Figure i.1.: "Serving as a bridge between two intense imaginative states" (John Berger, *Ways of Seeing,* 1972). Photographic Image, Vicinity of Grenfell Tower; Lancaster West Estate, North Kensington, London, June 2017.

A

Accumulation,
adsensory capital: xxxix; xl; xlvii; 4; 5; 10; 11;12;13; 131; 139; 155; 157; 161; 172; 173; 175; 177; 181; 183;
capitalising body: 185; 187; 189; 191; 195; 197; 199; 201; 205; 207; 209; 211; 213; 215; 216; 217; 219; 221; 223; 225; 227; 229; 231; 287; 300; 301.
capitalism: xxxviii; xxxix; xl; 5; 11; 12; 13; 127; 201; 202; 203; 205; 207; 223; 224; 227; 301;
Adsensory,
aleatory materialism: 11.
Aestheticisation of Urban Ecology,
regeneration: 9; 11; 13; 15; 17; 23; 88; 118;
Architectural Visualisation,
2D Architectural drawings: 9.
360-degree panoramic: 9.
3D rendering: 9; 12.
3D virtual reality: 9; 12.
architectural programs: 9.
photo-realist simulacra: 9.
sensory kinetic: 9
Triple D: 9; 10.
urban ecology: xxxi; 149; 151; 152; 153; 155; 156; 157; 158; 180.

B

Bath Press Site,
regeneration: 301; 362
Baudrillard, Jean,
System of Objects (1968): 67; 101; 102; 104; 212.
Bell, Daniel,
codification of knowledge: xl; 3; 5; 10; 11; 22.
Biosensors,
actuarial calculation: 208; 209; 212; 215; 216; 219.
monitoring body: 55' 211; 215; 219; 228.
Biotechnology,
wearable fitness technology:
Body,
biotechnology: xxxix; xl; 3; 5; 9; 11; 12; 13; 127; 135; 178; 180; 181; 205; 207; 211; 215; 219; 228; 233; 241; 269; 270; 277; 283; 300; 301.
capitalist production: 205; 207; 211; 215; 277; 283; 300; 301.
consumer capitalism: xxxix; xl; 3; 5; 9; 11; 12; 13; 127; 135; 178; 180.

C

Callon, Michel,
actor network theory: 125; 126.
Capital,
cultural capital: 12; 13; 176; 187; 195; 202; 272; 273; 277.
health capital: xxxix; xl; 11; 193; 207; 209; 215; 301.
immaterial capital: 12; 223.
social capital: xxxix; xlvii; 2; 10; 11; 12; 104; 139; 157; 199; 201; 204; 209; 211; 215; 255; 256; 264; 273; 277; 300.
Capital circulation,
capitalist accumulation: 11; 12; 201; 202; 203; 205; 207; 223; 224; 301.
Castells, Manuel,
network society: xl; 11; 270.
Cladding, Grenfell Tower,
aesthetics: vii; xxiii; 3; 22; 23; 24; 25; 26; 27; 28; 29; 31; 34; 35; 41.
Grenfell Tower Refurbishment: vii; xxiii; 3; 22; 23; 24; 25; 26; 27; 28; 29; 31; 34; 35; 41; 42; 51; 53; 54; 56; 55; 57- 81; 85-107; 109- 113; 116; 117; 118; 119; 120; 121; 122; 123; 126; 143;

144; 147; 148; 152; 153; 155;
156; 299; 300; 303; 304; 320;
325; 326; 327; 337; 346.
political economy of the sign: 117;
118; 119; 120; 121; 122; 123;
126; 143; 144; 147; 148; 152;
153; 155; 156; 299; 300; 303;
304; 320; 325; 326; 327; 337;
346.
Codification, Knowledge,
Bell, Daniel: xl; 3; 5; 10; 11; 22;
299; 301.
Critical Discourse Analysis,
discourse: 279.
paradigmatic: 29; 61; 123; 196; 209;
269; 279 -280.
semiosis: 61; 150; 152.
syntagmatic: 61.
Cum Ferre (c.f.),
Together bring (compare and
contrast): 95.

D

Disciplinary space and time,
    advertising inscriptive:
advertising. 5; 9; 11;12;13;67; 74;
102; 103; 105; 143; 144; 153;
179; 180; 195; 205; 215; 216;
217; 284; 301.
ethico-synoptics: xl.
hyper-rationalist: 213.
linear causality model: 213.
linear time: 95; 210; 211; 213; 214;
215; 217; 259.
modern governance: 3; 210; 280;
286.
objectification: 211; 279.
objectifying positivistic: 2.
panopticon: 213.
social time: 208-216.
subjectification: 208-216.
technologies, sign: 2; 3; 5; 9; 10; 11;
12; 81; 180; 207; 209; 210; 212;
213; 214; 217; 218; 219; 230;
277; 280; 282; 283; 284; 301.

E

ECO Brokerage,
flexible eligibility: 129; 134; 135;
136; 145.
government procurement service:
129; 134; 135; 136; 145.
reduce carbon emissions: 129; 134;
135; 136; 145.
ECO Obligated Supplier,
government procurement service:
128; 129; 133; 134; 136.
Elements,
technological rationality: 256.
Embodied labour time,
feminine time: 95; 261; 270; 271;
281.
gendered time: xxxix; 95; 260; 261;
274.
masculine time: 95; 271.
temporal clashes: 214; 217; 307.
Embodied time,
embodied labour: 10; 247; 277.
embodiment: xlii; 257; 258; 259;
262.
labour: 10; 13; 56; 61; 95; 100; 157;
177; 247; 257; 258; 259; 264;
265; 267; 268; 272; 301.
**Energy Company Obligation
(ECO),**
eco-funding: 36; 118; 128; 129;
130; 131; 132; 133; 134; 135;
136; 137; 138; 139; 140; 143;
144; 145; 160; 237.
energy efficiency: 3; 23; 117; 12;
123; 124; 125; 126; 127; 128;
129; 130; 131; 132; 133; 134;
135; 136; 137; 138; 139; 140;
141; 142; 143; 144; 145; 146;
147; 299.
Grenfell Tower eco-funding: 36;
118; 128; 131; 133; 134; 143;
152; 160.
Ofgem: 128; 133; 134; 135; 138;
137.

Energy Efficiency Measures (EEM),
eligibility, ECO: 124; 128; 129; 130; 131; 133; 134; 135; 136; 138; 139; 140; 141; 145.
energy suppliers funding: 124; 128; 129; 130; 131; 133; 134; 135; 136; 138; 139; 140; 141; 145.
Enterprise,
enterprise culture: 197; 200.
human capital: 197; 200.
neoliberalism: 197; 200.
Entrepreneurial self,
consumer citizenship: xl; 74.
neoliberal healthcare: xl.
Ethics of Care,
ecofeminism: 251-296.
Ethics of Justice,
ecofeminism: 251-296.
Ethico-synoptics,
bio-politics: xl.
healthcare citizenship: xl.
synoptics: xl.
Ethnographic Offline Methodology,
ethnography: xl; xii; xliii; xlvi; 5; 13; 301.
naturalism: xlii.

F

Feigning,
non-existent signs: 12; 13; 81.
simulation: 12; 13; 81; 100.
third-order simulacra: 12; 13; 81.
Financialisation,
interest bearing capital: vii; xxxviii; xl; xlvii; 4; 11; 13; 81; 171; 172-221; 255; 285; 287; 288; 290; 291.
Foucault, Michel,
Discipline and Punish: 2; 209; 210; 211; 213; 218.
technologies of power: xxxviii; 2; 210; 283.
technologies of production: 2; 209; 282; 283; 284.
technologies of the self: xxxviii; 2; 209; 211; 283.
technologies of the sign: xxxviii; xl; 2; 10; 100; 218; 283; 301.
temporality, disciplinary technology: 217.
Foucault, M.: *Of Other Spaces*:
coded elements: 10; 283.
codified classification: 10.
grid properties: 10.
linear perspectivism: 10.
other space: 10; 274.
perspectivist cartography: 10.
perspectivist nomenclature: 10.
proximity: xlv; 10; 40; 94; 116; 117.
space of emplacement: 10.
the site: 10; 34; 55; 153.

G

Garden Bridge, Activism,
@TCOSLondon: xxxii.
architectural community: xxx; xxxi; xxxii; 148.
architecturally political person: xxxi.
conservation, Thames: xivl; 197; 279; 284; 285; 286.
conservation, trees: 10; 175; 203; 234; 238; 247; 248; 252; 265; 275.
local Nimbys: xxxii.
politics architecture: xxxi.
society, culture architecture: xxxi.
Thames Central Open Spaces (TCOS): xxxii; xlvi; 232; 248; 285.
Garden Bridge, Architecture Activism,
@follyforlondon: xxx.
abridgetoofar.co.uk: xxx.
Will Hurst: xxxii.
Garden Bridge, Bridge Too Far,
abridgetoofar.co.uk: xxx.
spoof architectural competition:

xxxi.
Garden Bridge, Case Study,
architecture activism: xxxii; xlvi.
observation, South Bank, Thames: 225.
water ecology activism: 232; 288; 290.
Garden Bridge Ethics,
celebrity ecofeminism: 255-257; 264; 265.
ethic of care: 260; 261; 264; 265; 266; 268; 269; 270; 271; 272.
ethic of justice: 265; 267; 268; 271.
ethics of care, justice: 265; 267; 268; 271.
gendered time: xxxix; 260; 261.
Garden Bridge, Folly for London,
@follyforlondon: xxx.
architecture activism: xxxii.
Garden Bridge, Greenwash,
activist challenge: xxx.
Garden Bridge Trust: xxxii; 4; 173; 178; 179; 184; 186; 187; 189; 190; 197; 198; 199; 200; 201; 204; 207; 208; 209; 211; 215; 216; 217; 219; 225; 227; 228; 229; 230; 233; 234; 235; 236; 238; 239; 241; 242; 243; 244; 245; 254; 287; 300.
greenwash: 237; 238; 239.
recreational space: 177; 179; 199; 201; 219; 232.
Garden Bridge, Privatisation Space,
privatisation recreational space: 4; 173; 177; 199; 201; 230; 232; 277; 301.
Garden Bridge, Reclamation,
gentrification: 172-221; 222-250.
Gendered Time,
discursive basis: xxxix; 260; 261.
Gentrification, Post-industrial,
urban spaces: xl; xliii; 5; 10; 11; 13; 117; 205.
Governmental Rationalities,
insurantial technologies: 215; 217.

Grenfell Tower, Building Maintenance,
Lancaster West Estate: 88; 94; 115; 144; 147; 148; 161; 162; 163; 164; 165; 166; 167; 168; 169; 308; 319.
Grenfell Tower, Cladding,
aluminium cladding: 25; 26; 28; 30; 86; 116; 155; 158; 320.
BR 135: 25; 88.
building design: 25; 26; 28; 30; 86; 116; 155; 158; 320.
Celotex product (RS5000): 24; 25; 26; 30; 52; 337; 338.
Celotex Saint-Gobain: 25; 26; 327; 328.
Celotex: 24; 25; 28; 30; 52; 53; 54; 119; 120; 121.
cladding systems: 22; 24; 25; 30; 337.
corporate social responsibility: 25; 53; 199.
façade cladding: 20-50; 51-114; 115-170.
fire-retardant: 27.
glass reinforced concrete: 30.
insulated rainscreen: 25.
PIR insulation board: 25.
planning submission: 28.
procurement: 4; 30; 35; 55; 77; 78; 79; 93; 102; 103; 119; 120; 136; 158; 159.
Reynolux: 30.
Reyonbond: 30.
Reyondbond/reynolux: 30.
RS5000 fire resistance: 25.
Saint-Gobain: 25; 26; 337; 338.
Smoke Silver Metallic (colour No. E9107S): 30; 31.
zinc cladding: 28; 27; 28; 29; 30.
Grenfell Tower, Commemoration,
building, commemoration: 298-300.
building memorial: 297; 298; 299; 302; 328; 329; 330; 331.
Grenfell Tower, ECO,
Ofgem, administration: 128; 133;

134; 135; 138; 137.
Grenfell Tower ECO Funding,
carbon emissions: 118; 128; 129; 130; 131; 133; 143; 145.
energy company obligation (ECO): 118; 128129; 130; 131; 133; 134; 135; 136; 137; 139; 141; 144.
energy efficiency measures: 124; 128; 129; 130; 131; 133; 134; 135; 136; 138; 139; 140; 141; 145.
energy efficiency scheme: 122; 124; 128; 129; 130; 131; 133; 134; 135; 136; 137; 138; 139; 140; 141; 143; 144; 145.
energy supplier market share: 128; 133.
fuel poverty: 118; 128; 130; 131; 133; 134; 138; 140; 144.
home/residential installation: 3; 53; 121; 134.
targets obligated: 128; 133.
Grenfell Tower Enquiry,
Moore-Bick Sir Martin: 87; 94; 95; 100.
Grenfell Tower, Interviews/Observations,
artefacts, vicinity of Grenfell Tower: ix; x; xl; xii; xiii; xiv; xvi; 1; 15; 16; 17; 18; 19; 32; 33; 38; 39; 46; 47; 48; 49; 50; 51; 54; 55; 59; 64; 71; 83; 84; 115; 117; 161; 162; 163; 164; 166; 167; 168; 169.
Kensington and Chelsea local council: 303-327.
Grenfell Tower, KCTMO,
managerialism: 52-104; 155; 160.
Grenfell Tower Media,
cladding moral panic: 53; 54; 327.
media broadcast: 66; 67; 68; 69; 70; 73; 96; 97; 98.
Grenfell Tower, Refurbishment,
2014–2016 exterior fabrication: 23.
aesthetic gentrification: vii; 3; 5; 11;
13; 147; 149; 151; 153; 155.
axial feature: xl; 3; 10; 22.
cladding tiles: 3; 23.
cladding, moral panic: 53; 54.
cladding: vii; xxiii; 3; 22; 23; 24; 25; 26; 27; 28; 29; 30; 31; 34; 35; 41; 42; 51; 52; 53; 57; 59; 60; 61; 63; 65; 67; 69; 70; 71; 73; 75; 77; 79; 81; 83; 85; 86; 87; 89; 91; 93; 95; 97; 99; 101; 103; 104; 105; 107; 109; 111; 113; 116; 117; 118; 119; 120; 121; 122; 123; 126; 141; 142; 143; 144; 148; 152; 154; 155; 158; 299; 300; 304; 320; 325; 326; 327; 346.
combustible cladding: 89; 91; 93; 95; 97; 99; 101; 103; 104; 105; 107; 109; 111; 113; 116; 117; 118; 119; 120; 121; 122; 123; 126; 141; 142; 143; 144; 148; 152; 154; 155; 158; 299; 300; 304; 320; 325; 326; 327; 346.
exploitative political economy: 3; 24; 300.
external cladding: 30; 31; 34; 35; 41; 42; 51; 52; 53; 57; 59; 60; 61; 63; 65; 67; 69; 70; 71; 73; 75; 77; 79; 81; 83; 85; 86; 87; 89; 91; 93; 95; 97; 99; 101; 103; 104; 105; 107; 109; 111; 113; 116; 117; 118; 119; 120; 121; 122; 123; 126; 141; 142; 143; 144; 148; 152; 154; 155; 158.
facades: 71; 73; 75; 77; 79; 81; 83; 85; 86; 87; 89; 91; 93; 95; 97; 99; 101; 103; 104; 105; 107; 109; 111; 113; 116; 117; 118; 119; 120; 121; 122; 123; 126; 141; 142; 143; 144.
fenestration:29; 103.
Grenfell Tower, plant room: 29; 103.
invitation to tender: 36.
Kensington Council leadership: 21; 66; 73; 75; 89; 96; 303; 307;

311; 315.
neoliberal re-engineered: 3; 24.
nursery and boxing club: 27; 29; 103; 152.
polyethylene-insulated: 23; 299.
procurement: 55; 77; 78; 79; 93; 102; 103; 119; 120.
reconfiguration of lower 4: 29; 103.
refurbishment contract: 22; 26; 27; 30; 31; 34; 36; 55; 56; 57; 78; 118; 125; 131; 135; 142; 143; 144; 148; 147; 148; 158; 159; 160.

Grenfell Tower, Refurbishment Managerialism,
Grenfell Action Group Blog: 34; 58; 59; 141; 146.
Grenfell Action Group: 34-37.

Grenfell Tower, Regeneration,
Kensington Academy and Leisure Centre: 36; 37; 153.
Kensington and Chelsea Tenant Management Organisation (KCTMO):
Kirkham, Frances: 21.
Lakanal House: 21; 22.
regeneration programme: xxiii; 48; 180.

Grenfell Tower Residents' Associations,
Grenfell Action Group: 21; 34; 57; 58; 59; 60; 99; 104; 146.
Grenfell Community Association: 62; 66; 159.
Grenfell Housing Association: 57; 58; 62; 66; 149.

Ground Rent,
absolute boarder control: 227; 230.
rentier capitalism: 4; 177; 197.

Grounded Theory,
data analysis: xlviii.

H

Haptic,
haptic touch: xii; xvi; xviii; 19; 115; 162; 181; 221; 234.
haptic-sensory capital: xii; xvi; xviii; 19; 115; 162; 181; 221; 234.
haptic-sensory: xii; xvi; xviii; 19; 115; 162; 181; 221; 234.

HC 22nd June 2017,
building regulations: 21; 22; 23; 60.
Conservative-run council: 21; 22; 23; 60.
Corbyn, Jeremy: 21; 22; 23; 60.
Grenfell Action Group: 21; 22; 23; 60.
Grenfell Tower dispossessed: 21; 22; 23; 60.
Kensington and Chelsea Council: 21; 22; 23; 60.
Kensington and Chelsea Tenant Management Organisation: 21; 22; 23; 60.
Kirkham, Frances: 21; 22; 23; 60.
Lakanal House fire: 21; 22; 23; 60.
May, Theresa: 21; 22; 23; 60.

Heritage Industry,
gentrification of post-industrial: xl; xliii; 3; 5; 10; 11; 13; 20; 21; 23; 25; 27; 29; 31; 33; 35; 37; 39; 41; 43; 45; 47; 49; 51; 115; 117; 119; 121; 123; 125; 127; 129; 131; 133; 135; 137; 139; 141; 143; 145; 147; 149; 151; 153; 155; 157; 159; 161; 163; 165; 167; 169; 205; 219.
heritage space: xlvi; 177; 180; 181.
hermeneutics, phenomenology: 211; 214.

Heterotopic,
immaterial capital: 12.
market-based managerialism: 51-114.
mobile body: 127; 207.
skin: 165; 174.

High Frequency Trading (HFT),
digital capitalism: 349; 350; 351; 352.

Hodge, M,
Garden Bridge Review: 4; 173; 186; 245; 252; 253; 255; 261; 263; 265; 266; 269; 270; 271; 275; 276; 277; 300.
Lumley, J. EIR disclosure: 237; 240; 248; 252; 253; 255; 260; 261; 263; 264; 265; 266; 269; 270; 271; 272; 275; 276; 277.
Hyper-individualism,
social media: xlvi; 11; 12; 65; 66; 70.
Hyper-Mediated Urban Spaces,
gentrification: 37.
Trafalgar Square: xliii; xlviii; 10; 11; 301; 338.
Hyperreal signs,
advertising postmodern practices: 13; 81.
Hyper-reality,
second-order simulacra: 12; 13.

I

Individualism,
pseudo-individualistic: xxxix.
Individualistic rationality,
insurance: xxxix; xl; 306; 342; 358.
liberal society: xl; 3; 11; 22; 179; 301.
rational self-interest: 80.
Informationalism,
adsensory: 11.
algorithmic advertising: 81.
cartography: 10; 101.
codification: xl; 3; 5; 10; 11; 23.
façadism: 11; 117; 118.
finance capital: xl; xlvii; 177; 198; 228; 230; 285; 287; 292.
financialisation: xxxviii; xxxix; xl; xlvii; 4; 11; 13; 81; 171; 173; 177; 179; 181; 183; 185; 187; 189; 191; 193; 195; 197; 199; 201; 203; 205; 207; 209; 211; 215; 217; 219; 221; 255; 285; 287; 288; 290; 291; 292; 301.

individuation: 257; 258; 252; 263; 264; 268.
inscriptive advertising: xl; 11; 12; 217; 301.
knowledge-economy: 3; 10; 11; 24; 278; 300; 336; 342.
synoptics: xxxix; xl; 207; 208; 215; 218; 219.
timeless: x; xxxiii.
Insurantial Technology,
actuarial calculation: xxxix.
Intermediary,
actor network theory: xxxix; 117; 124; 131.
Interoperable,
social media: xlvi; 11; 12; 65; 66; 70.
Interpolate,
critical distance: 272.
Interpretative Data Analytics,
grounded theory: xlviii.

J

Cardiff, J.: *Artangel*; xliii.
Cardiff, J.: audio walk: xliii; 9.
juxtaposition: 151; 272.

K

KCHPSC 16th July 2013,
£11.278m budget: 34; 35; 36; 37.
£9.7m budget: 34; 35; 36; 37.
Grenfell Tower Refurbishment: 34; 35; 36; 37.
initial budget of £6m: 34; 35; 36; 37.
Leadbitter: 34; 35; 36; 37.
procurement process: 34; 35; 36; 37.
public consultation process: 34; 35; 36; 37.
residents' complaints: 34; 35; 36; 37.
Kensington Academy and Leisure Centre (KALC),
Bouygues UK: 36.

design team: 35; 36; 55; 101; 242.
Grenfell Tower regeneration: 36; 37; 153.
project management: 37; 146; 256.
Kensington and Chelsea Council Managerialism,
corporate governance: 74; 130; 131; 132; 133; 134; 135; 141; 142.
housing strategy: 57; 76; 77; 136.
procurement: 134; 135; 141; 142; 143; 144; 145; 148; 150; 152; 154; 156; 158; 159; 160.
refurbishment: xxii; xl; 11; 21; 22; 24; 25; 26; 27; 29; 30; 31; 34; 36; 52; 54; 55; 57; 90; 101; 102; 103; 116; 117; 118; 119; 120; 121; 122; 124; 125; 127; 128; 130; 131; 132; 133.

L

Labour,
absolute surplus-value: 76.
immaterial capital: 12.
labour time: xxxix; 11; 21; 22; 98; 208; 247; 274; 303.
necessary labour: 73; 196; 277; 323.
rentier capitalism: 4; 177; 197; 301.
surplus value: 76; 204; 205; 206.
Latour, Bruno,
actor network theory: xxxix; 117; 124; 131.
Lifestyle Insurance,
adsensory technology: xxxix; xl; 367.
Linear Time,
capital accumulation: 95; 211; 214; 215.
disciplinary technology: 95; 211; 214; 215.
Localism Act (2011),
community engagement: 29.
KCTMO community engagement: 29.

M

Managerialism,
displacement: 4; 89; 93; 116; 127; 128; 131; 132; 133; 173; 192; 300.
epistemology: 100.
ground-rent: 175; 203; 204; 207; 211; 223.
linear time: 95; 211; 214; 215.
positivistic management: 209; 211.
positivistic marketing critique of:
positivistic: xxxix; 2; 65; 209; 211.
programmatic: 149; 268.
Mathiesen, Thomas,
synoptics: xl; 208; 218 219.
McLuhan, Marshall,
"medium is the message": 65; 66.
Meta-industrial labour,
Salleh, A.: 196; 198; 277; 278.
Methodology,
actor network theory: xxxix; 117; 124; 131.
critical discourse analysis: 279.
management science interviews: xlvi; xlvii.
Methodology, Critical Ethnography
fieldwork: xl; xli; xlii; xliii; xlvi; xlviii; 5; 13; 301.
Methodology, Live Streaming
data coding: xli; xliii; xlvi.
Michel F.: *Technologies of the Self,*
sign systems: xxxviii; xxxix; 2; 12; 13; 24; 57; 74; 79; 80; 82; 101; 102; 121; 149; 151; 156; 158; 179; 208; 209; 210; 212; 255; 283; 284.
technologies of individual domination: xxxviii; 2; 3; 209; 210.
technologies of power and self: 77; xli; 2; 3; 210; 214; 280; 283.
technologies of power: xxxviii; xli; 2; 3; 100; 210; 213; 214; 218;

256; 277; 280; 282; 283; 284.
technologies of sign systems:
xxxviii; xxix; 2; 12; 13; 209;
210; 212; 283; 284.
technologies of the self: xxxviii;
xxix; xl; xli; xlvi; 2; 3; 9; 10;
180; 209; 210; 211; 212; 214;
217; 219; 257; 280; 283; 301.
technology of self: xxxviii; xxix; xl;
2; 3; 9; 180; 205; 209; 210; 212;
217; 219; 280; 301.

N

Network Society, Finance Capital:
computer networked healthcare:
xxxix; xl; 212.
consumer citizenship: xl; 74.
consumer healthcare citizenship: xl.
health capital: xxxix; xl; 11; 193;
207; 209; 215; 301.
managed narcissism: 263.
marketisation of health: xxxviii; 70;
75.
marketisation: xxxviii; 70; 75.
narcissism: 263.
national health service: xl.
neoliberalism: 178; 278.
social capital: 264.

O

Odih, P.: *Adsensory Financialisation,*
bio-sensing biotechnology: xxxix;
12.
body-tracking monitors: xxix; 207.
body, object: xxxix; xl; 11; 12; 13;
180; 215; 270; 275; 301; 304.
body, subject: xxxix; xl; 11; 13;
180; 215; 236; 269; 275; 301.
ethico-synoptics: xl; 219.
finance capital: xl; xlvii; 177; 198;
199; 228; 230; 254; 285; 287.
financialisation of health: xxxix; xl;
11; 81; 193; 207; 209; 215; 301.
financialisation of well-being:
xxxix; xl; 11; 81; 1977; 207;
215.
health and well-being: xxxix; xl; 11;
58; 81; 207; 215.
knowing of populations of bodies:
xl.
leisure industry: xxxix.
marketing healthcare: xxxix; xl.
private insurance: xl.
Online Ethnography,
connectivity: 11; 194.
virtual community: 178; 179; 181;
193; 198.

P

Panoptics,
Foucault, Michel: xl; 217; 218.
synoptics: xl; 208; 218; 219.
time, disciplinary technology:
xxxviii; 210; 211; 213; 215;
217; 218.
Phenomenology,
duality, disciplinary time: xxxviii.
of everyday life: xxxviii; xlii; 65;
217; 280.
phenomenological time: 217; 219.
Political Economy,
exploitative profit: 3; 24; 205; 223;
300.
façades: 3; 19; 22; 24; 30; 152; 156;
157; 174; 178; 300.
urban regeneration: 3; 10; 23; 24;
88; 118; 144; 152; 153; 157;
158; 159; 177; 300; 301.
Political Economy of the Sign,
consumer capitalism: 8; 12; 13; 74;
131; 134; 135; 137; 139; 159;
208; 216; 219; 250; 289; 290;
291.
models of simulacra: 13; 81; 179.
polyethylene aluminium cladding:
3; 23; 86; 155; 158; 299; 320.
post-industrial gentrification: 3; 5;
10; 11; 13; 20; 21; 23; 25; 27;

29; 31; 33; 35; 37; 39; 41; 43;
45; 47; 49; 51; 115; 117; 119;
119; 121; 123; 125; 127; 129;
131; 133; 135; 137; 139; 141;
143; 145; 147; 149; 151; 153;
155; 157; 159; 161; 163; 165;
167; 169; 205; 219; 299.
polyethylene aluminium,
best-value: 86; 155; 158; 320.
building refurbishment: 28; 30; 52;
88; 148; 155; 168; 320.
cladding panels: 28; 30; 52; 88; 148;
155; 168; 320.
exterior refurbishment: 86; 155;
158; 320.
Grenfell Tower: 86; 155; 158; 320.
semiological: 28; 30; 52; 88; 148;
155; 168; 320.
Privatisation Public Space,
ecofeminist: 252; 253; 255; 257;
259; 261; 283; 264; 265; 267;
269; 271; 273; 274; 275; 277;
278; 279; 281; 283; 285; 287;
289; 291; 293; 295; 301.
market-based: 278.
neoliberal: 89; 153; 155; 159; 178;
179; 300; 301.
public recreational. 4; 177; 179;
199; 201; 219; 230; 232; 260;
277; 301.
rentier capitalism: 4; 177; 197; 301.
urban ecology: 4; 118; 173; 178;
180; 181; 232; 301.
urban river space: 4; 230; 301.
Programmatic Digital,
body calibration: xxxix; xl; xlv; 3;
6; 9; 11; 12; 13; 127; 135; 178;
180; 181; 205; 207; 211; 215;
218; 219; 228; 233; 241; 269;
270; 277; 278; 283; 300.
Proliferation of Risk,
insurantial technology: xxxix; 215;
216; 217; 301.
positivistic epistemologies: xxxix;
2; 65; 209; 211.
Psychosomatic Capitalism,

simulacra, Brexit sign-systems: 12;
13; 81; 100; 119; 120; 121; 122;
245; 287; 288.
simulation: 12; 13; 81; 100.
UK's exit from European Union:
119; 120; 121; 122; 245; 287;
288.

Q

Qualitative Case Study, Garden Bridge,
environmental activists: xlvi; xxx-xxxvi.
expert practitioners: xlvi.
management consultations: xlvi.
Qualitative Case Study, Grenfell Tower,
ecological codification: 3; 11; 301.
environmental activists: xlvi.
expert practitioners: xlvi.
local government politicians: xlvi;
138.
management consultations: xlvi.
political activists: xlvi.
Tenant Management Organisation
(TMO): 21; 42; 43; 56; 66; 70;
75; 87; 88; 95; 96; 104; 131;
152; 158; 160.
thematic qualitative interview:
xlviii; 298; 299; 303.
urban regeneration: 3; 10; 23; 24;
88; 118; 144; 152; 153; 157;
158; 159; 177; 300; 301.
Qualitative, Organisational Analytics,
RBKC council meeting: 63; 65; 66;
68; 69; 70; 96; 339; 383.
Royal Borough of Kensington and
Chelsea: 21; 27; 28; 29; 34; 35;
60; 61; 63; 65; 66; 67; 87; 88;
93; 96; 98; 99; 100; 117; 141;
142; 153; 299; 303; 339.
simulacra of façade: 34-37; 67; 81;
101; 103; 153; 155.
Quasi-markets,

market analogues: 11; 74.

R

RBKC Grenfell Tower Tragedy,
rehousing: 143; 144.
RBKC Housing and Regeneration,
housing renewal: 34; 35.
regeneration: 3; 4l 9; 10; 11; 23; 24; 28; 29; 30; 35; 36; 37; 45; 56; 59; 63; 64; 70; 73; 88; 91; 93; 104; 117; 118; 122; 123; 141; 142; 144; 147; 152; 153; 157; 158; 159; 160; 177; 278.
social housing stock: 93; 95; 143; 305.
RBKC Leadership Team,
residents' satisfaction: 66.
Reductive Managerialism,
positivist epistemology: 66.
Refurbishment,
bare walls: xxiii.
cladding: vii; xxiii; 3; 22; 23; 24; 25; 26; 27; 28; 29; 31; 34; 35; 41.
Grenfell Tower interview: xxiii; xxiv; xlvi; xlviii; 40; 41; 45; 46;
social cleansing: 90; 93; 308; 322.
Regime of Accumulation,
digital advertising: xxxix; 67.
finance capital: xl; xlvii; 177; 198; 228; 230; 285; 287; 292.
Rent,
absolute boarder controls: vii; 171; 227; 230.
boarding: 52; 230.
rentier capitalism: 4; 177; 197; 301.
Resistance,
ecological activism: 269; 271; 272; 281.
housing activism: 22; 25; 34; 58; 104; 120; 121; 126 131.
technologies: 255; 256; 257.
Revelo: to reveal,
Revello: "to draw back", "to retract"

(Johnson and Todd 1837): 177.
reve'l (abbreviation of revello): 177.
Risk,
ecology: 121; 123; 156; 182; 183; 185; 186; 188; 191; 192; 194; 195; 208; 215; 217; 254; 256; 314.
tenant activism: 57; 95; 96.

S

Salleh, Ariel,
meta-industrial labour: 196; 198; 277; 278.
Simulacra,
first-order: 12; 67; 68; 97; 101; 103; 104; 153; 160; 208; 230; 266.
second-order: 12; 67; 82; 88; 97; 100; 101; 102; 103; 104; 153; 155; 160.
third-order: 12; 13; 81; 206; 238; 280; 256.
Simulation,
feigning: 12; 13; 81; 100.
Social Capital,
cultivation: 264.
cultural reproduction: 264.
synoptics,
ethico-synoptics: xl; 219.
many-watching-few: xl; 219.
many-watching-many: xl; 219.
synoptics: xl; 208; 218; 219.

T

Talk,
actor network theory: xxxix; 117; 124; 131.
disciplinary technology of production: 209.
phenomenology: xxxix; xlii; 10; 217.
Technological Rationality,
Culture industry: 66.
Marcuse, H.: *One Dimensional Man*: 66

Technology of Sign Systems,
technology of power: xxxviii; 2; 210; 213; 218; 256.
technology of production: 2; 205; 207; 209; 256; 280.
technology of the self: xxxix.
Time,
embodied: 95; 100; 177; 247; 259.
Translation,
actor network theory: xxxix; 117; 124; 131.

U

"Universal Code: Status" (Baudrillard 1968): 67.
Urban Ecology,
architectural: xxxi; 9; 118; 255.
design language: 9.
integrate ecology: 10; 214.
people, economy: 10; 91; 118; 256.
working landscapes: 20.
Use-value,
labour theory of value: 73.
Utopian Idealism,
codification of knowledge: xl; 3; 5; 10; 11; 22; 299; 301.

V

Valorised Labour Time,
embedded labour time: 274.
Virtual Ethnography,
off-line ethnographic: 11.
connectivity: 11; 194; 272.
Visualising Architecture,
2D architectural visualisation: 9-10.
3D architectural visualisation: 9-10.
Triple D: 9-10.

W

Wearable Fitness Technology,
bio-sensing: xxxix; 12.

X

xenophobia: 272.

Y

Yearsley, Ann,
Epicurean atomist physics: 39.

Z

zeitgeist: 114.

Figure i.2.: "The arc of the moral universe, although long, is bending toward justice" (Martin Luther King, Jr.,). Photographic Image, Vicinity of Grenfell Tower; Lancaster West Estate, North Kensington, London, June 2017.